COLLECTED ESSAYS

ARTHUR MILLER was not only one of America's most important play-wrights of the twentieth century, but also one of its most influential literary, cultural, and intellectual voices. Throughout his career, he consistently remained one of the country's leading public intellectuals, advocating tirelessly for social justice, global democracy, and the arts. Theater scholar Susan C. W. Abbotson introduces this volume as a selection of Miller's finest essays, organized in three thematic parts: essays on the theater, essays on specific plays including *Death of a Salesman* and *The Crucible*, and sociopolitical essays on topics spanning the Depression to the twenty-first century. Written with playful wit, clear-eyed intellect, and, above all, human dignity, these essays offer unmatched insight into the work of Arthur Miller and the turbulent times through which he guided his country.

PENGUIN CLASSICS 🐧 DELUXE EDITION

COLLECTED ESSAYS

ARTHUR MILLER (1915–2005) was born in New York City and studied at the University of Michigan. His plays include *All My Sons* (1947), *Death of a Salesman* (1949), *The Crucible* (1953), *A View from the Bridge* and *A Memory of Two Mondays* (1955), *After the Fall* and *Incident at Vichy* (1964), *The Price* (1968), *The Creation of the World and Other Business* (1972), and *The American Clock* (1980). His other works include *Focus*, a novel (1945); *The Misfits*, a cinema novel (1961); and the texts for *In Russia* (1969), *In the Country* (1977), and *Chinese Encounters* (1979), three books in collaboration with his wife, photographer Inge Morath. His memoirs include *Salesman in Beijing* (1984) and *Timebends*, an autobiography (1987). His short fiction includes the collection *I Don't Need You Any More* (1967), the novella *Homely Girl, A Life* (1995), and *Presence: Stories* (2007). His later work includes the plays *The Ride Down Mt. Morgan* (1991), *The Last Yankee* (1993), *Broken Glass* (1994), *Mr. Peters' Connections* (1999), and *Resurrection Blues* (2006); *Echoes Down the Corridor: Collected Essays, 1944–2000*; and *On Politics and the Art of Acting* (2001). Among numerous honors, he received the Pulitzer Prize for Drama and the John F. Kennedy Lifetime Achievement Award.

SUSAN C. W. ABBOTSON came to the United States from Britain in 1990 and started working at Rhode Island College in 1999, where she is now a professor, specializing in modern and contemporary drama. A leading scholar on the work of Arthur Miller, Dr. Abbotson has published three books and many articles on this seminal American writer. She has been president of the Arthur Miller Society, currently serves on its board, manages its website, and provides bibliographic information on Miller for several other databases. She is also the performance editor for *The Arthur Miller Journal*, was one of a panel of experts to discuss Arthur Miller on NPR's *On Point with Tom Ashbrook* shortly after the playwright's death, and has been invited to talk about Miller on other radio shows as well as at a number of area theaters. Dr. Abbotson has also published pieces on other playwrights, including Tennessee Williams, Sam Shepard, Thornton Wilder, Paula Vogel, Mae West, William Inge, August Wilson, and Eugene O'Neill. Her most recent work is *Modern American Drama: Playwriting in the 1950s*.

BY ARTHUR MILLER

PLAYS

The Golden Years
The Man Who Had All the Luck
All My Sons
Death of a Salesman
An Enemy of the People
The Crucible
A View from the Bridge
After the Fall
Incident at Vichy
The Price
The Creation of the World and
    Other Business
The Archbishop's Ceiling
The American Clock
Playing for Time
The Ride Down Mt. Morgan
Broken Glass
Mr. Peters' Connections
Resurrection Blues
Finishing the Picture

ONE-ACT PLAYS

A View from the Bridge (one-act version)
A Memory of Two Mondays
Fame
The Reason Why
Elegy for a Lady (in Two-Way Mirror)
Some Kind of Love Story
    (in Two-Way Mirror)
I Can't Remember Anything
    (in Danger: Memory!)
Clara (in Danger: Memory!)
The Last Yankee

SCREENPLAYS

The Misfits
Playing for Time
Everybody Wins
The Crucible

MUSICAL

Up from Paradise

AUTOBIOGRAPHY

Timebends: A Life

REPORTAGE

Situation Normal
In Russia (with Inge Morath)
In the Country (with Inge Morath)
Chinese Encounters (with Inge Morath)
Salesman in Beijing

FICTION

Focus (a novel)
Jane's Blanket (a children's story)
The Misfits (a cinema novel)
I Don't Need You Any More (stories)
Homely Girl, a Life
    (a novella and stories)
Presence: Collected Stories

COLLECTIONS

Arthur Miller's Collected Plays,
    Volumes I and II
The Portable Arthur Miller
Arthur Miller: Collected Plays
    1944–1961 (Tony Kushner,
    editor)
Arthur Miller: Collected Plays
    1964–1982 (Tony Kushner,
    editor)
Arthur Miller: Collected Plays
    1987–2004 with Stage and Radio
    Plays of the 1930s and '40s (Tony
    Kushner, editor)
The Penguin Arthur Miller

ESSAYS

Collected Essays
The Theater Essays of Arthur Miller
    (Robert A. Martin, editor)
Echoes Down the Corridor: Collected
    Essays, 1944–2000
    (Steven R. Centola, editor)
On Politics and the Art of Acting

VIKING
CRITICAL LIBRARY EDITIONS

Death of a Salesman
    (Gerald Weales, editor)
The Crucible
    (Gerald Weales, editor)

ARTHUR MILLER

Collected Essays

Introduction by SUSAN C. W. ABBOTSON

PENGUIN BOOKS

PENGUIN BOOKS

An imprint of Penguin Random House LLC
375 Hudson Street
New York, New York 10014
penguin.com

LIBRARY OF CONGRESS CATALOGING-IN-PUBLICATION DATA
Names: Miller, Arthur, 1915–2005, author. | Abbotson, Susan C. W., 1961–
writer of introduction.
Title: Collected essays / Arthur Miller ; introduction by Susan C. W. Abbotson.
Description: New York : Penguin Books, 2016. | Includes index.
Identifiers: LCCN 2016029622 (print) | LCCN 2016038652 (ebook) |
ISBN 9780143108498 (paperback) | ISBN 9781101992043
Subjects: LCSH: American drama—20th century—History and criticism—Theory, etc. |
BISAC: PERFORMING ARTS / Theater / History & Criticism. | LITERARY COLLECTIONS /
Essays. | BIOGRAPHY & AUTOBIOGRAPHY / Entertainment & Performing Arts.
Classification: LCC PS3525.I5156 A16 2016 (print) | LCC PS3525.I5156 (ebook) |
DDC 814/.52—dc23
LC record available at https://lccn.loc.gov/2016029622

Printed in the United States of America
1   3   5   7   9   10   8   6   4   2

Contents

Introduction

For Arthur Miller, theater was ever a serious business, and his essays exhibit the strong social and theatrical commitment and conviction that fed his drama, guided his life, and allowed him to be a perceptive commentator on the twentieth century through which he lived for all but fifteen years, as well as a prescient voice for the century to come. To read his essays is not only to learn more about the plays and the playwright, but to also learn much about the societies in which we live, and the core of human nature itself. As early as 1977, in his introduction to the first ever collection of Miller's theater essays, Robert A. Martin declared that "Miller's essays on drama and the theater may well represent the single most important statement of critical principles to appear in England and America by a major playwright since the Prefaces of George Bernard Shaw" (xx).

But Martin was only looking at the first thirty years of Miller's career, and there would be nearly another thirty during which Miller's scope and insights would broaden as well as deepen. His essays not only inform us of the values that shaped and inspired his artistic vision, but also present a series of provocative, balanced, and insightful commentaries on the world beyond theater. Miller's theatrical essays, both those explicating his own dramas, and those on the status and development of theater as a whole throughout the twentieth century and beyond, offer a formidable body of work that could hold its own against that of Aristotle, Gotthold Lessing, Vsevolod Meyerhold, or Bertolt Brecht. However, Miller also wrote beyond the confines of the theatrical scene and offered salient observations on a whole array of sociopolitical issues. We should not forget that when he first enrolled at the University of Michigan it was to study journalism, not playwriting, and that desire to be a commentator on human events never abated.

In 1977, Martin viewed Miller as "a writer of unusual talent and insight," and wrote of how Miller's "plays have been responsible in large part for extending the significance of the American theater beyond the horizons of its national origins, and for providing a standard of dramatic achievement for contemporary playwrights everywhere" (xix). Nineteen years later, in 1996, in his introduction to the revised and expanded version of *The Theater Essays of Arthur Miller*, Steven R. Centola posited that the characters in Miller's plays seem driven "to construct a society based on humanitarian and democratic principle, creating order out of chaos and giving meaning and dignity to human experience" (xlvii). He rightly concluded that Miller's essays do very much the same thing. But Miller does this in more than just his theater essays, which the scope of this collection is able to emphasize.

What is unique and special about this volume is its selection and organization. As a man who wrote and published essays for sixty years, Miller inevitably repeated himself on occasion, or tried to urge the same point in different words when his initial warning appeared to go unheard. An illustration of this tendency resides in the similarity of the included essays "Notes on Realism" and "About Theater Language." While their focus is slightly different, they both urge the reader to reconsider their perception of what is meant by "real" in drama. Previous volumes of his nonfiction writing have tended toward presenting everything he wrote, including selections from longer pieces and transcriptions of interviews. Given that the essay is in itself a distinct art form, this collection has (with two worthwhile exceptions) concentrated on actual essays to help better convey Miller's mastery of that form. Other volumes have also presented materials in a strict chronological order, or divided them into sections that cover topics within the periods of different plays he produced, with no other organizing feature. But Miller's work in this field can be divided into three distinct categories that have little to do with chronology, and that is what this volume does. It begins by selecting the most important statements Miller made pertaining to theater technique and the state of the theater as a whole, then follows this with a selection of essays that are key to understanding specific plays he created. The final section presents Miller's commentary on a variety of important social and political issues. By creating this topic-based organization, the hope is to allow the reader to be able to better focus on the reader's personal area of concern, and the book's conciseness can, ironically, better convey the sheer scope of Miller's interests.

ON THE THEATER

Some of Miller's most famous essays are those he wrote early in his career concerning his definition of tragedy. As we can see from his comments in a later piece "Sorting Things Out" (1977), he created a furor that he later almost regretted, but only "almost." In "Tragedy and the Common Man," printed in the *New York Times* just two weeks after *Death of a Salesman* opened on Broadway in 1949, and the follow-up, "The Nature of Tragedy," printed a month later in the *New York Herald Tribune*, Miller controversially redefined forever the way American dramatists, in particular, would define the genre. Reinventing traditional Aristotelian definitions of tragedy, which Miller saw as having become misunderstood by a skeptical modern audience with different value systems from the ancient Greeks, Miller insisted that while they should remain complex figures, tragic heroes no longer need be high-born, intelligent, or even likable. For Miller, "In the tragic view the need of man to wholly realize himself is the only fixed star." Thus, tragedy could be wrought from the travails of any human being who refuses against great odds to give up personal dignity and what they deem as their "rightful position" in society. Such characterizations are sufficient to create catharsis and establish the promise of humankind's potential that Miller saw as central to tragedy, and to lead the audience to examine, and seek to fix, the social faults that caused the protagonist's destruction.

However, Miller wished to say more about the modern theater and its techniques than argue the ways in which tragedy might be written; he wished to have a bigger impact, and to show how theater could effectively respond to the deepest needs of any society, and do so in a variety of ways without becoming overtly polemic. In its consideration of the problems faced by mid-twentieth-century American theater, "Introduction to the Collected Plays" is a major work toward that aim. Miller explains his "organic" process of playwriting, the need for playwrights to remain connected to the concerns of their audiences, and his humanistic goals of working toward the improvement of society. While "Introduction to the Collected Plays" is one of the longest modern American essays on theater in general (as well as offering several insights into his writing process for many of Miller's best-known plays), he wrote several other seminal midcentury pieces that further expanded his attempt to redefine drama for what he saw as a new age of theater.

Initially intended as a preface to *A View from the Bridge* and *A Memory of Two Mondays*, "On Social Plays" keenly articulates Miller's understanding that true social drama, which in his opinion is the most valuable kind of drama to write, must explore the notion of how we can live as both individuals and contributing members of society. He also connects this outlook to his vision of tragedy. Aside from challenging limiting definitions of realism and expressionism, "The Family in Modern Drama" explains the difference between plays that just deal with family and those that take on a wider society, with his stated goal being a genre that combines the two by using the family as a microcosmic study of the macrocosm. "There lies within the dramatic form," he boldly concludes, "the ultimate possibility of raising truth-consciousness of mankind to a level of such intensity as to transform those who observe it." For Miller, drama is clearly all about connections, between private and social lives, art and form, the past, present, and future. While 1958's "The Shadows of the Gods" succinctly outlines various influences on Miller's work and his connection to other American dramatists, its emphasis is on Miller's agenda to revitalize what he viewed as a theater fast becoming "absurd, repetitious, and decayed." Disdaining narrow introspection or comforting sentimentality, he asks for plays that are infused with a deeper sociopolitical context. Using his experiences during the Great Depression and knowledge of the Holocaust as springboards, Miller shares two of his foundational beliefs. First, in the power of a past from which no one can truly escape, which ensures the birds will always come "home to roost," and, second, that each person has a potential capacity for evil and needs to accept this fact. In Miller's worldview, no one can be truly innocent, and it is foolish for any dramatist to pretend otherwise.

While the above three essays best relay Miller's essential beliefs regarding human nature, and the place and promise of drama in the world, other, lesser-known pieces, such as "Ibsen and the Drama of Today," "Tennessee Williams' Legacy: An Eloquence," "The Good Old American Apple Pie," and "Notes on Realism" place those theories more carefully within the frame of other writers, theatrical trends, and exigencies. The pieces on Ibsen and Williams offer excellent encapsulations of what it is in each of these playwrights that Miller most admires, while "Good Old Apple Pie" focuses on Miller's disdain for theatrical censorship, especially within a nation purporting itself to be a democracy. Finally, "Notes on Realism" warns against oversimplifying what is meant by the term, and asserts the need for bedrock realism in drama for it to be fully effective. This essay is clearly a rewrite of the earlier "About Theater Language," but here Miller has both honed and broadened his original argument with additional commentary, and left out specific observations of *The Last Yankee*. "Subsidized Theatre" is included as most representative of several essays Miller wrote bemoaning the inadequacies and shortfalls of the ways in which theater is treated and perceived in America, and his suggested solutions.

Another important aspect of Miller's work that is becoming more widely recognized is his close attention to how language is used to dramatic purpose. The essays "About Theater Language" and "On Screenwriting and Language: Introduction to *Everybody Wins*" consider the demands of the written word on both stage and screen. Miller suggests that prose is the language of "the individual and private life" and poetry "the language of the man in crowds, in society." Suggesting that prose provides a play's feeling and poetry its thought, Miller asserts a need for the language of plays to maintain a balance between the two to be the most effective. In the playwright's opinion, the realism of a play, created through the natural speech of its characters, while necessary to engage an audience, should only ever pertain to its veneer, for a play that does not offer deeper challenges through a stylized, poetic lift in its language is doomed to be merely entertaining. "About Theater Language" continues to illustrate these points using *The Last Yankee*. Given the difference in media, in "On Screenwriting and Language," Miller suggests that writing for films becomes less about words and more about images, as metaphoric language is replaced by visual symbolism. But while the screenwriter subsequently focuses more on realistic dialogue, the end product, ironically, has the potential to be more successfully poetic than a play.

ON HIS WORKS

While it is useful to consider a playwright's broader view of his profession, it is also advantageous to have a line into their viewpoint regarding what they themselves have written. Thus, this collection includes several essays that Miller wrote referencing specific plays of his own, from early works, including *Golden Years* and *The Man Who Had All the Luck* to later ones, such as *The Archbishop's Ceiling* and *The American Clock*. Given the sheer volume of Miller's output, not every work is included here, but the best known are given ample coverage, and several others are included to represent the wide range of his oeuvre. Presented chronologically according to when the works they discuss were produced or published, the pieces selected for such plays as *Death of a Salesman* and *The Crucible* were written over a span of more than forty years to offer an evolving view of Miller's perception of their prolonged impact. Given the consistent aims and tropes of Miller's drama, many of the explanations and opinions in these pieces could be applied to other of his works than the ones highlighted for commentary.

Of the early works, the introduction to *The Golden Years* and *The Man Who Had All the Luck* explains each play's metaphorical basis, how they relate to each other, and how well they hold up. Meanwhile, in "The Face in the Mirror: Anti-Semitism Then and Now" Miller explains the genesis of his 1945 novel, *Focus*, and considers how far its concerns continue to apply forty years on, especially in the light of the creation of Israel and the changing map of Jews throughout the world. While Miller wrote about his conception of *All My Sons* extensively in "Introduction to the Collected Plays," the extract "Belief in America," from an early nonfiction book he published in 1944, *Situation Normal . . .* , offers a telling experience that clearly gave Miller the idea for the army experiences of *All My Son*'s Chris Keller, beyond the heroism of Miller's own brother, Kermit.

The book, as a whole, with its central focus on the difficulties of returning veterans, offers a still timely depiction of the price those who go to war continue to pay, and is an early example of Miller's social concerns beyond the stage.

In 1950, Miller was asked by Fredric March and Florence Eldridge to write a translation of Henrik Ibsen's *Enemy of the People* that they could perform on Broadway as a subtle complaint against the smear campaign they felt was being developed against them during that period of the "Red Scare." In his preface to this adaptation, Miller explains his aim to make the play relevant to Americans by focusing his translation on the "question of whether the democratic guarantees protecting political minorities ought to be set aside in time of crisis" to try to expose the collateral damage that comes with majority rule. In the later piece "Ibsen's Warning," Miller points out how the play has become even more relevant over the years as pollution and contamination have become so much more prevalent issues than in Ibsen's day.

Death of a Salesman and *The Crucible* are Miller's best-known plays, and in addition to the detailed descriptions he gives regarding his conception of each in his "Introduction to the Collected Plays," they are also represented by several pieces, written over a period of years, to illustrate both plays' continued relevance and impact. The extract from Miller's 1987 autobiography, *Timebends: A Life*, is the best rendition of the play's evolution in Miller's mind, and its subsequent creation on the actual stage with the aid of Elia Kazan. His later preface from the 1991 edition of *Salesman in Beijing*—the journal Miller wrote in 1984 to relate his experience directing a landmark production of *Salesman* at the Beijing People's Arts Theatre in China—alongside a 1999 piece "*Salesman* at Fifty," evoke the wide and long-lasting impact of the play, seemingly applicable to all cultures and periods of history.

Four pieces that discuss *The Crucible* have been included: "Brewed in *The Crucible*," "Again They Drink from the Cup of Suspicion," "It Could Happen Here—And Did," and "*The Crucible* in History." These collectively assert the play's relevance beyond McCarthyism and Miller's intent to write a play that conveyed a universal relevance. The longevity and growth of its production history fully support such claims, and in "It Could Happen Here" Miller suggests possible reasons for its endurance. "*The Crucible* in History" is included as Miller's fullest explanation of the cultural forces and historical context of the 1950s that impacted *The Crucible* when it was being written, while also allowing that when these conditions replay in rising dictatorships elsewhere, they prove the play remains relevant.

Miller's introduction to *A View from the Bridge* and foreword to *After the Fall*, as well as his discussion of "Guilt and *Incident at Vichy*" and "*The Price*—The Power of the Past," all offer discerning perceptions of the plays and the personal and social concerns that influenced their creation. His explanations of the development of *A View from the Bridge* from a one- to a two-act play, the relation of Lee Harvey Oswald and the biblical Adam to *After the Fall*, the connections between Nazis and those who killed the three civil rights workers in 1964 Mississippi to what occurs in *Incident at Vichy*, and his view of *The Price* as a response to both the growing absurdism of the 1960s and to Vietnam expand our understanding of each play's wider resonance. Originally published as "Our Guilt for the World's Evil," "Guilt and *Incident at Vichy*" also asserts Miller's central belief that anyone who stands by and allows evil to occur is as guilty as the perpetrators. In a similar way, "Conditions of Freedom: Two Plays of the Seventies" offers a telling picture of the social milieu that spawned both *The Archbishop's Ceiling* and *The American Clock*. The title reflects Miller's belief in the need for a social contract before any freedom can be safely entertained. Post-Watergate and having experienced the surveillance undergone by so-called dissident writers in other countries, Miller wrote *The Archbishop's Ceiling* to expose the potential damage caused by such polarizing conduct, and to argue for the freedom of art as paramount to human advancement. Making analogies between the self-ish and hedonistic 1920s and 1970s, Miller explains how he wrote about the Great Depression in *The American Clock* as a warning of what to expect if behaviors were not altered, but also as an example of how an active democracy might be able to save the day. In all cases we see clearly how Miller's plays addressed key issues of the periods in which they were written, even while illustrating issues of the past and maintaining an evident prescience of the future. It is partly this ability to make clear connections between past, present, and future that allows his works their continued resonance and relevance.

The section on specific plays concludes with the brief preface for *Mr. Peters' Connections*, a play Miller wrote toward the end of his career but one whose very construction, described here, provides an interesting connection back to both *Death of a Salesman* and *After the Fall*, earlier plays through which Miller strove to create an entirely new form of drama that convincingly conveyed the simultaneity of past, present, and even future in an individual's psyche. It speaks to Miller's lifelong desire to perfect a new form of theater that would truly allow the audience to see the complexity inside a character's head and transcend the constraints of strict chronology. For Miller, time was both fluid and mutable, and *Mr. Peters' Connections* was a play imbued with that understanding.

ON SOCIETY AND POLITICS

Miller, however, did not just offer insights into the theater and his own work, but also contributed important essays on a variety of sociopolitical topics, including juvenile delinquency, McCarthyism and other American social issues and politics, the Holocaust, and world politics. Often outspoken, he consistently supported his arguments using his humanistic sympathies, which allowed him to view each case beyond what he saw as narrow nationalistic beliefs. While remaining staunchly proud of the potential of American democracy, he continued to criticize whenever he saw that falling short, and he became to all intents a true citizen of the world. He was also not above a few deliciously satirical pieces regarding such matters as communist paranoia, the death penalty, and congressional lobbying. While these pieces offer insights into the man beyond the plays, they also flesh out the attitudes and beliefs that helped shape Miller's art.

Juvenile Delinquency

One little-known aspect of American culture about which Miller was concerned for much of his life was difficulties regarding juvenile delinquency, which he viewed as the country's "most notable and violent manifestation of social nihilism" and in urgent need of address. During 1955, he spent several weeks among youth gangs in New York collecting material for a documentary, but fears of a socialist agenda prevented it from getting the necessary council approval for production. Three years later he published "Bridge to a Savage World" in *Esquire*, describing the intent and content of the project. Recognizing that much of the problem was being caused by the supreme negativity under which many of these supposed thugs had been raised, Miller insists that love and compassion are insufficient cures, and a new kind of engaged social work needs to be encouraged that moves away from the office and meets the youths on their own terms in the streets. Those willing to take such a risk might be able to offer the bridge that can lead such youths back to productive, safer lives. In the "The Bored and the Violent," Miller responds to a book he had recently read that, while a little disorganized, at least presented delinquents in a refreshingly unromantic way. Differentiating between rich and slum delinquents, Miller posits that delinquents of all kinds are still being misunderstood, and that many are less hardened rebels than bored and frightened teenagers who are incapable of independent thought and join gangs as an act of conformism rather than rebellion. If viewed anew in this light, and approached from a psychological or even spiritual rather than physically punitive standpoint, he suggests that better progress might be made against the problems of delinquency.

The McCarthy Era

"Many Writers: Few Plays," "The Night Ed Murrow Struck Back," and "1956 and All This" collectively offer insights into Miller's take on the McCarthy era and the trials of living under the dangerous bludgeon of the House Un-American Activities Committee and "Red Scare" paranoia of the period. "Many Writers: Few Plays" points to the ways in which the pressures of the McCarthy era witch hunts (as they are now seen), led to the virtual silencing of many American writers out of fear of being targeted, and calls for an end to such temerity. "The Night Ed Murrow Struck Back" reflects on what Miller felt was the outlandish lunacy of McCarthyism, while acknowledging its hold and its impact on himself. The playwright's admiration of Murrow comes from his recognition of the broadcaster's refusal to be cowed by the climate of fear that had been created in the country, and his optimistic support of American values that had in reality all but disappeared. "1956 and All This" critiques isolationist American foreign policy of the period and calls for a better understanding between cultures, which Miller suspects would lessen the nation's fears about communism and a third world war. America, he feels, would be better off helping those in poverty than continuing to pursue a cold war.

Conditions in America

Always deeply concerned with the conditions of living in America, Miller's Jewish upbringing, albeit more secular than religious, is crucial to his outlook on the world and his art. The early essay "Concerning Jews Who Write," written in 1948 for *Jewish Life* but long overlooked, outlines Miller's identification as a Jew, and his commitment to the defense of Jewish culture. Taking a broader approach, in "Miracles" Miller offers his opinions on the sociopolitical situation in America in general, from the 1930s through to the 1960s, drawing connections between the different decades.

Miller became personally involved in American politics when he agreed to serve as Eugene McCarthy's delegate at the 1968 Democratic National Convention in Chicago. Beset by internal disagreement and external rioting, "The Battle of Chicago: From the Delegates' Side" reports on Miller's experience. Passing commentary on the damaging lack of communication between all parties involved, Miller turns this descriptive piece into a general defense of the right to freedom of speech, and a call for a stronger commitment toward morality and substance among politicians. Just as Henrik Ibsen once presented the "life-lies" of individuals who created alternative realities for themselves to avoid facing unpleasant truths, "The Limited Hang-Out: The Dialogues of Nixon as a Drama of the Antihero" exposes what Miller essentially saw as the growing "life-lie" running through the American political system. He points to the rottenness of politicians he saw as ruining a decent political system by constantly trying to blame others rather than take personal responsibility. If Nixon had only been honest, he suggests, he might have saved himself, but it seemed not in his nature to be so.

Delving further into the nation's political system, Miller surprised and shocked his listeners when asked to deliver the Jefferson lecture in 2001, with the acerbic "American Playhouse: Politics and the Art of Acting." While pointing out humorous connections between American presidents and actors, Miller ultimately calls for the public to question the authenticity of its political leaders and demand a more substantive theater as a corrective to the distorted politics of the time. He would later expand this to a book-length piece, but included here is the original speech that contains the essential argument. In "Clinton in Salem," Miller draws interesting connections between what he saw as the circus surrounding then–President Clinton's sexual disgrace and the Salem witch trials, concluding that with changing social mores the general public was less prone to the real political manipulation behind the event.

The Holocaust

Two major catastrophic events of the twentieth century that impacted Miller and his work were the Great Depression and the Holocaust. While he speaks at length about the Great Depression in his autobiography, *Timebends: A Life*, "The Nazi Trials and the German Heart" offers a fuller explanation of the impact he felt from the Holocaust, which would change his opinion of human nature forever. Miller points out how the apparent ordinariness of the defendants at trial should warn us against the banality of evil and to be more vigilant in the future, as there is no one who is not capable of killing another under certain conditions; though these are conditions, he insists, which we can also strive to eliminate. Our moral response to the Holocaust, as Miller had insisted in the piece he originally wrote for the *New York Times Magazine* in 1965 ("Our Guilt for the World's Evil," reprinted here under the title "Guilt and *Incident at Vichy*") should color our responses to continued injustices from juvenile delinquency and civil rights to the treatment of Vietcong prisoners.

Politics Abroad

After his marriage to photographer Ingeborg Morath in 1962, Miller was encouraged by his new wife to get more involved in politics on a worldwide level. In 1965, he was elected the President of PEN, an international literary organization formed to defend writers from intimidation. Through this, he went on missions to several countries to solicit better rights for authors. He grew more and more interested in political and social policy beyond American shores, and this "Politics Abroad" section reflects some of this wider interest. Aside from longer works of reportage on China and Russia that he published with his wife (as an accompaniment to her photography), his essays appeared in *The Nation*, *Harper's*, *The New Republic*, and *Esquire*. Miller liked to use his observations of other nations to better assess the strengths and weaknesses of his own. Several of his essays deal with the negative effects of censorship and demand the necessary freedom of artists to create, while others work to point out the intrinsic similarities between different nations and people bound by a common humanity. Miller remains ever critical of the misuse of power and the treatment of any individual as less than equal in his quest to assert the right to freedom for all within an equitable social contract, in which the rights of the individual remain balanced against the needs of the larger society.

"Dinner with the Ambassador" tells of Miller's 1985 trip to Turkey with fellow playwright Harold Pinter on behalf of PEN, during which he speaks out against the complacency of the United States against unjust foreign censorship, as writers in Turkey are being imprisoned and tortured while the U.S. ambassador makes polite conversation at a local dinner party. He warns that by suppressing knowledge of such occurrences, America becomes as guilty of censorship as Turkey. "What's Wrong with This Picture?" describes a postcard he had received from Vaclav Havel and his wife sent from the Czech Republic. He uses this image to reflect on the foolish injustice within any nation that treats such decent and engaged writers as if they were criminals, for that nation endangers the health of its own cultural life in the doing.

Noting similarities between the racism of South Africa and New

York City, after having the opportunity to interview Nelson Mandela in 1991, in "The Measure of the Man" Miller expresses his admiration for the African leader's lack of rancor regarding his past treatment and ability to see past color and class—traits he views clearly as worthy of emulation. Meanwhile, "The Parable of the Stripper" relates an ironic anecdote during which the members of a group of Yugoslavian artists, committed to equality for all, each expose their own innate tribalism when asked to identify the ethnicity of a stripper. "Uneasy About the Germans: After the Wall" allows Miller to discuss two notions close to his heart—his strong belief in the democratic system and his insistence that the past should never be forgotten. Not that he sees any signs of it failing, but Miller voices a suspicion of the authenticity of Germany's embrace of democracy, given both its historical proclivity toward more authoritarian regimes, and the fact that, rather than fought for, this political system was imposed upon its citizens. Albeit hopeful that Germans can better internalize this transformation, he asks that both they and others remain vigilant.

Recalling again that notion of the "life-lie," "The Sin of Power" Miller tells us, "is to not only distort reality but to convince people that the false is true." Miller argues this is something of which both Soviets and Americans are guilty, although he maintains that Americans remain freer to challenge this and should do so to the best of their ability to ensure the rights of the individual cannot be trampled. In 2000, Miller was part of a group of "cultural visitors" invited to Cuba, and he wrote of this experience in "A Visit with Castro." He likens Castro to an outmoded Don Quixote, who has clearly lost touch with reality, and whose enchantment with power has perverted his original ambition. The American embargo, he concludes, rather than helping the situation, is actually assisting Castro in keeping things the way he wants. Written in 2003, "Why Israel Must Choose Justice" was Miller's acceptance speech for receiving the Jerusalem Prize, in part for his "activities in defense of civil rights." It created controversy for its hard-line approach to Israeli politics of the time, calling for the state of Israel to reconsider its settlement policy, which Miller viewed as working against the spirit of her original charter and felt could only undercut Israel's future safety. Just as Israel was created for Jews as an act of justice and repayment for the suffering of the Holocaust, Miller felt that

Israel's response toward the Palestinians should reflect its baseline humanistic values rather than become so aggressively territorial.

Satire

Miller's use of satire points to an aspect of Miller that is all too often overlooked; the man could be very funny. Feeding off Jonathan Swift's 1729 satire of the callous attitude toward Irish famine, by which he instructs the Irish to eat their own babies, Miller's "A Modest Proposal for the Pacification of the Public" mocks the way 1950s paranoia caused civil rights to be trampled and people condemned on flimsy to no evidence, by suggesting that everyone should be sent to jail at the age of eighteen for two years until they can prove their patriotism, and determines different levels of "treachery." "Get It Right: Private Executions," meanwhile, is a pointed dig at supporters of the death penalty, and no doubt dropped the seed that would later become the comical satiric play *Resurrection Blues*. In it, he suggests criminals should be executed in large sporting arenas, and admission charges could help pay for the prison system and provide compensation for victims. His "hope" is that growing tired of such spectacles, people would reassess the efficacy of maintaining the death penalty, since it has clearly not reduced the number of murders committed and only adds to the death total. "Let's Privatize Congress" berates Congress for its many hypocrisies over issues such as health care, the environment, and education, and the rise of private economic interests in the country's governance. By making Congress a private enterprise, he jokes, representatives can have their salaries paid by whichever business wants their vote, and we will have full transparency and avoid the costs of expensive campaigns and the "inconvenience" of voting.

While described by some as the "moral conscience" of America, it is evident from his essays that while Miller attempts to take the moral path, he is also fully aware of his own potential biases, which he examines through his writing with true surgical precision. Forthright and willing to tackle even the most sensitive issues with a calm deliberation, he writes to make sense of the world for himself as much as for his reader. Quite often we see how his initial stance becomes adapted by the essay's conclusion as he draws in an accretion of detail to support this alternate view. While only including selected essays, the breadth and scope of this collection is underscored by the varied approaches and topics covered. Whether he is winking at us in playful humor or seriously addressing a concern in measured prose, Miller is always, as fellow playwright Edward Albee observed at Miller's memorial service in 2005, "a writer who mattered. A lot."

SUSAN C. W. ABBOTSON

ON THE THEATER

Sorting Things Out: Foreword to
The Theater Essays of Arthur Miller
1977

I find it hard to read through these essays without wanting to make changes on each page and often in each sentence. Nothing written about the theater ever comes out right, the thing is forever escaping its commentators.

I am a little surprised that I have written so much on the subject in the past thirty years, and it is hard now to remember what drove me to it. I think it may have been the feeling that it was being trivialized in most published commentary at a time when I thought it the most important thing in the world. It could be of some great importance, I still think, if we ever get it beyond the childish delights of the commercial hit-flop situation.

I have not so much changed my opinions about certain issues as added to what I believed, but I have often wished that I had never written a word on the subject of tragedy. I am not a scholar, not a critic, and my interest in the phenomenon was and is purely practical, so that having delivered myself of certain views I only unwittingly entered an arena of near-theological devoutness which I had not known existed. The damage having been done, however, there is no further reason to withhold new thoughts, which may or may not line up with those of the ancients and their modern heirs.

I have not yet seen a convincing explanation of why the tragic mode seems anachronistic now, nor am I about to attempt one. But it has often seemed to me that what tragedy requires—of the artist first and of the audience thereafter—is a kind of grief without which the tragic area somehow cannot be approached. Instead of grief we have come to substitute irony and even comedy, black or otherwise. I am too lazy to go back to Aristotle, but I do not recall his mentioning grief; most probably because he took for granted that his hero's catastrophe would entail that emotion all by itself.

It is probably not that we have lost the capacity to grieve, but that we have misplaced the ritual through which grief can be shown to others and shared. Of course the waning of organized religion is a factor, but I wonder if it is not more a result than a cause. And I wonder, too, if we are awkward about grieving because the loss of one person evokes in us only the paradoxical fact of death without the straightforward and clear image of a sacred identity that has vanished. Rather, we know that nothing and no one is truly sacred, but that a biological set of forces have been used up so that there is something faintly fatuous, something perhaps operatic, in the kind of grief-outbreak which underlies the real tragedies as they approach their moments of terror and death.

If we are this way—rationalized and beyond the reach of public grief—it is interesting to wonder why it has happened. And inevitably there arise the images of the carnage of two world wars, the many revolutions and counter-revolutions, the Nazi Holocaust—this, after all, has been the most spendthrift of all centuries with human lives. Perhaps the public psyche has simply been overloaded and, like an electrical circuit, has blown its fuse and gone cold under the weight of too many impulses. So that the tragic proposal is simply presumptuous—this making so much out of one death when we know it is meaningless. In other words, in an important respect we have ceased to feel.

I would agree, except that we can still respond to the old trage-dies as much as people apparently did in early times. Is this merely nostalgia? It doesn't seem so in the theater.

My own view, or at least my leaning, is toward a less alarming explanation. Clearly, however tragedy is defined or explained, it must allow the hero to speak for himself. This may sound so rudi-mentary as not to be worth discussing, but in contemporary drama few major characters are allowed this privilege, it being assumed that something like naturalism is one thing we can't have. What we have instead are forms of authorial ironical comment or directorial interpretation of the character's situation total enough to wipe out his autonomy entirely. We are being spared the incoherence of the character's feeling for the coherence of our own interpretation, which allows us to observe the outlines of suffering without very much participation in it. Thus, it is absurd to attempt the kind of protest that tragedy always has entailed, a cry against heaven, fate, or what you will. That cry may still be implicit, but it has been stylized into a glance upwards or even a grin and a cough. From one or another philosophical points of view this makes lots of sense, but is it really the viewpoint of the sufferer or of the one observing him? If we could get this sorted out, we might well see tragic emotions forming again.

What I think has been forgotten is that the objectivity of a Shakespeare is expressed through his form—the balancing of responsibility between various persons, interests, and forces—but that the sufferings that result are not at all objectified, dried up, or gentled. It may be we have lost the art of tragedy for want of a certain level of self-respect, finally, and are in disgrace with ourselves. Compared to the tragic emotion, the others are covered with a certain embarrassment, even shame, as though suffering were a sign of one's failure or a loss of dignity, like being caught with a hole in one's stocking at an affair of state. People not free enough to weep or cry out are not fit subjects for tragedy, at least not on the stage, and weeping without self-respect is mere self-pity.

As for the sociology in these pieces, I still support its main point, the need to subsidize the American theater. I have had far more experience with such theaters abroad than I had decades ago, and I would add now that a mixed private and public theater would be the most useful rather than a monopoly by either type. A subsidy is a form of power that always tends toward bureaucratization and needs challenging from outside the organization. We are still, at this writing, paying less for the upkeep of theater art than any other viable nation.

Finally, there is a question of tone in these pieces—an overemphasis here and there on what has already been proved. I would ask the reader to remember that an unspoken gentleman's agreement was prevalent in the 1940s and '50s, if not earlier, under which every playwright had to present himself to critics and the public as a pure entertainer, a man in an aesthetic daze who barely knew the name of the president or how to negotiate a subway turnstile. This image was good for business, conforming to the Anglo-Saxon tradition of the separation of church and state, poesy and instruction, form and meaning. A play, needless to say, could not teach without exploding into its several parts, so that the most authentically aesthetic of experiences was necessarily the one without any perceptible reference to society or life as it was lived. The exception was George Bernard Shaw, but only because he was funny, and funny in a definitely aristocratic manner that gave him license to preach the virtues of a socialism of wits and a capitalism whose horrors were familiar, somehow warm, and somehow bearable after all.

Thus, the lessons of a play, its meaning and theme, had to spread out like a contagion if they were to be aesthetic, in which case few would be aware they were even infected. In a word, what I was trying to do was to objectify the social situation of our theater, and even of some of the creative procedures that produced one style of playwriting or another, rather than leaving these matters—as our critics normally did—to temperament and taste without deeper reason or cause.

Nevertheless and notwithstanding, the theater is first of all imitation, mimickry. If anything contrary is found in these pieces, it was not intended to be there. We need food, sex, and an image. The rest is commentary on these.

Tragedy and the Common Man
1949

In this age few tragedies are written. It has often been held that the lack is due to a paucity of heroes among us, or else that modern man has had the blood drawn out of his organs of belief by the skepticism of science, and the heroic attack on life cannot feed on an attitude of reserve and circumspection. For one reason or another, we are often held to be below tragedy—or tragedy above us. The inevitable conclusion is, of course, that the tragic mode is archaic, fit only for the very highly placed, the kings or the kingly, and where this admission is not made in so many words it is most often implied.

I believe that the common man is as apt a subject for tragedy in its highest sense as kings were. On the face of it this ought to be obvious in the light of modern psychiatry, which bases its analysis upon classic formulations, such as the Oedipus and Orestes complexes, for instances, which were enacted by royal beings, but which apply to everyone in similar emotional situations.

More simply, when the question of tragedy in art is not at issue, we never hesitate to attribute to the well-placed and the exalted the very same mental processes as the lowly. And finally, if the exaltation of tragic action were truly a property of the high-bred character alone, it is inconceivable that the mass of mankind should cherish tragedy above all other forms, let alone be capable of understanding it.

As a general rule, to which there may be exceptions unknown to me, I think the tragic feeling is evoked in us when we are in the presence of a character who is ready to lay down his life, if need be, to secure one thing—his sense of personal dignity. From Orestes to

Hamlet, Medea to Macbeth, the underlying struggle is that of the individual attempting to gain his "rightful" position in his society.

Sometimes he is one who has been displaced from it, sometimes one who seeks to attain it for the first time, but the fateful wound from which the inevitable events spiral is the wound of indignity, and its dominant force is indignation. Tragedy, then, is the consequence of a man's total compulsion to evaluate himself justly.

In the sense of having been initiated by the hero himself, the tale always reveals what has been called his "tragic flaw," a failing that is not peculiar to grand or elevated characters. Nor is it necessarily a weakness. The flaw, or crack in the character, is really nothing— and need be nothing—but his inherent unwillingness to remain passive in the face of what he conceives to be a challenge to his dignity, his image of his rightful status. Only the passive, only those who accept their lot without active retaliation, are "flawless." Most of us are in that category.

But there are among us today, as there always have been, those who act against the scheme of things that degrades them, and in the process of action everything we have accepted out of fear or insensitivity or ignorance is shaken before us and examined, and from this total onslaught by an individual against the seemingly stable cosmos surrounding us—from this total examination of the "unchangeable" environment—comes the terror and the fear that is classically associated with tragedy.

More important, from this total questioning of what has previously been unquestioned, we learn. And such a process is not beyond the common man. In revolutions around the world, these past thirty years, he has demonstrated again and again this inner dynamic of all tragedy.

Insistence upon the rank of the tragic hero, or the so-called nobility of his character, is really but a clinging to the outward forms of tragedy. If rank or nobility of character was indispensable, then it would follow that the problems of those with rank were the particular problems of tragedy. But surely the right of one monarch to capture the domain from another no longer raises our passions, nor are our concepts of justice what they were to the mind of an Elizabethan king.

The quality in such plays that does shake us, however, derives from the underlying fear of being displaced, the disaster inherent in being torn away from our chosen image of what and who we are in this world. Among us today this fear is as strong, and perhaps stronger, than it ever was. In fact, it is the common man who knows this fear best.

Now, if it is true that tragedy is the consequence of a man's total compulsion to evaluate himself justly, his destruction in the attempt posits a wrong or an evil in his environment. And this is precisely the morality of tragedy and its lesson. The discovery of the moral law, which is what the enlightenment of tragedy consists of, is not the discovery of some abstract or metaphysical quantity.

The tragic right is a condition of life, a condition in which the human personality is able to flower and realize itself. The wrong is the condition which suppresses man, perverts the flowing out of his love and creative instinct. Tragedy enlightens—and it must, in that it points the heroic finger at the enemy of man's freedom. The thrust for freedom is the quality in tragedy which exalts. The revolutionary questioning of the stable environment is what terrifies. In no way is the common man debarred from such thoughts or such actions.

Seen in this light, our lack of tragedy may be partially accounted for by the turn which modern literature has taken toward the purely psychiatric view of life, or the purely sociological. If all our miseries, our indignities, are born and bred within our minds, then all action, let alone the heroic action, is obviously impossible.

And if society alone is responsible for the cramping of our lives, then the protagonist must needs be so pure and faultless as to force us to deny his validity as a character. From neither of these views can tragedy derive, simply because neither represents a balanced concept of life. Above all else, tragedy requires the finest appreciation by the writer of cause and effect.

No tragedy can therefore come about when its author fears to question absolutely everything, when he regards any institution, habit or custom as being either everlasting, immutable or inevitable. In the tragic view the need of man to wholly realize himself is the only fixed star, and whatever it is that hedges his nature and lowers it is ripe for attack and examination. Which is not to say that tragedy must preach revolution.

The Greeks could probe the very heavenly origin of their ways and return to confirm the rightness of laws. And Job could face God in anger, demanding his right and end in submission. But for a moment everything is in suspension, nothing is accepted, and in this stretching and tearing apart of the cosmos, in the very action of so doing, the character gains "size," the tragic stature which is spuriously attached to the royal or the highborn in our minds. The commonest of men may take on that stature to the extent of his willingness to throw all he has into the contest, the battle to secure his rightful place in his world.

There is a misconception of tragedy with which I have been struck in review after review, and in many conversations with writers and readers alike. It is the idea that tragedy is of necessity allied to pessimism. Even the dictionary says nothing more about the word than that it means a story with a sad or unhappy ending. This impression is so firmly fixed that I almost hesitate to claim that in truth tragedy implies more optimism in its author than does comedy, and that its final result ought to be the reinforcement of the onlooker's brightest opinions of the human animal.

For, if it is true to say that in essence the tragic hero is intent upon claiming his whole due as a personality, and if this struggle must be total and without reservation, then it automatically demonstrates the indestructible will of man to achieve his humanity.

The possibility of victory must be there in tragedy. Where pathos rules, where pathos is finally derived, a character has fought a battle he could not possibly have won. The pathetic is achieved when the protagonist is, by virtue of his witlessness, his insensitivity or the very air he gives off, incapable of grappling with a much superior force.

Pathos truly is the mode for the pessimist. But tragedy requires a nicer balance between what is possible and what is impossible. And it is curious, although edifying, that the plays we revere, century after century, are the tragedies. In them, and in them alone, lies the belief—optimistic, if you will, in the perfectibility of man.

It is time, I think, that we who are without kings, took up this bright thread of our history and followed it to the only place it can possibly lead in our time—the heart and spirit of the average man.

The Nature of Tragedy
1949

There are whole libraries of books dealing with the nature of tragedy. That the subject is capable of interesting so many writers over the centuries is part proof that the idea of tragedy is constantly changing, and more, that it will never be finally defined.

In our day, however, when there seems so little time or inclination to theorize at all, certain elemental misconceptions have taken hold of both critics and readers to a point where the word has often been reduced to an epithet. A more exact appreciation of what tragedy entails can lead us all to a finer understanding of plays in general, which in turn may raise the level of our theater.

The most common confusion is that which fails to discriminate between the tragic and the pathetic. Any story, to have validity on the stage, must entail conflict. Obviously the conflict must be between people. But such a conflict is of the lowest, most elementary order; this conflict purely *between* people is all that is needed for melodrama and naturally reaches its apogee in physical violence. In fact, this kind of conflict defines melodrama.

The next rung up the ladder is the story which is not only a conflict between people, but at the same time within the minds of the combatants. When I show you why a man does what he does, I may do so melodramatically; but when I show why he almost did not do it, I am making drama.

Why is this higher? Because it more closely reflects the actual process of human action. It is quite possible to write a good melodrama without creating a single living character; in fact, melodrama becomes diffused wherever the vagaries and contradictions of real characterizations come into play. But without a living character it is not possible to create drama or tragedy. For as soon as one investigates not only why a man is acting, but what is trying to prevent him from acting—assuming one does so honestly—it becomes extremely difficult to contain the action in the forced and arbitrary form of melodrama.

Now, standing upon this element of drama we can try to reach toward tragedy. Tragedy, first of all, creates a certain order of feeling in the audience. The pathetic creates another order of feeling. Again, as with drama and melodrama, one is higher than the other. But while drama may be differentiated psychologically from melodrama—the higher entailing a conflict *within* each character— to separate tragedy from the mere pathetic is much more difficult. It is difficult because here society enters in.

Let me put it this way. When Mr. B., while walking down the street, is struck on the head by a falling piano, the newspapers call this a tragedy. In fact, of course, this is only the pathetic end of Mr. B. Not only because of the accidental nature of his death; that is elementary. It is pathetic because it merely arouses our feelings of sympathy, sadness, and possibly of identification. What the death of Mr. B. does not arouse is the tragic feeling.

To my mind the essential difference, and the precise difference, between tragedy and pathos is that tragedy brings us not only sadness, sympathy, identification and even fear; it also, unlike pathos, brings us knowledge or enlightenment.

But what sort of knowledge? In the largest sense, it is knowledge pertaining to the right way of living in the world. The manner of Mr. B. 's death was not such as to illustrate any principle of living. In short, there was no illumination of the ethical in it. And to put it all in the same breath, the reason we confuse the tragic with the pathetic, as well as why we create so few tragedies, is twofold: in the first place many of our writers have given up trying to search out the right way of living, and secondly, there is not among us any commonly accepted faith in a way of life that will give us not only material gain but satisfaction.

Our modern literature has filled itself with an attitude which implies that despite suffering, nothing important can really be learned by man that might raise him to a happier condition. The probing of the soul has taken the path of behaviorism. By this method it is sufficient for an artist simply to spell out the anatomy of disaster. Man is regarded as essentially a dumb animal moving through a preconstructed maze toward his inevitable sleep.

Such a concept of man can never reach beyond pathos, for enlightenment is impossible within it, life being regarded as an immutably disastrous fact. Tragedy, called a more exalted kind of consciousness, is so called because it makes us aware of what the character might have been. But to say or strongly imply what a man might have been requires of the author a soundly based, completely believed vision of man's great possibilities. As Aristotle said, the poet is greater than the historian because he presents not only things as they were, but foreshadows what they might have been. We forsake literature when we are content to chronicle disaster.

Tragedy, therefore, is inseparable from a certain modest hope regarding the human animal. And it is the glimpse of this brighter possibility that raises sadness out of the pathetic toward the tragic.

But again, to take up a sad story and discover the hope that may lie buried in it, requires a most complete grasp of the characters involved. For nothing is so destructive of reality in literature as thinly motivated optimism. It is my view—or my prejudice—that when a man is seen whole and round and so characterized, when he is allowed his life on the stage over and beyond the mould and purpose of the story, hope will show its face in his, just as it does, even so dimly, in life. As the old saying has it, there is some good in the worst of us. I think that the tragedian, supposedly the saddest of citizens, can never forget this fact, and must strive always to posit a world in which that good might have been allowed to express itself instead of succumbing to the evil. I began by saying that tragedy would probably never be wholly defined. I end by offering you a definition. It is not final for me, but at least it has the virtue of keeping mere pathos out.

You are witnessing a tragedy when the characters before you are wholly and intensely realized, to the degree that your belief in their reality is all but complete. The story in which they are involved is such as to force their complete personalities to be brought to bear upon the problem, to the degree that you are able to understand not only why they are ending in sadness, but how they might have avoided their end. The demeanor, so to speak, of the story is most serious—so serious that you have been brought to the state of outright fear for the people involved, as though for yourself.

And all this, not merely so that your senses shall have been stretched and your glands stimulated, but that you may come away with the knowledge that man, by reason of his intense effort and desire, which you have just seen demonstrated, is capable of flowering on this earth.

Tragedy arises when we are in the presence of a man who has missed accomplishing his joy. But the joy must be there, the promise of the right way of life must be there. Otherwise pathos reigns, and an endless, meaningless, and essentially untrue picture of man is created—man helpless under the falling piano, man wholly lost in a universe which by its very nature is too hostile to be mastered.

In a word, tragedy is the most accurately balanced portrayal of the human being in his struggle for happiness. That is why we revere our tragedies in the highest, because they most truly portray us. And that is why tragedy must not be diminished through confusion with other modes, for it is the most perfect means we have of showing us who and what we are, and what we must be—or should strive to become.

Introduction to the *Collected Plays*
1957

I

As a writer of plays I share with all specialists a suspicion of gener-
alities about the art and technique of my craft, and I lack both the
scholarly patience and the zeal to define terms in such a way as to
satisfy everyone. The only other course, therefore, is to stop along
the way to say what *I* mean by the terms I use, quite certain as I do
so that I will be taken to task by no small number of people, but
hopeful at the same time that something useful may be said about
this art, a form of writing which generates more opinions and fewer
instructive critical statements than any other. To be useful it seems
impossible not to risk the obvious by returning always to the fundamental nature of theater, its historic human function, so to speak.
For it seems odd, when one thinks of it, that an art which has always
been so expensive to produce and so difficult to do well should have
survived in much the same general form that it possessed when it
began. This is especially striking now, when almost alone among
the arts the theater has managed to live despite the devouring mech-
anization of the age, and, in some places and instances, even to
thrive and grow. Under these circumstances of a very long if frequently interrupted history, one may make the assumption that the
drama and its production must represent a well-defined expression
of profound social needs, needs which transcend any particular
form of society or any particular historic moment. It is therefore
possible to speak of fundamentals of the form too when its only

tools of importance never change, there being no possibility of drama without mimicry, conflict, tale, or speech.

My approach to playwriting and the drama itself is organic; and to make this glaringly evident at once it is necessary to separate drama from what we think of today as literature. A drama ought not be looked at first and foremost from literary perspectives merely because it uses words, verbal rhythm, and poetic image. These can be its most memorable parts, it is true, but they are not its inevitable accompaniments. Nor is it only convention which from Aristotle onward decreed that the play must be dramatic rather than narrative in concept and execution. A Greek's seat was harder than an American's and even he had to call a halt to a dramatic presentation after a couple of hours. The physiological limits of attention in a seated position enforce upon this art an interconnected group of laws, in turn expressed by aesthetic criteria, which no other writing art requires. But it is not my intention here to vivisect dramatic form or the techniques of playwriting. I only want to take advantage of this rare opportunity—a collected edition—to speak for myself as to my own aims; not to give my estimates of what can portentously be called the dramatic problem in this time, but simply to talk in workaday language about the problem of how to write so that one's changing vision of people in the world is more accurately represented in each succeeding work.

A few of the inevitable materials of the art dictate to me certain aesthetic commitments which may as well be mentioned at the outset, for they move silently but nevertheless with potent influence through the plays in this book as well as in my thoughts about them. These plays were written on the assumption that they would be acted before audiences. The "actor" is a person, and he no sooner appears than certain elementary questions are broached. Who is he? What is he doing here? How does he live or make his living? Who is he related to? Is he rich or poor? What does he think of himself? What do other people think of him, and why? What are his hopes and fears; and what does he say they are? What does he claim to want, and what does he really want?

The actor brings questions onto the stage just as any person does when we first meet him in our ordinary lives. Which of them a play chooses to answer, and how they are answered, are the ruling and highly consequential imperatives which create the style of the play, and control what are later called the stylistic levels of its writing. If, for instance, the actor is masked as he appears and his body movements are constricted and highly ordered, we instantly expect that the common surfaces of life will also be breached by the kinds of questions he or the play will respond to. He will very probably speak about the theme or essential preoccupation of the play directly and without getting to it by circuitous routes of naturalistic detail. If he appears in the costume of his trade, class, or profession, however, we expect that he or the play will give us the answers to his common identity, and if they do not they risk our dissatisfaction and frustration. In a word, the actor's appearance on the stage in normal human guise leads us to expect a realistic treatment. The play will either be intent upon rounding out the characters by virtue of its complete answers to the common questions, or will substitute answers to a more limited group of questions which, instead of being "human," are thematic and are designed to form a symbol of meaning rather than an apparency of the "real." It is the nature of the questions asked and answered, rather than the language used— whether verse, ordinary slang, or colorless prose—that determines whether the style is realistic or non-realistic. When I speak of style, therefore, this is one of the relationships I intend to convey. In this sense the tragedies of Shakespeare are species of realism, and those of Aeschylus and Sophocles are not. We know a great deal more about Macbeth and Hamlet, apart from their functions as characters in their particular given dramas, than we can ever surmise about Oedipus the king, or the heroes and heroines of Strindberg's plays. To put it another way, when the career of a person rather than the detail of his motives stands at the forefront of the play, we move closer to non-realistic styles, and vice versa. I regard this as the one immovable and irremediable quality which goes to create one style or another. And there is always an organic connection rather than a temperamental choice involved in the style in which a play is written and must be performed. The first two plays in this book were written and performed with the intention of answering as many of the common questions as was possible.

The Crucible, *A Memory of Two Mondays*, and *A View from the Bridge* were not so designed, and to this extent they are a departure from realism.

Another decisive influence upon style is the conception and manipulation of time in a play. Broadly speaking, where it is conceived and used so as to convey a natural passage of hours, days, or months, the style it enforces is pressed toward realism. Where action is quite openly freed so that things mature in a moment, for instance, which would take a year in life, a true license for non-realistic styles is thereby won. As is obvious, the destruction of temporal necessity occurs in every play if only to a rudimentary degree; it is impossible that in life people should behave and speak in reference to a single thematic point for so continuous a time. Events, therefore, are always collapsed and drawn together in any drama. But as the collapsing process becomes more self-evident, and as the selection of events becomes less and less dominated by the question of their natural maturation, the style of the play moves further and further away from realism. *All My Sons* attempts to account for time in terms of months, days, and hours. *Death of a Salesman* explodes the watch and the calendar. *The Crucible* is bound by natural time— or strives to appear so.

The compacting of time destroys the realistic style not only because it violates our sense of reality, but because collapsing time inevitably emphasizes an element of existence which in life is not visible or ordinarily felt with equivalent power, and this is its symbolic meaning. When a criminal is arraigned, for instance, it is the prosecutor's job to symbolize his behavior for the jury so that the man's entire life can be characterized in one way and not in another. The prosecutor does not mention the accused as a dog lover, a good husband and father, a sufferer from eczema, or a man with the habit of chewing tobacco on the left and not the right side of his mouth. Nor does he strive to account for the long intervals of time when the accused was behaving in a way quite contrary to that symbolic characterization. The prosecutor is collapsing time—and destroying realism—by fastening only on those actions germane to the construction of his symbol. To one degree or another every play must do this or we should have to sit in a theater for years in order to appreciate a character and his story. But where the play does pretend to give us details of hours, months, and years which are not clearly and avowedly germane to the symbolic meaning, we come closer and closer to what is called a realistic style. In passing, I should say that the Greek "unity" of time imposed on the drama was not arbitrary but a concomitant of the preponderant Greek interest in the fate and career of the hero rather than his private characteristics, or, to put it another way, his social and symbolic side rather than his family role.

Another material, so to speak, of drama is not describable in a word, and has a less direct influence on style. I mention it, however, because it is probably the single most powerful influence on my way of writing and enforces on me a kind of taste and approach to the art which marks these plays. It is necessary, if one is to reflect reality, not only to depict why a man does what he does, or why he nearly didn't do it, but why he cannot simply walk away and say to hell with it. To ask this last question of a play is a cruel thing, for evasion is probably the most developed technique most men have, and in truth there is an extraordinarily small number of conflicts which we must, at any cost, live out to their conclusions. To ask this question is immediately to impose on oneself not, perhaps, a style of writing but at least a kind of dramatic construction. For I understand the symbolic meaning of a character and his career to consist of the kind of commitment he makes to life or refuses to make, the kind of challenge he accepts and the kind he can pass by. I take it that if one could know enough about a human being one could discover some conflict, some value, some challenge, however minor or major, which he cannot find it in himself to walk away from or turn his back on. The structure of these plays, in this respect, is to the end that such a conflict be discovered and clarified. Idea, in these plays, is the generalized meaning of that discovery applied to men other than the hero. Time, characterizations, and other elements are treated differently from play to play, but all to the end that that moment of commitment be brought forth, that moment when, in my eyes, a man differentiates himself from every other man, that moment when out of a sky full of stars he fixes on one star. I take it, as well, that the less capable a man is of walking away from the central conflict of the play, the closer he approaches a tragic existence. In turn, this implies that the closer a man

approaches tragedy the more intense is his concentration of emotion upon the fixed point of his commitment, which is to say the
closer he approaches what in life we call fanaticism. From this
flows the necessity for scenes of high and open emotion, and plays
constructed toward climax rather than the evocation of a mood
alone or of bizarre spectacle. (The one exception among these plays
is *A Memory of Two Mondays*—as will be seen later.)

From such considerations it ought to be clear that the common
tokens of realism and non-realism are in themselves not acceptable
as criteria. That a play is written prosaically does not make it a
realistic play, and that the speech is heightened and intensified by
imagery does not set it to one side of realism necessarily. The underlying poem of a play I take to be the organic necessity of its parts. I
find in the arbitrary not poetry but indulgence. (The novel is
another matter entirely.) A very great play can be mimed and still
issue forth its essential actions and their rudiments of symbolic
meaning; the word, in drama, is the transformation into speech of
what is *happening*, and the fiat for intense language is intensity of
happening. We have had more than one extraordinary dramatist
who was a cripple as a writer, and this is lamentable but not ruin-
ous. Which is to say that I prize the poetic above else in the theater,
and because I do I insist that the poem truly be there.

II

The assumption—or presumption—behind these plays is that life
has meaning. I would now add, as their momentary commentator,
that what they meant to me at the time of writing is not in each
instance the same as what they mean to me now in the light of further experience. Plato, by banning artists from citizenship in his
ideal republic, expressed at least a partial truth; the intention
behind a work of art and its effects upon the public are not always
the same. Worse yet, in his conscious intention the artist often conceals from himself an aim which can be quite opposed to his fond-
est beliefs and ideas. Those more tempted by an evil, for instance,
are more likely to feel deeply about it than those who have only
known the good. From this, two ironic propositions logically flow.

The first is that a play's "idea" may be useful as a unifying force empowering the artist to evoke a cogent emotional life on the stage, but that in itself it has no aesthetic value, since, after all, it is only a means to an end. The second is that since every play means something—even the play which denies all meaning to existence—the "idea" of a play is its measure of value and importance and beauty, and that a play which appears merely to exist to one side of "ideas" is an aesthetic nullity.

Idea is very important to me as a dramatist, but I think it is time someone said that playwrights, including the greatest, have not been noted for the new ideas they have broached in their plays. By new I mean an original idea invented by the playwright, quite as such things are created, if infrequently, by scientists, and occasionally by philosophers. Surely there is no known philosophy which was first announced through a play, nor any ethical idea. No social concept in Shaw's plays could have been much of a surprise to the Webbs and thousands of other Socialists of the time; nor can Ibsen, Chekhov, Strindberg, or O'Neill be credited with inventing any new thoughts. As a matter of fact, it is highly unlikely that a new idea could be successfully launched through a play at all, and this for several good reasons.

A genuine invention in the realm of ideas must first emerge as an abstruse and even partial concept. Be it Christianity, Darwinism, Marxism, or any other that can with reason be called original it has always been the product of proofs which, before they go to form a complete and new concept, require years and often generations of testing, research, and polemic. At first blush a new idea appears to be very close to insanity because to be new it must reverse important basic beliefs and assumptions which, in turn, have been institutionalized and are administered by one or another kind of priesthood with a vested interest in the old idea. Nor would the old idea be an idea at all, strictly speaking, if some goodly section of the population did not believe in it. If only because no dramatic structure can bear the brunt of the incredulity with which any really new idea is greeted, the play form would collapse under the burdens of having to deliver up the mountain of proof required for a new idea to be believed. And this would be true even if the audience were all philosophers—perhaps even truer, for the philosopher requires proofs even more exact than the layman does.

The dramatic form is a dynamic thing. It is not possible to dally in it for reflection. The polemical method, as well as the scientific exposition, the parable, or the ethical teaching, all depend upon a process which, in effect, says, "What you believe is wrong for these reasons; what the truth is is as follows." Tremendous energy must go into destroying the validity of the ancient proposition, and destroying it from an absolutely opposite viewpoint. An idea, if it is really new, is a genuine humiliation for the majority of the people; it is an affront not only to their sensibilities but to their deepest convictions. It offends against the things they worship, whether God or science or money.

The conflict between a new idea and the very notion of drama is remorseless and not resolvable because, among other things, plays are always performed before people sitting en masse and not alone. To a very large degree, much greater than is generally realized, we react *with* a surrounding crowd rather than against it; our individual criteria of truth are set to one side and we are no longer at the mercy of a performance alone, but of the surrounding reaction to it. A man walking down a deserted street sees another man beating a horse; he does not like this, he is possibly revolted by it, even angered. Perhaps he walks on, or perhaps he stops to remonstrate with the horsewhipper, who then perhaps threatens *him* with the same whip. Depending on the character of the man, he either fights or decides it is none of his business, really, and goes on about his life. The same man on the same street, but this time a busy street with many people, sees the same scene of cruelty. He is now behaving in public; he cries out and hears his cries echoed; he is encouraged; he moves in to stop the cruelty and when he himself is threatened the conflict in him over whether to back off or to fight is much higher and more intense, for now he is surrounded by the administrators of shame or the bestowers of honor—his fellow men. He is no longer looking at the same scene in the same way; the very significance of the experience is changed and more likely than not his own actions. So it is in the theater. Inevitably, to one degree or another, we see what we see on the stage not only with our own eyes but with the eyes of others. Our standards of right and wrong, good taste and bad, must in some way come into either conflict or agreement with social standards, and a truth, however true, is no longer merely itself, but itself plus the conventional reaction to it; and in the case of a genuinely new idea the conventional reaction, by definition, will come down on it like a ton of bricks, and it is finished, however beautifully written.

If plays have not broached new ideas, they have enunciated not-yet-popular ideas which are already in the air, ideas for which there has already been a preparation by non-dramatic media. Which is to say that once an idea is "in the air" it is no longer an idea but a feeling, a sensation, an emotion, and with these the drama can deal. For one thing, where no doubt exists in the hearts of the people, a play cannot create doubt: where no desire to believe exists, a play cannot create a belief. And again, this springs from the nature of dramatic form and its inevitable dynamism; it must communicate as it proceeds and it literally has no existence if it must wait until the audience goes home to think before it can be appreciated. It is the art of the present tense par excellence.

Thus it is that the forms, the accents, the intentions of the plays in this book are not the same from play to play. I could say that my awareness of life was not the same and leave it at that, but the truth is wider, for good or for ill. It is also that the society to which I responded in the past decade was constantly changing, as it is changing while I write this sentence. These plays, in one sense, are my response to what was "in the air," they are one man's way of saying to his fellow men, "This is what you see every day, or think or feel; now I will show you what you really know but have not had the time, or the disinterestedness, or the insight, or the information to understand consciously." Each of these plays, in varying degrees, was begun in the belief that it was unveiling a truth already known but unrecognized as such. My concept of the audience is of a public each member of which is carrying about with him what he thinks is an anxiety, or a hope, or a preoccupation which is his alone and isolates him from mankind; and in this respect at least the function of a play is to reveal him to himself so that he may touch others by virtue of the revelation of his mutuality with them. If only for this reason I regard the theater as a serious business, one that makes or should make man more human, which is to say, less alone.

III

When *All My Sons* opened on Broadway, it was called an "Ibsenesque" play. Some people liked it for this reason and others did not. Ibsen is relevant to this play but what he means to me is not always what he means to others, either his advocates or his detractors. More often than not, these days, he is thought of as a stage carpenter with a flair for ideas of importance. The whole aim of shaping a dramatic work on strict lines which will elicit a distinct meaning reducible to a sentence is now suspect. "Life" is now more complicated than such a mechanical contrasting of forces can hope to reflect. Instead, the aim is a "poetic" drama, preferably one whose ultimate thought or meaning is elusive, a drama which appears not to have been composed or constructed, but which somehow comes to life on a stage and then flickers away. To come quickly to the point, our theater inclines toward the forms of adolescence rather than analytical adulthood. It is not my place to deal in praise or blame, but it seems to me that a fair judge would be compelled to conclude, as a minimum, that the run of serious works of the past decade have been written and played under an intellectually—as well as electrically—diffused light. It is believed that any attempt to "prove" something in a play is somehow unfair and certainly inartistic, if not gauche, more particularly if what is being proved happens to be in any overt way of social moment. Indeed, one American critic believes that the narrowness of the theater audience—as compared with that for the movies and television—is the result of the masses' having been driven away from the theater by plays that preached.

This is not, of course, a new attitude in the world. Every major playwright has had to make his way against it, for there is and always will be a certain amount of resentfulness toward the presumption of any playwright to teach. And there will never be a satisfactory way of explaining that no playwright can be praised for his high seriousness and at the same time be praised for not trying to teach; the very conception of a dramatic theme inevitably means that certain aspects of life are selected and others left out, and to imagine that a play can be written disinterestedly is to believe that one can make love disinterestedly.

The debatable question is never whether a play ought to teach but whether it is art, and in this connection the basic criterion—purely technical considerations to one side—is the passion with which the teaching is made. I hasten to add the obvious—that a work cannot be judged by the validity of its teaching. But it is entirely misleading to state that there is some profound conflict between art and the philosophically or socially meaningful theme. I say this not out of a preference for plays that teach but in deference to the nature of the creative act. A work of art is not handed down from Olympus from a creature with a vision as wide as the world. If that could be done a play would never end, just as history has no end. A play must end, and end with a climax, and to forge a climax the forces in life, which are of infinite complexity, must be made finite and capable of a more or less succinct culmination. Thus, all dramas are to that extent arbitrary—in comparison with life itself—and embody a viewpoint if not an obsession on the author's part. So that when I am told that a play is beautiful and (or because) it does not try to teach anything, I can only wonder which of two things is true about it: either what it teaches is so obvious, so inconsiderable as to appear to the critic to be "natural," or its teaching has been embedded and articulated so thoroughly in the action itself as not to appear as an objective but only a subjective fact.

All My Sons was not my first play but the eighth or ninth I had written up to the mid-forties. But for the one immediately preceding it, none of the others were produced in the professional theater, and since the reader can have little knowledge of this one—which lasted less than a week on Broadway—and no knowledge at all of the others, a word is in order about these desk-drawer plays, particularly the failure called *The Man Who Had All the Luck*.

This play was an investigation to discover what exact part a man played in his own fate. It deals with a young man in a small town who, by the time he is in his mid-twenties, owns several growing businesses, has married the girl he loves, is the father of a child he has always wanted, and is daily becoming convinced that as his desires are gratified he is causing to accumulate around his own head an invisible but nearly palpable fund, so to speak, of retribution. The law of life, as he observes life around him, is that people are always frustrated in some important regard; and he conceives that he must be too, and the play is built around his conviction of impending disaster. The disaster never comes, even when, in effect, he tries to bring it on in order to survive it and find peace. Instead, he comes to believe in his own superiority, and in his remarkable ability to succeed.

Now, more than a decade later, it is possible for me to see that far from being a waste and a failure this play was a preparation, and possibly a necessary one, for those that followed, especially *All My Sons* and *Death of a Salesman*, and this for many reasons. In the more than half-dozen plays before it I had picked themes at random—which is to say that I had had no awareness of any inner continuity running from one of these plays to the next, and I did not perceive myself in what I had written. I had begun with a play about a family, then a play about two brothers caught on either side of radicalism in a university, then a play about a psychologist's dilemma in a prison where the sane were inexorably moving over to join the mad, a play about a bizarre ship's officer whose desire for death led him to piracy on the seas, a tragedy on the Cortes-Montezuma conflict, and others. Once again, as I worked on *The Man Who Had All the Luck*, I was writing, I would have said, about what lay outside me. I had heard the story of a young man in a midwestern town who had earned the respect and love of his town and great personal prosperity as well, and who, suddenly and for no known reason, took to suspecting everyone of wanting to rob him, and within a year of his obsession's onset had taken his own life.

In the past I had rarely spent more than three months on a play. Now the months went by with the end never in sight. After nearly ten years of writing, I had struck upon what seemed a bottomless pit of mutually canceling meanings and implications. In the past I had had less difficulty with forming a "story" and more with the exploration of its meanings. Now, in contrast, I was working with an overwhelming sense of meaning, but however I tried I could not make the drama continuous and of a piece; it persisted, with the beginning of each scene, in starting afresh as though each scene were the beginning of a new play. Then one day, while I was lying on a beach, a simple shift of relationships came to mind, a shift which did not and could not solve the problem of writing *The Man*

Who Had All the Luck, but, I think now, made at least two of the plays that followed possible, and a great deal else besides.

What I saw, without laboring the details, was that two of the characters, who had been friends in the previous drafts, were logically brothers and had the same father. Had I known then what I know now I could have saved myself a lot of trouble. The play was impossible to fix because the overt story was only tangential to the secret drama its author was quite unconsciously trying to write. But in writing of the father-son relationship and of the son's search for his relatedness there was a fullness of feeling I had never known before; a crescendo was struck with a force I could almost touch. The crux of *All My Sons*, which would not be written until nearly three years later, was formed; and the roots of *Death of a Salesman* were sprouted.

The form of *All My Sons* is a reflection and an expression of several forces, of only some of which I was conscious. I desired above all to write rationally, to write so that I could tell the story of the play to even an unlettered person and spark a look of recognition on his face. The accusation I harbored against the earlier play was that it could not make sense to common-sense people. I have always been in love with wonder, the wonder of how things and people got to be what they are, and in *The Man Who Had All the Luck* I had tried to grasp wonder, I had tried to make it on the stage, by writing wonder. But wonder had betrayed me and the only other course I had was the one I took—to seek cause and effect, hard actions, facts, the geometry of relationships, and to hold back any tendency to express an idea in itself unless it was literally forced out of a character's mouth; in other words, to let wonder rise up like a mist, a gas, a vapor from the gradual and remorseless crush of factual and psychological conflict. I went back to the great book of wonder, *The Brothers Karamazov*, and I found what suddenly I felt must be true of it: that if one reads its most colorful, breathtaking, wonderful pages, one finds the thickest concentration of hard facts. Facts about the biographies of the characters, about the kind of bark on the moonlit trees, the way a window is hinged, the exact position of Dmitri as he peers through the window at his father, the precise description of his father's dress. Above all, the precise collision of inner themes during, not before or after, the high dramatic scenes. And quite as suddenly I noticed in Beethoven the holding back of climax until it was ready, the grasp of the rising line and the unwillingness to divert to an easy climax until the true one was ready. If there is one word to name the mood I felt it was *Forgo*. Let nothing interfere with the shape, the direction, the intention. I believed that I had felt too much in the previous play and understood too little.

I was turning thirty then, the author of perhaps a dozen plays, none of which I could truly believe were finished. I had written many scenes, but not a play. A play, I saw then, was an organism of which I had fashioned only certain parts. The decision formed to write one more, and if again it turned out to be unrealizable, I would go into another line of work. I have never loved the brick and mortar of the theater, and only once in my life had I been truly engrossed in a production—when Ruth Gordon played in the Jed Harris production of *A Doll's House*. The sole sense of connection with theater came when I saw the productions of the Group Theatre. It was not only the brilliance of ensemble acting, which in my opinion has never been equaled since in America, but the air of union created between actors and the audience. Here was the promise of prophetic theater which suggested to my mind the Greek situation when religion and belief were the heart of drama. I watched the Group Theatre from fifty-five-cent seats in the balcony, and at intermission time it was possible to feel the heat and the passion of people moved not only in their bellies but in their thoughts. If I say that my own writer's ego found fault with the plays, it does not detract from the fact that the performances were almost all inspiring to me, and when I heard that the Group was falling apart it seemed incredible that a society of saints—which they were to me, artistically, even as I had never met one of them—should be made up of people with less than absolute dedication to their cause.

All My Sons was begun several years after the Group had ceased to be, but it was what I can only call now a play written for a prophetic theater. I am aware of the vagueness of the term but I cannot do very well at defining what I mean. Perhaps it signifies a theater, a play, which is meant to become part of the lives of its audience— a play seriously meant for people of common sense, and relevant to both their domestic lives and their daily work, but an experience which widens their awareness of connection—the filaments to the past and the future which lie concealed in "life."

My intention in this play was to be as untheatrical as possible. To that end any metaphor, any image, any figure of speech, however creditable to me, was removed if it even slightly brought to consciousness the hand of a writer. So far as was possible nothing was to be permitted to interfere with its artlessness.

It seems to me now that I had the attitude of one laying siege to a fortress in this form. The sapping operation was to take place without a sound beneath a clear landscape in the broad light of a peaceful day. Nor was this approach arbitrary. It grew out of a determination to reverse my past playwriting errors, and from the kind of story I happened to have discovered.

During an idle chat in my living room, a pious lady from the Middle West told of a family in her neighborhood which had been destroyed when the daughter turned the father into the authorities on discovering that he had been selling faulty machinery to the Army. The war was then in full blast. By the time she had finished the tale I had transformed the daughter into a son and the climax of the second act was full and clear in my mind.

I knew my informant's neighborhood, I knew its middle-class ordinariness, and I knew how rarely the great issues penetrate such environments. But the fact that a girl had not only wanted to, but had actually moved against an erring father transformed into fact and common reality what in my previous play I had only begun to hint at. I had no awareness of the slightest connection between the two plays. All I knew was that somehow a hard thing had entered into me, a crux toward which it seemed possible to move in strong and straight lines. Something was crystal clear to me for the first time since I had begun to write plays, and it was the crisis of the second act, the revelation of the full loathesomeness of an antisocial action.

With this sense of dealing with an existing objective fact, I began to feel a difference in my role as a writer. It occurred to me that I must write this play so that even the actual criminal, on reading it, would have to say that it was true and sensible and as real as his life. It began to seem to me that what I had written until then, as well as almost all the plays I had ever seen, had been written for a theatrical performance, when they should have been written as a kind of testimony whose relevance far surpassed theatrics.

For these reasons the play begins in an atmosphere of undisturbed normality. Its first act was later called slow, but it was designed to be slow. It was made so that even boredom might threaten, so that when the first intimation of the crime is dropped a genuine horror might begin to move into the heart of the audience, a horror born of the contrast between the placidity of the civilization on view and the threat to it that a rage of conscience could create.

It took some two years to fashion this play, chiefly, I think now, because of a difficulty not unconnected with a similar one in the previous play. It was the question of relatedness. The crime in *All My Sons* is not one that is about to be committed but one that has long since been committed. There is no question of its consequences being ameliorated by anything Chris Keller or his father can do; the damage has been done irreparably. The stakes remaining are purely the conscience of Joe Keller and its awakening to the evil he has done, and the conscience of his son in the face of what he has discovered about his father. One could say that the problem was to make a fact of morality, but it is more precise, I think, to say that the structure of the play is designed to bring a man into the direct path of the consequences he has wrought. In one sense, it was the same problem of writing about David Beeves in the earlier play, for he too could not relate himself to what he had done. In both plays the dramatic obsession, so to speak, was with the twofold nature of the individual—his own concept of his deeds, and what turns out to be the "real" description of them. *All My Sons* has often been called a moral play, and it is that, but the concept of morality is not quite as purely ethical as it has been made to appear, nor is it so in the plays that follow. That the deed of Joe Keller at issue in *All My Sons* is his having been the cause of the death of pilots in war obscures the other kind of morality in which the play is primarily interested. Morality is probably a faulty word to use in the connection, but what I was after was the wonder in the fact that consequences of actions are as real as the actions themselves, yet we rarely take them into consideration as we perform actions, and we cannot hope to do so fully when we must always act with only partial knowledge of consequences. Joe Keller's trouble, in a word, is not that he cannot tell right from wrong but that his cast of mind cannot admit that he, personally, has any viable connection with his world, his universe, or his society. He is not a partner in society, but an incorporated member, so to speak, and you cannot sue personally the officers of a corporation. I hasten to make clear here that I am not merely speaking of a literal corporation but the concept of a man's becoming a function of production or distribution to the point where his personality becomes divorced from the actions it propels.

The fortress which *All My Sons* lays siege to is the fortress of unrelatedness. It is an assertion not so much of a morality in terms of right and wrong, but of a moral world's being such because men cannot walk away from certain of their deeds. In this sense Joe Keller is a threat to society and in this sense the play is a social play. Its "socialness" does not reside in its having dealt with the crime of selling defective materials to a nation at war—the same crime could easily be the basis of a thriller which would have no place in social dramaturgy. It is that the crime is seen as having roots in a certain relationship of the individual to society, and to a certain indoctrination he embodies, which, if dominant, can mean a jungle existence for all of us no matter how high our buildings soar. And it is in this sense that loneliness is socially meaningful in these plays.

To return to Ibsen's influence upon this play, I should have to split the question in order to make sense of it. First, there was the real impact of his work upon me at the time: this consisted mainly in what I then saw as his ability to forge a play upon a factual bedrock. A situation in his plays is never stated but revealed in terms of hard actions, irrevocable deeds; and sentiment is never confused with the action it conceals. Having for so long written in terms of what people felt rather than what they did, I turned to his works at the time with a sense of homecoming. As I have said, I wanted then to write so that people of common sense would mistake my play for life itself and not be required to lend it some poetic license before it could be believed. I wanted to make the moral world as real and evident as the immoral one so splendidly is.

But my own belief is that the shadow of Ibsen was seen on this play for another reason, and it is that *All My Sons* begins very late in its story. Thus, as in Ibsen's best-known work, a great amount of time is taken up with bringing the past into the present. In passing,

I ought to add that this view of action is presently antipathetic to our commonly held feeling about the drama. More than any other quality of realism, or, to be more exact, of Ibsenism as a technique, this creates a sense of artificiality which we now tend to reject, for in other respects realism is still our reigning style. But it is no longer acceptable that characters should sit about discussing events of a year ago, or ten years ago, when in "life" they would be busy with the present. In truth, the effort to eliminate antecedent material has threatened to eliminate the past entirely from any plays. We are impatient to get on with it—so much so that anyone making a study of some highly creditable plays of the moment would be hard put to imagine what their characters were like a month before their actions and stories begin. *All My Sons* takes its time with the past, not in deference to Ibsen's method as I saw it then, but because its theme is the question of actions and consequences, and a way had to be found to throw a long line into the past in order to make that kind of connection viable.

That the idea of connection was central to me is indicated again in the kind of revision the play underwent. In its earlier versions the mother, Kate Keller, was in a dominating position; more precisely, her astrological beliefs were given great prominence. (The play's original title was *The Sign of the Archer*.) And this, because I sought in every sphere to give body and life to connection. But as the play progressed the conflict between Joe and his son Chris pressed astrology to the wall until its mysticism gave way to psychology. There was also the impulse to regard the mystical with suspicion, since it had, in the past, given me only turgid works that could never develop a true climax based upon revealed psychological truths. In short, where in previous plays I might well have been satisfied to create only an astrologically obsessed woman, the obsession now had to be opened up to reveal its core of self-interest and intention on the character's part. Wonder must have feet with which to walk the earth.

But before I leave this play it seems wise to say a few more words about the kind of dramatic impulse it represents, and one aspect of "Ibsenism" as a technique is the quickest path into that discussion. I have no vested interest in any one form—as the variety of forms I have used attests—but there is one element in Ibsen's method which

I do not think ought to be overlooked, let alone dismissed as it so often is nowadays. If his plays, and his method, do nothing else they reveal the evolutionary quality of life. One is constantly aware, in watching his plays, of process, change, development. I think too many modern plays assume, so to speak, that their duty is merely to show the present countenance rather than to account for what happens. It is therefore wrong to imagine that because his first and sometimes his second acts devote so much time to a studied revelation of antecedent material, his view is static compared to our own. In truth, it is profoundly dynamic, for that enormous past was always heavily documented to the end that the present be comprehended with wholeness, as a moment in a flow of time, and not—as with so many modern plays—as a situation without roots. Indeed, even though I can myself reject other aspects of his work, it nevertheless presents barely and unadorned what I believe is the biggest single dramatic problem, namely, how to dramatize what has gone before. I say this not merely out of technical interest, but because dramatic characters, and the drama itself, can never hope to attain a maximum degree of consciousness unless they contain a viable unveiling of the contrast between past and present, and an awareness of the process by which the present has become what it is. And I say this, finally, because I take it as a truth that the end of drama is the creation of a higher consciousness and not merely a subjective attack upon the audience's nerves and feelings. What is precious in the Ibsen method is its insistence upon valid causation, and this cannot be dismissed as a wooden notion.

This is the "real" in Ibsen's realism for me, for he was, after all, as much a mystic as a realist. Which is simply to say that while there are mysteries in life which no amount of analyzing will reduce to reason, it is perfectly realistic to admit and even to proclaim that hiatus as a truth. But the problem is not to make complex what is essentially explainable; it is to make understandable what is complex without distorting and oversimplifying what cannot be explained. I think many of his devices are, in fact, quite arbitrary; that he betrays a Germanic ponderousness at times and a tendency to over-prove what is quite clear in the first place. But we could do with more of his basic intention, which was to assert nothing he had not proved, and to cling always to the marvelous spectacle of life forcing one event out of the jaws of the preceding one and to reveal its elemental consistencies with surprise. In other words, I contrast his realism not with the lyrical, which I prize, but with sentimentality, which is always a leak in the dramatic dike. He sought to make a play as weighty and living a fact as the discovery of the steam engine or algebra. This can be scoffed away only at a price, and the price is a living drama.

IV

I think now that the straightforwardness of the *All My Sons* form was in some part due to the relatively sharp definition of the social aspects of the problem it dealt with. It was conceived in wartime and begun in wartime; the spectacle of human sacrifice in contrast with aggrandizement is a sharp and heartbreaking one. At a time when all public voices were announcing the arrival of that great day when industry and labor were one, my personal experience was daily demonstrating that beneath the slogans very little had changed. In this sense the play was a response to what I felt "in the air." It was an unveiling of what I believed everybody knew and nobody publicly said. At the same time, however, I believed I was bringing news, and it was news which I half expected would be denied as truth.

When, in effect, it was accepted, I was gratified, but a little surprised. The success of a play, especially one's first success, is somewhat like pushing against a door which is suddenly opened from the other side. One may fall on one's face or not, but certainly a new room is opened that was always securely shut until then. For myself, the experience was invigorating. It suddenly seemed that the audience was a mass of blood relations, and I sensed a warmth in the world that had not been there before. It made it possible to dream of daring more and risking more. The Wonderful was no longer something that would inevitably trap me into disastrously confusing works, for the audience sat in silence before the unwinding of *All My Sons* and gasped when they should have, and I tasted that power which is reserved, I imagine, for playwrights, which is to know that by one's invention a mass of strangers has been publicly transfixed.

As well, the production of the play was an introduction to the acting art and its awesome potentials. I wanted to use more of what lay in actors to be used. To me, the most incredible spectacle of this first successful production was the silence it enforced. It seemed then that the stage was as wide and free and towering and laughingly inventive as the human mind itself, and I wanted to press closer toward its distant edges. A success places one among friends. The world is friendly, the audience is friendly, and that is good. It also reveals, even more starkly than a failure—for a failure is always ill-defined—what remains undone.

The wonder in *All My Sons* lay in its revelation of process, and it was made a stitch at a time, so to speak, in order to weave a tapestry before our eyes. What it wanted, however, was a kind of moment-to-moment wildness in addition to its organic wholeness. The form of the play, I felt, was not sensuous enough in itself. Which means that its conception of time came to appear at odds with my own experience.

The first image that occurred to me, which was to result in *Death of a Salesman*, was of an enormous face the height of the proscenium arch which would appear and then open up, and we would see the inside of a man's head. In fact, *The Inside of His Head* was the first title. It was conceived half in laughter, for the inside of his head was a mass of contradictions. The image was in direct opposition to the method of *All My Sons*—a method one might call linear or eventual in that one fact or incident creates the necessity for the next. The *Salesman* image was from the beginning absorbed with the concept that nothing in life comes "next" but that everything exists together and at the same time within us; that there is no past to be "brought forward" in a human being, but that he is his past at every moment and that the present is merely that which his past is capable of noticing and smelling and reacting to.

I wished to create a form which, in itself as a form, would literally be the process of Willy Loman's way of mind. But to say "wished" is not accurate. Any dramatic form is an artifice, a way of transforming a subjective feeling into something that can be comprehended through public symbols. Its efficiency as a form is to be judged—at least by the writer—by how much of the original vision and feeling is lost or distorted by this transformation. I wished to speak of the salesman most precisely as I felt about him, to give no part of that feeling away for the sake of any effect or any dramatic necessity. What was wanted now was not a mounting line of tension, nor a gradually narrowing cone of intensifying suspense, but a bloc, a single chord presented as such at the outset, within which all the strains and melodies would already be contained. The strategy, as with *All My Sons*, was to appear entirely unstrategic but with a difference. This time, if I could, I would have told the whole story and set forth all the characters in one unbroken speech or even one sentence or a single flash of light. As I look at the play now its form seems the form of a confession, for that is how it is told, now speaking of what happened yesterday, then suddenly following some connection to a time twenty years ago, then leaping even further back and then returning to the present and even speculating about the future.

Where in *All My Sons* it had seemed necessary to prove the connections between the present and the past, between events and moral consequences, between the manifest and the hidden, in this play all was assumed as proven to begin with. All I was doing was bringing things to mind. The assumption, also, was that everyone knew Willy Loman. I can realize this only now, it is true, but it is equally apparent to me that I took it somehow for granted then. There was still the attitude of the unveiler, but no bringing together of hitherto unrelated things; only pre-existing images, events, confrontations, moods, and pieces of knowledge. So there was a kind of confidence underlying this play which the form itself expresses, even a naïveté, a self-disarming quality that was in part born of my belief in the audience as being essentially the same as myself. If I had wanted, then, to put the audience reaction into words, it would not have been "What happens next and why?" so much as "Oh, God, of course!"

In one sense a play is a species of jurisprudence, and some part of it must take the advocate's role, something else must act in defense, and the entirety must engage the Law. Against my will, *All My Sons* states, and even proclaims, that it is a form and that a writer wrote it and organized it. In *Death of a Salesman* the original impulse was to make that same proclamation in an immeasurably more violent, abrupt, and openly conscious way. Willy Loman does not merely suggest or hint that he is at the end of his strength and of his justifications, he is hardly on the stage for five minutes when he says so; he does not gradually imply a deadly conflict with his son, an implication dropped into the midst of serenity and surface calm, he is avowedly grappling with that conflict at the outset. The ultimate matter with which the play will close is announced at the outset and is the matter of its every moment from the first. There is enough revealed in the first scene of *Death of a Salesman* to fill another kind of play which, in service to another dramatic form, would hold back and only gradually release it. I wanted to proclaim that an artist had made this play, but the nature of the proclamation was to be entirely "inartistic" and avowedly unstrategic; it was to hold back nothing, at any moment, which life would have revealed, even at the cost of suspense and climax. It was to forgo the usual preparations for scenes and to permit—and even seek—whatever in each character contradicted his position in the advocate-defense scheme of its jurisprudence. The play was begun with only one firm piece of knowledge and this was that Loman was to destroy himself. How it would wander before it got to that point I did not know and resolved not to care. I was convinced only that if I could make him remember enough he would kill himself, and the structure of the play was determined by what was needed to draw up his memories like a mass of tangled roots without end or beginning.

As I have said, the structure of events and the nature of its form are also the direct reflection of Willy Loman's way of thinking at this moment of his life. He was the kind of man you see muttering to himself on a subway, decently dressed, on his way home or to the office, perfectly integrated with his surroundings excepting that unlike other people he can no longer restrain the power of his experience from disrupting the superficial sociality of his behavior. Consequently he is working on two logics which often collide. For instance, if he meets his son Happy while in the midst of some memory in which Happy disappointed him, he is instantly furious at Happy, despite the fact that Happy at this particular moment deeply desires to be of use to him. He is literally at that terrible moment when the voice of the past is no longer distant but quite as loud as the voice of the present. In dramatic terms the form, therefore, *is* this process, instead of being a once-removed summation or indication of it.

The way of telling the tale, in this sense, is as mad as Willy and as abrupt and as suddenly lyrical. And it is difficult not to add that the subsequent imitations of the form had to collapse for this particular reason. It is not possible, in my opinion, to graft it onto a character whose psychology it does not reflect, and I have not used it since because it would be false to a more integrated—or less disintegrating—personality to pretend that the past and the present are so openly and vocally intertwined in his mind. The ability of people to down their past is normal, and without it we could have no comprehensible communication among men. In the hands of writers who see it as an easy way to elicit anterior information in a play it becomes merely a flashback. There are no flashbacks in this play but only a mobile concurrency of past and present, and this, again, because in his desperation to justify his life Willy Loman has destroyed the boundaries between now and then, just as anyone would do who, on picking up his telephone, discovered that this perfectly harmless act had somehow set off an explosion in his basement. The previously assumed and believed-in results of ordinary and accepted actions, and their abrupt and unforeseen—but apparently logical—effects, form the basic collision in this play, and, I suppose, its ultimate irony.

It may be in place to remark, in this connection, that while the play was sometimes called cinematographic in its structure, it failed as a motion picture. I believe that the basic reason—aside from the gross insensitivity permeating its film production—was that the dramatic tension of Willy's memories was destroyed by transferring him, literally, to the locales he had only imagined in the play. There is an inevitable horror in the spectacle of a man losing consciousness of his immediate surroundings to the point where he engages in conversations with unseen persons. The horror is lost—and drama becomes narrative—when the context actually becomes his imagined world. And the dream evaporates because psychological truth has been amended, a truth which depends not only on what images we recall but in what connections and contexts we recall them. The setting on the stage was never shifted, despite the many changes in locale, for the precise reason that, quite simply, the mere fact that a man forgets where he is does not mean that he has really moved. Indeed, his terror springs from his never-lost awareness of time and place. It did not need this play to teach me that the screen is time-bound and earth-bound compared to the stage, if only because its preponderant emphasis is on the visual image, which, however rapidly it may be changed before our eyes, still displaces its predecessor, while scene-changing with words is instantaneous; and because of the flexibility of language, especially of English, a preceding image can be kept alive through the image that succeeds it. The movie's tendency is always to wipe out what has gone before, and it is thus in constant danger of transforming the dramatic into narrative. There is no swifter method of telling a "story" but neither is there a more difficult medium in which to keep a pattern of relationships constantly in being. Even in those sequences which retained the real backgrounds for Willy's imaginary confrontations the tension between now and then was lost. I suspect this loss was due to the necessity of shooting the actors close-up—effectively eliminating awareness of their surroundings. The basic failure of the picture was a formal one. It did not solve, nor really attempt to find, a resolution for the problem of keeping the past constantly alive, and that friction, collision, and tension between past and present was the heart of the play's particular construction.

A great deal has been said and written about what *Death of a Salesman* is supposed to signify, both psychologically and from the socio-political viewpoints. For instance, in one periodical of the far Right it was called a "time bomb expertly placed under the edifice of Americanism," while the *Daily Worker* reviewer thought it entirely decadent. In Catholic Spain it ran longer than any modern play and it has been refused production in Russia but not, from time to time, in certain satellite countries, depending on the direction and velocity of the wind. The Spanish press, thoroughly controlled by Catholic orthodoxy, regarded the play as commendable proof of the spirit's death where there is no God. In America, even as it was being cannonaded as a piece of Communist propaganda, two of the largest manufacturing corporations in the country invited me to address their sales organizations in conventions assembled, while the road company was here and there picketed by the Catholic War Veterans and the American Legion. It made only a fair impression in London, but in the area of the Norwegian

Arctic Circle fishermen whose only contact with civilization was the radio and the occasional visit of the government boat insisted on seeing it night after night—the same few people—believing it to be some kind of religious rite. One organization of salesmen raised me up nearly to patronsainthood, and another, a national sales managers' group, complained that the difficulty of recruiting salesmen was directly traceable to the play. When the movie was made, the producing company got so frightened it produced a sort of trailer to be shown before the picture, a documentary short film which demonstrated how exceptional Willy Loman was; how necessary selling is to the economy; how secure the salesman's life really is; how idiotic, in short, was the feature film they had just spent more than a million dollars to produce. Fright does odd things to people.

On the psychological front the play spawned a small hill of doctoral theses explaining its Freudian symbolism, and there were innumerable letters asking if I was aware that the fountain pen which Biff steals is a phallic symbol. Some, on the other hand, felt it was merely a fountain pen and dismissed the whole play. I received visits from men over sixty from as far away as California who had come across the country to have me write the stories of their lives, because the story of Willy Loman was exactly like theirs. The letters from women made it clear that the central character of the play was Linda; sons saw the entire action revolving around Biff or Happy, and fathers wanted advice, in effect, on how to avoid parricide. Probably the most succinct reaction to the play was voiced by a man who, on leaving the theater, said, "I always said that New England territory was no damned good." This, at least, was a fact.

That I have and had not the slightest interest in the selling profession is probably unbelievable to most people, and I very early gave up trying even to say so. And when asked what Willy was selling, what was in his bags, I could only reply, "Himself." I was trying neither to condemn a profession nor particularly to improve it, and, I will admit, I was little better than ignorant of Freud's teachings when I wrote it. There was no attempt to bring down the American edifice nor to raise it higher, to show up family relations or to cure the ills afflicting that inevitable institution. The truth, at least of my aim—which is all I can speak of authoritatively—is much simpler and more complex.

The play grew from simple images. From a little frame house on a street of little frame houses, which had once been loud with the noise of growing boys, and then was empty and silent and finally occupied by strangers. Strangers who could not know with what conquistadorial joy Willy and his boys had once re-shingled the roof. Now it was quiet in the house, and the wrong people in the beds.

It grew from images of futility—the cavernous Sunday afternoons polishing the car. Where is that car now? And the chamois cloths carefully washed and put up to dry, where are the chamois cloths?

And the endless, convoluted discussions, wonderments, arguments, belittlements, encouragements, fiery resolutions, abdications, returns, partings, voyages out and voyages back, tremendous opportunities and small, squeaking denouements—and all in the kitchen now occupied by strangers who cannot hear what the walls are saying.

The image of aging and so many of your friends already gone and strangers in the seats of the mighty who do not know you or your triumphs or your incredible value.

The image of the son's hard, public eye upon you, no longer swept by your myth, no longer rousable from his separateness, no longer knowing you have lived for him and have wept for him.

The image of ferocity when love has turned to something else and yet is there, is somewhere in the room if one could only find it.

The image of people turning into strangers who only evaluate one another.

Above all, perhaps, the image of a need greater than hunger or sex or thirst, a need to leave a thumbprint somewhere on the world. A need for immortality, and by admitting it, the knowing that one has carefully inscribed one's name on a cake of ice on a hot July day.

I sought the relatedness of all things by isolating their unrelatedness, a man superbly alone with his sense of not having touched, and finally knowing in his last extremity that the love which had always been in the room unlocated was now found.

The image of a suicide so mixed in motive as to be unfathomable and yet demanding statement. Revenge was in it and a power of love, a victory in that it would bequeath a fortune to the living and a flight from emptiness. With it an image of peace at the final curtain, the peace that is between wars, the peace leaving the issues above ground and viable yet.

And always, throughout, the image of private man in a world full of strangers, a world that is not home nor even an open battleground but only galaxies of high promise over a fear of falling.

And the image of a man making something with his hands being a rock to touch and return to. "He was always so wonderful with his hands," says his wife over his grave, and I laughed when the line came, laughed with the artist-devil's laugh, for it had all come together in this line, she having been made by him though he did not know it or believe in it or receive it into himself. Only rank, height of power, the sense of having won he believed was real—the galaxy thrust up into the sky by projectors on the rooftops of the city he believed were real stars.

It came from structural images. The play's eye was to revolve from within Willy's head, sweeping endlessly in all directions like a light on the sea, and nothing that formed in the distant mist was to be left uninvestigated. It was thought of as having the density of the novel form in its interchange of viewpoints, so that while all roads led to Willy the other characters were to feel it was their play, a story about them and not him.

There were two undulating lines in mind, one above the other, the past webbed to the present moving on together in him and sometimes openly joined and once, finally, colliding in the showdown which defined him in his eyes at least—and so to sleep.

Above all, in the structural sense, I aimed to make a play with the veritable countenance of life. To make one the many, as in life, so that "society" is a power and a mystery of custom and inside the man and surrounding him, as the fish is in the sea and the sea inside the fish, his birthplace and burial ground, promise and threat. To speak commonsensically of social facts which every businessman knows and talks about but which are too prosaic to mention or are usually fancied up on the stage as philosophical problems. When a man gets old you fire him, you have to, he can't do the work. To speak and even to celebrate the common sense of businessmen, who love the personality that wins the day but know that you've got to have the right goods at the right price, handsome and well-spoken as you are. (To some, these were scandalous and infamous arraignments of society when uttered in the context of art. But not to the businessmen themselves; they knew it was all true and I cherished their clear-eyed talk.)

The image of a play without transitional scenes was there in the beginning. There was too much to say to waste precious stage time with feints and preparations, in themselves agonizing "structural" bridges for a writer to work out since they are not why he is writing. There was a resolution, as in *All My Sons*, not to waste motion or moments, but in this case to shear through everything up to the meat of a scene; a resolution not to write an unmeant word for the sake of the form but to make the form give and stretch and contract for the sake of the thing to be said. To cling to the process of Willy's mind as the form the story would take.

The play was always heroic to me, and in later years the academy's charge that Willy lacked the "stature" for the tragic hero seemed incredible to me. I had not understood that these matters are measured by Greco-Elizabethan paragraphs which hold no mention of insurance payments, front porches, refrigerator fan belts, steering knuckles, Chevrolets, and visions seen not through the portals of Delphi but in the blue flame of the hot-water heater. How could "Tragedy" make people weep, of all things?

I set out not to "write a tragedy" in this play, but to show the truth as I saw it. However, some of the attacks upon it as a pseudo-tragedy contain ideas so misleading, and in some cases so laughable, that it might be in place here to deal with a few of them.

Aristotle having spoken of a fall from the heights, it goes without saying that someone of the common mould cannot be a fit tragic hero. It is now many centuries since Aristotle lived. There is no more reason for falling down in a faint before his *Poetics* than before Euclid's geometry, which has been amended numerous times by men with new insights; nor, for that matter, would I choose to have my illnesses diagnosed by Hippocrates rather than the most ordinary graduate of an American medical school, despite the Greek's genius. Things do change, and even a genius is limited by his time and the nature of his society.

I would deny, on grounds of simple logic, this one of Aristotle's contentions if only because he lived in a slave society. When a vast number of people are divested of alternatives, as slaves are, it is rather inevitable that one will not be able to imagine drama, let alone tragedy, as being possible for any but the higher ranks of society. There is a legitimate question of stature here, but none of rank, which is so often confused with it. So long as the hero may be said to have had alternatives of a magnitude to have materially changed the course of his life, it seems to me that in this respect at least, he cannot be debarred from the heroic role.

The question of rank is significant to me only as it reflects the question of the social application of the hero's career. There is no doubt that if a character is shown on the stage who goes through the most ordinary actions, and is suddenly revealed to be the President of the United States, his actions immediately assume a much greater magnitude, and pose the possibilities of much greater meaning, than if he is the corner grocer. But at the same time, his stature as a hero is not so utterly dependent upon his rank that the corner grocer cannot outdistance him as a tragic figure— providing, of course, that the grocer's career engages the issues of, for instance, the survival of the race, the relationships of man to God—the questions, in short, whose answers define humanity and the right way to live so that the world is a home, instead of a battle- ground or a fog in which disembodied spirits pass each other in an endless twilight.

In this respect *Death of a Salesman* is a slippery play to catego- rize because nobody in it stops to make a speech objectively stating the great issues which I believe it embodies. If it were a worse play, less closely articulating its meanings with its actions, I think it would have more quickly satisfied a certain kind of criticism. But it was meant to be less a play than a fact; it refused admission to its author's opinions and opened itself to a revelation of process and the operations of an ethic, of social laws of action no less powerful in their effects upon individuals than any tribal law administered by gods with names. I need not claim that this play is a genuine solid-gold tragedy for my opinions on tragedy to be held valid. My purpose here is simply to point out a historical fact which must be taken into account in any consideration of tragedy, and it is the sharp alteration in the meaning of rank in society between the present time and the distant past. More important to me is the fact that this particular kind of argument obscures much more relevant considerations.

One of these is the question of intensity. It matters not at all whether a modern play concerns itself with a grocer or a president if the intensity of the hero's commitment to his course is less than the maximum possible. It matters not at all whether the hero falls from a great height or a small one, whether he is highly conscious or only dimly aware of what is happening, whether his pride brings the fall or an unseen pattern written behind clouds; if the intensity, the human passion to surpass his given bounds, the fanatic insistence upon his self-conceived role—if these are not present there can only be an outline of tragedy but no living thing. I believe, for myself, that the lasting appeal of tragedy is due to our need to face the fact of death in order to strengthen ourselves for life, and that over and above this function of the tragic viewpoint there are and will be a great number of formal variations which no single definition will ever embrace.

Another issue worth considering is the so-called tragic victory, a question closely related to the consciousness of the hero. One makes nonsense of this if a "victory" means that the hero makes us feel some certain joy when, for instance, he sacrifices himself for a "cause," and unhappy and morose because he dies without one. To begin at the bottom, a man's death is and ought to be an essentially terrifying thing and ought to make nobody happy. But in a great variety of ways even death, the ultimate negative, can be, and appear to be, an assertion of bravery, and can serve to separate the death of man from the death of animals; and I think it is this distinction which underlies any conception of a victory in death. For a society of faith, the nature of the death can prove the existence of the spirit, and posit its immortality. For a secular society it is perhaps more difficult for such a victory to document itself and to make itself felt, but, conversely, the need to offer greater proofs of the humanity of man can make that victory more real. It goes without saying that in a society where there is basic disagreement as to the right way to live, there can hardly be agreement as to the right way to die, and both life and death must be heavily weighted with meaningless futility.

It was not out of any deference to a tragic definition that Willy Loman is filled with a joy, however broken-hearted, as he approaches his end, but simply that my sense of his character dictated his joy, and even what I felt was an exultation. In terms of his character, he has achieved a very powerful piece of knowledge, which is that he is loved by his son and has been embraced by him and forgiven. In this he is given his existence, so to speak—his fatherhood, for which he has always striven and which until now he could not achieve. That he is unable to take this victory thoroughly to his heart, that it closes the circle for him and propels him to his death, is the wage of his sin, which was to have committed himself so completely to the counterfeits of dignity and the false coinage embodied in his idea of success that he can prove his existence only by bestowing "power" on his posterity, a power deriving from the sale of his last asset, himself, for the price of his insurance policy.

I must confess here to a miscalculation, however. I did not realize while writing the play that so many people in the world do not see as clearly, or would not admit, as I thought they must, how futile most lives are; so there could be no hope of consoling the audience for the death of this man. I did not realize either how few would be impressed by the fact that this man is actually a very brave spirit who cannot settle for half but must pursue his dream of himself to the end. Finally, I thought it must be clear, even obvious, that this was no dumb brute heading mindlessly to his catastrophe.

I have no need to be Willy's advocate before the jury which decides who is and who is not a tragic hero. I am merely noting that the lingering ponderousness of so many ancient definitions has blinded students and critics to the facts before them, and not only in regard to this play. Had Willy been unaware of his separation from values that endure he would have died contentedly while polishing his car, probably on a Sunday afternoon with the ball game coming over the radio. But he was agonized by his awareness of being in a false position, so constantly haunted by the hollowness of all he had placed his faith in, so aware, in short, that he must somehow be filled in his spirit or fly apart, that he staked his very life on the ultimate assertion. That he had not the intellectual fluency to verbalize his situation is not the same thing as saying that he lacked awareness, even an overly intensified consciousness that the life he had made was without form and inner meaning.

To be sure, had he been able to know that he was as much the victim of his beliefs as their defeated exemplar, had he known how much of guilt he ought to bear and how much to shed from his soul, he would be more conscious. But it seems to me that there is of necessity a severe limitation of self-awareness in any character, even the most knowing, which serves to define him as a character, and more, that this very limit serves to complete the tragedy and, indeed, to make it at all possible. Complete consciousness is possible only in a play about forces, like *Prometheus*, but not in a play about people. I think that the point is whether there is a sufficient awareness in the hero's career to make the audience supply the rest. Had Oedipus, for instance, been more conscious and more aware of the forces at work upon him he must surely have said that he was not really to blame for having cohabited with his mother since neither he nor anyone else knew she was his mother. He must surely decide to divorce her, provide for their children, firmly resolve to investigate the family background of his next wife, and thus deprive us of a very fine play and the name for a famous neurosis. But he is conscious only up to a point, the point at which guilt begins. Now he is inconsolable and must tear out his eyes. What is tragic about this? Why is it not even ridiculous? How can we respect a man who goes to such extremities over something he could in no way help or prevent? The answer, I think, is not that we respect the man, but that we respect the Law he has so completely broken, wittingly or not, for it is that Law which, we believe, defines us as men. The confusion of some critics viewing *Death of a Salesman* in this regard is that they do not see that Willy Loman has broken a law without whose protection life is insupportable if not incomprehensible to him and to many others; it is the law which says that a failure in society and in business has no right to live. Unlike the law against incest, the law of success is not administered by statute or church, but it is very nearly as powerful in its grip upon men. The confusion increases because, while it is a law, it is by no means a wholly agreeable one even as it is slavishly obeyed, for to fail is no longer to belong to society, in his estimate. Therefore, the path is opened for those who wish to call Willy merely a foolish man even as they themselves are living in obedience to the same law that killed him. Equally, the fact that Willy's law—the belief, in other words, which administers guilt to him—is not a civilizing statute whose destruction menaces us all; it is, rather, a deeply believed and deeply suspect "good" which, when questioned as to its value, as it is in this play, serves more to raise our anxieties than to reassure us of the existence of an unseen but humane metaphysical system in the world. My attempt in the play was to counter this anxiety with an opposing system which, so to speak, is in a race for Willy's faith, and it is the system of love which is the opposite of the law of success. It is embodied in Biff Loman, but by the time Willy can perceive his love it can serve only as an ironic comment upon the life he sacrificed for power and for success and its tokens.

V

A play cannot be equated with a political philosophy, at least not in the way a smaller number, by simple multiplication, can be assimilated into a larger. I do not believe that any work of art can help but be diminished by its adherence at any cost to a political program, including its author's, and not for any other reason than that there is no political program—any more than there is a theory of tragedy—which can encompass the complexities of real life. Doubtless an author's politics must be one element, and even an important one, in the germination of his art, but if it is art he has created it must by definition bend itself to his observation rather than to his opinions or even his hopes. If I have shown a preference for plays which seek causation not only in psychology but in society, I may also believe in the autonomy of art, and I believe this because my experience with *All My Sons* and *Death of a Salesman* forces the belief upon me. If the earlier play was Marxist, it was a Marxism of a strange hue. Joe Keller is arraigned by his son for a willfully unethical use of his economic position; and this, as the Russians said when they removed the play from their stages, bespeaks an assumption that the norm of capitalist behavior is ethical or at least can be, an assumption no Marxist can hold. Nor does Chris propose to liquidate the business built in part on soldiers' blood; he will run it himself, but cleanly.

The most decent man in *Death of a Salesman* is a capitalist (Charley) whose aims are not different from Willy Loman's. The great difference between them is that Charley is not a fanatic. Equally, however, he has learned how to live without that frenzy, that ecstasy of spirit which Willy chases to his end. And even as Willy's sons are unhappy men, Charley's boy, Bernard, works hard, attends to his studies, and attains a worthwhile objective. These people are all of the same class, the same background, the same neighborhood. What theory lies behind this double view? None whatever. It is simply that I knew and know that I feel better when my work is reflecting a balance of the truth as it exists. A muffled debate arose with the success of *Death of a Salesman* in which attempts were made to justify or dismiss the play as a Left-Wing piece, or as a Right-Wing manifestation of decadence. The presumption underlying both views is that a work of art is the sum of its author's political outlook, real or alleged, and more, that its political implications are valid elements in its aesthetic evaluation. I do not believe this, either for my own or other writers' works.

The most radical play I ever saw was not *Waiting for Lefty* but *The Madwoman of Chaillot*. I know nothing of Giradoux's political alignment, and it is of no moment to me; I am able to read this play, which is the most open indictment of private exploitation of the earth I know about. By the evidence of his plays, Shaw, the socialist, was in love not with the working class, whose characters he could only caricature, but with the middle of the economic aristocracy, those men who, in his estimate, lived without social and economic illusions. There is a strain of mystic fatalism in Ibsen so powerful as to throw all his scientific tenets into doubt, and a good measure besides of contempt—in this radical—for the men who are usually called the public. The list is long and the contradictions are embarrassing until one concedes a perfectly simple proposition. It is merely that a writer of any worth creates out of his total perception, the vaster part of which is subjective and not within his intellectual control. For myself, it has never been possible to generate the energy to write and complete a play if I know in advance everything it signifies and all it will contain. The very impulse to write, I think, springs from an inner chaos crying for order, for meaning, and that meaning must be discovered in the process of writing or the work lies dead as it is finished. To speak, therefore, of a play as though it were the objective work of a propagandist is an almost biological kind of nonsense, provided, of course, that it is a play, which is to say a work of art.

VI

In the writing of *Death of a Salesman* I tried, of course, to achieve a maximum power of effect. But when I saw the devastating force with which it struck its audiences, something within me was shocked and put off. I had thought of myself as rather an optimistic man. I looked at what I had wrought and was forced to wonder whether I knew myself at all if this play, which I had written half in laughter and joy, was as morose and as utterly sad as its audiences found it. Either I was much tougher than they, and could stare at calamity with fewer terrors, or I was harboring within myself another man who was only tangentially connected with what I would have called my rather bright viewpoint about mankind. As I watched and saw tears in the eyes of the audience I felt a certain embarrassment at having, as I thought then, convinced so many people that life was not worth living—for so the play was widely interpreted. I hasten to add now that I ought not have been embarrassed, and that I am convinced the play is not a document of pessimism, a philosophy in which I do not believe.

Nevertheless, the emotionalism with which the play was received helped to generate an opposite impulse and an altered dramatic aim. This ultimately took shape in *The Crucible*, but before it became quite so definite and formed into idea, it was taking hold of my thoughts in a purely dramatic and theatrical context. Perhaps I can indicate its basic elements by saying that *Salesman* moves with its arms open wide, sweeping into itself by means of a subjective process of thought-connection a multitude of observations, feelings, suggestions, and shadings much as the mind does in its ordinary daily functions. Its author chose its path, of course, but, once chosen, that path could meander as it pleased through a world that was well recognized by the audience. From the theatrical viewpoint that play desired the audience to forget it was in a theater even as it broke the bounds, I believe, of a long convention of realism. Its expressionistic elements were consciously used as such, but since the approach to Willy Loman's characterization was consistently and rigorously subjective, the audience would not ever be aware— if I could help it—that they were witnessing the use of a technique which had until then created only coldness, objectivity, and a highly styled sort of play. I had willingly employed expressionism but always to create a subjective truth, and this play, which was so manifestly "written," seemed as though nobody had written it at all but that it had simply "happened." I had always been attracted and repelled by the brilliance of German expressionism after World War I, and one aim in *Salesman* was to employ its quite marvelous shorthand for humane, "felt" characterizations rather than for purposes of demonstration for which the Germans had used it.

These and other technical and theatrical considerations were a preparation for what turned out to be *The Crucible*, but "what was in the air" provided the actual locus of the tale. If the reception of *All My Sons* and *Death of a Salesman* had made the world a friendly place for me, events of the early fifties quickly turned that warmth into an illusion. It was not only the rise of "McCarthyism" that moved me, but something which seemed much more weird and mysterious. It was the fact that a political, objective, knowledgeable campaign from the far Right was capable of creating not only a terror, but a new subjective reality, a veritable mystique which was gradually assuming even a holy resonance. The wonder of it all struck me that so practical and picayune a cause, carried forward by such manifestly ridiculous men, should be capable of paralyzing thought itself, and worse, causing to billow up such persuasive clouds of "mysterious" feelings within people. It was as though the whole country had been born anew, without a memory even of certain elemental decencies which a year or two earlier no one would have imagined could be altered, let alone forgotten. Astounded, I watched men pass me by without a nod whom I had known rather well for years; and again, the astonishment was produced by my knowledge, which I could not give up, that the terror in these people was being knowingly planned and consciously engineered, and yet that all they knew was terror. That so interior and subjective an emotion could have been so manifestly created from without was a marvel to me. It underlies every word in *The Crucible*.

I wondered, at first, whether it must be that self-preservation and the need to hold on to opportunity, the thought of being exiled and "put out," was what the fear was feeding on, for there were people who had had only the remotest connections with the Left who were quite as terrified as those who had been closer. I knew of one man who had been summoned to the office of a network executive and, on explaining that he had had no Left connections at all, despite the then current attacks upon him, was told that this was precisely the trouble; "You have nothing to give them," he was told, meaning he had no confession to make, and so he was fired from his job and for more than a year could not recover the will to leave his house.

It seemed to me after a time that this, as well as other kinds of social compliance, is the result of the sense of guilt which individuals strive to conceal by complying. Generally it was guilt, in this historic instance, resulting from their awareness that they were not as Rightist as people were supposed to be; that the tenor of public pronouncements was alien to them and that they must be somehow discoverable as enemies of the power overhead. There was a new religiosity in the air, not merely the kind expressed by the spurt in church construction and church attendance, but an official piety which my reading of American history could not reconcile with the free-wheeling iconoclasm of the country's past. I saw forming a kind of interior mechanism of confession and forgiveness of sins which until now had not been rightly categorized as sins. New sins were being created monthly. It was very odd how quickly these were accepted into the new orthodoxy, quite as though they had been there since the beginning of time. Above all, above all horrors, I saw accepted the notion that conscience was no longer a private matter but one of state administration. I saw men handing conscience to other men and thanking other men for the opportunity of doing so.

I wished for a way to write a play that would be sharp, that would lift out of the morass of subjectivism the squirming, single, defined process which would show that the sin of public terror is that it divests man of conscience, of himself. It was a theme not unrelated to those that had invested the previous plays. In *The Crucible*, however, there was an attempt to move beyond the discovery and unveiling of the hero's guilt, a guilt that kills the personality. I had grown increasingly conscious of this theme in my past work, and aware too that it was no longer enough for me to build a play, as it were, upon the revelation of guilt, and to rely solely upon a fate which exacts payment from the culpable man. Now guilt appeared to me no longer the bedrock beneath which the probe could not penetrate. I saw it now as a betrayer, as possibly the most real of our illusions, but nevertheless a quality of mind capable of being overthrown.

I had known of the Salem witch hunt for many years before "McCarthyism" had arrived, and it had always remained an inexplicable darkness to me. When I looked into it now, however, it was with the contemporary situation at my back, particularly the mystery of the handing over of conscience which seemed to me the central and informing fact of the time. One finds, I suppose, what one seeks. I doubt I should ever have tempted agony by actually writing a play on the subject had I not come upon a single fact. It was that Abigail Williams, the prime mover of the Salem hysteria, so far as the hysterical children were concerned, had a short time earlier been the house servant of the Proctors and now was crying out Elizabeth Proctor as a witch; but more—it was clear from the record that with entirely uncharacteristic fastidiousness she was refusing to include John Proctor, Elizabeth's husband, in her accusations despite the urgings of the prosecutors. Why? I searched the records of the trials in the courthouse at Salem but in no other instance could I find such a careful avoidance of the implicating stutter, the murderous, ambivalent answer to the sharp questions of the prosecutors. Only here, in Proctor's case, was there so clear an attempt to differentiate between a wife's culpability and a husband's.

The testimony of Proctor himself is one of the least elaborate in the records, and Elizabeth is not one of the major cases either. There could have been numerous reasons for his having been ultimately apprehended and hanged which are nowhere to be found.

After the play opened, several of his descendants wrote to me; and one of them believes that Proctor fell under suspicion because, according to family tradition, he had for years been an amateur inventor whose machines appeared to some people as devilish in their ingenuity, and—again according to tradition—he had had to conceal them and work on them privately long before the witch hunt had started, for fear of censure if not worse. The explanation does not account for everything, but it does fall in with his evidently liberated cast of mind as revealed in the record; he was one of the few who not only refused to admit consorting with evil spirits, but who persisted in calling the entire business a ruse and a fake. Most, if not all, of the other victims were of their time in conceding the existence of the immemorial plot by the Devil to take over the visible world, their only reservation being that they happened not to have taken part in it themselves.

It was the fact that Abigail, their former servant, was their accuser, and her apparent desire to convict Elizabeth and save John, that made the play conceivable for me.

As in any such mass phenomenon, the number of characters of vital, if not decisive, importance is so great as to make the dramatic problem excessively difficult. For a time it seemed best to approach the town impressionistically, and, by a mosaic of seemingly disconnected scenes, gradually to form a context of cause and effect. This I believe I might well have done had it not been that the central impulse for writing at all was not the social but the interior psychological question, which was the question of that guilt residing in Salem which the hysteria merely unleashed, but did not create. Consequently, the structure reflects that understanding, and it centers in John, Elizabeth, and Abigail.

In reading the record, which was taken down verbatim at the trial, I found one recurring note which had a growing effect upon my concept, not only of the phenomenon itself, but of our modern way of thinking about people, and especially of the treatment of evil in contemporary drama. Some critics have taken exception, for instance, to the unrelieved badness of the prosecution in my play. I understand how this is possible, and I plead no mitigation, but I was up against historical facts which were immutable. I do not think that either the record itself or the numerous commentaries upon it reveal any mitigation of the unrelieved, straightforward, and absolute dedication to evil displayed by the judges of these trials and the prosecutors. After days of study it became quite incredible how perfect they were in this respect. I recall, almost as in a dream, how Rebecca Nurse, a pious and universally respected woman of great age, was literally taken by force from her sickbed and ferociously cross-examined. No human weakness could be displayed without the prosecution's stabbing into it with greater fury. The most patent contradictions, almost laughable even in that day, were overridden with warning not to repeat their mention. There was a sadism here that was breathtaking.

So much so, that I sought but could not at the time take hold of a concept of man which might really begin to account for such evil. For instance, it seems beyond doubt that members of the Putnam family consciously, coldly, and with malice aforethought conferred in private with some of the girls, and told them whom it was desirable to cry out upon next. There is and will always be in my mind the spectacle of the great minister, and ideological authority behind the prosecution, Cotton Mather, galloping up to the scaffold to beat back a crowd of villagers so moved by the towering dignity of the victims as to want to free them.

It was not difficult to foresee the objections to such absolute evil in men; we are committed, after all, to the belief that it does not and cannot exist. Had I this play to write now, however, I might proceed on an altered concept. I should say that my own—and the critics'—unbelief in this depth of evil is concomitant with our unbelief in good, too. I should now examine this fact of evil as such. Instead, I sought to make Danforth, for instance, perceptible as a human being by showing him somewhat put off by Mary Warren's turnabout at the height of the trials, which caused no little confusion. In my play, Danforth seems about to conceive of the truth, and surely there is a disposition in him at least to listen to arguments that go counter to the line of the prosecution. There is no such swerving in the record, and I think now, almost four years after the writing of it, that I was wrong in mitigating the evil of this man and the judges he represents. Instead, I would perfect his evil to its utmost and make an open issue, a thematic consideration of it in the play. I believe now, as I did not conceive then, that there are people dedicated to evil in the world; that without their perverse example we should not know the good. Evil is not a mistake but a fact in itself. I have never proceeded psychoanalytically in my thought, but neither have I been separated from that humane if not humanistic conception of man as being essentially innocent while the evil in him represents but a perversion of his frustrated love. I posit no metaphysical force of evil which totally possesses certain individuals, nor do I even deny that given infinite wisdom and patience and knowledge any human being can be saved from himself. I believe merely that, from whatever cause, a dedication to evil, not mistaking it for good, but knowing it as evil and loving it as evil, is possible in human beings who appear agreeable and normal. I think now that one of the hidden weaknesses of our whole approach to dramatic psychology is our inability to face this fact—to conceive, in effect, of Iago.

The Crucible is a "tough" play. My criticism of it now would be that it is not tough enough. I say this not merely out of deference to the record of these trials, but out of a consideration for drama. We are so intent upon getting sympathy for our characters that the consequences of evil are being muddied by sentimentality under the guise of a temperate weighing of causes. The tranquility of the bad man lies at the heart of not only moral philosophy but dramaturgy as well. But my central intention in this play was to one side of this idea, which was realized only as the play was in production. All I sought here was to take a step not only beyond the realization of guilt, but beyond the helpless victimization of the hero.

The society of Salem was "morally" vocal. People then avowed principles, sought to live by them and die by them. Issues of faith, conduct, society, pervaded their private lives in a conscious way. They needed but to disapprove to act. I was drawn to this subject because the historical moment seemed to give me the poetic right to create people of higher self-awareness than the contemporary sense affords. I had explored the subjective world in Salesman and I wanted now to move closer to a conscious hero.

The decidedly mixed reception to the play was not easily traceable, but I believe there are causes for it which are of moment to more than this play alone. I believe that the very moral awareness of the play and its characters—which are historically correct—was repulsive to the audience. For a variety of reasons I think that the

Anglo-Saxon audience cannot believe the reality of characters who live by principles and know very much about their own characters and situations, and who say what they know. Our drama, for this among other reasons, is condemned, so to speak, to the emotions of subjectivism, which, as they approach knowledge and self-awareness, become less and less actual and real to us. In retrospect I think that my course in *The Crucible* should have been toward greater self-awareness and not, as my critics have implied, toward an enlarged and more pervasive subjectivism. The realistic form and style of the play would then have had to give way. What new form might have evolved I cannot now say, but certainly the passion of knowing is as powerful as the passion of feeling alone, and the writing of the play broached the question of that new form for me.

The work of Bertolt Brecht inevitably rises up in any such quest. It seems to me that, while I cannot agree with his concept of the human situation, his solution of the problem of consciousness is admirably honest and theatrically powerful. One cannot watch his productions without knowing that he is at work not on the periphery of the contemporary dramatic problem, but directly upon its center—which is again the problem of consciousness.

VII

The Crucible, then, opened up a new prospect, and, like every work when completed, it left behind it unfinished business. It made a new freedom possible, and it also threw a certain light upon the difference between the modern playwriting problem of meaning and that of the age preceding the secularization of society. It is impossible to study the trial record without feeling the immanence of a veritable pantheon of life values in whose name both prosecution and defense could speak. The testimony is thick with reference to Biblical examples, and even as religious belief did nothing to temper cruelty—and in fact might be shown to have made the cruel crueler—it often served to raise this swirling and ludicrous mysticism to a level of high moral debate; and it did this despite the fact that most of the participants were unlettered, simple folk. They lived and would die more in the shadow of the other world than in the light of this one (and it is no mean irony that the theocratic prosecution should seek out the most religious people for its victims).

The longer I dwelt on the whole spectacle, the more clear became the failure of the present age to find a universal moral sanction, and the power of realism's hold on our theater was an aspect of this vacuum. For it began to appear that our inability to break more than the surfaces of realism reflected our inability—playwrights and audiences—to agree upon the pantheon of forces and values which must lie behind the realistic surfaces of life. In this light, realism, as a style, could seem to be a defense against the assertion of meaning. How strange a conclusion this is when one realizes that the same style seventy years ago was the prime instrument of those who sought to illuminate meaning in the theater, who divested their plays of fancy talk and improbable locales and bizarre characters in order to bring "life" onto the stage. And I wondered then what was true. Was it that we had come to fear the hard glare of life on the stage and under the guise of an aesthetic surfeited with realism were merely expressing our flight from reality? Or was our condemned realism only the counterfeit of the original, whose most powerful single impetus was to deal with man as a social animal? Any form can be drained of its informing purpose, can be used to convey, like the Tudor façades of college dormitories, the now vanished dignity and necessity of a former age in order to lend specious justification for a present hollowness. Was it realism that stood in the way of meaning or was it the counterfeit of realism?

Increasingly over the past five years and more the poetic plays, so-called, some of them much admired by all sorts of critics, were surprisingly full of what in the university years ago was called "fine" writing. If one heard less of the creak of plot machinery there was more of the squeak of self-pity, the humming of the poetic poseur, the new romance of the arbitrary and the uncompleted. For one, I had seen enough of the "borrowings" of the set, the plot, the time-shifting methods, and the lighting of *Death of a Salesman* to have an intimate understanding of how a vessel could be emptied and still purveyed to the public as new wine. Was realism called futile now because it needed to illuminate an exact meaning behind it, a conviction that was no more with us? Confusion, the inability to describe one's sense of a thing, often issues in a genuine poetry of feeling, and feeling was now raised up as the highest good and the ultimate attainment in drama. I had known that kind of victory myself with *Salesman*; but was there not another realm even higher, where feeling took awareness more openly by the hand and both equally ruled and were illuminated? I had found a kind of self-awareness in the bloody book of Salem and had thought that since the natural, realistic surface of that society was one already immersed in the questions of meaning and the relations of men to God, to write a realistic play of that world was already to write in a style beyond contemporary realism. That more than one critic had found the play "cold" when I had never written more passionately was by this time an acceptable and inevitable detail of my fate, for, while it will never confess to it, our theater is trained—actors, directors, audience, and critics—to take to its heart anything that does not prick the mind and to suspect everything that does not supinely reassure.

If *Salesman* was written in a mood of friendly partnership with the audience, *The Crucible* reminded me that we had not yet come to terms. The latter play has been produced more often than any of the others, and more successfully the more time elapses from the headline "McCarthyism" which it was supposed to be "about." I believe that on the night of its opening, a time when the gale from the Right was blowing at its fullest fury, it inspired a part of its audience with an unsettling fear and partisanship which deflected the sight of the real and inner theme, which, again, was the handing over of conscience to another, be it woman, the state, or a terror, and the realization that with conscience goes the person, the soul immortal, and the "name." That there was not one mention of this process in any review, favorable or not, was the measure of my sense of defeat, and the impulse to separate, openly and without concealment, the action of the next play, *A View from the Bridge*, from its generalized significance. The engaged narrator, in short, appeared.

I had heard its story years before, quite as it appears in the play, and quite as complete, and from time to time there were efforts to break up its arc, to reshuffle its action so that I might be able to find what there was in it which drew me back to it again and again—until it became like a fact in my mind, an unbreakable series of actions that went to create a closed circle impervious to all interpretation. It was written experimentally not only as a form, but as an exercise in interpretation. I found in myself a passionate detachment toward its story as one does toward a spectacle in which one is not engaged but which holds a fascination deriving from its monolithic perfection. If this had happened, and if I could not forget it after so many years, there must be some meaning in it for me, and I could write what had happened, why it had happened, and to one side, as it were, express as much as I knew of my sense of its meaning for me. Yet I wished to leave the action intact so that the onlooker could seize the right to interpret it entirely for himself and to accept or reject my reading of its significance.

That reading was the awesomeness of a passion which, despite its contradicting the self-interest of the individual it inhabits, despite every kind of warning, despite even its destruction of the moral beliefs of the individual, proceeds to magnify its power over him until it destroys him.

I have not dealt with the business of production until now because it is a subject large enough for separate treatment, but at this point it is unavoidable. *A View from the Bridge* was relatively a failure in New York when it was first produced; a revised version, published in this volume, became a great success in London not long afterward. The present version is a better play, I think, but not that much better; and the sharp difference between the impressions each of the productions created has a bearing on many themes that have been treated here.

Certain objective factors ought to be mentioned first. In New York, the play was preceded by *A Memory of Two Mondays*. That one of its leading performers on opening night completely lost his bearings and played in a state bordering on terror destroyed at the outset any hope that something human might be communicated by this evening in the theater. *A Memory of Two Mondays* was dismissed so thoroughly that in one of the reviews, and one of the most important, it was not even mentioned as having been played. By the time *A View from the Bridge* came on, I suppose the critics were certain that they were witnessing an aberration, for there had been no suggestion of any theatrical authority in the first play's performance. It was too much to hope that the second play could retrieve what had been so completely dissipated by the first.

A Memory of Two Mondays is a pathetic comedy; a boy works among people for a couple of years, shares their troubles, their victories, their hopes, and when it is time for him to be on his way he expects some memorable moment, some sign from them that he has been among them, that he has touched them and been touched by them. In the sea of routine that swells around them they barely note his departure. It is a kind of letter to that subculture where the sinews of the economy are rooted, that darkest Africa of our society from whose interior only the sketchiest messages ever reach our literature or our stage. I wrote it, I suppose, in part out of a desire to relive a sort of reality where necessity was open and bare; I hoped to define for myself the value of hope, why it must arise, as well as the heroism of those who know, at least, how to endure its absence. Nothing in this book was written with greater love, and for myself I love nothing printed here better than this play.

Nevertheless, the fact that it was seen as something utterly sad and hopeless as a comment on life quite astonishes me still. After all, from this endless, timeless, will-less environment, a boy emerges who will not accept its defeat or its mood as final, and literally takes himself off on a quest for a higher gratification. I suppose we simply do not want to see how empty the lives of so many of us are even when the depiction is made hopefully and not at all in despair. The play speaks not of obsession but of rent and hunger and the need for a little poetry in life and is entirely out of date in those respects—so much so that many took it for granted it had been written a long time ago and exhumed.

It shares with *A View from the Bridge* the impulse to present rather than to represent an interpretation of reality. Incident and character are set forth with the barest naïveté, and action is stopped abruptly while commentary takes its place. The organic impulse behind *Salesman*, for instance, and *All My Sons* is avowedly split apart; for a moment I was striving not to make people forget they were in a theater, not to obliterate an awareness of form, not to forge a pretense of life, but to be abrupt, clear, and explicit in setting forth fact as fact and art as art so that the sea of theatrical sentiment, which is so easily let in to drown all shape, meaning, and perspective, might be held back and some hard outline of a human dilemma be allowed to rise and stand. *A Memory of Two Mondays* has a story but not a plot, because the life it reflects appears to me to strip people of alternatives and will beyond a close and tight periphery in which they may exercise a meager choice.

The contradiction in my attitude toward these two plays and what was hoped for them is indicated by the experience of the two productions of *A View from the Bridge*, the one a failure and "cold," the other quite the opposite. In writing this play originally I obeyed the impulse to indicate, to telegraph, so to speak, rather than to explore and exploit what at first had seemed to me the inevitable and therefore unnecessary emotional implications of the conflict. The Broadway production's setting followed the same impulse, as it should have, and revealed nothing more than a platform to contain the living room, the sea behind the house, and a Grecian-style pediment overhanging the abstract doorway to the house. The austerity of the production, in a word, expressed the reticence of the writing.

This version was in one act because it had seemed to me that the essentials of the dilemma were all that was required, for I wished it to be kept distant from the empathic flood which a realistic portrayal of the same tale and characters might unloose.

On seeing the production played several times I came to understand that, like the plays written previously, this one was expressing a very personal preoccupation and that it was not at all apart from my own psychological life. I discovered my own relationships to what quite suddenly appeared as, in some part, an analogy to situations in my life, a distant analogy but a heartening proof that under the reticence of its original method my own spirit was attempting to speak. So that when a new production was planned for London it was not possible to let the original go on as it was. Now there were additional things to be said which it became necessary to say because I had come to the awareness that this play had not, as I had almost believed before, been "given" to me from without, but that my life had created it.

Therefore, many decisive alterations, small in themselves but nonetheless great in their over-all consequences, began to flow into the conception of the play. Perhaps the two most important were an altered attitude toward Eddie Carbone, the hero, and toward the two women in his life. I had originally conceived Eddie as a phenomenon, a rather awesome fact of existence, and I had kept a certain distance from involvement in his self-justifications. Consequently, he had appeared as a kind of biological sport, and to a degree a repelling figure not quite admissible into the human family. In revising the play it became possible to accept for myself the implication I had sought to make clear in the original version, which was that however one might dislike this man, who does all sorts of frightful things, he possesses or exemplifies the wondrous and humane fact that he too can be driven to what in the last analysis is a sacrifice of himself for his conception, however misguided, of right, dignity, and justice. In revising it I found it possible to move beyond contemplation of the man as a phenomenon into an acceptance for dramatic purposes of his aims themselves. Once this occurred the autonomous viewpoints of his wife and niece could be expressed more fully and, instead of remaining muted counterpoints to the march of Eddie's career, became involved forces pressing him forward or holding him back and eventually forming, in part, the nature of his disaster. The discovery of my own involvement in what I had written modified its original friezelike character and the play moved closer toward realism and called up the emphatic response of its audience.

The conception of the new production was in accordance with this new perspective. Peter Brook, the London director, designed a set which was more realistically detailed than the rather bare, if beautiful, New York background, and at the same time emphasized the environment of the neighborhood. Its central idea was to bring the people of the neighborhood into the foreground of the action. Two high wings closed to form the face of the house where Eddie lived, a brick tenement, and when opened revealed a basement living room. Overhead and at the sides and across the back were stairways, fire escapes, passages, quite like a whole neighborhood constructed vertically. The easier economics of the London theater made it possible to use many more neighbors than the three or four extras we could hire in New York, and there was a temperate but nevertheless full flow of strangers across the stage and up and down its stairways and passages. The maturing of Eddie's need to destroy Rodolpho was consequently seen in the context which could make it of real moment, for the betrayal achieves its true proportions as it flies in the face of the mores administered by Eddie's conscience—which is also the conscience of his friends, co-workers, and neighbors and not just his own autonomous creation. Thus his "oddness" came to disappear as he was seen in context, as a creature of his environment as well as an exception to it; and where originally there had been only a removed sense of terror at the oncoming catastrophe, now there was pity and, I think, the kind of wonder which it had been my aim to create in the first place. It was finally possible to mourn this man.

Perhaps more than any other production experience, this helped to resolve for me one important question of form and meaning. I warn, however, that like everything else said here this is highly personal, and even as I avow it know that there are other paths and other standards which can issue in a worthwhile kind of dramatic experience. For myself, the theater is above all else an instrument of passion. However important considerations of style and form have been to me, they are only means, tools to pry up the well-worn, "inevitable" surfaces of experience behind which swarm the living thoughts and feelings whose expression is the essential purpose of art. I have stood squarely in conventional realism; I have tried to expand it with an imposition of various forms in order to speak more directly, even more abruptly and nakedly of what has moved me behind the visible façades of life. Critics have given me more praise than a writer can reasonably hope for, and more condemnation than one dares believe one has the power to survive. There are certain distillations which remain after the dross rises to the top and boils away, certain old and new commitments which, despite the heat applied to them and the turmoil that has threatened to sweep them away, nevertheless remain, some of them purified.

A play, I think, ought to make sense to common-sense people. I know what it is to have been rejected by them, even unfairly so, but the only challenge worth the effort is the widest one and the tallest one, which is the people themselves. It is their innate conservatism which, I think, is and ought to be the barrier to excess in experiment and the exploitation of the bizarre, even as it is the proper aim of drama to break down the limits of conventional unawareness and acceptance of outmoded and banal forms.

By whatever means it is accomplished, the prime business of a play is to arouse the passions of its audience so that by the route of passion may be opened up new relationships between a man and men, and between men and Man. Drama is akin to the other inventions of man in that it ought to help us to know more, and not merely to spend our feelings.

The ultimate justification for a genuine new form is the new and heightened consciousness it creates and makes possible—a consciousness of causation in the light of known but hitherto inexplicable effects.

Not only in the drama, but in sociology, psychology, psychiatry, and religion, the past half century has created an almost overwhelming documentation of man as a nearly passive creation of environment and family-created psychological drives. If only from the dramatic point of view, this dictum cannot be accepted as final and "realistic" any more than man's ultimate position can be accepted as his efficient use by state or corporate apparatus. It is more "real," however, for drama to "liberate" itself from this vise by the route of romance and the spectacle of free will and a new heroic formula than it is "real" now to represent man's defeat as the ultimate implication of an overwhelming determinism.

Realism, heightened or conventional, is neither more nor less an artifice, a species of poetic symbolization, than any other form. It is merely more familiar in this age. If it is used as a covering of safety against the evaluation of life it must be overthrown, and for that reason above all the rest. But neither poetry nor liberation can come merely from a rearrangement of the lights or from leaving the skeletons of the flats exposed instead of covered by painted cloths; nor can it come merely from the masking of the human face or the transformation of speech into rhythmic verse, or from the expunging of common details of life's apparencies. A new poem on the stage is a new concept of relationships between the one and the many and the many and history, and to create it requires greater attention, not less, to the inexorable, common, pervasive conditions of existence in this time and this hour. Otherwise only a new self-indulgence is created, and it will be left behind, however poetic its surface.

A drama worthy of its time must first, knowingly or by instinctive means, recognize its major and most valuable traditions and where it has departed from them. Determinism, whether it is based on the iron necessities of economics or on psychoanalytic theory seen as a closed circle, is a contradiction of the idea of drama itself as drama has come down to us in its fullest developments. The idea of the hero, let alone the mere protagonist, is incompatible with a drama whose bounds are set in advance by the concept of an unbreakable trap. Nor is it merely that one wants arbitrarily to find a hero and a victory. The history of man is a ceaseless process of overthrowing one determinism to make way for another more faithful to life's changing relationships. And it is a process inconceivable without the existence of the will of man. His will is as much a fact as his defeat. Any determinism, even the most scientific, is only that stasis, that seemingly endless pause, before the application of man's will administering a new insight into causation.

The analogy to physics may not be out of place. The once-irreducible elements of matter, whose behavior was seen as fixed and remorseless, disintegrated under the controlled bombardment of atomic particles until so fine a perception as the scale of atomic weights appears as a relatively gross concept on the road to man's manipulation of the material world. More to the point: even as the paths, the powers, and the behavior of smaller and smaller elements and forces in nature are brought into the fields of measurement, we are faced with the dialectical irony that the act of measurement itself changes the particle being measured, so that we can know only what it is at the moment when it receives the impact of our rays, not what it was before it was struck. The idea of realism has become wedded to the idea that man is at best the sum of forces working upon him and of given psychological forces within him. Yet an innate value, an innate will, does in fact posit itself as real not alone because it is devoutly to be wished, but because, however closely he is measured and systematically accounted for, he is more than the sum of his stimuli and is unpredictable beyond a certain point. A drama, like a history, which stops at this point, the point of conditioning, is not reflecting reality. What is wanted, therefore, is not a poetry of escape from process and determinism, like that mood play which stops where feeling ends or that inverted romanticism which would mirror all the world in the sado-masochistic relationship. Nor will the heightening of the intensity of language alone yield the prize. A new poem will appear because a new balance has been struck which embraces both determinism and the paradox of will. If there is one unseen goal toward which every play in this book strives, it is that very discovery and its proof—that we are made and yet are more than what made us.

On Social Plays
1955

A Greek living in the classical period would be bewildered by the dichotomy implied in the very term "social play." Especially for the Greek, a drama created for public performance had to be "social." A play to him was by definition a dramatic consideration of the way men ought to live. But in this day of extreme individualism even that phrase must be further defined. When we say "how men ought to live," we are likely to be thinking of psychological therapy, of ridding ourselves individually of neurotic compulsions and destructive inner tendencies, of "learning how to love" and thereby gaining "happiness."

It need hardly be said that the Greek dramatist had more than a passing interest in psychology and character on the stage. But for him these were means to a larger end, and the end was what we isolate today as social. That is, the relations of man as a social animal, rather than his definition as a separated entity, was the dramatic goal. Why this should have come to be is a large historical question which others are more competent to explain, as several already have. For our purposes it will be sufficient to indicate one element in the life of classical Greece that differs so radically from anything existing in the modern world as to throw a bright light on certain of our attitudes which we take for granted and toward which we therefore are without a proper perspective.

The Greek citizen of that time thought of himself as belonging not to a "nation" or a "state" but to a *polis*. The polis were small units, apparently deriving from an earlier tribal social organization, whose members probably knew one another personally because they were relatively few in number and occupied a small territory. In war or peace the whole people made the vital decisions, there being no profession of politics as we know it; any man could be elected magistrate, judge, even a general in the armed forces. It was an amateur world compared to our stratified and specialized one, a world in which everyone knew enough about almost any profession to practice it, because most things were simple to know. The thing of importance for us is that these people were *engaged*, they could not imagine the good life excepting as it brought each person into close contact with civic matters. They were avid argufiers. Achilles was blessed by the gods with the power to fight well and make good speeches. The people had a special sense of pride in the polis and thought that it in itself distinguished them from the barbarians outside who lived under tyrannies.

The preoccupation of the Greek drama with ultimate law, with the Grand Design, so to speak, was therefore an expression of a basic assumption of the people, who could not yet conceive, luckily, that any man could long prosper unless his polis prospered. The individual was at one with his society; his conflicts with it were, in our terms, like family conflicts the opposing sides of which nevertheless shared a mutuality of feeling and responsibility. Thus the drama written for them, while for us it appears wholly religious, was religious for them in a more than mystical way. Religion is the only way we have any more of expressing our genuinely social feelings and concerns, for in our bones we as a people do not otherwise believe in our oneness with a larger group. But the religiousness of the Greek drama of the classical time was more worldly; it expressed a social concern, to be sure, but it did so on the part of a people already unified on earth rather than the drive of a single individual toward personal salvation. The great gap we feel between religious or "high" emotion and the emotions of daily life was not present in their mass affairs. The religious expression was not many degrees higher for them than many other social expressions, of which their drama is the most complete example.

It is necessary to add that as the polis withered under the impact of war and historical change, as commerce grew and a differentiation of interest separated man from man, the Greek drama found it more and more difficult to stand as a kind of universal mass

statement or prayer. It turned its eye inward, created more elabo-
rated characterizations, and slowly gave up some of its former loft-
iness. Men, as H. D. F. Kitto has said in *The Greeks*, replaced Man
in the plays. Nevertheless, to the end the Greek drama clearly conceived its right function as something far wider than a purely private examination of individuality for the sake of the examination
or for art's sake. In every dramatic hero there is the idea of the
Greek people, their fate, their will, and their destiny.

In today's America the term "social play" brings up images which
are historically conditioned, very recent, and, I believe, only incidentally pertinent to a fruitful conception of the drama. The term
indicates to us an attack, an arraignment of society's evils such as
Ibsen allegedly invented and was later taken up by left-wing playwrights whose primary interest was the exposure of capitalism for
the implied benefit of socialism or communism. The concept is tired
and narrow, but its worst effect has been to confuse a whole generation of playwrights, audiences, and theater workers.

If one can look at the idea of "social drama" from the Greek
viewpoint for one moment, it will be clear that there can be only
either a genuinely social drama or, if it abdicates altogether, its true
opposite, the antisocial and ultimately antidramatic drama.

To put it simply, even oversimply, a drama rises in stature and
intensity in proportion to the weight of its application to all manner of men. It gains its weight as it deals with more and more of the
whole man, not either his subjective or his social life alone, and the
Greek was unable to conceive of man or anything else except as a
whole. The modern playwright, at least in America, on the one
hand is importuned by his most demanding audience to write
importantly, while on the other he is asked not to bring onto the
stage images of social function, lest he seem like a special pleader
and therefore inartistic. I am not attempting a defense of the social
dramas of the thirties, most of which were in fact special pleadings
and further from a consideration of the whole man than much of
the antisocial drama is. I am trying only to project a right conception of what social drama was and what it ought to be. It is, I
think, the widest concept of drama available to us thus far.

When, however, a contemporary dramatist is drawn for but a
moment toward a concept of form even remotely Greek, certain

lacks become evident—a certain abyss even begins to appear around him. When you are writing in the name of a people unified in a self-conscious and rather small band, when you yourself as a writer are not an individual entrepreneur offering wares to a hostile marketplace but a member of a group who is in other ways no different from the rest—when, in short, the dramatic form itself is regarded as inevitably a social expression of the deepest concerns of all your fellow men—your work is bound to be liberated, freed of even the hypothesis of partisanship, if only because partisanship cannot thrive where the idea of wholeness is accepted. Thus in such a situation what we call social matters become inseparable from subjective psychological matters, and the drama is once again whole and capable of the highest reach.

If one considers our own drama of the past forty years in comparison with that of classical Greece, one elemental difference—the difference which seems to me to be our crippling hobble—will emerge. The single theme to which our most ambitious plays can be reduced is frustration. In all of them, from O'Neill's through the best of Anderson, Sidney Howard, and the rest, the underlying log jam, so to speak, the unresolvable paradox, is that, try as he will, the individual is doomed to frustration when once he gains a consciousness of his own identity. The image is that of the individual scratching away at a wall beyond which stands society, his fellow men. Sometimes he pounds at the wall, sometimes he tries to scale it or even blow it up, but at the end the wall is always there, and the man himself is dead or doomed to defeat in his attempt to live a human life.

The tragic victory is always denied us because, I believe, the plays cannot project with any conviction what the society, in the playwrights' views at any rate, has failed to prove. In Greece the tragic victory consisted in demonstrating that the polis—the whole people—had discovered some aspect of the Grand Design which also was the right way to live *together*. If the American playwrights of serious intent are in any way the subconscience of the country, our claims to have found that way are less than proved. For when the Greek thought of the right way to live it was a whole concept; it meant a way to live that would create citizens who were brave in war, had a sense of responsibility to the polis in peace, and were also developed as individual personalities.

It has often seemed to me that the Soviet Russians have studied classical Greece and have tried to bridge with phraseology profound differences between their social organization and that of Greece, while demanding of their writers what in effect is a Greek social drama. The word "cosmopolitan," as Kitto points out, was invented in Greece when the small polis were disintegrating, and when the drama itself was beginning to turn inward, away from the largest questions of social fate to the fate of individuals alone. It was invented to describe a new kind of man, a man whose allegiance was not primarily to his society, his polis, but to others of like mind anywhere in the world. With it goes an intimation—or more—of skepticism, of self-removal, that presages the radical separation of man from society which the American drama expresses ultimately through themes of frustration. To supplant the polis and allegiance to it, the Soviets have a thousand kinds of social organizations, and, for all one knows, the individual Russian might well feel a sense of connection with civic affairs which the West does not afford its citizens. The crucial difference, however, is that only the most theoretical Russian can trace the effects, if any, of his personality upon the policies of his country, while the Greek could literally see what he had done when he made his speech and swayed or failed to sway his fellow men.

Thus the Russian drama after the Revolution, much as ours, is a drama of frustration, the inability of industrialized men to see themselves spiritually completed through the social organization. But in the Soviet case the frustration is not admitted; it is talked away in large phrases having to do with a victory of the people through tragic sacrifice. The fact remains, however, that nowhere in the world where industrialized economy rules—where specialization in work, politics, and social life is the norm—nowhere has man discovered a means of connecting himself to society except in the form of a truce with it. The best we have been able to do is to speak of a "duty" to society, and this implies sacrifice or self-deprivation. To think of an individual fulfilling his subjective needs through social action, to think of him as living most completely when he lives most socially, to think of him as doing this, not as a social worker acting out of conscientious motives, but naturally, without guilt or sense of oddness—this is difficult for us to imagine, and when we can, we know at the same time that only a few, perhaps a blessed few, are so constructed as to manage it.

As with Greece, so with us—each great war has turned men further and further away from preoccupation with Man and drawn them back into the family, the home, the private life and the preoccupation with sexuality. It has happened, however, that at the same time our theater has exhausted the one form that was made to express the private life—prose realism. We are bored with it; we demand something more, something "higher," on the stage, while at the same time we refuse, or do not know how, to live our private lives excepting as ego-centers. I believe it is this paradox that underlies the kind of struggle taking place in the drama today—a struggle at one and the same time to write of private persons privately and yet lift up their means of expression to a poetic—that is, a social—level. You cannot speak in verse of picayune matters—at least not on the stage—without sounding overblown and ridiculous, and so it should be. Verse reaches always toward the general statement, the wide image, the universal moment, and it must be based upon wide concepts—it must speak not merely of men but of Man. The language of dramatic verse is the language of a people profoundly at one with itself; it is the most public of public speech. The language of prose is the language of the private life, the kind of private life men retreat to when they are at odds with the world they have made or been heirs to.

The social drama, then—at least as I have always conceived it—is the drama of the whole man. It seeks to deal with his differences from others not *per se*, but toward the end that, if only through drama, we may know how much the same we are, for if we lose that knowledge we shall have nothing left at all. The social drama to me is only incidentally an arraignment of society. *A Streetcar Named Desire* is a social drama; so is *The Hairy Ape*, and so are practically all O'Neill's other plays. For they ultimately make moot, either weakly or with full power, the ancient question, how are we to live? And that question is in its Greek sense, its best and most humane sense, not merely a private query.

The social drama, as I see it, is the main stream and the antisocial drama a bypass. I can no longer take with ultimate seriousness a drama of individual psychology written for its own sake, however full it may be of insight and precise observation. Time is moving; there is a world to make, a civilization to create that will move toward the only goal the humanistic, democratic mind can ever accept with honor. It is a world in which the human being can live as a naturally political, naturally private, naturally engaged person, a world in which once again a true tragic victory may be scored.

But that victory is not really possible unless the individual is more than theoretically capable of being recognized by the powers that lead society. Specifically, when men live, as they do under any industrialized system, as integers who have no weight, no *person*, excepting as either customers, draftees, machine tenders, ideologists, or whatever, it is unlikely (and in my opinion impossible) that a dramatic picture of them can really overcome the public knowledge of their nature in real life. In such a society, be it communistic or capitalistic, man is not tragic, he is pathetic. The tragic figure must have certain innate powers which he uses to pass over the boundaries of the known social law—the accepted mores of his people—in order to test and discover necessity. Such a quest implies that the individual who has moved onto that course must be somehow recognized by the law, by the mores, by the powers that design—be they anthropomorphic gods or economic and political laws—as having the worth, the innate value, of a whole people asking a basic question and demanding its answer. We are so atomized socially that no character in a play can conceivably stand as our vanguard, as our heroic questioner. Our society—and I am speaking of every industrialized society in the world—is so complex, each person being so specialized an integer, that the moment any individual is dramatically characterized and set forth as a hero, our common sense reduces him to the size of a complainer, a misfit. For deep down we no longer believe in the rules of the tragic contest; we no longer believe that some ultimate sense can in fact be made of social causation, or in the possibility that any individual can, by a heroic effort, make sense of it. Thus the man that is driven to question the moral chaos in which we live ends up in our estimate as a possibly commendable but definitely odd fellow, and probably as a compulsively driven neurotic. In place of a social aim which called an all-around excellence—physical, intellectual, and moral—the ultimate good, we have set up a goal which can best be characterized as "happiness"—namely, staying out of trouble. This concept is the end result of the truce which all of us have made with society. And a truce implies two enemies. When the truce is broken it means either that the individual has broken out of his ordained place as an integer, or that the society has broken the law by harming him unjustly—that is, it has not left him alone to be a peaceful integer. In the heroic and tragic time the act of questioning the-way-things-are implied that a quest was being carried on to discover an ultimate law or way of life which would yield excellence; in the present time the quest is that of a man made unhappy by rootlessness and, in every important modern play, by a man who is essentially a victim. We have abstracted from the Greek drama its air of doom, its physical destruction of the hero, but its victory escapes us. Thus it has even become difficult to separate in our minds the ideas of the pathetic and of the tragic. And behind this melting of the two lies the overwhelming power of the modern industrial state, the ignorance of each person in it of anything but his own technique as an economic integer, and the elevation of that state to a holy, quite religious sphere.

What, after all, are our basic social aims as applied to the individual? Americans are often accused of worshiping financial success, but this is, first of all, not an American monopoly, and, second, it does not as a concept make clear what is causing so much uneasiness and moral pain. My own belief, at any rate, is that America has merely arrived first at the condition that awaits every country that takes her economic road without enforcing upon every development of industrial technique certain quite arbitrary standards of value.

The deep moral uneasiness among us, the vast sense of being only tenuously joined to the rest of our fellows, is caused, in my view, by the fact that the person has value as he fits into the pattern of efficiency, and for that alone. The reason *Death of a Salesman*, for instance, left such a strong impression was that it set forth unremittingly the picture of a man who was not even especially "good" but whose situation made clear that at bottom we are alone, valueless, without even the elements of a human person, when once we fail to fit the patterns of efficiency. Under the black shadow of that gigantic necessity, even the drift of some psychoanalytic practice is toward the fitting-in, the training of the individual whose soul has revolted, so that he may once again "take his place" in society— that is, do his "work," "function," in other words, accommodate himself to a scheme of things that is not at all ancient but very new in the world. In short, the absolute value of the individual human being is believed in only as a secondary value; it stands well below the needs of efficient production. We have finally come to serve the machine. The machine must not be stopped, marred, left dirty, or outmoded. Only men can be left marred, stopped, dirty, and alone. Our pity for the victim is mixed, I think. It is mixed with an air of self-preserving superiority—we, thank God, know how to fit in, therefore this victim, however pitiful, has himself to thank for his fate. We believe, in other words, that to fit into the patterns of efficiency is the ultimate good, and at the same time we know in our bones that a crueler concept is not easy to arrive at.

Nor may the exponents of socialism take heart from this. There is no such thing as a capitalist assembly line or drygoods counter. The disciplines required by machines are the same everywhere and will not be truly mitigated by old-age pensions and social-security payments. So long as modern man conceives of himself as valuable only because he fits into some niche in the machine-tending pattern, he will never know anything more than a pathetic doom.

The implications of this fact spread throughout our culture, indeed, throughout the culture of the industrialized parts of the world. Be it in music, literature, drama, or whatever, the value of a work is, willy nilly, equated with its mass "acceptance," i.e., its efficiency. All the engines of economic law are, like the mills of the gods, working toward that same end. The novel of excellence that could once be published without financial loss if it sold two or three thousand copies can no longer be published, because the costs of production require that every book sell at least ten, twelve, or fifteen thousand copies. The play that might have been produced at a decent profit if it could fill half a house for a few months can no longer be produced, for the costs of production require a play to draw packed houses from the first night.

When one has the temerity to suggest that the Greek theater was subsidized, that so much of the world's great music, art, and literature was stubbornly patronized by people who found honor in helping to bring beauty onto the earth, one is not quite suspect, to be sure, but the suggestion nevertheless has an unreal air, an air of being essentially at odds and possibly in dangerous conflict with some unspoken sense of values. For we do believe that a "good" thing, be it art or toothpaste, proves its goodness by its public acceptance. And at the same time we know, too, that something dark and dreadful lies within this concept.

The problem, then, of the social drama in this generation is not the same as it was for Ibsen, Chekhov, or Shaw. They, and the left-wing playwrights of the thirties who amplified their findings and repeated their forms, were oriented either toward an arraignment of some of the symptoms of efficiency men or toward the ultimate cure by socialism. With the proliferation of machine techniques in the world, and the relative perfection of distributing techniques, in America first and the rest of the world soon, the time will shortly be upon us when the truth will dawn. We shall come to see, I think, that Production for Profit and Production for Use (whatever their relative advantages—and each has its own) leave untouched the problem which the Greek drama put so powerfully before mankind. How are we to live? From what fiat, from what ultimate source are we to derive a standard of values that will create in man a respect for himself, a real voice in the fate of his society, and, above all, an aim for his life which is neither a private aim for a private life nor one which sets him below the machine that was made to serve him?

The social drama in this generation must do more than analyze and arraign the social network of relationships. It must delve into the nature of man as he exists to discover what his needs are, so that those needs may be amplified and exteriorized in terms of social concepts. Thus, the new social dramatist, if he is to do his work, must be an even deeper psychologist than those of the past, and he must be conscious at least of the futility of isolating the psychological life of man lest he fall always short of tragedy, and return, again and again and again, to the pathetic swampland where the waters are old tears and not the generative seas from which new kinds of life arise.

It is a good time to be writing because the audience is sick of the old formulations. It is no longer believed—and we may be thankful for it—that the poor are necessarily virtuous or the rich necessarily decayed. Nor is it believed that, as some writers would put it, the rich are necessarily not decayed and the poor necessarily the carriers of vulgarity. We have developed so democratic a culture that in America neither the speech of a man nor his way of dressing nor even his ambitions for himself inevitably mark his social class. On the stage social rank tells next to nothing about the man any more. The decks are cleared. There is a kind of perverse unity forming among us, born, I think, of the discontent of all classes of people with the endless frustration of life. It is possible now to speak of a search for values, not solely from the position of bitterness, but with a warm embrace of mankind, with a sense that at bottom every one of us is a victim of this misplacement of aims.

The debilitation of the tragic drama, I believe, is commensurate with the fracturing and the aborting of the need of man to maintain a fruitful kind of union with his society. Everything we learn, everything we know or deem valuable for a man to know, has been thrown into the creation of a machine technology. The nuclear bomb, as a way of waging war, is questioned only now—because we have it, because we have invented it: not before both sides knew how to make it. Both sides have the bomb and both sides have the machine. Some day the whole world will have both and the only force that will keep them from destructive use will be a force strange to machine psychology, a force born of will—the will of man to survive and to reach his ultimate, most conscious, most knowing, most fulfilled condition, his fated excellence.

History has given the social drama its new chance. Ibsen and Shaw had to work through three acts to prove in the fourth that, even if we are not completely formed by society, there is little left that society does not affect. The tremendous growth in our consciousness of social causation has won for these writers their victory in this sense: it has given to us a wider consciousness of the causes that form character. What the middle of the twentieth century has taught us is that theirs was not the whole answer. It is not enough any more to know that one is at the mercy of social pressures; it is necessary to understand that such a sealed fate cannot be accepted. Nor is courage alone required now to question this complex, although without courage nothing is possible, including real

dramatic writing. It is necessary to know that the values of commerce, values which were despised as necessary but less than noble
in the long past, are now not merely perversely dominant everywhere but claimed as positive moral goodness itself. The question
must begin to be asked; not whether a new thing will work or pay,
not whether it is more efficient than its predecessor, more popular,
and more easily accepted; but what it will do to human beings. The
first invention of man to create that response in all nations was the
atomic bomb. It is the first "improvement" to have dramatized for
even the numbest mind the question of value. Over the past decade
this nation and this world have been gripped by an inner debate on
many levels, a debate raised to consciousness by this all-destroying
"improvement." Alongside it is the "improvement" called automa-
tion, which will soon displace workers who mass-produce in industry. The conquest of poverty and hunger is the order of the day; the
refusal of the dark peoples to live in subjection to the white is
already a fact. The world, I think, is moving toward a unity, a unity
won not alone by the necessities of the physical developments themselves, but by the painful and confused re-assertion of man's inherited will to survive. When the peace is made, and it will be made,
the question Greece asked will once again be a question not
reserved for philosophers and dramatists; it will be asked by the
man who can live out his life without fear of hunger, joblessness,
disease, the man working a few hours a day with a life-span probability of eighty, ninety, or perhaps a hundred years. Hard as it is
for most people, the sheer struggle to exist and to prosper affords a
haven from thought. Complain as they may that they have no time
to think, to cultivate themselves, to ask the big questions, most men
are terrified at the thought of not having to spend most of their
days fighting for existence. In every sphere, and for a hundred hard
reasons, the ultimate questions are once again becoming moot,
some because without the right answers we will destroy the earth,
others because the peace we win may leave us without the fruits of
civilized life. The new social drama will be Greek in that it will
face man as a social animal and yet without the petty partisanship
of so much of past drama. It will be Greek in that the "men" dealt
with in its scenes—the psychology and characterizations—will be
more than ends in themselves and once again parts of a whole, a

whole that is social, a whole that is Man. The world, in a word, is moving into the same boat. For a time, their greatest time, the Greek people were in the same boat—their polis. Our drama, like theirs, will, as it must, ask the same questions, the largest ones. Where are we going now that we are together? For, like every act man commits, the drama is a struggle against his mortality, and meaning is the ultimate reward for having lived.

A NOTE ON THESE PLAYS

A Memory of Two Mondays is about several things. It is about mortality, first, in that the young man caught in the warehouse cannot understand what point there can be, beyond habit and necessity, for men to live this way. He is too young to find out, but it is hoped that the audience will glimpse one answer. It is that men live this way because they must serve an industrial apparatus which feeds them in body and leaves them to find sustenance for their souls as they may.

This play is a mortal romance. It expresses a preoccupation with the facts that everything we do in this fragmented world is so quickly wiped away and the goals, when won, are so disappointing. It is also the beginning of a further search and it lays the basis for a search. For it points the different roads people do take who are caught in warehouses, and in this play the warehouse is our world—a world in which things are endlessly sent and endlessly received; only time never comes back.

It is an abstract realism in form. It is in one act because I have chosen to say precisely enough about each character to form the image which drove me to write the play—enough and no more.

It is in one act, also, because I have for a long time wished I could turn my back on the "demands" of the Broadway theater in this regard. There are perfectly wonderful things one can say in one sentence, in one letter, one look, or one act. On Broadway this whole attitude has been suspect, regarded as the means taken by fledglings to try their wings. My ambition is to write shorter and shorter plays. It is harder to hit a target with one bullet—perhaps that is why.

A *View from the Bridge* is in one act because, quite simply, I did not know how to pull a curtain down anywhere before its end. While writing it, I kept looking for an act curtain, a point of pause, but none ever developed. Actually it is practically a full-length play in number of pages, needing only the addition of a little material to make it obvious as such.

That little material, that further elaboration, is what seemed to me, however, exactly what it ought not to have. Like *A Memory of Two Mondays*, this play has been in the back of my head for many years. And, as with the former, I have been asking of it why it would not get any longer. The answer occurred finally that one ought to say on the stage as much as one knows, and this, quite simply, is what I know about these subjects.

This is not to say that there is nothing more I could tell about any of the people involved. On the contrary, there is a great deal— several plays' worth, in fact. Furthermore, all the cues to great length of treatment are there in *A View from the Bridge*. It is wide open for a totally subjective treatment, involving, as it does, several elements which fashion has permitted us to consider down to the last detail. There are, after all, an incestuous motif, homosexuality, and, as I shall no doubt soon discover, eleven other neurotic patterns hidden within it, as well as the question of codes. It would be ripe for a slowly evolving drama through which the hero's antecedent life forces might, one by one, be brought to light until we know his relationships to his parents, his uncles, his grandmother, and the incident in his life which, when revealed toward the end of the second act, is clearly what drove him inevitably to his disaster.

But as many times as I have been led backward into Eddie's life, "deeper" into the subjective forces that made him what he evidently is, a counter-impulse drew me back. It was a sense of form, the shape of this work which I saw first sparely, as one sees a naked mast on the sea, or a barren cliff. What struck me first about this tale when I heard it one night in my neighborhood was how directly, with what breathtaking simplicity, it did evolve. It seemed to me, finally, that its very bareness, its absolutely unswerving path, its exposed skeleton, so to speak, was its wisdom and even its charm and must not be tampered with. In this instance to cleave to his story was to cleave to the man, for the naïveté with which Eddie

Carbone attacked his apparent enemy, its very directness and suddenness, the kind of blatant confession he could make to a near-
stranger, the clarity with which he saw a wrong course of
action—these *qualities* of the events themselves, their texture,
seemed to me more psychologically telling than a conventional
investigation in width which would necessarily relax that clear,
clean line of his catastrophe.

This play falls into a single act, also, because I saw the characters
purely in terms of their action and because they are a kind of people who, when inactive, have no new significant definition as people. I use the word "significant" because I am tired of documentation
which, while perfectly apt and evidently reasonable, does not add
anything to our comprehension of the tale's essence. In so writing,
I have made the assumption that the audience is like me and would
like to see, for once, a fine, high, always visible arc of forces moving
in full view to a single explosion.

There was, as well, another consideration that held ornamenta-
tion back. When I heard this tale first it seemed to me that I had
heard it before, very long ago. After a time I thought that it must be
some re-enactment of a Greek myth which was ringing a long-
buried bell in my own subconscious mind. I have not been able to
find such a myth and yet the conviction persists, and for that reason I wished not to interfere with the mythlike march of the tale.
The thought has often occurred to me that the two "submarines,"
the immigrants who come to Eddie from Italy, set out, as it were,
two thousand years ago. There was such an iron-bound purity in
the autonomic egocentricity of the aims of each of the persons
involved that the weaving together of their lives seemed almost the
work of a fate. I have tried to press as far as my reason can go
toward defining the objective and subjective elements that made
that fate, but I must confess that in the end a mystery remains for
me and I have not attempted to conceal that fact. I know a good
many ways to explain this story, but none of them fills its outline
completely. I wrote it in order to discover its meanings completely,
and I have not got them all yet, for there is a wonder remaining for
me even now, a kind of expectation that derives, I think, from a
sense of having somehow stumbled upon a hallowed tale.

The form of this play, finally, had a special attraction for me because once the decision was made to tell it without an excess line, the play took a harder, more objective shape. In effect, the form announces in the first moments of the play that only that will be told which is cogent, and that this story is the only part of Eddie Carbone's life worth our notice and therefore no effort will be made to draw in elements of his life that are beneath these, the most tense and meaningful of his hours. The form is what it is because its aim is to recreate my own feeling toward this tale—namely, wonderment. It is not designed primarily to draw tears or laughter from an audience but to strike a particular note of astonishment at the way in which, and the reasons for which, a man will endanger and risk and lose his very life.

The Family in Modern Drama
1956

Most people, including the daily theater reviewers, have come to assume that the forms in which plays are written spring either from nowhere or from the temperamental choice of the playwrights. I am not maintaining that the selection of a form is as objective a matter as the choice of let us say a raincoat instead of a linen suit for a walk on a rainy day; on the contrary, most playwrights, including myself, reach rather instinctively for that form, that way of telling a play, which seems inevitably right for the subject at hand. Yet I wonder whether it is all as accidental, as "free" a choice, as it appears to be at a superficial glance. I wonder whether there may not be within the ideas of family on the one hand, and society on the other, primary pressures which govern our notions of the right form for a particular kind of subject matter.

It has gradually come to appear to me over the years that the spectrum of dramatic forms, from Realism over to the Verse Drama, the Expressionistic techniques, and what we call vaguely the Poetic Play, consists of forms which express human relationships of a particular kind, each of them suited to express either a primarily familial relation at one extreme, or a primarily social relation at the other.

When we think of Realism we think of Ibsen—and if we don't we ought to, because in his social plays he not only used the form but pressed it very close to its ultimate limits. What are the main characteristics of this form? We know it by heart, of course, since most of the plays we see are realistic plays. It is written in prose; it makes believe it is taking place independently of an audience which views it through a "fourth wall," the grand objective being to make everything seem true to life in life's most evident and apparent sense. In contrast, think of any play by Aeschylus. You are never under an illusion in his plays that you are watching "life"; you are watching a play, an art work.

Now at the risk of being obvious I must remind you that Realism is a style, an artful convention, and not a piece of reportage. What, after all, is real about having all the furniture in a living room facing the footlights? What is real about people sticking to the same subject for three consecutive hours? Realism is a style, an invention quite as consciously created as Expressionism, Symbolism, or any of the other less familiar forms. In fact, it has held the stage for a shorter period of time than the more poetic forms and styles which dominate the great bulk of the world repertoire, and when it first came into being it was obvious to all as a style, a poet's invention. I say this in order to make clear that Realism is neither more nor less "artistic" than any other form. The only trouble is that it more easily lends itself in our age to hack work, for one thing because more people can write passable prose than verse. In other ages, however, as for instance in the lesser Elizabethan playwrights, hack work could also make of the verse play a pedestrian and uninspired form.

As with any artist, Ibsen was writing not simply to photograph scenes from life. After all, at the time he wrote *A Doll's House* how many Norwegian or European women had slammed the door upon their hypocritical relations with their husbands? Very few. So there was nothing, really, for him to photograph. What he was doing, however, was projecting through his personal interpretation of common events what he saw as their concealed significance for society. In other words, in a perfectly "realistic" way he did not report so much as project or even prophesy a meaning. Put in playwriting terms, he created a symbol on the stage.

We are not ordinarily accustomed to juxtaposing the idea of a symbol with the idea of Realism. The symbolic action, symbolic speech, have come to be reserved in our minds for the more poetic forms. Yet Realism shares equally with all other ways of telling a play this single mission. It must finally arrive at a meaning symbolic of the underlying action it has set forth. The difference lies in its method of creating its symbol as opposed to the way the poetic forms create theirs.

Now then, the question arises: Why, if Ibsen and several other playwrights could use Realism so well to make plays about modern life, and if in addition the modern American audience is so quickly at home with the form—why should playwrights over the past thirty years be so impatient with it? Why has it been assaulted from every side? Why do so many people turn their backs on it and revere instead any kind of play which is fanciful or poetic? At the same time, why does Realism always seem to be drawing us all back to its arms? We have not yet created in this country a succinct form to take its place. Yet it seems that Realism has become a familiar bore; and by means of cutout sets, revolving stages, musical backgrounds, new and more imaginative lighting schemes, our stage is striving to break up the old living room. However, the perceiving eye knows that many of these allegedly poetic plays are Realism underneath, tricked up to look otherwise. I am criticizing nobody, only stating that the question of form is a deeper one, perhaps, than we have been willing to admit.

As I have indicated, I have come to wonder whether the force or pressure that makes for Realism, that even requires it, is the magnetic force of the family relationship within the play, and the pressure which evokes in a genuine, unforced way the un-realistic modes is the social relationship within the play. In a generalized way we commonly recognize that forms do have some extratheatrical, common-sense criteria; for instance, one of the prime difficulties in writing modern opera, which after all is lyric drama, is that you cannot rightly sing so many of the common thoughts of common life. A line like "Be sure to take your bath, Gloria," is difficult to musicalize, and impossible to take seriously as a sung concept. But we normally stop short at recognition of the ridiculous in this problem. Clearly, a poetic drama must be built upon a poetic idea, but I wonder if that is the whole problem. It is striking to me, for instance, that Ibsen, the master of Realism, while writing his realistic plays in quite as serious a frame of mind as in his social plays, suddenly burst out of the realistic frame, out of the living room, when he wrote *Peer Gynt*. I think that it is not primarily the living room he left behind, in the sense that this factor had made a poetic play impossible for him, but rather the family context. For Peer Gynt is first of all a man seen alone; equally, he is a man confronting non-familial, openly social relationships and forces.

I warn you not to try to apply this rule too mechanically. A play, like any human relationship, has a predominant quality, but it also contains powerful elements which, although secondary, may not be overlooked, and may in fact be crucial in the development of that relationship. I offer this concept, therefore, as a possible tool and not as a magic key to the writing or understanding of plays and their forms.

I have used Ibsen as an example because he wrote in several forms; another equally experimental dramatist was O'Neill. It ought to be noted that O'Neill himself described his preoccupation as being not with the relations between man and man, but with those between man and God. What has this remark to do with dramatic form? Everything, I think. It is obvious, to begin with, that Ibsen's mission was to create not merely characters, but a context in which they were formed and functioned as people. That context, heavily and often profoundly delineated, was his society. His very idea of fate, for instance, was the inevitability residing in the conflict between the life force of his characters struggling with the hypocrisies, the strangling and abortive effects of society upon them. Thus, if only to create a climax, Ibsen had to draw society in his plays as a realistic force embodied in money, in social mores, in taboos, and so on, as well as an internal, subjective force within his characters.

O'Neill, however, seems to have been seeking for some fate-making power behind the social force itself. He went to ancient Greece for some definition of that force; he reached toward modern religion and toward many other possible sources of the poetic modes. My point here, however, is that so long as the family and family relations are at the center of his plays his form remains—indeed, it is held prisoner by—Realism. When, however, as for instance in *The Hairy Ape* and *Emperor Jones*, he deals with men out in society, away from the family context, his forms become alien to Realism, more openly and self-consciously symbolic, poetic, and finally heroic.

Up to this point I have been avoiding any question of content except that of the family relation as opposed to relations out in the world—social relations. Now I should like to make the bald statement that all plays we call great, let alone those we call serious, are ultimately involved with some aspect of a single problem. It is this: How may a man make of the outside world a home? How and in what ways must he struggle, what must he strive to change and overcome within himself and outside himself if he is to find the safety, the surroundings of love, the ease of soul, the sense of identity and honor which, evidently, all men have connected in their memories with the idea of family?

One ought to be suspicious of any attempt to boil down all the great themes to a single sentence, but this one—"How may a man make of the outside world a home?"—does bear watching as a clue to the inner life of the great plays. Its aptness is most evident in the modern repertoire; in fact, where it is not the very principle of the play at hand we do not take the play quite seriously. If, for instance, the struggle in *Death of a Salesman* were simply between father and son for recognition and forgiveness it would diminish in importance. But when it extends itself out of the family circle and into society, it broaches those questions of social status, social honor and recognition, which expand its vision and lift it out of the merely particular toward the fate of the generality of men.

The same is true—although achieved in different ways—of a play like *A Streetcar Named Desire*, which could quite easily have been limited to a study of psychopathology were it not that it is placed clearly within the wider bounds of the question I am discussing. Here Blanche Dubois and the sensitivity she represents has been crushed by her moving out of the shelter of the home and the family into the uncaring, anti-human world outside it. In a word, we begin to partake of the guilt for her destruction, and for Willy's, because the blow struck against them was struck outside the home rather than within it—which is to say that it affects us more because it is a social fact we are witnessing.

The crucial question has an obverse side. If we look at the great plays—at *Hamlet*, *Oedipus*, *Lear*—we must be impressed with one fact perhaps above all others. These plays are all examining the concept of loss, of man's deprivation of a once-extant state of bliss unjustly shattered—a bliss, a state of equilibrium, which the hero (and his audience) is attempting to reconstruct or to recreate with new, latter-day life materials. It has been said often that the central theme of the modern repertoire is the alienation of man, but the idea usually halts at the social alienation—he cannot find a satisfying role in society. What I am suggesting here is that while this is true of our plays, the more or less hidden impulse antedating social alienation, the unsaid premise of the very idea of "satisfaction," is the memory of both playwright and audience of an enfolding family and of childhood. It is as though both playwright and audience believed that they had once had an identity, a *being*, somewhere in the past which in the present has lost its completeness, its definitiveness, so that the central force making for pathos in these large and thrusting plays is the paradox which Time bequeaths to us all: we cannot go home again, and the world we live in is an alien place.

One of the forms most clearly in contrast to Realism is Expressionism. I should like now to have a look at its relevancy to the family-social complex.

The technical arsenal of Expressionism goes back to Aeschylus. It is a form of play which manifestly seeks to dramatize the conflict of either social, religious, ethical, or moral forces *per se*, and in their own naked roles, rather than to present psychologically realistic human characters in a more or less realistic environment. There is, for instance, no attempt by Aeschylus to create the psychology of a violent "character" in *Prometheus Bound*, or of a powerful one; rather he brings on two figures whose names are Power and Violence, and they behave, as the *idea* of Power and the *idea* of Violence ought to behave, according to the laws of Power and Violence. In Germany after the First World War, playwrights sought to dramatize and unveil the social condition of man with similar means. For instance, in *Gas I* and *Gas II* Georg Kaiser placed the figure of man against an image of industrial society but without the slightest attempt to characterize the man except as a representative of one or the other of the social classes vying for control of the machine. There are, of course, numerous other examples of the same kind of elimination of psychological characterization in favor of what one might call the presentation of forces. In *The Great God Brown*, for instance, as well as in *The Hairy Ape*, O'Neill reached toward this very ancient means of dramatization without psychology—without, one might say, behavior as we normally know it. *Everyman* is another work in that long line.

In passing, I must ask you to note that expressionist plays—which is to say plays preoccupied with the open confrontation of moral, ethical, or social forces—seem inevitably to cast a particular kind of shadow. The moment realistic behavior and psychology disappear from the play all the other appurtenances of Realism vanish too. The stage is stripped of knickknacks; instead it reveals symbolic *designs*, which function as overt pointers toward the moral to be drawn from the action. We are no longer under quite the illusion of watching through a transparent fourth wall. Instead we are constantly reminded, in effect, that we are watching a theater piece. In short, we are not bidden to lose our consciousness of time and place, the consciousness of ourselves, but are appealed to through our intelligence, our faculties of knowing rather than of feeling.

This difference in the area of appeal is the difference between our familial emotions and our social emotions. The two forms not only spring from different sectors of human experience but end up by appealing to different areas of receptivity within the audience. Nor is this phenomenon confined to the play.

When one is speaking to one's family, for example, one uses a certain level of speech, a certain plain diction perhaps, a tone of voice, an inflection suited to the intimacy of the occasion. But when one faces an audience of strangers, as a politician does, for instance—and he is the most social of men—it seems right and proper for him to reach for the well-turned phrase, even the poetic word, the aphorism, the metaphor. And his gestures, his stance, his tone of voice, all become larger than life; moreover, his character is not what gives him these prerogatives, but his role. In other words, a confrontation with society permits us, or even enforces upon us, a certain reliance upon ritual. Similarly with the play.

The implications of this natural wedding of form with inner relationships are many, and some of them are complex. It is true to say, I think, that the language of the family is the language of the private life—prose. The language of society, the language of the public life, is verse. According to the degree to which the play partakes of either relationship, it achieves the right to move closer or further away from either pole. I repeat that this "right" is given by some common consent which in turn is based upon our common experience in life.

It is interesting to look at a couple of modern plays from this viewpoint and to see whether critical sense can be made of them. T. S. Eliot's *The Cocktail Party*, for instance, drew from most intelligent auditors a puzzled admiration. In general, one was aware of a struggle going on between the apparencies of the behavior of the people and what evidently was the preoccupation of the playwright. There were a Husband and a Wife whom we were evidently expected to accept in that commonly known relationship, especially since the setting and the mode of speech and much of its diction were perfectly real if inordinately cultivated for a plebeian American audience. Even the theme of the play was, or should have been, of importance to most of us. Here we were faced with the alternative ways of giving meaning to domestic existence, one of them being through the cultivation of self, partly by means of the psychoanalytic ritual; the other and victorious method being the martyrization of the self, not for the sake of another, or as a rebuke to another, as martyrdom is usually indulged in in family life, but for the sake of martyrdom, of the disinterested action whose ultimate model was, according to the author, Jesus Christ. The heroine is celebrated for having been eaten alive by ants while on a missionary work among savages, and the very point is that there was no point—she converted nobody at all. Thus she gained her self by losing self or giving it away. Beyond the Meaningless she found Meaning at last.

To say the least, Eliot is manifestly an apt writer of verse. The inability of this play to achieve a genuine poetic level cannot therefore be laid to the usual cause—the unpoetic nature of the playwright's talent. Indeed, *Murder in the Cathedral* is a genuine poetic play, so he had already proved that he could achieve a wholeness of poetic form. I believe that the puzzlement created by *The Cocktail Party*, the sense of its being drawn in two opposite directions, is the result of the natural unwillingness of our minds to give to the Husband-Wife relation— a family relation—the prerogatives of the poetic mode, especially when the relationship is originally broached, as it is in this play, through any means approaching Realism.

Whether consciously or not, Eliot himself was aware of this dichotomy and wrote, and has said that he wrote, a kind of line which would not seem obtrusively formal and poetic to the listening ear. The injunction to keep it somehow unpoetic was issued by the central family situation, in my opinion. There was no need to mask his poetry at all in *Murder in the Cathedral*, because the situation is social, the conflict of a human being with the world. That earlier play had the unquestioned right to the poetic because it dealt with man as a public figure and could use the public man's style and diction.

We recognize now that a play can be poetic without verse, and it is in this middle area that the complexities of tracing the influence of the family and social elements upon the form become more troublesome. *Our Town* by Thornton Wilder is such a play, and it is important not only for itself but because it is the progenitor of many other works.

This is a family play which deals with the traditional family figures, the father, mother, brother, sister. At the same time it uses this particular family as a prism through which is reflected the author's basic idea, his informing principle—which can be stated as the indestructibility, the everlastingness, of the family and the community, its rhythm of life, its rootedness in the essentially safe cosmos despite troubles, wracks, and seemingly disastrous, but essentially temporary, dislocations.

Technically, it is not arbitrary in any detail. Instead of a family living room or a house, we are shown a bare stage on which actors set chairs, a table, a ladder to represent a staircase or an upper floor, and so on. A narrator is kept in the foreground as though to remind us that this is not so much "real life" as an abstraction of it—in other words, a stage. It is clearly a poetic rather than a realistic play. What makes it that? Well, let us first imagine what would make it more realistic.

Would a real set make it realistic? Not likely. A real set would only discomfit us by drawing attention to what would then appear to be a slightly unearthly quality about the characterizations. We should probably say, "People don't really act like that." In addition, the characterization of the whole town could not be accomplished with anything like its present vividness if the narrator were removed, as he would have to be from a realistic set, and if the entrances and exits of the environmental people, the townspeople, had to be justified with the usual motives and machinery of Realism.

The preoccupation of the entire play is quite what the title implies— the town, the society, and not primarily this particular family—and every stylistic means used is to the end that the family foreground be kept in its place, merely as a foreground for the larger context behind and around it. In my opinion, it is this larger context, the town and its enlarging, widening significance, that is the bridge to the poetic for this play. Cut out the town and you will cut out the poetry.

The play is worth examining further against the Ibsen form of Realism to which it is inevitably related if only in contrast. Unlike Ibsen, Wilder sees his characters in this play not primarily as personalities, as individuals, but as forces, and he individualizes them only enough to carry the freight, so to speak, of their roles as forces. I do not believe, for instance, that we can think of the brother in this play, or the sister or the mother, as having names other than Brother, Sister, Mother. They are not given that kind of particularity or interior life. They are characterized rather as social factors, in their roles of Brother, Sister, Mother, in Our Town. They are drawn, in other words, as forces to enliven and illuminate the author's symbolic vision and his theme, which is that of the family as a timeless, stable quantity which has not only survived all the turmoil of time but is, in addition, beyond the possibility of genuine destruction.

The play is important to any discussion of form because it has achieved a largeness of meaning and an abstraction of style that created that meaning, while at the same time it has moved its audiences subjectively—it has made them laugh and weep as abstract plays rarely if ever do. But it would seem to contradict my contention here. If it is true that the presentation of the family on the stage inevitably forces Realism upon the play, how did this family play manage to transcend Realism to achieve its symbolistic style?

Every form, every style, pays its price for its special advantages. The price paid by *Our Town* is psychological characterization forfeited in the cause of the symbol. I do not believe, as I have said, that the characters are identifiable in a psychological way, but only as figures in the family and social constellation, and this is not meant in criticism, but as a statement of the limits of this form. I would go further and say that it is not *necessary* for every kind of play to do every kind of thing. But if we are after ultimate reality we must make ultimate demands.

I think that had Wilder drawn his characters with a deeper configuration of detail and with a more remorseless quest for private motive and self-interest, for instance, the story as it stands now would have appeared oversentimental and even sweet. I think that if the play tested its own theme more remorselessly, the world it creates of a timeless family and a rhythm of existence beyond the disturbance of social wracks would not remain unshaken. The fact is that the juvenile delinquent is quite directly traced to the breakup of family life and, indeed, to the break in that ongoing, steady rhythm of community life which the play celebrates as indestructible.

I think, further, that the close contact which the play established with its audience was the result of its coincidence with the deep longing of the audience for such stability, a stability which in daylight out on the street does not truly exist. The great plays pursue the idea of loss and deprivation of an earlier state of bliss which the characters feel compelled to return to or to recreate. I think this play forgoes the loss and suffers thereby in its quest for reality, but that the audience supplies the sense of deprivation in its own life experience as it faces what in effect is an idyl of the past. To me, therefore, the play falls short of a form that will press into reality to the limits of reality, if only because it could not plumb the psychological interior lives of its characters and still keep its present form. It is a triumph in that it does open a way toward the dramatization of the larger truths of existence while using the common materials of life. It is a truly poetic play.

Were there space, I should like to go into certain contemporary works with a view to the application in them of the forces of society and family—works by Clifford Odets, Tennessee Williams,

Lillian Hellman, William Saroyan, and others. But I will jump to the final question I have in mind. If there is any truth in the idea of a natural union of the family and Realism as opposed to society and the poetic, what are the reasons for it?

First, let us remind ourselves of an obvious situation, but one which is often overlooked. The man or woman who sits down to write a play, or who enters a theater to watch one, brings with him in each case a common life experience which is not suspended merely because he has turned writer or become part of an audience. We—all of us—have a role anteceding all others: we are first sons, daughters, sisters, brothers. No play can possibly alter this given role.

The concepts of Father, Mother, and so on were received by us unawares before the time we were conscious of ourselves as selves. In contrast, the concepts of Friend, Teacher, Employee, Boss, Colleague, Supervisor, and the many other social relations came to us long after we gained consciousness of ourselves, and are therefore outside ourselves. They are thus in an objective rather than a subjective category. In any case, what we feel is always more "real" to us than what we know, and we feel the family relation while we only know the social one. Thus the former is the very apotheosis of the real and has an inevitability and a foundation indisputably actual, while the social relation is always relatively mutable, accidental, and consequently of a profoundly arbitrary nature to us.

Today the difficulty in creating a form that will unite both elements in a full rather than partial onslaught on reality is the reflection of the deep split between the private life of man and his social life. Nor is this the first time in history that such a separation has occurred. Many critics have remarked upon it, for instance, as a probable reason for the onset of Realism in the later Greek plays, for it is like a rule of society that, as its time of troubles arrives, its citizens revert to a kind of privacy of life that excludes society, as though man at such times would like to banish society from his mind. When this happens, man excludes poetry too.

All of which, while it may provide a solution, or at least indicate the mansion where the solution lives, only serves to point to the ultimate problem more succinctly. Obviously, the playwright cannot create a society, let alone one so unified as to allow him to portray man in art as a monolithic creature. The playwright is not a reporter, but in a serious work of art he cannot set up an image of man's condition so distant from reality as to violate the common sense of what reality is. But a serious work, to say nothing of a tragic one, cannot hope to achieve truly high excellence short of an investigation into the whole gamut of causation of which society is a manifest and crucial part. Thus it is that the common Realism of the past forty or fifty years has been assaulted—because it could not, with ease and beauty, bridge the widening gap between the private life and the social life. Thus it is that the problem was left unsolved by Expressionism, which evaded it by forgoing psychological realism altogether and leaping over to a portrayal of social forces alone. Thus it is that there is now a certain decadence about many of our plays; in the past ten years they have come more and more to dwell solely upon psychology, with little or no attempt to locate and dramatize the social roles and conflicts of their characters. For it is proper to ascribe decay to that which turns its back upon society when, as is obvious to any intelligence, the fate of mankind is social.

Finally, I should say that the current quest after the poetic as poetic is fruitless. It is the attempt to make apples without growing trees. It is seeking poetry precisely where poetry is not: in the private life viewed entirely within the bounds of the subjective, the area of sensation, or the bizarre and the erotic. From these areas of the private life have sprung the mood plays, the plotless plays for which there is much admiration as there is much relief when one turns from a problem to a ramble in the woods. I do not ask you to disdain such plays, for they are within the realm of art; I say only that the high work, the tragic work, cannot be forged waywardly, while playing by ear. There is a charm in improvisation, in letting one chord suggest the other and ending when the moment wanes. But the high order of art to which drama is fated will come only when it seeks to account for the total condition of man, and this cannot be improvised.

Whatever is said to describe a mood play, one point must be made: such plays all have in common an air of self-effacement—which is to say that they wish to seem as though they had not only no plot but no writer. They would convince us that they "just happen," that no directing hand has arranged matters—contrary to the Ibsen plays, for instance, or, for that matter, the Shakespearean play or the Greek.

Furthermore, the entire operation is most moody when the characters involved have the least consciousness of their own existence. The mood play is a play in hiding. A true plot is an assertion of meaning. The mood play is not, as it has been mistaken for, a rebellion of any kind against the so-called well-made play, especially when Ibsen is widely held to be a writer of well-made plays. For there is as much subjectivity and inner poetry in *Hedda Gabler*—I daresay a lot more—as in any of these mood plays. What is really repulsive in Ibsen to one kind of contemporary mind is not openly mentioned: it is his persistent search for an organizing principle behind the "moods" of existence and not the absence of mood in his work.

An art form, like a person, can achieve greatness only as it accepts great challenges. Over the past few decades the American theater, in its best moments, has moved courageously and often beautifully into the interior life of man, an area that had most often been neglected in the past. But now, I think, we are in danger of settling for tears, as it were—for any play that "moves" us, quite as though the ultimate criterion of the art were lachrymosity. For myself, I find that there is an increasing reliance upon what pass for realistic, even tough, analytical picturizations of existence, which are really quite sentimental underneath; and the sentiment is getting thicker, I think, and an end in itself. Sentimentalism is perfectly all right, but it is nowhere near a great challenge, and to pursue it, even under the guise of the exotic atmosphere and the celebration of the sensuous, is not going to bring us closer to the fated mission of the drama.

What, after all, is that mission? I may as well end with such a question because it underlies and informs every word I have written. I think of it so: Man has created so many specialized means of unveiling the truth of the world around him and the world within him—the physical sciences, the psychological sciences, the disciplines of economic and historical research and theory. In effect, each of these attacks on the truth is partial. It is within the rightful sphere of the drama—it is, so to speak, its truly just employment and its ultimate design—to embrace the many-sidedness of man. It is as close to being a total art as the race has invented. It can tell, like science, what is—but more, it can tell what ought to be. It can depict, like painting, in designs and portraits, in the colors of the day or night; like the novel it can spread out its arms and tell the story of a life, or a city, in a few hours—but more, it is dynamic, it is always on the move as life is, and it is perceived like life through the motions, the gestures, the tones of voice, and the gait and nuance of living people. It is the singer's art and the painter's art and the dancer's art, yet it may hew to fact no less tenaciously than does the economist or the physician. In a word, there lies within the dramatic form the ultimate possibility of raising the truth-consciousness of mankind to a level of such intensity as to transform those who observe it.

The problem, therefore, is not simply an aesthetic one. As people, as a society, we thirst for clues to the past and the future; least of all, perhaps, do we know about the present, about what *is*. It is the present that is always most evasive and slippery, for the present always threatens most directly our defenses against seeing what we are, and it is the present, always the present, to which the dramatic form must apply or it is without interest and a dead thing, and forms do die when they lose their capacity to open up the present. So it is its very nature to bring us closer to ourselves if only it can grow and change with the changing world.

In the deepest sense, I think, to sophisticated and unsophisticated alike, nothing is quite so real to us, so extant, as that which has been made real by art. Nor is this ironical and comic. For the fact is that art is a function of the civilizing act quite as much as is the building of the water supply. American civilization is only recently coming to a conscious awareness of art not as a luxury but as a necessity of life. Without the right dramatic form a genuine onslaught upon the veils that cloak the present is not possible. In the profoundest sense I cannot create that form unless, somewhere in you, there is a wish to know the present and a demand upon me that I give it to you.

For at bottom what is that form? It is the everlastingly sought balance between order and the need of our souls for freedom; the relatedness between our vaguest longings, our inner questions, and private lives and the life of the generality of men which is our society and our world. How may man make for himself a home in that vastness of strangers and how may he transform that vastness into a home? This, as I have repeated, is the question a form must solve anew in every age. This, I may say, is the problem before you too.

The Shadows of the Gods
1958

I see by the papers that I am going to talk today on the subject of the literary influences on my work. It is probably a good subject, but it isn't what Harold Clurman and I discussed when he asked if I would speak here. What he had in mind was something else. I am supposed to widen your horizons by telling something about the frame of reference I used when I started to write, and that included books I read, or music I heard, or whatnot.

I doubt whether anybody can widen horizons by making a speech. It is possible, perhaps, by writing a play. Still, I may be able to suggest an approach to our theater which—even if it is not valid for everyone—will not be quite the same as that of the various critics; and if nothing else is accomplished here maybe it will at least appear that there is another way of looking at drama.

Tolstoy wrote a book called *What Is Art?* The substance of it is that almost all the novels, plays, operas, and paintings were not art but vanity, and that the rhythm with which a Russian peasant swung a scythe was more artful than all the dance on Moscow stages, and the paintings of peasants on the sides of their wagons more genuine than all the paintings in the museums. The thing that disheartened him most, I believe, was that inevitably artistic creation became a profession, and the artist who may have originated as a natural quickly became self-conscious and exploited his own gifts for money, prestige, or just for want of an honest profession.

Yet, Tolstoy went on writing. The truth, I suppose, is that soon or late we are doomed to know what we are doing, and we may as well accept it as a fact when it comes. But the self-knowledge of professionalism develops only as a result of having repeated the same themes in different plays. And for a whole theater the time for self-appraisal comes in the same way. We are, I believe, at the end of a period. Certain things have been repeated sufficiently for one to speak of limitations which have to be recognized if our theater is not to become absurd, repetitious, and decayed.

Now one can no sooner speak of limitations than the question of standards arises. What seems like a limitation to one man may be an area as wide as the world to another. My standard, my viewpoint, whether it appears arbitrary, or true and inevitable, did not spring out of my head unshaped by any outside force. I began writing plays in the midst of what Allan Seager, an English teacher friend of mine at Michigan, calls one of the two genuinely national catastrophes in American history—the Great Depression of the thirties. The other was the Civil War. It is almost bad manners to talk about depression these days, but through no fault or effort of mine it was the ground upon which I learned to stand.

There are a thousand things to say about that time but maybe one will be evocative enough. Until 1929 I thought things were pretty solid. Specifically, I thought—like most Americans—that somebody was in charge. I didn't know exactly who it was, but it was probably a businessman, and he was a realist, a no-nonsense fellow, practical, honest, responsible. In 1929 he jumped out of the window. It was bewildering. His banks closed and refused to open again, and I had twelve dollars in one of them. More precisely, I happened to have withdrawn my twelve dollars to buy a racing bike a friend of mine was bored with, and the next day the Bank of the United States closed. I rode by and saw the crowds of people standing at the brass gates. Their money was inside! And they couldn't get it. And they would never get it. As for me, I felt I had the thing licked.

But about a week later I went into the house to get a glass of milk and when I came out my bike was gone. Stolen. It must have taught me a lesson. Nobody could escape that disaster.

I did not read many books in those days. The depression was my book. Years later I could put together what in those days were only feelings, sensations, impressions. There was the sense that everything had dried up. Some plague of invisible grasshoppers was eating money before you could get your hands on it. You had to be a Ph. D. to get a job in Macy's. Lawyers were selling ties. Everybody

was trying to sell something to everybody else. A past president of
the Stock Exchange was sent to jail for misappropriating trust
funds. They were looking for runaway financiers all over Europe
and South America. Practically everything that had been said and
done up to 1929 turned out to be a fake. It turns out that there had
never been anybody in charge.

What the time gave me, I think now, was a sense of an invisible
world. A reality had been secretly accumulating its climax according to its hidden laws to explode illusion at the proper time. In that
sense 1929 was our Greek year. The gods had spoken, the gods,
whose wisdom had been set aside or distorted by a civilization that
was to go onward and upward on speculation, gambling, graft, and
the dog eating the dog. Before the crash I thought "Society" meant
the rich people in the Social Register. After the crash it meant the
constant visits of strange men who knocked on our door pleading
for a chance to wash the windows, and some of them fainted on the
back porch from hunger. In Brooklyn, New York. In the light of
weekday afternoons.

I read books after I was seventeen, but already, for good or ill, I
was not patient with every kind of literature. I did not believe, even
then, that you could tell about a man without telling about the
world he was living in, what he did for a living, what he was like
not only at home or in bed but on the job. I remember now reading
novels and wondering, What do these people do for a living? When
do they work? I remember asking the same questions about the few
plays I saw. The hidden laws of fate lurked not only in the characters of people, but equally if not more imperiously in the world
beyond the family parlor. Out there were the big gods, the ones
whose disfavor could turn a proud and prosperous and dignified
man into a frightened shell of a man whatever he thought of himself, and whatever he decided or didn't decide to do.

So that by force of circumstance I came early and unawares to be
fascinated by sheer process itself. How things connected. How the
native personality of a man was changed by his world, and the
harder question, how he could in turn change his world. It was not
academic. It was not even a literary or a dramatic question at first.
It was the practical problem of what to believe in order to proceed
with life. For instance, should one admire success—for there were

sucessful people even then. Or should one always see through it as an illusion which only existed to be blown up, and its owner destroyed and humiliated? Was success immoral?—when everybody else in the neighborhood not only had no Buick but no breakfast? What to believe?

An adolescent must feel he is on the side of justice. That is how human indignation is constantly renewed. But how hard it was to feel justly, let alone to think justly. There were people in the neighborhood saying that it had all happened because the workers had not gotten paid enough to buy what they had produced, and that the solution was to have Socialism, which would not steal their wages any more the way the bosses did and brought on this depression. It was a wonderful thought with which I nearly drove my grandfather crazy. The trouble with it was that he and my father and most of the men I loved would have to be destroyed.

Enough of that. I am getting at only one thought. You can't understand anything unless you understand its relations to its context. It was necessary to feel beyond the edges of things. That much, for good or ill, the Great Depression taught me. It made me impatient with anything, including art, which pretends that it can exist for its own sake and still be of any prophetic importance. A thing becomes beautiful to me as it becomes internally and externally organic. It becomes beautiful because it promises to remove some of my helplessness before the chaos of experience. I think one of the reasons I became a playwright was that in dramatic form everything must be openly organic, deeply organized, articulated from a living center. I used long ago to keep a book in which I would talk to myself. One of the aphorisms I wrote was, "The structure of a play is always the story of how the birds came home to roost." The hidden will be unveiled; the inner laws of reality will announce themselves; I was defining my impression of 1929 as well as dramatic structure.

When I was still in high school and ignorant, a book came into my hands, God knows how, *The Brothers Karamazov*. It must have been too rainy that day to play ball. I began reading it, thinking it was a detective story. I have always blessed Dostoevsky for writing in a way that any fool could understand. The book, of course, has

no connection with the depression. Yet it became closer, more intimate to me, despite the Russian names, than the papers I read every
day. I never thought to ask why, then. I think now it was because of
the father and son conflict, but something more. It is always probing beyond its particular scenes and characters for the hidden laws,
for the place where the gods ruminate and decide, for the rock
upon which one may stand without illusion, a free man. Yet the
characters appear liberated from any systematic causation.

The same yearning I felt all day for some connection with a hidden logic was the yearning in this book. It gave me no answers but
it showed that I was not the only one who was full of this kind of
questioning, for I did not believe—and could not after 1929—in
the reality I saw with my eyes. There was an invisible world of
cause and effect, mysterious, full of surprises, implacable in its
course. The book said to me:

"There is a hidden order in the world. There is only one reason
to live. It is to discover its nature. The good are those who do this.
The evil say that there is nothing beyond the face of the world, the
surface of reality. Man will only find peace when he learns to live
humanly, in conformity to those laws which decree his human
nature."

Only slightly less ignorant, I read Ibsen in college. Later I heard
that I had been reading problem plays. I didn't know what that
meant. I was told they were about social problems, like the inequality of women. The women I knew about had not been even slightly
unequal; I saw no such problem in *A Doll's House*. I connected
with Ibsen not because he wrote about problems, but because he
was illuminating process. Nothing in his plays exists for itself, not
a smart line, not a gesture that can be isolated. It was breathtaking.

From his work—read again and again with new wonders crop-
ping up each time—as well as through Dostoevsky's, I came to an
idea of what a writer was supposed to be. These two issued the
license, so to speak, the only legitimate one I could conceive, for
presuming to write at all. One had the right to write because other
people needed news of the inner world, and if they went too long
without such news they would go mad with the chaos of their lives.
With the greatest of presumption I conceived that the great writer

was the destroyer of chaos, a man privy to the councils of the hidden gods who administer the hidden laws that bind us all and destroy us if we do not know them. And chaos, for one thing, was life lived oblivious of history.

As time went on, a lot of time, it became clear to me that I was not only reporting to others but to myself first and foremost. I wrote not only to find a way into the world but to hold it away from me so that sheer, senseless events would not devour me.

I read the Greeks and the German Expressionists at the same time and quite by accident. I was struck by the similarity of their dramatic means in one respect—they are designed to present the hidden forces, not the characteristics of the human beings playing out those forces on the stage. I was told that the plays of Aeschylus must be read primarily on a religious level, that they are only lay dramas to us now because we no longer believe. I could not understand this because one did not have to be religious to see in our own disaster the black outlines of a fate that was not human, nor of the heavens either, but something in between. Like the howling of a mob, for instance, which is not a human sound but is nevertheless composed of human voices combining until a metaphysical force of sound is created.

I read O'Neill in those days as I read everything else—looking to see how meaning was achieved. He said something in a press conference which in the context of those years seemed to be a challenge to the social preoccupations of the thirties. He said, "I am not interested in the relations of man to man, but of man to God." I thought that very reactionary. Until, after repeated and repeated forays into one play of my own after another, I understood that he meant what I meant, not ideologically but dramatically speaking. I too had a religion, however unwilling I was to be so backward. A religion with no gods but with godlike powers. The powers of economic crisis and political imperatives which had twisted, torn, eroded, and marked everything and everyone I laid eyes on.

I read for a year in economics, discovered my professors dispensing their prejudices which were no better founded than my own; worse yet, an economics that could measure the giant's footsteps but could not look into his eyes.

I read for a year in history, and lost my last illusion on a certain afternoon at two-thirty. In a lecture class a student at question time rose to ask the professor if he thought Hitler would invade Austria. For fifteen minutes the professor, by no means a closet historian but a man of liberal and human interests, proved why it was impossible for Hitler to invade Austria. It seems there were treaties forbidding this which went back to the Congress of Vienna, side agreements older than that, codicils, memoranda, guarantees— and to make a long story short, when we got out at three o'clock there was an extra being hawked. Hitler had invaded Austria. I gave up history. I knew damned well Hitler was going to invade Austria.

In that sense it was a good time to be growing up because nobody else knew anything either. All the rules were nothing but continuations of older rules. The old plays create new plays, and the old histories create new histories. The best you could say of the academic disciplines was that they were breathlessly running after the world. It is when life creates a new play that the theater moves its limbs and wakens from its mesmerized fixation on ordinary reality; when the present is caught and made historic.

I began by speaking of standards. I have labored the point long enough to state it openly. My standard is, to be sure, derived from my life in the thirties, but I believe that it is as old as the drama itself and was merely articulated to me in the accent of the thirties. I ask of a play, first, the dramatic question, the carpenter-builder's question—What is its ultimate force? How can that force be released? Second, the human question—What is its ultimate relevancy to the survival of the race?

Before proceeding with these two queries I want to jump ahead to say that my object remains to throw some light on our dramatic situation today, the challenge, so to speak, which I think lies before us. I will pause for a moment or two in order to say a few things about a writer who has been, along with Ibsen, an enormous influence upon our theater whether we know it or not.

It is hard to imagine any playwright reading Chekhov without envying one quality of his plays. It is his balance. In this, I think he is closer to Shakespeare than any dramatist I know. There is less distortion by the exigencies of the telescoping of time in the theater, there is less stacking of the cards, there is less fear of the ridiculous, there is less fear of the heroic. His touch is tender, his eye is warm, so warm that the Chekhovian legend in our theater has become that of an almost sentimental man and writer whose plays are elegies, postcripts to a dying age. In passing, it must be said that he was not the only Russian writer who seemed to be dealing with all his characters as though he were related to them. It is a quality not of Chekhov alone but of much Russian literature, and I mention it both to relate him to this mood and to separate him from it.

Chekhov is important to us because he has been used as a club against two opposing views of drama. Sometimes he seems—as he evidently does to Walter Kerr—to have encouraged dramatists to an overly emphasized introspection if not self-pity. To this kind of viewpoint, he is the playwright of inaction, of perverse self-analysis, of the dark blue mood. In the thirties he was condemned by many on the Left as lacking in militancy, and he was confused with the people he was writing about.

His plays, I think, will endure, but in one sense he is as useless as a model as the frock coat and the horse and carriage. Our civilization is immeasurably more strident than his and to try to recreate his mood would be to distort our own. But more important, I think, is that—whatever the miseries of his characters—their careers are played out against a tradition of which they are quite conscious, a tradition whose destruction is regarded by them as the setting of their woes. Whether or not it was ever objectively true is beside the point, of course; the point is that they can look back to a time when the coachman was young and happy to be a coachman, when there was a large, firmly entrenched family evenly maturing over the slow-passing years, when, in a word, there was an order dominated by human relations. Now—to put it much more briefly than its complexity warrants—the Cherry Orchard is cut down by a real estate man, who, nice fellow that he may be, simply has to clear land for a development.

The closest we have ever gotten to this kind of relation to a tradition is in Tennessee Williams, when a disorganized refugee from a plantation arrives in our civilization some eighty years after the plantation itself has been destroyed. We cannot reproduce Chekhov if only because we are long past the time when we believe in the primacy of human relations over economic necessity. We have given up what was still in his time a live struggle. We believe—or at least take it completely for granted—that wherever there is a conflict between human relations and necessity, the outcome is not only inevitable but even progressive when necessity wins, as it evidently must.

The main point I would make here in relation to our theater, however, is that while Chekhov's psychological insight is given full play, and while his greatest interest is overwhelmingly in the spiritual life of his characters, his farthest vision does not end with their individual psychology. Here is a speech to remind you—and it is only one of a great many which do not at all fit with the conventional characterization of these allegedly wispy plays—concerned with nothing more than realistic character drawing and introspection. In *Three Sisters* Vershinin speaks:

> What else am I to say to you at parting? What am I to theorize about? (Laughs) Life is hard. It seems to many of us blank and hopeless; but yet we must admit that it goes on getting clearer and easier, and it looks as though the time were not far off when it will be full of happiness. (Looks at his watch.) It's time for me to go! In old days men were absorbed in wars, filling all their existence with marches, raids, victories, but now all that is a thing of the past, leaving behind it a great void which there is so far nothing to fill; humanity is searching for it passionately, and of course will find it. Ah, if only it could be quickly. If, don't you know, industry were united with culture and culture with industry. . . . (Looks at his watch.) But, I say, it's time for me to go. . . .

In other words, these plays are not mere exercises in psychology. They are woven around a very critical point of view, a point of view not only toward the characters, but toward the social context in which they live, a point of view which—far from being some arbitrary angle, as we have come to call such things—is their informing principle. I haven't the time here to investigate the plays one by one and it is not the business of the moment. All I have said comes down to this: that with all our technical dexterity, with all our lighting effects, sets, and a theater more solvent than any I know about, yes, with all our freedom to say what we will—our theater is narrowing its vision year by year, it is repeating well what it has done well before.

I can hear already my critics complaining that I am asking for a return to what they call problem plays. That criticism is important only because it tells something important about the critic. It means that he can only conceive of man as a private entity, and his social relations as something thrown at him, something "affecting" him only when he is conscious of society. I hope I have made one thing clear to this point—and it is that society is inside of man and man is inside society, and you cannot even create a truthfully drawn psychological entity on the stage until you understand his social relations and their power to make him what he is and to prevent him from being what he is not. The fish is in the water and the water is in the fish.

I believe we have arrived in America at the end of a period because we are repeating ourselves season after season, despite the fact that nobody seems to be aware of it. In almost every success there is a striking similarity of mood and of mode. There is one play after another in which a young person, usually male, usually sensitive, is driven either to self-destructive revolt or impotency by the insensitivity of his parents, usually the father. A quick and by no means exhaustive look brings to mind, *Look Homeward Angel, Dark at the Top of the Stairs, Cat on a Hot Tin Roof, A Hatful of Rain*. I wish to emphasize at once that I am not here as a critic of these plays as plays, nor do I intend to equate their worth one with the other. I am rather looking at them as a stranger, a man from Mars, who would surely have to wonder at so pervasive a phenomenon.

Now I am not saying there is anything "wrong" with this theme, if only because I have written more than once on it myself. It lies at the heart of all human development, and its echoes go to *Hamlet*, to *Romeo and Juliet*, to *Oedipus Rex*. What I am critical of is that our theater is dealing almost exclusively with affects. Where the parent stands the world ends, and where the son stands is where the world should begin but cannot because he is either made impotent, or he revolts, or more often runs away. What is there wrong with this? Does it not happen all the time? It must, or so many playwrights would not be repeating the theme, and it would not have the fascination it evidently does for so many audiences.

What is wrong is not the theme but its failure to extend itself so as to open up ultimate causes. The fact, for one thing, is not merely the frustration of the children, or even the bankruptcy of moral authority in the parents, but also their common awareness in our time of some hidden, ulterior causation for this. If only because this theme is so recurrent, the phenomenon has the right to be called a generalized social one. Therefore, it is proper in this instance to say that the potential vision of these plays is not fulfilled and their potential aesthetic size and perfection is left unrealized. And perhaps even more important, there is implicit in this cut-down vision a decay of nerve, a withering of power to grasp the whole world on the stage and shake it to its foundations as it is the historic job of high drama to do. The mystery of our condition remains, but we know much more about it than appears on our stage.

I am not asking for anything new, but something as old as the Greek drama. When Chekhov, that almost legendary subjectivist, has Vershinin—and many others in his plays—objectifying the social questions which his play has raised, he is merely placing himself within the great tradition which set its art works fully in view of the question of the survival of the race. It is we who are the innovators, or more precisely, the sports, when we refuse to reflect on our stage a level of objective awareness at least as great as exists commonly in our lives outside.

I am asking for the world to be brought into the stage family, to be sure, but I begin and I end from the viewpoint of the dramatist, the dramatist seeking to intensify the power of his plays and his theater. There is something dramatically wrong, for instance, when an audience can see a play about the Nazi treatment of a group of Jews hiding in an attic, and come away feeling the kind of—I can only call it gratification—which the audiences felt after seeing *The Diary of Anne Frank*. Seeing this play I was not only an audience or even a Jew, but a dramatist, and it puzzled me why it was all so basically reassuring to watch what must have been the most harrowing kind of suffering in real life.

As a constructor of plays I had nothing technical of consequence to add. And I found myself putting to this play the question I have put to you—what is its relevancy to the survival of the race? Not the American race, or the Jewish race, or the German race, but the human race. And I believe the beginning of an answer has emerged. It is that with all its truth the play lacks the kind of spread vision, the over-vision beyond its characters and their problems, which could have illuminated not merely the cruelty of Nazism but something even more terrible. We see no Nazis in this play. Again, as with the plays I have mentioned, it is seen from the viewpoint of the adolescent, a poignant and human viewpoint to be sure, but surely a limited one. The approach of the Nazi is akin to the approach of a childhood Demon.

What was necessary in this play to break the hold of reassurance upon the audience, and to make it match the truth of life, was that we should see the bestiality in our own hearts, so that we should know how we are brothers not only to these victims but to the Nazis, so that the ultimate terror of our lives should be faced— namely our own sadism, our own ability to obey orders from above, our own fear of standing firm on humane principle against the obscene power of the mass organization. Another dimension was waiting to be opened up behind this play, a dimension covered with our own sores, a dimension revealing us to ourselves.

Once this dimension had been unveiled we could not have watched in the subtly perverse comfort of pathos; our terror would no longer be for these others but for ourselves, once that part of ourselves which covertly conspires with destruction was made known. Then, for one thing, even tragedy would have been possible, for the issue would not have been why the Nazis were so cruel, but why human beings—ourselves, us—are so cruel. The pathetic is the refusal or inability to discover and face ultimate relevancy for the race; it is therefore a shield against ultimate dramatic effect.

In this instance the objection will be raised that I am demanding a different kind of play than *Diary* was intended to be. I am. I make this demand, if one can presume so far, even though I believe that the original book was very faithfully followed by the dramatists who adapted it. Who am I to argue with the martyred girl who wrote the original document? Her right to her point of view is irreproachable. I agree that it is irreproachable. I repeat, as a matter of fact, what I said earlier—that the adolescent viewpoint is and should be precious to us. In this instance, first of all, I am treating the play as a separate work, as another play opening in New York. Secondly, I am using it to show that even when the adolescent viewpoint is most perfectly announced and movingly dramatized, it nevertheless has a nature, an inner dynamic which prevents it from seeing what it cannot see and still be itself.

It is necessary, in short, to be able to appreciate a thing for what it is, and to see what it is not and what it might be. Our present failure to distinguish between low and high altitude, between amplitude and relative narrowness, leaves us—as it leaves the critics for the most part—at the mercy of "affects"; which is to say that if a small play of minor proportions achieves its affects well, it is as good as a large play of greater proportions.

One consequence of this inability to distinguish between the sizes of things, so to speak, is to condemn ourselves ultimately to minor art. For it is always more likely that small things of shallow breath will show fewer defects than the large, and if the perfecting of affects, regardless of their larger relevancies or irrelevancies, is to be our criterion, as it threatens now to be, we shall turn the theater into a kind of brooding conceit, a showplace for our tricks, a proving ground for our expertise, a shallows protected from the oceans.

I repeat that I am not here as a critic of individual plays but of the dramatic viewpoint which I believe imposes by no means unbreakable limitations upon them. They are limitations which tend to force repetitions of mood, mode, style, yes, and even the lighting and setting of one play after another, even as they are written by writers in their individual isolation. While on the one hand we prize the original work, the new creation, we are surprisingly unconscious of the sameness of so much that passes for new. But the new, the truly new dramatic poem will be, as it has always been, a new organization of the meaning, the generalized significance of the action.

A moment ago I threw together several plays for the purposes of this discussion, one of which I should like now to set apart. In every way but one *Cat on a Hot Tin Roof* differs from *Diary of Anne Frank*, as well as from the others mentioned. Williams has a long reach and a genuinely dramatic imagination. To me, however, his greatest value, his aesthetic valor, so to speak, lies in his very evident determination to unveil and engage the widest range of causation conceivable to him. He is constantly pressing his own limit. He creates shows, as all of us must, but he possesses the restless inconsolability with his solutions which is inevitable in a genuine writer. In my opinion, he is properly discontented with the total image some of his plays have created. And it is better that way, for when the image is complete and self-contained it is usually arbitrary and false.

It is no profound thing to say that a genuine work of art creates not completion, but a sustained image of things in tentative balance. What I say now is not to describe that balance as a false or illusory one, but one whose weighing containers, so to speak, are larger and greater than what has been put into them. I think, in fact, that in *Cat on a Hot Tin Roof*, Williams in one vital respect made an assault upon his own viewpoint in an attempt to break it up and reform it on a wider circumference.

Essentially it is a play seen from the viewpoint of Brick, the son. He is a lonely young man sensitized to injustice. Around him is a world whose human figures partake in various ways of grossness, Philistinism, greed, money-lust, power-lust. And—with his mean-spirited brother as an example—it is a world senselessly reproducing itself through ugly children conceived without the grace of genuine affection, and delivered not so much as children but as inheritors of great wealth and power, the new perpetuators of inequity.

In contrast, Brick conceives of his friendship with his dead friend as an idealistic, even gallant and valorous and somehow morally elevated one, a relationship in which nothing was demanded, but what was given was given unasked, beyond the realm of price, of value, even of materiality. He clings to this image as to a banner of purity to flaunt against the world, and more precisely, against the decree of nature to reproduce himself, to become in turn the father, the master of the earth, the administrator of the tainted and impure world. It is a world in whose relations—especially between the sexes—there is always the element of the transaction, of materiality.

If the play confined itself to the psychiatry of impotence, it could be admired or dismissed as such. Williams' plays are never really that, but here in addition, unlike his other plays, there is a father.

Not only is he the head of a family, but the very image of power, of materiality, of authority. And the problem this father is given is how he can infuse his own personality into the prostrated spirit of his son so that a hand as strong as his own will guide his fortune when he is gone—more particularly, so that his own immortality, his civilization will be carried on.

As the play was produced, without the surface realism of living-room, bedroom, walls, conventional light—in an atmosphere, instead, of poetic conflict, in a world that is eternal and not merely this world—it provided more evidence that Williams' preoccupation extends beyond the surface realities of the relationships, and beyond the psychiatric connotations of homosexuality and impotence. In every conceivable fashion there was established a goal beyond sheer behavior. We were made to see, I believe, an ulterior pantheon of forces and a play of symbols as well as of characters.

It is well known that there was difficulty in ending this play, and I am certainly of no mind to try it. I believe I am not alone in saying that the resolutions wherein Brick finally regains potency was not understandable on the stage. But my feeling is that even if this were more comprehensively motivated so that the psychiatric development of the hero were persuasively completed, it in itself could not embrace the other questions raised in the play.

We are persuaded as we watch this play that the world around Brick is in fact an unworthy collection of unworthy motives and greedy actions. Brick refuses to participate in this world, but he cannot destroy it either or reform it and he turns against himself. The question here, it seems to me, the ultimate question is the right of society to renew itself when it is, in fact, unworthy. There is, after all, a highly articulated struggle for material power going on here. There is literally and symbolically a world to win or a world to forsake and damn. A viewpoint is necessary, if one is to raise such a tremendous issue, a viewpoint capable of encompassing it. This is not a study in cynicism where the writer merely exposes the paradoxes of all sides and is content to end with a joke. Nor, again, is it mere psychiatry, aiming to show us how a young man reclaims his sexuality. There is a moral judgment hanging over this play which never quite comes down. A tempting analogy would be that of a Hamlet who takes up his sword and neither fights nor refuses to fight but marries an Ophelia who does not die.

Brick, despite his resignation from the race, has thrown a challenge to it which informs the whole play, a challenge which the father and the play both recognize and ignore. But if it is the central challenge of the play—as the play seems to me to emphasize—then the world must either prove its worthiness to survive, or its unworthiness must lie dramatically proved, to justify Brick's refusal to renew it—or, like a Hamlet who will neither do battle nor put down his sword, it must condemn Brick to inaction and perhaps indifference to its fate.

Because of Williams' marvelous ability, I for one would be willing to listen—and perhaps to him alone—even as he pronounced ultimate doom upon the race—a race exemplified in his play by the meanest of motives. This is a foundation grand enough, deep enough, and worthy of being examined remorselessly and perhaps even shaken and smashed. Again, as with *The Diary of Anne Frank*, had the implicit challenge ripened, we should no longer be held by our curiosity or our pity for someone else, but by that terror which comes when we must in truth justify our most basic assumptions. The father in this play, I think, must be forced to the wall in justification of his world, and Brick must be forced to his wall in justification of his condemning that world to the ultimate biological degree. The question of society's right to insist upon its renewal when it is unworthy is a question of tragic grandeur, and those who have asked this question of the world know full well the lash of its retaliation.

Quite simply, what I am asking is that the play pursue the ultimate development of the very questions it asks. But for such a pursuit, the viewpoint of the adolescent is not enough. The father, with the best will in the world, *is* faced with the problem of a son he loves best refusing to accept him and his spirit. Worse yet, it is to the least worthy son that that spirit must be handed if all else fails. Above the father's and the son's individual viewpoints the third must emerge, the viewpoint, in fact, of the audience, the society, and the race. It is a viewpoint that must weigh, as I have said, the question of its own right to biological survival—and one thing more, the question of the fate of the sensitive and the just in an impure world of power. After all, ultimately someone must take charge; this is the tragic dilemma, but it is beyond the viewpoint of adolescence. Someone must administer inequity or himself destroy that world by refusing to renew it, or by doing battle against its injustice, or by declaring his indifference or his cynicism. The terms upon which Brick's potency returns are left waiting to be defined and the play is thus torn from its climax.

Again, I am not criticizing this play, but attempting to mark the outlines of its viewpoint—which is an extension of our theater's viewpoint to its present limits. Nor is this an entirely new and unheralded idea. Be it Tolstoy, Dostoevsky, Hemingway, you, or I, we are formed in this world when we are sons and daughters and the first truths we know throw us into conflict with our fathers and mothers. The struggle for mastery—for the freedom of manhood or womanhood as opposed to the servility of childhood—is the struggle not only to overthrow authority but to reconstitute it anew. The viewpoint of the adolescent is precious because it is revolutionary and insists upon justice. But in truth the parent, powerful as he appears, is not the source of injustice but its deputy.

A drama which refuses or is unable to reach beyond this façade is denying itself its inherited chance for greatness. The best of our theater is standing tiptoe, striving to see over the shoulders of father and mother. The worst is exploiting and wallowing in the self-pity of adolescence and obsessive keyhole sexuality. The way out, as the poet has said, is always *through*. We will not find it by huddling closer to the center of the charmed circle, by developing more and more naturalism in our dialogue and our acting, that "slice-of-life" reportage which is to life what an overheard rumor is to truth; nor by setting up an artificial poetic style, nor by once again shocking the householders with yet other unveilings of domestic relations and their hypocrisies. Nor will we break out by writing problem plays. There is an organic aesthetic, a tracking of impulse and causation from the individual to the world and back again which must be reconstituted. We are exhausting the realm of affects, which is the world of adolescence taken pure.

The shadow of a cornstalk on the ground is lovely, but it is no denial of its loveliness to see as one looks on it that it is telling the

time of the day, the position of the earth and the sun, the size of our
planet and its shape, and perhaps even the length of its life and ours
among the stars. A viewpoint bounded by affects cannot engage
the wider balance of our fates where the great climaxes are found.

In my opinion, if our stage does not come to pierce through
affects to an evaluation of the world it will contract to a lesser psychiatry and an inexpert one at that. We shall be confined to writing
an *Oedipus* without the pestilence, an *Oedipus* whose catastrophe
is private and unrelated to the survival of his people, an *Oedipus*
who cannot tear out his eyes because there will be no standard by
which he can judge himself; and *Oedipus*, in a word, who on learning of his incestuous marriage, instead of tearing out his eyes, will
merely wipe away his tears thus to declare his loneliness. Again,
where a drama will not engage its relevancy for the race, it will halt
at pathos, that tempting shield against ultimate dramatic effect,
that counterfeit of meaning.

Symbolically, as though sensing that we are confined, we have
removed the doors and walls and ceilings from our sets. But the
knowing eye still sees them there. They may truly disappear and
the stage will open to that symbolic stature, that realm where the
father is after all not the final authority, that area where he is the
son too, that area where religions are made and the giants live, only
when we see beyond parents, who are, after all, but the shadows of
the gods.

A great drama is a great jurisprudence. Balance is all. It will
evade us until we can once again see man as whole, until sensitivity
and power, justice and necessity are utterly face to face, until
authority's justifications and rebellion's too are tracked even to
those heights where the breath fails, where—because the largest
point of view as well as the smaller has spoken—truly the rest is
silence.

Ibsen and the Drama of Today
1994

I am not scholar enough—or journalist either—to be able to say with any real certainty what Ibsen's influence is today. I have only impressions, which may or may not be accurate.

I don't believe that many of today's playwrights look to his methods as models, but his standing as a modern has nevertheless improved, I think, over the past thirty or forty years. When I began writing plays in the late thirties, he was a favorite of the Left for his radical politics and rebellious mind. His work, however, not often performed, was frequently regarded as quaintly methodical onion-peeling. If you had the patience to labor through it, an Ibsen play was more like argument in a legal case than an entertainment. Such was the prejudice and ignorance of the time, his most important lack was thought to be the poetic spirit; it was fashionable, as it still is in some places today, to call him more of a carpenter than the visionary architect that Shaw, among others, thought him to be. What the young avant-garde wanted in the thirties, positioned as ever against clunky Broadway realism, was the lyrical voice. Clifford Odets and Sean O'Casey specifically, were the more or less Marxist prophets while Saroyan, a premature or closet absurdist, sang basically for his supper. In the Broadway/West End mainstream Maxwell Anderson and Christopher Fry were trying to wring popular drama from unconventional word usage, reviving even Elizabethan iambics. These were very different writers but they were all attempting to sing the language on the stage, as Yeats had done for a more recondite audience and Eliot, too. All of these were self-conscious artists rather than stage shopsmiths, but they would all have no doubt thought that Ibsen's time had passed.

Ibsen's language, lyrical as it may sound in Scandinavia, does not sing in translation, although his ideas often do. Of course, they were only Ibsen's realistic social plays that were produced but these became his stamp, his mysticism having been more or less overlooked and his metaphysical side likewise. Probably his more social plays, like the genre itself, are fundamentally optimistic—demanding change, which is itself an upbeat notion and therefore easy to grasp, while his deepest personal thought is the opposite; symbolist, mythic, muffled in pessimism as it surveys the changeless sea, the sky, aging, cowardice, the classic brick walls against which philosophy has always broken its head.

It is the quasi-journalistic element therefore which came down to later generations, at least in America. He seemed to write about "issues," rather than circumstance. Especially in the Leftist tide of the thirties his stance was translated into an anti-capitalist militancy, but occasionally his apparent elitism seemed relevant to Fascism. For example, a small controversy developed over whether *An Enemy of the People* had a Fascistic tendency with its admittedly confusing claims for an elite of the intellect which must be trusted to lead ordinary folk. Nowadays the wheel has turned once more and probably something similar is happening now that political correctness is (again) in vogue. But *An Enemy of the People*, it seems to me, is really about Ibsen's belief that there is such a thing as a truth and that it bears something like holiness within it, regardless of the cost its discovery at any one moment entails. And the job of the elite is to guard and explain that holiness without compromise or stint.

For myself, I was deeply stirred by his indignation at the social lies of his time, but it was in his structures that I was thrilled to find his poetry. His plays were models of a stringent economy of means to create immense symphonic images of tragic proportions. It wasn't that things fit together but that *everything* fit together, like a natural organism, a human being, for example, or a rose. His works had an organic intensity making them, or most of them, undeniable. To me he was a reincarnation of the Greek dramatic spirit, especially its obsessive fascination with past transgressions as the seeds of current catastrophe. In this slow unfolding was wonder, even god. Past and present were drawn into a single continuity, and thus a secret moral order was being limned. He and the

Greeks were related also through their powerful integrative impulse which, at least in theory, could make possible a total picture of a human being—character sprang from action, and like a spiritual CAT scan the drama could conceivably offer up a human being seen from within and without at the same. (In fact, my *Death of a Salesman* would proceed in that fashion.) Present dilemma was simply the face that the past had left visible. Every catastrophe was the story of how the birds came home to roost, and I still believe that a play without a past is a mere shadow of a play, just as a man or woman whose past is largely blank or ineptly drawn is merely a suggestion of a man or a woman, and a trivialization to boot.

I don't know what exactly has happened to the concept of the past in contemporary dramaturgy, but it is rarely there any more. Things happen, God knows why. Maybe we are just too tired of thinking, or maybe meaning itself has become an excrescence. But most likely it is that we have too often been wrong about what important things mean.

Perhaps it comes down to our loss of confidence in our ability to lay a finger on the inevitable in life; in the name of freedom and poetry it is now customary to declare, in effect, that our existence is itself a surprise and that surprise is the overwhelmingly central principle of life. Or maybe we are just surfeited with entertainment and prefer to lie back and let our brains enjoy a much needed rest.

The triumph of the past-less art is of course the film. A film persona requires no past or any other proof of his existence; he need only be photographed and he is palpably *there*.

The past keeps coming back to our art, however, if only in the parodistic form of the detective or crime story, probably our most popular fictional entertainment. The crime exists, or is about to happen, and we have to move backwards to find out whose general character fits the crime, who has dropped hints of his dire tendency, and so forth. It is the tragic event scrubbed clean of its visionary moral values, its sole job being the engendering of anxiety and fear. (Detective fiction also reassures us about the stability of our civilization, but that's another story.)

The so-called Absurd theater, in a different way, also helped make any obsession with the past seem quaint, and Ibsen with it. The proof of a character's existence was simply his awareness of his ironical situation, that was all and that was enough. Character itself, which surely must mean individuation, smacked of realism, and in its stead were interchangeable stickmen whose individuation lay in their varying attitudes and remarks about the determining force, the situation. Without a past the present, and its anxieties, was all that was left to talk about. And the situation of the stickman is of course so utterly overwhelming—war, or concentration camps, or economic disaster—that what individually he may have had, his will or lack of will, his self-doubt or assurance, his faith or cynicism is squashed out, leaving only the irony of humans continuing to exist at all.

So that the quality we instantly recognized as supremely human was not characterological definition, which requires a history, but its very absence; whatever his personality, it is without significance because it doesn't affect history—that is, his kindness, his dreams of a different kind of life, his love, his devotion to duty or to another human being simply do not matter as he is marched towards the flames. It may be the Holocaust clinched the case for reducing personality to a laughable affectation. I am inclined to believe this to be so, even for people who never think about the events in Eastern Europe directly. The Holocaust—the story of a great nation turned criminal on a vast scale—implicitly defeated us, broke confidence in our claims to being irrevocably in the camp of what was once securely called humanity, and left us with absurdity as the defining human essence.

Again, the concept of a gradually in-gathering, swelling, evidentiary, revelatory explosion is now reserved for thrillers, by and large; but instead of insights we have clues, mechanically dropped most of the time, to both lead us on and astray. We are given, if you will, the skeleton of the Ibsen form without the soul or the flesh.

The revolt—or rather the loss of interest in what is commonly thought of as Ibsenism—also imagines itself to be a revolt against the well-made play, quite as though Ibsen was not himself the first to attack that kind of play. Instead of being well-made his plays are true. That is the difference. They follow the psycho-moral dilemma, not the plot. But we have arrived at a point where, as indicated, the very notion of inevitability is itself highly suspect—in short, no one can know why great events happen, let alone why

the shifts and changes in human attitudes take place. Under the
rubric of a new freedom and a deeper wisdom we have turned
against the rational, claiming the delightful license to simply
express feeling and impressions, the more randomly the better to
create surprise, the ultimate aesthetic value.

In short, Strindberg has won the philosophical battle with Ibsen
and Ibsenism. The poet of instinct and the impromptu, of the paradoxical surprise, his mission is not to save anyone or a society, but
simply to rip the habit of hypocrisy from the human heart and cant
from the life of the mind. He is the destroying rebel chopping off
the ever-growing heads of a thousand-armed dragon, a pessimistic
labor to be sure. Ibsen, quite otherwise, is the revolutionary groping for a new system, an optimistic business, for when the old is
destroyed, the new construct implies rational decisions, and above
all hope.

And who can gainsay Strindberg any more? Apart from the Holocaust are we not witnesses to the implosion of the Soviet Union,
the most "rationally" run society, falling in upon itself, a fraud and
a farce? And what has survived but old, chaotic, irrational capitalism, blinding itself to its poor behind the glaring lights of its packed
store windows, and hiding its spiritual starvation under the shiny
bonnets of its marvellous cars? How to rationally account for *this*
surprise—the victory of the decadent doomed and the disgrace
of the historically "inevitable victors," the "new men" who stand
revealed as medieval fief-holders when they were not actual gangsters and killers of the dream?

Compare this awesome moral chaos, this wracking collapse of
the comfortably predictable, with Ibsen's methodical unravelling of
motives and the interplay of social and psychological causation, all
of it speaking of rational control! They cannot jibe, our reality and
his. So he must seem outmoded, a picturesque mind out of a more
orderly time.

Perhaps that is why he seems to be coming back, at least his prestige as a modern, if not precisely his methods. For while it is purely
a sense of the new mood on my part, it does seem that the taste for
"real plays" rather than only fun effusions has begun to stir again.
Of course, there are still old-fashioned critics who think that anything that has a beginning and end is out of date, but there are

young playwrights who would disagree and are looking to life rather than the theater for their inspiration, and life, of course, includes not only surprise but the consequences flowing from our actions or structure, in other words.

Perhaps I ought to add here that in these past dozen years my most Ibsen-influenced play, *All My Sons*, written nearly fifty years ago, is more and more frequently and more widely produced now and the reviewers no longer feel obliged to dismiss its structure as not-modern. I have had to wonder whether this is partly due to the number of investigations of official malfeasance in the papers all the time, and the spectacle of men of stature and social influence being brought down practically every week by revelations excavated from the hidden past. From the heights of Wall Street, the Pentagon, the White House, big business, the same lesson seems to fly out at us—the past lives! As does Ibsen, the master of the explosive force when it bombs in the present, and above all, with the soul-rot that comes of the hypocrisy of its denial.

Needless to say, I have not attempted in this short note to deal with Ibsen as poet and creator of mythic plays, beginning with the opening of his career. For one thing, those plays remain to be interpreted for modern audiences, their mythology having little obvious meaning for most people outside Scandinavia.

Tennessee Williams' Legacy: An Eloquence and Amplitude of Feeling
1984

So long as there are actors at work in the world, the plays of Tennessee Williams will live on. The autocratic power of fickle taste will not matter in his case; his texture, his characters, his dramatic personality are unique and are as permanent in the theatrical vision of this century as the stars in the sky.

It is usually forgotten what a revolution his first great success meant to the New York theater. *The Glass Menagerie* in one stroke lifted lyricism to its highest level in our theater's history, but it broke new ground in another way. What was new in Tennessee Williams was his rhapsodic insistence that form serve his utterance rather than dominating and cramping it. In him the American theater found, perhaps for the first time, an eloquence and an amplitude of feeling. And driving on this newly discovered lyrical line was a kind of emotional heroism; he wanted not to approve or disapprove but to touch the germ of life and to celebrate it with verbal beauty.

His theme is perhaps the most pervasive in American literature, where people lose greatly in the very shadow of the mountain from whose peak they might have had a clear view of God. It is the romance of the lost yet sacred misfits, who exist in order to remind us of our trampled instincts, our forsaken tenderness, the holiness of the spirit of man.

Despite great fame, Williams never settled into a comfortable corner of the literary kitchen. It could only have been the pride born of courage that kept him at playwriting after the professional theater to which he had loaned so much dignity, so much aspiration, could find no place for his plays. But he never lost his humor and a phenomenal generosity toward other artists. A few months before his death, I had a letter from him about a play of mine that had had some of the most uncomprehending reviews of my career. I had not seen Tennessee in years, but out of darkness came this clasp of a hand, this sadly laughing voice telling me that he had seen and understood and loved my play, and in effect, that we had both lived to witness a chaos of spirit, a deafness of ear and a blindness of eye, and that one carried on anyway.

His audience remained enormous, worldwide. Hundreds of productions of his plays have gone on each year—but not on the Broadway that his presence had glorified. He would end as he had begun, on the outside looking in—as he once put it, scratching on the glass. But of course, past the suffering the work remains, the work for which alone he lived his life, the gift he made to his actors, his country, and the world.

The Good Old American Apple Pie
1993

What a strange irony it is that at the very moment when all over Europe and Latin America repressive regimes have been driven out of power and with them their censors from office, that we Americans should be increasingly discovering the uses of censorship over our own writers and artists. The devil, as was once said, has many disguises; defeated in one place he pops up somewhere else.

Evidently there are many Americans who still do not understand why censorship and democracy cannot live happily together. What so many seem to forget is that a censor does not merely take something out, he puts something in, something of his own in a work that does not belong to him. His very purpose is to change a work to his own tastes and preconceptions.

Many forget that when they read a work that has passed through censorship, they are putting themselves in the hands of an anonymous person whose name appears nowhere and cannot be held responsible for what is published.

Perhaps we can appreciate what censorship really means by looking at a strange story that took place in Britain at the end of the eighteenth century.

A teenager named William Henry Ireland, illegitimate son of a wealthy London antique dealer, desperate to get into his father's good graces, came home one day claiming to have been given various papers in Shakespeare's hand, as well as a lock of hair of Shakespeare's wife, by a stranger whose carriage had nearly run him down on the street. Following the near accident, he and this stranger had become friends, according to young William, and as a token of the man's regard for him he had been given these invaluable papers and the lock of hair.

The elder Ireland immediately had the handwriting on the papers checked by the authorities who pronounced it Shakespeare's, and the ink and paper were without question of the Elizabethan period, nearly two centuries old. All London was agog, and the boy and his father became overnight sensations. Naturally, young Ireland, until now utterly ignored by everyone, got enthusiastic and announced that his new friend had a whole trunkful of Shakespeare's original manuscripts which he promised he might let the boy have one day.

After producing various forged snippets of Shakespeare's love notes, and a few of the Bard's "lost" verses, young Ireland (would-be poet and idolizer of the late Thomas Chatterton, another young forger-poet) proclaimed that his benefactor had decided to give him nothing less than the original manuscript of *King Lear*, but only in due time. And sure enough, after some weeks young Ireland showed up with that very manuscript. A gathering was instantly convoked in the Ireland living room where the new discovery was read to a dozen of the most authoritative literary critics, noble patrons of the arts, and cultural leaders of the time.

At the end, James Boswell, the famous biographer of Samuel Johnson, fell to his knees before the manuscript to thank God that at long last the true Shakespeare had been revealed to the world, a Shakespeare who was positive and cheerful rather than brooding and dark and defeatist, a Shakespeare who scorned foul language and never brought up sex or bodily functions, a Shakespeare who was clearly a true Christian gentleman rather than the barbaric, foul-mouthed rotter whose works had always embarrassed decent people with their obscenities and blood-covered view of mankind and the English nation.

Of course what young Ireland had done was to clean up *King Lear* to suit the narrow middle-class tastes of his time. It was a time when revolution was gathering in France, threatening to British stability, if not the idea of monarchy itself. Ireland's major fix was to brighten up the end so that the aged king, rather than raving on the heath, swamped in his madness and abandoned by the world, was reunited with his daughters in a comforting sentimental scene of mutual Christian forgiveness, whereupon they all lived happily ever after. The paper on which this version was written was indeed authentic, the young forger having snipped off sheets of it from the blank ends of Elizabethan wills and deeds in the files of the London law office where he worked as a clerk. The antique ink he had produced himself after months of lonely experiment.

Only one critic, Edmund Malone, saw through the forgery, but he did not expose the fraud by analyzing ink or paper but rather the mawkishness of the "newly discovered" alterations, the shallow naïveté behind their versification. But as important as any technical doubts was his conviction that the spirit behind this "new-found authentic *King Lear*" was pawky, narrow-minded, fearful of sexuality and the lustiness of the English tongue, and fearful too of the play's awesome image of human judgment's frailty, and the collapse of the very foundations in reason of government itself. The real *King Lear* reduces man to his elemental nature, stripping him of rank and money and his protective morality, in order to present a vision of the essence of humankind with no ameliorating illusions. In place of these challenges the "newly discovered" play was a story of reassurance fit for family entertainment, one that offers comfort by turning a far-ranging tragedy into a story of misunderstandings which are pleasantly cleared up at the end.

In a word, young William Ireland did what censorship always attempts to do—force a work to conform to what *some* people want life to look like even if it means destroying the truth the work is written to convey.

Had the Ireland forgery been left uncontested, we can be sure that *King Lear* as a play would never have survived the hour. Many critics then and since have thought it a nasty work with an improbably black estimate of humanity, but succeeding generations have come to treasure it precisely for its truthfulness to life's worst as well as its best.

What Ireland did was erase the doubts about life that were in the original play and were so discomforting to the upper class of Britain at the time.

Censorship is as old as America. The Puritans forbade the reading of novels—or, indeed, anything but scripture—as one of the condemned "vain pursuits." A reader nowadays would find it impossible to recognize in those novels what could possibly have aroused the Puritan fathers to such fury against them. But closer to our time, there is hardly a master writer who has not felt the censor's lash, from James Joyce to Gustave Flaubert to D. H. Lawrence to Hemingway and Fitzgerald, to William Faulkner and a long, long list that just about comprises the roster of world literature. Someone somewhere could doubtless find reasons for moral outrage in a McDonald's menu or a phone book.

Of course there is no denying that there are people who misuse freedom to appeal to the sinister in us, our brutality, scorn for justice, or concealed violence and lust. By exploiting our suppressed feelings people with no interest in anything but making an illicit buck can prosper, for example, by exploiting human sexual curiosity even if it victimizes children.

But the problem, clearly, is that when we legitimize censorship of what we agree is antisocial art we come very close to legitimizing it for real art. For example, right now some three hundred and fifty lines of *Romeo and Juliet* are customarily removed from American school textbooks because they are about sex. There is a similar emasculation of the two other most commonly taught Shakespeare plays, *Julius Caesar* and *Macbeth*. In other words, lines of very high poetry are forbidden American students who, it is assumed, will think that much less often about sex. Of course this is ridiculous; all this censoring does is deprive them of realizing that there is something sublime and beautiful in sex and that it is not merely dirty. It throws them entirely to the mercies of suggestive videos and rock lyrics and really raw pornography which apparently nothing will stop, and will certainly not be slowed by censoring *Romeo and Juliet*.

The purported aim of censorship is always to preserve public morality but we ought not forget that for those who advocate censorship pornography is by no means necessarily the only kind of immoral communication. If it becomes established policy that blotting out certain sexual images in art is acceptable, then there is nothing in principle to stop the censoring of other "immoral" expression.

I have had some experience with "moral" censorship myself. In 1947, my play *All My Sons* was about to open in the Colonial Theatre, Boston, for its first performances before coming to Broadway. The Catholic Church at that time exercised censorship over the Boston theaters and threatened to issue a condemnation of the play unless a certain line were eliminated from it. I should add that the raunchiest burlesque shows in America were playing on the Boston

"Strip" at the time, but these apparently were not bothersome to the moral authorities. What troubled them terribly was the line, "A man can't be a Jesus in this world!" spoken by Joe Keller, a character who has knowingly shipped defective engine parts to the Air Force resulting in twenty-odd fighter planes crashing and who is now pleading for his son's forgiveness. The name of Jesus was forbidden utterance on the Boston stage, no matter that in this case it was used to indicate Jesus' high moral standard. I refused to change the line, as much because I could not think of a substitute as anything else, but the hypocrisy of the complaint was painful to contemplate, given the level of entertainment of the Boston "Strip" a few blocks from my theater.

In 1962, when my film *The Misfits* was previewed by religious censors, the gravest displeasure was expressed with a scene in which Marilyn Monroe, in a mood of despair and frustration—fully clothed, it should be said—walks out of a house and embraces a tree trunk. In all seriousness this scene was declared to be masturbation, and unless it was cut the picture would be classified as condemned and a large part of the audience barred from seeing it. Once again it was necessary to refuse to oblige a censor, but I would not have had that privilege had I lived in a different kind of country. Experiences like these have helped me to stand against censorship.

Life is not reassuring; if it were we would not need the consolations of religion, for one thing. Literature and art are not required to reassure when in reality there is no reassurance, or to serve up "clean and wholesome" stories in all times and all places. Those who wish such art are welcome to have it, but those who wish art to symbolize how life really is, in order to understand it and perhaps themselves, also have a right to their kind of art.

I would propose to censors and their supporters that they write the stories and paint or shoot the pictures they approve of, and let them offer them to the public in open competition with the stories and pictures of those whose works they want to suppress.

Let them write a new *Romeo and Juliet* that is wholesome and unoffending and put it on a stage and invite the public to come and enjoy it as millions have enjoyed Shakespeare's play for three hundred years. Who knows?—maybe they will win out.

But of course they cannot accept this challenge; censorship is an attack on healthy competition. It comes down to a refusal to enter the arena and instead to wipe out the competitor by sanctions of suppressive writs and the police power.

I write this as one who is often disgusted by certain displays that call themselves art and are really raids on the public's limitless sexual curiosity, purely for the purpose of making money. As an artist I sometimes wonder at my having to compete with this easy and specious way of attracting attention and gaining a public following. And I will not deny my belief that there may ultimately be a debasement of public taste as the result of the incessant waves of sexual exploitation in films and other media.

But bad as this is, it is not as bad as censorship, because the censor is given a police power no individual ought to have in a democracy—the power not only to keep bad art from the public, but good art, too; the power not only to protect people from lies but from uncomfortable truths. That way lies not wholesomeness, not community values, but the domination of the many by the few acting in the name of the many. Nobody said it was easy to be a free people, but censorship not only makes it harder, it makes it in the end impossible.

Probably because we in general enjoy freedom to express ourselves we are unaware of not only the power that a censor takes but the hypocrisy that inevitably accompanies it. In the winter of 1965 I interviewed a lady in her Moscow offices, one Madame Elena Furtseva, then head of all culture of the Soviet Union. In theory and often in practice this woman and the committee she headed had the power to shut down any play before or during its run in a theater, or to cancel a film or suppress a novel or book of poems or whatever. She could also promote certain books if she so pleased. She had been Khrushchev's special friend and when he was ousted she cut her wrists but was saved and restored to her job.

Behind her chair was a long table piled high with at least a hundred books lying on their sides. Each volume had a few slips of paper sticking out of its pages which I deduced marked passages of censorable writing which her assistants were submitting to her to decide upon.

She looked quite exhausted and I remarked sympathetically on this. "Well I have so much I must read, you see," she said, and gestured toward the possibly offending books behind her.

With nothing to lose—my U.S. passport snug in my pocket, I ventured: "You know, I have never met writers anywhere who are as patriotic as your Russian writers. Whatever their criticisms, they have a deep love of country. Why don't you make an experiment; don't tell anybody but let's say for one month just don't read anything. See what happens. Maybe nothing will happen. Then you won't have to be reading all this stuff every day."

She tried hard for a sophisticated smile but it came out looking hard and painful. And then she said something interesting: "The Soviet worker cannot be asked to pay for the paper and ink to print ideas that go counter to his interests and his moral ideas of right and wrong."

I can't help thinking of that statement when I hear people saying that the American taxpayers ought not be asked to pay for artworks that offend their tastes or their ideas of right and wrong. The fundamental fallacy in such a statement is quite simple and inexorable; how did Madame Furtseva know what the Soviet worker thought was right and wrong, moral or immoral? How *could* she know when no one but her and her assistants were allowed to read possibly offending works?

Indeed, for nearly three-quarters of a century Soviet writing has been kept remarkably chaste, with very strict rules about depicting sex, while at the same time the Soviet abortion rate was rising to the highest in the world. It was also very strict about barring negative pictures of Soviet conditions in all the media and forbade any genuine attack on the system. After three-quarters of a century of such censorship the Soviet system appears to have collapsed. Why? Because reality does not go away when a censor draws a line through a sentence or tears a page out of *Romeo and Juliet*.

If there is a way to curb pornography, if there is any possibility of preventing people from lathering after obscene material, it can only be the result of changing their tastes. If they don't want the stuff it won't be profitable and it will vanish. I doubt that day will ever come, no matter what, but surely cursing the darkness never brought light. Through education raising the intelligence level of the population, sensitizing people to real rather than cosmetic feeling, enhancing mutual respect between the sexes and between races—these are the paths to decency, not calling in the cops to drive out the bad guys.

There is an analogy here to the narcotics problem. We spend tens of millions on planes to spot smugglers, more millions to wipe out Peruvian coca crops, more millions on narcotics police; but of course the narcotics keep coming in because Americans want dope. Meantime, an addict who wants to get rid of the habit has to wait as long as a couple of years to get placed in a rehabilitation clinic because these are underfunded.

Censoring Shakespeare won't make us good and may possibly make us a little more stupid, a little more ignorant about ourselves, a little further from the angels. The day must come when we will stop being so foolish. Why not now?

Notes on Realism
1999

Twenty-five years ago I used to defend Broadway against its detractors, because it was where American theatrical innovation almost always began, the rest of the country timorously following behind. Now the Broadway producer is scared stiff, and in those rare cases when he does produce a serious play—Harold Pinter's *Betrayal*, or Tony Kushner's *Angels in America*—it needs to have proven itself somewhere else, such as Texas or London. A play likely to alienate some part of the audience, as so many great plays have done, or whose style is strange or requires some effort to penetrate, simply will not get produced on today's Broadway. George Bernard Shaw once remarked that businessmen always want to talk about art, but playwrights want to talk about business. This is inevitable, especially now, when one knows, for example, that a play like my *Crucible* would be inconceivable, with its cast of twenty-one and its four large sets. Put another way, the aesthetic of that kind of play is beyond the reach now of the commercial theater, though it would be a mistake to think that serious, expensive-to-mount plays like this were exactly welcome in the theater of the Forties or earlier. On the contrary, producers then as now prayed for the next *Life with Father*, a genial comedy with a smaller cast and one set. The difference is that there existed then a handful of producers, most notably Kermit Bloomgarden and Robert Whitehead, who longed for artistically ambitious and socially interesting plays and could put their money where their mouth was. The nub of the problem is that a "straight" play could be mounted in those times for well under $50,000, as opposed to the $1 million or more frequently required today.

Directly and more subtly, theatrical economics translates into theatrical style, unless one is thinking of closet drama put on for a few recondite friends. Fantastic production costs have combined almost lethally with the rise to near total domination of a single paper, the *New York Times*, and its critic over a play's fate, so that stylistic innovation has been left to small and Off-Broadway venues, where the risk of financial loss is lessened. It seems to me that a resulting confusion has crept into the reviewing and discussion of the various styles of playwriting in fashion today. "Realism" is now a put-down; "poetic" is praise. "Experimental" is attractive; "traditional" is not. "Metaphorical" is intriguing, though perhaps not so much as "lyrical," "nonlinear," "dreamlike," and "surreal." It is almost as if "realism" can hardly be poetic, or as if the "poetic" is not, at its best, more real than the merely "realistic" and, at its worst, more conventional beneath its elusive or unfathomable skin. It would be impossible in a small essay to comb out all this fur, but perhaps at least some of the fundamental fault lines, as well as the overlaps among various approaches to the art, can be illuminated by examining a tiny bit of the history of age-old stylistic strategies employed by playwrights to trap reality on the stage.

Perhaps the obvious needs stating first: There is no such thing as "reality" in any theatrical exhibition that can properly be called a play. The reason for this is that stage time is not, and cannot be, street time. In street time, Willy Loman's story would take sixty-two years to play out instead of two and a half hours. Thus, whether a play strives for straight realism or for some more abstracted style, with the very act of condensation the artificial enters even as the first of its lines is being written. The only important question is the nature of that artificiality and how it is acknowledged by the play, and what ought to be judged is not the extent to which the artifice is "nonlinear" or "metaphorical" or "dreamlike" but rather its efficiency in getting across the playwright's vision of life. This in turn raises questions about a style's suitability to its subject and about the kind of language—what variation on "real" speech—the playwright chooses.

When I began writing plays in the late Thirties, "realism" was the reigning style in the English-language commercial theater, which was just about all the theater there was at the time in America and Britain. Theater could still be thought of then as a popular art, though one knew (and this was long before television) that something of its mass appeal had gone out of it, and a lot of its Twenties glamour, too. In general, one blamed the movies, which had stolen theater's audience and thus its civic power, such as it was, as well as its cultural influence. Despite the obvious fact that our audience was predominantly middle class, we continued to believe that we were making theater for an audience comprising a representative variety of New York City people and even beyond; in other words, theatergoers of many different cultural and educational levels. In New York, where plays had a ticket price of 55 cents to $4.40 (as opposed to $40 to $100 today), one somehow took for granted that a professor might be sitting next to a housewife, a priest beside a skilled worker, or a grammar school teacher, or a business executive, or a student. This perception of a democratic audience, accurate or not, influenced the writing of plays directed at the commonsensical experience of everyday people. (Black or Asian or Hispanic faces were not represented, of course, but these were beyond the consciousness of the prevailing culture.) Even into the Forties, production costs were relatively within reason; plays such as *All My Sons* or *Death of a Salesman*, for example, cost between $20,000 and $40,000 to produce, a budget small enough to be raised among half a dozen modest contributors who could afford to lose their investment with some embarrassment but reasonably little pain, given the killing they occasionally would make.

We were torn, those of us who tried to convince ourselves that we were carrying on the time-honored tradition of theater as a civic art rather than as a purely commercial exercise, because to attract even the fitful interest of a Broadway producer, and thus to engage the audience, we had to bow to realism, even if we admired and wished to explore the more "poetic" forms. An Expressionist like the German Ernst Toller, for example, would not have been read past his sixth page by a Broadway producer or, for that matter, by a producer in London. There is not one "important" playwright of Toller's era who was then, or is now, welcome in the commercial theater, not Chekhov, not Ibsen, not Hauptmann, not Pirandello, Strindberg, Turgenev, or even Shaw.

To perform a Beckett play like *Waiting for Godot* in the proximity of today's Broadway, one has to have a cast of movie stars for a very short run, as was done a little while back at Lincoln Center with Robin Williams, Steve Martin, F. Murray Abraham, Bill Irwin, and Lukas Haas. Things were probably worse half a century ago or more.

One need only read Eugene O'Neill's letters castigating the "showshop" mentality of Broadway and the narrow compass of the American theater audience's imagination, or Shaw's ridiculing of British provincialism, to understand that for some mysterious reason the Anglo-Saxon culture has regarded theater as an entertainment first and last, an art of escape with none of the Continental or Russian involvement in moral or philosophical obligations. The English-language theater was, in fact, almost pridefully commercial; it was a profit-making enterprise wedded to a form whose "realistic" veneer would be universally recognized. Musicals were the exception—they alone had the happy license to part from reality, at least to some extent—but for straight plays even satire was uncommercial enough to merit George Kaufman's definition of it as what closes on Saturday night.

The point is that what we think of as "straight realism" was tiresome half a century ago but nonetheless went unquestioned as a reflection of life by audience and reviewer alike. At a time when "experimental" is all that need be said of a play for it to gain serious consideration, it is not a bad idea to confess that an extraordinarily few such researches have achieved any kind of enduring life. It is not quite enough to know how to escape restrictions; sooner or later one also has to think of arriving somewhere.

American theater's one formal innovation in the Thirties, and probably the single exception to realism's domination, was the WPA's Living Newspaper. An epic in presentational form, written like movies by groups of writers under an editor-producer rather than individually, the Living Newspaper dealt exuberantly with social issues such as public ownership of electrical power, labor unions, agriculture, and medicine, and was extremely popular. The WPA was government-subsidized, using unemployed actors, designers, and technicians, and had no need to make a profit, so a show could call upon large casts and elaborate production elements. And the ticket price was low. It could send Orson Welles, for example, into Harlem storefronts with a big cast playing *Macbeth*, charging a quarter a seat. Theater-for-profit was hardly affected by what might be called this epic-populist approach, because, then as now, it was simply too expensive to produce commercially.

My own first playwriting attempt was purely mimetic, a realistic play about my own family. It won me some prizes and productions, but, interestingly, I could not wait to turn at once to a stylized treatment of life in a gigantic prison—modeled on Jackson state penitentiary in Michigan, near Ann Arbor, where I was in school. Jackson, with something like six thousand inmates, was the largest prison in the United States. I had visited the place over weekends with a friend, who, having taken one psychology course in college, was appointed its lone psychologist. The theme of my play, *The Great Disobedience*, was that prisons existed to make desperate workingmen insane. There was a chorus of sane prisoners chanting from a high overpass above the stage and a counterchorus of the insane trying to draw the other into their ranks. Inevitably, I discovered a strange problem of dramatic language, which could not engage so vast a human disaster with speech born in a warm kitchen. And this led to the question of whether the essential pressure toward poetic dramatic language, if not toward stylization itself, came from the inclusion of society as a major element in a play's story or vision. Manifestly, prose realism was the language of the individual and of private life; poetry, the language of the man in the crowd, in society. Put another way, prose was the language of family relations; it was the inclusion of the larger world beyond that naturally opened a play to the poetic. Was it possible to create a style that would at once deeply engage an American audience that insisted on a recognizable reality of characters, locales, and themes while at the same time opening the stage to considerations of public morality and the mythic social fates—in short, to the invisible?

Of course, this was hardly my preoccupation alone. I doubt there was ever a time when so much discussion went on about form and style. T. S. Eliot was writing his verse plays; Auden and Isherwood, their own. The poetic mimesis of Sean O'Casey was most popular, and W. B. Yeats's dialogue was studied and praised, if not very often produced. The realism of Broadway—and the Strand and the Boulevard theater of France—was detested by the would-be poetic dramatists of my generation, just as it had always been since it came into vogue in the nineteenth century. What did this realism really come down to? A play devoid of symbolic or metaphysical persons and situations, its main virtue verisimilitude, with no revolutionary implications for society. Quite simply, conventional realism was conventional because it avowedly or implicitly supported convention. But it could just as easily do something quite different, or so it seemed. We thought of it as the perfect style for an unchallenging, simple-minded, linear, middle-class, conformist view of life. What I found confusing at the time, however, was that it was not so very long before the term "realism" came to be applied to the revolutionary style of playwrights like Ibsen, Chekhov, and, quite frequently, Strindberg, writers whose whole thrust was in opposition to the bourgeois status quo and the hypocrisies on which it stood.

Clifford Odets, for a few years in the mid-Thirties, was more wildly and lavishly celebrated than any playwright before or since. For younger writers such as myself, Odets was the trailblazer not just because of his declared radicalism but because of the fact that his plays were so manifestly *written*. But there was a misapprehension behind his popularity, too; since his characters were the very exemplars of realistic theater, lacking strangeness or stylish elegance, Odets was called a realist—indeed, a kind of reporter, no less, of Jewish life in the Bronx. I had never lived in the Bronx, but the speech of Brooklyn Jews could not have been much different, and it had no resemblance whatever to the way Odets's people spoke:

> I'm super-disgusted with you!
> A man hits his wife and it is the first step to fascism!
> Look in the papers! On every side the clouds of war—
> Ask yourself a pertinent remark: could a boy make a living playing this instrument [a violin] in our competitive civilization today?
> I think I'll run across the street and pick up an eight-cylinder lunch.

Odets was turning dialogue into his personal jazz, and the surprised audience roared with delight. But had any Bronxite—or anyone else—ever really exclaimed, "God's teeth, no!" or, "What exhaust pipe did he crawl out of?" or, "I feel like I'm shot from a cannon"?

Inevitably, in a theater defined by realism, this had to be

mistakenly labeled as simply a kind of reported news from the netherworld. But of course it was a poet's invented diction, with slashes of imagery of a sort never heard before, onstage or off. Odets's fervent ambition was to burst the bounds of Broadway while remaining inside its embrace, there being no other theatrical place in America for him to go. When the time came, as it probably had to, when some of the surprise was no longer there and when critics took the same pleasure in putting him down as they had in building him up, he found himself homeless on Broadway, and he left for the movies.

I suppose his fate may have had some effect on my own explorations into "alternative" forms as I came out of the Thirties. All I knew for sure was that the word "poetry" wasn't enough if a play's underlying structure was a fractured one, a concept not fully realized. A real play was the discovery of the unity of its contradictions, and the essential poetry, the first poetry, was the synthesis of even the least of its parts to form a symbolic meaning. A certain consistency was implicit. The oak does not sprout maple leaves, and a certain kind of self-conscious lyricism does not belong in a realistic work. In short, I had come to believe that if one could create a very strong unity in a work, any audience could be led anywhere. Ideally, a good play must offer as sound an emotional proof of its thesis as a law case does factually, and you couldn't really do that with words alone, lovely as they might be.

Odets's contribution, ironically, was not his realistic portrayal of social reality—his alleged aim—but his willingness to be artificial; he brought back artificiality, if you will, just as ten years later Tennessee Williams did so with his birdsong from the magnolias. But Williams had an advantage: his language could be far more faithful to its real-world sources. Southern people really did love to talk, and often elaborately, and in accents much like Amanda's in *The Glass Menagerie*:

> But Laura is, thank heavens, not only pretty but also very domestic. I'm not at all. I never was a bit. I never could make a thing but angel-food cake. Well, in the South we had so many servants. Gone, gone, gone. All vestige of gracious living! Gone completely! I wasn't prepared for what the future brought me. All my gentlemen callers

were sons of planters and so of course I assumed that I would be married to one and raise my family on a large piece of land with plenty of servants. But man proposes—and woman accepts the proposal! To vary that old, old saying a little bit—I married no planter! I married a man who worked for the telephone company! That gallantly smiling gentleman over there! [*Points to husband's picture*] A telephone man who—fell in love with long distance! Now he travels and I don't even know where!

This, too, was called realism, but then how did it differ from the conventional realistic play? Clearly the very action of Williams's plays, certainly the best of them, was working toward the building of a symbolic meaning that would express both the psychological development of his characters and his personal specter of a menacing America struggling with its own repressed sexuality. His earliest work is shot through with the left-wing attitudes of the time, which he managed gradually to fuse with his own vulnerability, his pain and anxiety at being overwhelmed and defeated by a crazy violence that underlay the American, one might say the whole Western, ethos. Without that confession of his pain and anxiety— his tragic vision—his words alone would have seemed, I think, flowery and excessively romantic.

To consider such writers as purely private, self-involved persons is to disserve the truth. Odets when he began thought his egalitarian Marxism would heal America and create its new community, and Williams unfurled the banner of a forlorn but gallant resistance to the mendacity and the violence aimed at the oddball, the poet, the sexual dissident. But it may as well be admitted that in their different ways both men in the bitter end unwittingly collaborated with the monster they believed was trying to destroy them.

O'Neill, of course, was an aesthetic rebel, but his socialism was private and did not inform his plays (though *The Hairy Ape* is surely an anti-capitalist work). It was his formal experiments and tragic ambience that set him apart. But O'Neill was a totally isolated phenomenon in the Broadway theater as a maker and user of new and old theatrical forms. Odets, on the other hand, while describing himself as a man of the Left, was, with the possible exception of his first produced play, *Waiting for Lefty*, no innovator where form was concerned. His was a poetic realism, but it was still bound to recognizably real types in actual social relationships. And this was perhaps inevitable; as both actor and revolutionary he had his eye on the great public and the reconstitution of power once a failed capitalism had been brought down. In the Depression, it was all but impossible for a Left writer not to think of the act of writing as a fulcrum for social change. Odets saw himself not only as a political realist but as an anarchic poet, a word-nurse (he kept a file of startling locutions) whose novel twists of language would lift his work into the skies. O'Neill, on the other hand, was not the revolutionary but the rebel, a despairing anarchist who, if he glimpsed any salvation, knew that it could come only with the tragic cleansing of the life-lie that is permanently ensconced in the human condition. Since, unlike Odets, he did not obligate himself to even foreshadow some new and better polity in place of the present corrupt one, he was free to explore all sorts of theatrical means by which to set forth the extant situation of the damned—that is, the Americans. Moreover, if O'Neill wanted his plays to register in the here and now, as he surely did, they need not necessarily be popular to justify his having written them, for he was hunting the sounding whale of ultimate meaning, and he expected to suffer for it (and to be misunderstood) as his models, like Strindberg, had. As much as any playwright could be, O'Neill seemed hardened to the possibility of failure, pledged as he was to drag the theater into the unfamiliar world of spirit and metaphysic.

A critical or box-office failure for Odets meant rejection of a far more personal kind, a spit in the eye by an ungrateful and self-satisfied bourgeois society. A failed play was a denial of what Odets was owed, for he was chasing the public no differently than did his bourgeois and nonrevolutionary contemporaries, a public as fickle as it always was and is. O'Neill could say, as he did, that he was interested in relations not among men but between Man and God. For America, in his view, was damned, from virtue estranged by fixations on gain, racism, social climbing, and the rest of the materialist agenda.

A good style for O'Neill was basically a question of the apt use of metaphor, imagery, and argot. "I wish to God I could write like that!" he wrote to O'Casey, who, incidentally, would no doubt have called himself a "realistic" writer in the sense that he was trying to turn Irish attention to Irish reality. But like Williams, O'Casey came from a culture that loved talk and sucked on language like a sweet candy:

> MRS. GOGAN: Oh, you've got a cold on you, Fluther.
> FLUTHER: Ah, it's only a little one.
> MRS. GOGAN: You'd want to be careful, all th' same. I knew a woman, a big lump of a woman, red-faced and round-bodied, a little awkward on her feet; you'd think, to look at her, she could put out her two arms an' lift a two-storied house on th' top of her head; got a ticklin' in her throat, an' a little cough, an' th' next mornin' she had a little catchin' in her chest, an' they had just time to wet her lips with a little rum, an' off she went.

Even in the most mundane of conversational exchanges, O'Casey sought, and as often as not found, the lift of poetry. Indeed, that was the whole point—that the significantly poetic sprang from the raw and real experience of ordinary people. J. M. Synge, O'Casey's forerunner at the turn of the century, had struck a similar chord. Synge was in a supremely conscious revolt against the banality of most theater language. As he wrote, the popular imagination was still

> fiery and magnificent, and tender; so that those of us who wish to write start with a chance that is not given to writers in places where the springtime of the local life has been forgotten, and the harvest is a memory only, and the straw has been turned into bricks.

Synge rejected the then-dominant Ibsen and Zola for their realism with "joyless and pallid words" and instead, as in *Riders to the Sea*, when the women are lamenting the deaths of so many of their men working the angry sea, wrote

> MAURYA: In the big world the old people do be leaving things after them for their sons and children, but in this place it is the young men do be leaving things behind for them that do be old.

Here it might be useful to remember that James Joyce, another Irish poet, revered Ibsen notwithstanding the pallor of his words in

English, for Joyce had, by learning Ibsen's Norwegian, penetrated the poetic structure of the plays and their outcry against the spiritual failure of the modern world.

The advent of the Absurd and of Beckett and his followers both obscured and illuminated the traditional discussion of theater style. The Beckett difference, as it might be called, was to introduce humble people, or social sufferers—bums, in fact—with the plainest of language arranged so as to announce and develop pure theme. His could be called a presentational thematic play, announcing what it was about and never straying very far from what it sought to prove or what his instinct had led him to confirm. Beckett had parted with the time-honored tradition of inferential playwriting, in which the author's thematic intentions were inferred from a seemingly autonomous story whose climax consisted of the joining together of story and the finally revealed underlying theme. With Beckett, the story *was* the theme, inseparably so, from page one. Moreover, he blatantly interpreted the story himself in his dialogue.

By the Fifties, the notion that an elevated tone or diction was required for an escape from common realism was discarded in favor of the most common, undecorated speech. But it was not the traditional speech of realistic plays. Rather, it was a speech bent almost out of recognition by a surreal deracination. The Absurdist approach at first seemed to me to be celebrating the impotence of human hopes, even the futility of action itself. All but the flimsiest connectiveness between utterances was eventually eliminated, creating an atmosphere of sinister danger (in Pinter) or (in Beckett) the threatening sense of immanence familiar from bad dreams. Man was unique because he tripped over himself, and it was quite as though the emphatic absence of purpose in the characters had created a loss of syntax. I take it that in later years Beckett took pains to clarify this impression of human futility, emphasizing the struggle against inertia as his theme. In any case, however ridiculous so much of his dialogue is, the tenderness of feeling in his work is emphatically not that of the cynic or the hard ironist.

Beckett fused style and meaning organically, the dominating theme of *Godot* being stasis and the struggle to overcome humanity's endlessly repetitious paralysis before the need to act and change.

We hear this theme as blatantly as a train announcement and as stripped clean as a bleached bone.

ESTRAGON: Then adieu.
POZZO: Adieu.
VLADIMIR: Adieu.
POZZO: Adieu.
VLADIMIR: Adieu.
POZZO: Adieu.
ESTRAGON: Adieu.
Silence.
POZZO: And thank you.
VLADIMIR: Thank *YOU*.
POZZO: Not at all.
ESTRAGON: Yes yes.
POZZO: No no.
VLADIMIR: Yes yes.
ESTRAGON: No no.
Silence.
POZZO: I don't seem to be able . . . (*long hesitation*) . . . to depart.
ESTRAGON: Such is life.

This is a vaudeville at the edge of the cliff, but vaudeville anyway, so I may be forgiven for being reminded of Jimmy Durante's ditty—"Didja ever get the feelin' that you wanted to go? But you wanted to stay? But you wanted to go?" Here is a language shorn of metaphor, simile, everything but its instructions, so the listener may hear the theme like a nail drawn across a pane of glass. *Godot* does not make the mistake of so many of its imitators; in its flight from realism it does not leave structure behind.

My own tendency has been to shift styles according to the nature of my subject. *All My Sons, The Crucible, A View from the Bridge, Death of a Salesman, The Price, The American Clock*, my earliest work like *The Golden Years*, about the destruction of Mexico by the Spaniards, and the more recent plays like *The Creation of the World, Some Kind of Love Story, The Last Yankee*, and *Broken Glass* all differ greatly in their language. I have done this in order to find speech that springs naturally out of the characters and their backgrounds rather than imposing a general style. If my approach to playwriting is partly literary, I hope it is well hidden.

It is necessary to employ the artificial in order to arrive at the real. More than one actor in my plays has told me that it is surprisingly difficult to memorize their dialogue. The speeches sound like real, almost reported talk when in fact they are intensely composed, compressed into a sequential inevitability that seems natural but isn't. But all this, important though it may be, is slightly to one side of the point. Experimental or traditional, the real question to ask of a work is whether it brings news, something truly felt by its author, an invention on his part or an echo.

The struggle with what might be called reportorial realism, written "the way people talk," is at least as old as the century. And although realism can land us further from common reality than can the most fantastic caprice, in the end stylization in the theater will be justified not by its novelty—at least not for long—but by the degree to which it illuminates how life works in our time. How a thing is said is only as new as what it is saying. The proof of this is the deep pile of experimental plays of two, three, five, ten years ago, which can only be appreciated anymore by the scholar-specialist. It is a pile, incidentally, no smaller than the one for so many conventionally realistic plays of the same era. Finding truth is no easier now when we are totally free to use any stylistic means at hand than it was a century or half a century ago, when a play had to be "real" to be read at all and had to make sense to sensible people.

Call it a question of personal taste rather than principle, but I think that in theater work there is an optimum balance between two kinds of approaches: One is the traditional attempt to fill characters with acknowledged emotion, "as in life." The other is in effect to evacuate emotion from characters, merely referring to their subjective life rather than acting it out, the so-called camp style. In his speculative prose, Brecht, for one, called for such a drying-out of script and acting, but except in his most agitprop and forgettable plays he failed or declined to practice this method. The strict containment not of emotion but of emotionalism is the hallmark of the Greek tragic plays, of Molière and Racine and the

Japanese Noh plays, whereas Shakespeare, it seems to me, is the balance, the fusion of idea and feeling. In short, it is by no means the abstracting of emotion I dislike; it is the lack of feeling and the substitution of fashionably alienated ironies in its place.

There has been a plethora of plays in recent years whose claim to modernity is based on indicated rather than felt emotion. The assumption, I suppose, is that this *sec* quality lends a play an intellectuality it may or may not have earned and in any case rescues it from the banality of work aimed at the audience's belly rather than its head. The big devil to be avoided is sentimentality, emotion unearned.

Theater, like politics, is always the art of the possible. And when economics makes it impossible to employ more than four or five actors in a single unchanging set, when competition for actors by TV and films prevents them from maturing in theater work, when the cost of advertising makes it effectively impossible for a play to survive without nearly unanimous critical praise, it seems to me a shame to dismiss a play that is not camp simply because it moves an audience. Can't it be art if it moves people? If the pun can be pardoned, man lives not by head alone, and the balance between the two modes, one aimed at the mind and one the flesh, as it were, is what will interpret life more fully. After all, at least part of what we ask of a modern play is to show us what life now *feels* like.

Ultimately, every assault on the human mystery falls back to the ground, changing little, but the flight of the arrow continues claiming our attention over a longer time when its direction is toward the castle of reality rather than the wayward air.

Subsidized Theatre
1947/2000

The commercial system of theatrical production in New York is some two centuries old. In contrast, theatre has been carried on in various parts of the West for a couple of thousand years but under very different production circumstances. The New York system is thus a sport, something created to reflect a vibrant capitalism with its joy in risk-taking and the excitement of the win-all-or-lose-all rodeo. We have arrived—in New York—at the expiration time of that theatrical way of life as far as straight plays are concerned. The system no longer works for non-musical theatre and hasn't in years. The time has come to consider alternatives.

I have sometimes wondered if there ever was what one could call a "healthy" theatrical circumstance. The classical Greek situation, turning out one masterpiece after another, usually appears to us as serene, like some great ship cruising stormy seas unperturbed by the tons of water crashing down on its decks. But then one recalls stories of the *choreaqi*, the men of wealth chosen for the honor of paying the bills for the chorus, who tried as best they could to duck the distinction. And to read almost any twenty pages of Aristophanes is to sense the backbiting and posturing and nastiness surrounding Greek theatre. Much the same mess seems to have prevailed in Elizabethan times, and Molière's, Strindberg's, Chekhov's, Shaw's, O'Casey's, just as in our own.

Theatre production these days is a problem with not even an acceptable definition let alone a solution. The theatre owner will tell you that it is simply that costs are too high even as he takes fifty-two percent of the gross. Nor is the stagehand or author or actor likely to look to himself for the source of the difficulty. All one can say is that the play that cost less than forty thousand to produce a generation ago now comes in at a million and a half or even two million and rising, the price of a ticket soaring from four or six dollars to seventy-five and up. It is a system which has almost literally eaten its own body alive.

In the belly of the beast, as always, is the money and the conflicts it breeds. Where the state finances production, as it partially does in England and other parts of the world, its built-in urge to censor has to be curbed; where private investment does so, it is greed that must be bridled lest it lead down into the swamp of theatrical triviality where the great mass of the public is alleged to live and hence the promise of the biggest returns. Theatre is born to trouble as the sparks fly upward, but we are in more than trouble now and an altogether new spirit will have to infuse those interested in changing—perhaps saving is the word—the production of plays on a professional level.

Amid the gratitude, which I share, for the annual arrival of fine British plays on and off Broadway, it is useful to remember that every one of them, practically with no exceptions, came out of subsidized theatres. It is not possible to imagine that a Pinter, a Stoppard, a Hare, a Frayn, would have been nurtured in London's commercial West End. They are all too chancey and their audiences admittedly too limited to warrant investment-for-profit. The British public, in short, has been financing a significant part of New York's theatre for a long time now.

The minds of probably most American politicians—and even some critics and editorialists—seem to curdle at the idea of subsidizing any art, least of all theatre. To them, subsidized theatre seems to imply a crutch to help hold erect failed artists who can't make it in the tough, Darwinian for-profit arena. After all, a good number of people have gotten rich on doing theatre work, why can't these mendicants? And besides, isn't theatre attendance on Broadway higher than ever? And if almost all the increase has gone to musicals, then so be it—the public has decided it doesn't want straight plays. The system operates like any other market and if one can't manage on its terms maybe he ought to give up and go into another line of work.

With the richest theatre in America unable to produce a single new straight play season after season, leaving only a very occasional revival on the boards in that category, one is given the reason as being the failure of playwrights who somehow have forgotten how to do the job. That hundreds, thousands of plays are written in this country every year, without a single one good enough for professional production in our greatest entertainment city, is nothing short of a statistical marvel. So extreme is the situation that one is driven to drastic explanations; is it possible, one wonders, that this generation of New York producers, who will travel to England or even Australia to sign up a new hit play, are not competent to read and judge a script but only its reviews, or by having sat in the midst of a laughing or weeping audience to decide to reach for their contracts? I find this illiteracy far more likely than the idea that the playwriting art has simply gone to earth forever in a United States of two hundred and fifty million souls.

For reasons I can't pretend to understand, there are never more than a handful of playwrights in any age. Poets, novelists, essayists show up in numbers, but playwrights come in two's and three's. We presently have many more than this handful but the most commercialized theatre in the world has no place for them. Can it be that the commercial organization of professional theatre is, in fact, preventing the flowering of theatre, most especially in New York, where theatre is so important to the economy as well as the spirit of the place?

But why bother even to complain about the Broadway theatre when it is clearly so artistically bankrupt where production of original straight plays is concerned? There are good reasons for caring, most of them forgotten. In the two- or three-hundred seat off-Broadway theatre, whatever its charm, it is next to impossible to produce plays with casts larger than half a dozen, not to mention those requiring multiple sets. Thus, the esthetic of playwriting itself is affected by this total commercialization, and playwriting becomes of necessity a constricted technique. I do not believe that, for example, most of my own plays would have found production on today's Broadway, and what would one do with *The Crucible* on a shoebox stage with its twenty-one characters and several sets? I don't think *Salesman* would have been produced by the present breed of Broadway producers because it is too sad—and in fact even in 1949 there was pressure to find a more upbeat title, the producer actually paying to poll theatre audiences asking if they'd like to see a play called *Death of a Salesman*. Practically none, quite naturally, said they would. Off-Broadway has its uses but creating plays of breadth and physical size is not one of them. Broadway theatres, on the other hand, once welcomed plays of size, which of course is not to deny that in any age the producer's dream is a very funny play with a cast of two in one set.

As things stand now, it is almost impossible to imagine an actor making a lifelong career acting in the theatre. The off-Broadway theatre is basically subsidized by people without families to support, its young underpaid actors whose eye is really on television or films, not theatre. Much is made of the great British actors, but almost without exception the Oliviers, Richardsons, Gielguds, Gambons, Guinnesses came out of subsidized theatres where they developed their craft in great roles in classic plays. There is no play in New York where anything like this kind of muscle building is possible. We have wonderfully talented actors who do incredible things in the three- or four-week rehearsal period normally allowed them, but if a bottom-line theatre, which is what we have, cannot afford longer rehearsals it doesn't justify making a virtue of our deprivation.

If we have theatres, we don't have Theatre, which is not real estate but a collection of people of talent whose main interest and devotion is the creation of something beautiful. This is difficult to discuss because it is basically about an atmosphere. Playwrights as different as Clifford Odets and Eugene O'Neill have hated the absolute commercialization of New York theatre, and it is hard to think of any artist who has loved it, including some who have made fortunes out of it. My own impression is that the atmosphere has in some ways degenerated even further than when the earlier generation complained of it. Perhaps it is the immensity of the investment required now, but where there was once a certain comity between producer and artist, a certain collaborative equality between people with different but complimentary functions, it seems now like merely one more employer-employee relationship. A real power shift seems to be taking place. Producers speak now of having "given" a production to an author, quite as though profit-making were not at all involved in driving the deal but the generosity and largesse of one who is not only the holder of a lease on a theatre building but the proprietor of the art itself. There is some dangerous, if superficial, logic in this; the businessman is always around but the author, director, and actors vanish sometimes for years before they show up again with a new play and new roles. So that the illusion can easily grow that the business of theatre is business, and the art rather incidental. Indeed, the pressure is actually on now by certain producers to junk the traditional royalty arrangements with authors, who of course have for several generations retained ownership and control of their scripts, and to replace it with the producer's taking over if not actual ownership then the right to make any script changes he desires. Some think we are moving into the Hollywood system, where the producer buys or commissions scripts and the author moves down to the bottom of the totem pole, without control or contractual rights once he is paid. Indeed, the Hollywood system sprang from the old Broadway practice of producers buying plays and even attaching their names to them as authors, as the famed John Golden did for many a year before the Dramatists Guild was organized to protect writers.

Broadway has been pronounced dead too many times for me to do so again, but one thing is new—its impotence before the challenge to produce new plays. It is now a secondhand merchandiser of plays from abroad or, on occasion, one of the off-Broadway theatres. That there is an audience there can be no question—the success of revivals of famous, proven works over the past decade has shown that a sizable number of people want to see straight plays on Broadway. It is the production system that has broken. It needs replacement by a new, broader vision, a rededication to essentials— the writer, the director, the actor, the audience. Whoever can bring these elements together deserves praise and gratitude, but excepting for occasional flukes, the risks have clearly grown too great now for private capital alone to manage anymore. Something not particularly novel, of course, but rather as old as theatre itself awaits us—at least partial subsidization of production by either private or public funds or a mixture of both.

Having worked in two great state-subsidized theatres—in China and Sweden, where I directed *Death of a Salesman*—I can testify to some of their failings as well as their virtues. Inevitably, their worst problem, I think, is bureaucracy. People nestle into state jobs and can't be blasted out of them regardless of competency or even sobriety. (In Stockholm I had two drunks operating a hidden platform on my *Salesman* set, and on their cue to lower a bed they were found in the basement playing a bleary, oblivious card game. As union men they could not be fired, but one of them felt he had so humiliated himself that he resigned his position.) It is hard to see any ready solution to this dilemma. But friction arises with anything that moves, and these theatres are nevertheless often capable of work far beyond what any New York theatre can presently contemplate. Ingmar Bergman's *Peer Gynt* and the *Teahouse* of the Beijing People's Art Theatre, which I happened to see, were of a conceptual grandeur, a lyricism and exactitude of acting that simply cannot be achieved in our hit-and-run, semihysterical production process. They were reminders once again that every play of the European masters of the nineteenth and twentieth centuries has come out of subsidized theatres. From Brecht to Strindberg and Ibsen and reaching back to Shakespeare and the Greeks, there was a partial or complete state subsidy or, as in Elizabethan times, a noble patronage supporting the art.

But there may not necessarily be one single solution to the problem. It has to be said that in our hazardous, high-stakes gambling house called Broadway the thrill of the dice throw can be exhilarating, and in times past when productions did not yet bear killing costs the flow of new American plays was greatly admired by theatre folk in other countries. But that was then and this is now.

My own experience indicates that the best system is most probably a mixed one, with the private commercial theatre coexisting with the subsidized one. Their functions may often overlap but in general the private theatre would most likely offer entertainment while the other would be free to pursue its more difficult theatrical dreams.

The subsidized theatre can indeed settle into an institutionalized stupor if allowed to drift that way, but the British, for one, have shown that it need not, or at least not for long. In any case, if there are other alternatives than I have named to the present system, let them be heard and debated.

Theatre is not going to die. To paraphrase Carl Sandburg, there will always be the young strangers, people desperate to act, to interpret what they have seen, and now and again a writer gathering stray beams of light into a flaming focal point. Most of these now dream of the filmic media, but some of that attraction is due to the present theatre system which ignores or repels the young rather than working to open itself to them. Whole generations have passed now which have gone through the taste-forming years of youth without having seen a play, but only film. Would people want music who have never heard music? A responsible subsidized theatre would, as it does elsewhere, open the world of plays to students. If it was always at bottom an entertainment machine devised to make money and fame for a few, commercial production nevertheless did keep open a certain space for writers, directors, and actors with serious intentions and visions of a world they passionately wished to make real. No more. That whole developmental function has simply been passed along to off-Broadway and academia while commercial Broadway waits to skim off some floating drops of cream.

✑

About Theater Language:
Afterword to *The Last Yankee*
1994

I

When I began writing plays in the late thirties, something called realism was the undisputed reigning style in the American commercial theater—which was just about all the theater there was in this country. The same was more or less the case in Britain. If not a mass art, theater then could still be thought of at least as a popular one, although everyone knew—long before television—that something of its common appeal had gone out of it, and a lot of its twenties' glamor, too. One blamed the movies, which had stolen so much of the audience and thus theater's old dominance as a cultural influence. Notwithstanding the obvious fact that the audience was predominantly middle class, we continued to imagine that we were making plays for people of many different educational and cultural levels, a representative variety of the city and even the country. If this was never really true, there was certainly no thought of appealing to a clique of college graduates or to academics and their standards. A *New York Times* critic like George S. Kaufman had both feet in show business and became the most popular writer of comedies of the period, while Brooks Atkinson may have had one eye on Aristotle but understood that his readers were Americans impatient with any theatrical enterprise that required either education or patience. Outside New York there were at least the remains of the twenties' touring wheel, theaters in many smaller cities regularly attended by quite ordinary citizens eager for last year's Broadway hits, albeit with replacement casts. In New York, with a ticket price of 55 cents to four dollars and forty cents, one somehow took for granted that a professor might be sitting next to a housewife, a priest beside a skilled worker or perhaps a grammar-school teacher, a small or large business executive beside a student. This conception of the demotic audience, accurate or not, influenced the writing of plays directed at the commonsensical experience of everyday people. Missing were black or Asian or Hispanic faces, of course, but they were beyond the consciousness of the prevailing culture. As for production costs, even into the forties they were within reason; plays like *All My Sons* or *Death of a Salesman*, for example, cost between twenty and forty thousand to produce, a budget small enough to be raised by half a dozen modest contributors, who might lose all, with some embarrassment but reasonably little pain, or make a killing.

Radicals—people like myself, trying to convince ourselves that we were carrying on the age-old tradition of theater as a civic art rather than a purely commercial one—were in a conflict; to attract even the fitful interest of a Broadway producer, and subsequently to engage the audience, we had to bow to realism, even if the poetic forms were what we really admired or at least wished to explore. An Expressionist like the German Ernst Toller, for example, would not have been read past his sixth page by a Broadway producer or, for that matter, one in London. Among the playwrights one thinks of as important, not one was—or is now—welcome in the commercial theater. Not Chekhov, not Ibsen, not Hauptmann, not Pirandello, Strindberg, Turgenev—not even Shaw. To so much as think of performing a Beckett play like *Waiting for Godot* in the general proximity of Broadway a cast of movie stars and a short run are essential—Lincoln Center pulled it off in 1988—and things were probably a bit worse half a century ago. One need only read O'Neill's letters of complaint at the "showshop" of Broadway and the narrow compass of the American audience's imagination—or in Britain, Shaw's ridicule of his countrymen's provincialism—to understand the problem; for some mysterious reason the Anglo-Saxon culture regarded theater as an entertainment first and last, an art of escape with none of the Continental or Russian interest in moral and philosophical opportunities or obligations. Very occa-

sionally in America there was an *Adding Machine* by the young
Elmer Rice, but such a breakout from conventional realism was
rare enough to be brought up in conversation for years after, like a
calf born with five legs. The English-language theater was pridefully commercial, a profit-making enterprise which wed it to a form
whose surfaces of familiar reality would be universally recognized.
Captain Shotover's outcry, "I like to know where I am!" could have
been sewn to the flag of this theater. Only musicals had the happy
license to stretch reality, at least to some extent. But for straight
plays, even satire was too strange to prosper; George Kaufman
defined satire as what closes on Saturday night.

The point here is that what we think of as "straight realism" was
tiresome half a century ago, indeed longer ago than that, but it was
accepted by the audiences and almost all the reviewers as a reflection of life. Nonetheless, it should be remembered that realism has
emerged at various moments to very capably express the essence of
an era. At a time when "experimental" is all the virtue a play needs
in order to gain serious consideration, it is not a bad idea to confess
that an extraordinarily few such researches have achieved any kind
of enduring life. It is not quite enough to know how to escape; one
has also to think of arriving somewhere.

In the thirties, probably the single exception—at least that I was
aware of—to realism's domination was the WPA's *Living Newspaper*, the one formal innovation of American theater. An epic in
more or less presentational form, written like movies by groups of
writers, rather than individually, it dealt in an overtly exuberant
spirit with social issues like public ownership of electrical power,
labor unions, agriculture, and medicine, and was extremely popular. Significantly, the WPA was government-subsidized, and did not
have to make a profit. Using unemployed actors, designers, technicians, a show could call upon large casts and elaborate scenery and
production elements. And the ticket was low-priced. The WPA
could send Orson Welles, for example, into Harlem storefronts
with a big cast playing *Doctor Faustus*, charging a quarter a seat.
But theater-for-profit was hardly affected by what might be called
this epic-populist approach—it was simply too expensive to produce.

I mention these mundane matters because they profoundly affect style in the theater, which, like politics, is always the art of the possible.

There were at least a dozen playwrights regularly feeding the commercial theater in the years before World War II, and all but perhaps Odets and Hellman would have pridefully declared that their sole purpose was to entertain. Those playwrights were sophisticated and no doubt knew all about the Continental theater tradition, and its aspiring to the philosophical condition, something like that of the Greeks or, in a different way, the Elizabethans. The Theater Guild, for one, had been started in the twenties in part to bring that kind of theater to America, the theater of Pirandello, Schnitzler, Ibsen, and Strindberg.

In the thirties, one American styled himself a political revolutionary, and that was Clifford Odets. O'Neill, of course, had been the aesthetic rebel but his socialism was private rather than informing his plays, although *The Hairy Ape* is surely an anticapitalist work. It was his formal experiments and tragic mood that set him apart. O'Neill was a totally isolated phenomenon in the Broadway theater as a maker and user of new and old theatrical forms.

Odets, on the other hand, while describing himself as "a man of the Left," was, with the possible exception of his first play, *Waiting for Lefty*, no innovator where form was concerned. He attempted a poetic realism but it was still trying to represent real people in actual social relationships. And this was perhaps inevitable given his actor's temperament as well as his Marxist commitment; he had the revolutionary's eye on the great public, on the reconstitution of power once a failed capitalism had been brought down—for such was the Marxist and non-Marxist Left position on the proper moral obligation of the artist. But by temperament he was a poet seeking words that would lift him into a takeoff, regardless of his realist political commitments. O'Neill, on the other hand, was not the revolutionary but the rebel with a despairing anarchism in his heart. If he glimpsed any salvation, it was not to arrive in a more benign reconstitution of political power but in the tragic cleansing of the life-lie permanently ensconced in the human condition. Since he took no responsibility in theory for a new and better policy to take the place of the corrupted present one, he was free to explore all sorts of theatrical means by which to set forth the situation of the damned. Moreover, if O'Neill wanted his plays to register, and he surely did, they need not be popular to justify his having written them, for he was hunting the sounding whale of ultimate meaning, and he expected to suffer for it; oppositely, a critical or box-office failure for Odets meant rejection of a very personal kind, a spit in the eye by an ungrateful, self-satisfied bourgeois society. A failed play for Odets was a denial of what he was owed, for he was chasing the public no differently from his bourgeois nonrevolutionary contemporaries. O'Neill could say, and he did, that he was not interested in relations between men, but between Man and God. For America, in his view, was damned and if there were a few individuals who behaved justly and well, it was not because they belonged to a particular social class or held a generous or unselfish political viewpoint, but by virtue of a grace whose source is beyond definition.

II

The realism of Broadway—and the Strand and the Boulevard theater of France—was detested by the would-be poetic dramatists of my generation, just as it had always been since it came into vogue in the nineteenth century. What did this realism really come down to? A play representing real rather than symbolic or metaphysical persons and situations, its main virtue verisimilitude, with no revolutionary implications for society or even a symbolic statement of some general truth. Quite simply, conventional realism was conventional because it implicitly supported the conventions of society, but it could just as easily do something quite different, or so it seemed to me. Nevertheless, we thought it the perfect style for an unchallenging, simpleminded, linear middle-class conformist view of life. What I found confusing at the time, however, was that not so very long before, the name "realism" had been applied to the revolutionary style of playwrights like Ibsen, Chekhov, and quite frequently Strindberg, writers whose thrust was in opposition to the bourgeois status quo and the hypocrisies on which it stood, or, in Chekhov's case, the futilities of the Czarist system.

My own first playwriting attempt was purely mimetic, a realistic play about my own family. It won me some prizes and productions, but, interestingly, I turned at once to a stylized treatment of life in a gigantic prison, modeled on Jackson State Penitentiary in Michigan—near Ann Arbor, where I was in school—the largest prison in the United States, which I had visited over weekends with a friend who was its lone psychologist. The theme of that play was that prisons existed to make desperate workingmen insane. There was a chorus of sane prisoners chanting from a high overpass above the stage, and a counterchorus of the insane trying to draw the other into their ranks. It was inevitable that I had to confront the problem of dramatic language, for it was impossible to engage so vast a human disaster with speech born in a warm kitchen. I gradually came to wonder if the essential pressure toward poetic dramatic language—if not of stylization itself—came from the inclusion of society as a major element in the play's story or vision. Manifestly, prose realism was the language of the individual and private life, poetry the language of man in crowds, in society. Put another way, prose is the language of family relations; it is the inclusion of the larger world beyond that naturally opens a play to the poetic.

But I wanted to succeed, I wanted to emerge and grip an audience. Minds might be illuminated by speeches thrown at them but it was by being moved that one was changed. And so the problem was that our audiences were trained, as it were, in a pawky realism and were turned off by stylistic novelty, by "art." How to find a style that would at one and the same time deeply engage an American audience, which insisted on a recognizable reality of characters, locales, and themes, while opening the stage to considerations of public morality and the mythic social fates—in short, the invisible?

Of course, this was not my preoccupation alone. I doubt there was ever a time when there was so much discussion about form and style. T. S. Eliot was writing his verse plays, and Auden and Isherwood theirs; the poetic mimesis of Sean O'Casey was most popular; and W. B. Yeats's dialogue was studied, if not very often produced. The impulse to poetry reached into the ex-newspaperman and realistic writer Maxwell Anderson, whose attempts to imitate Elizabethan prosody with contemporary characters and social themes were widely celebrated, as curious by some, as moving experiences by others.

To be just to Odets, it was he who challenged the Broadway theater's addiction to verisimilitude by his idiosyncratic dialogue. And he was surely the first American playwright to be celebrated—and more wildly and lavishly than any other before him—for his writing style. For younger writers such as myself, Odets for a couple of years was the trailblazer; he was bringing the suffering of the Great Depression onto the Broadway stage and making audiences listen. If he had not solved the problem of a contemporary American style, he had dared to invent an often wildly stylized stage speech. But I suppose that since his characters lacked elegance or strangeness, were, in fact, the very exemplars of realistic theater, Odets was called a realist—indeed, a kind of reporter of Jewish life in the Bronx. I may not have lived in the Bronx but the speech of Brooklyn Jews certainly bore no resemblance to that of Odets's characters.

> CARP [in *Golden Boy*]: I'm superdisgusted with you! . . . A man hits his wife and it's the first step to fascism! Look in the papers! On every side the clouds of war! . . . Ask yourself a pertinent remark; could a boy make a living playing this instrument [a violin] in our competitive civilization today?
> ROXY: I think I'll run across the street and pick up an eight-cylinder sandwich.

The audiences roared with delight at these inventions. It was as though Odets were trying to turn dialogue into jazz. And his devotees went to his plays especially to pick up his latest deliciously improbable remarks and repeat them to their friends. Had any Bronxite—or anyone else in the century—really exclaimed, "God's teeth, no!" "What exhaust pipe did he crawl out of?" Lorna: "I feel like I'm shot from a cannon."

Inevitably, in a theater bounded by realism, this had to be mistakenly labeled as accurate reportage, news from the netherworld. But, of course, it was an invented diction of a kind never heard before on stage—or off, for that matter. Odets's fervent ambition was to burst the bounds of Broadway while remaining inside its embrace, and if, as time went on, his lines began to seem self-consciously labored, no longer springing from characters but manifestly from the author and his will-to-poeticize, he at a minimum had made language the identifying mark of a playwright in America, and that was something that hadn't happened before.

Admittedly, I did not look at his style with objectivity but for its potential usefulness in breaking through the constricted realism of our theater then. Odets was tremendously exciting to young writers. I was troubled by a tendency in his plays toward overtheatricalized excess, however—lines sometimes brought laughter where there should have been outrage, or pity, or some deeper emotion than amusement—and at times the plots verged on the schematic. Odets often overrhapsodized at the climaxes when he should have been reaching to ancillary material that was not there. He wrote terrific scenes, blazing speeches and confrontations which showed what theater could be, but with the exception, perhaps, of *Awake and Sing* and the racy *Golden Boy* he never wrote a play that lifted inexorably to its climatic revelation.

I came out of the thirties unsure whether there could be a viable counterform to the realism around me. All I knew for sure was that a good play must move forward in its depths as rapidly as on its surfaces; word-poetry wasn't enough if there was a fractured poetry in the structure, the gradually revealed illuminating idea behind the whole thing. A real play was the discovery of the unity of its contradictions; the essential poetry was the synthesis of even the least of its parts to form a symbolic meaning. Of course, the problem had much to do with language but more primary was how to penetrate my own feelings about myself and the time in which I lived. Ideally, a good play must show as sound an emotional proof of its thesis as a case at law shows factual proof, and you can't do that with words alone, lovely as they might be.

Odets's contribution, ironically was not his realistic portrayal of society—his alleged aim—but his willingness to be artificial; he brought back artificiality, if you will, just as ten years later Tennessee Williams did with his birdsong from the magnolias. But Williams had an advantage—his language could be far more faithful to its sources in reality. Southern people did love to talk, and in the accents Williams captured (as in *The Glass Menagerie*):

AMANDA: . . . But Laura is, thank heavens, not only pretty but also very domestic. I'm not at all. I never was a bit. I never could make a thing but angel-food cake. Well, in the South we had so many servants. Gone, gone, gone. All vestige of gracious living! Gone completely! I wasn't prepared for what the future brought me. All by gentlemen callers were sons of planters and so of course I assumed that I would be married to one and raise my family on a large piece of land with plenty of servants. But man proposes—and woman accepts the proposal!—To vary that old, old saying a little bit—I married no planter! I married a man who worked for the telephone company!—That gallantly smiling gentleman over there! (*Points to husband's picture.*) A telephone man who—fell in love with long distance! Now he travels and I don't even know where! . . .

This too was called realism, and it probably was in the sense that there were people who talked like this. But then how did it differ from the conventional realistic play? Clearly, it was that the very action of Williams's plays, certainly the best of them, was working toward the building of symbolic meaning that would embrace both the psychological development of his characters and his personal specter of a menacing America struggling with its own sexuality and the anomie born of its dire materialism. In a word, Williams's style arose from his pain and anxiety at being overwhelmed and defeated by a gross violence that underlay the American—one might say the whole Western—ethos.

Their obsession with words notwithstanding, it was their need to communicate their resistance to something deathdealing in the culture that finally pressed Odets and Williams to address the big public and made them playwrights rather than sequestered poets. Stylistic invention without an implicit commitment of some kind to a more human vision of life is a boat without rudder or cargo or destination—or worse, it is the occupation of the dilettante. Odets, when he began, thought his egalitarian Marxism would heal America and create its new community, but that ideology devolved into a rote religion before the thirties had even passed. Williams unfurled the banner of a forlorn but resisting heroism to the violence against the oddball, the poet, and sexual dissident. But it may as well be admitted that in their different ways both men in the end unwittingly collaborated with the monster they saw as trying to destroy them.

The plays these men wrote were shields raised against the many-arrowed darkness, but in the end there was little from outside to give them the spiritual support to complete their creative lives. Odets's best work ended with his rejection by Broadway and his move to Hollywood; Williams, likewise rejected, kept nevertheless to his trade, experimenting with forms and new methods that drew no encouragement from reviewers unable or unwilling to notice that the theater culture had boxed in a writer of greatness who was struggling to find an audience in the passing crowd of a generation other than his own. At his strongest he had spoken for and to the center of society, in a style it could relate to, an enhanced, visionary realism. In the end a writer has no one to blame for his failings, not even himself, but the brutally dismissive glee of critics toward Williams's last plays simply laid more sticks on his burden. Toward the end he was still outside, scratching on the glass, as he had once put it, and it was the shadowed edges of life that drew him, the borderland where how things are said is everything, and everything has been said before.

The advent of the Absurd and of Beckett and his followers both obscured and illuminated the traditional elements of the discussion of theater style. For O'Neill a good style was basically a question of the apt use of metaphor and argot. "God, if I could write like that!" he wrote to O'Casey, who, incidentally, would no doubt have labeled himself a realistic writer in the sense that he was giving his audiences the substance of their life conflicts. But like Williams, O'Casey came from a culture which loved talk and sucked on language like a sweet candy.

> MRS. GROGAN: Oh, you've got a cold on you, Fluther.
> FLUTHER: Oh, it's only a little one.
> MRS. GROGAN: You'd want to be careful, all th' same. I knew a woman, a big lump of a woman, red-faced and round-bodied, a little awkward on her feet; you'd think, to look at her, she could put out her two arms an' lift a two-storied house on th' top of her head; got a ticklin' in her throat, an' a little cough, an' th' next mornin' she

had a little catchin' in her chest, an' they had just time to wet her
lips with a little rum, an' off she went. (*Juno and the Paycock*)

Even in the most mundane of conversational exchanges O'Casey
sought, and as often as not found, the lift of poetry. Indeed, that
was the whole point—that the significantly poetic sprang from the
raw and real experience of ordinary people. J. M. Synge, O'Casey's
forerunner at the turn of the century, had struck a similar chord;
Synge was in a supremely conscious revolt against the banality of
most theater language. As John Gassner noted, in Ireland the popular imagination was still, according to Synge, "fiery and magnificent, and tender; so that those of us who wish to write start with a
chance that is not given to writers in places where the springtime of
local life has been forgotten, and the harvest is a memory only, and
the straw has been turned into bricks."

Synge rejected the then-dominant Ibsen and Zola for the "joyless
and pallid words" of their realism and as in *Riders to the Sea*, when
the women are lamenting the deaths of so many of their men working the angry sea:

MAURYA: In the big world the old people do be leaving things after
them for their sons and children, but in this place it is the young
men do be leaving things behind for them that do be old.

As far as style is concerned, the Beckett difference, as it might be
called, was to introduce humble people—bums, in fact, or social
sufferers—with the plainest of language, but arranged so as to
announce and develop pure theme. His could be called a presentational thematic play, announcing what it was about and never straying very far from what it was conceived of to prove, or what his
instinct had led him to confirm. Beckett had parted with inferential
playwriting, where speeches inferred the author's thematic intentions while hewing to an apparently autonomous story building to a
revelatory climax that united story and theme. In Beckett the story
was the theme, inseparably so. Moreover, as will be shown in a
moment, he interpreted the theme himself in his dialogue.

If—instead of the prewar poetic drama's requirement of an

elevated tone or diction—the most common speech was now prized, it was not the speech of realistic plays. It was a speech skewed almost out of recognition by a surreal commitment to what at first had seemed to be the impotence of human hopes, and hence the futility of action itself. All but the flimsiest connections between speeches were eliminated, creating an atmosphere of sinister danger (in Pinter) or immanence (in Beckett). It was quite as though the emphatic absence of purpose in the characters had created a loss of syntax. It seems that in later years Beckett took pains to clarify this impression of human futility, emphasizing the struggle *against* inertia as his theme. In any case, however ridiculous so much of his dialogue exchanges are, the tenderness of feeling in his work is emphatically not that of the cynic or the hard ironist.

The dominating theme of *Godot* is stasis and the struggle to overcome humanity's endlessly repetitious paralysis before the need to act and change. We hear it plainly and stripped clean of plot or even incident.

ESTRAGON: Then adieu.
POZZO: Adieu.
VLADIMIR: Adieu.
POZZO: Adieu.
Silence. No one moves.
VLADIMIR: Adieu.
POZZO: Adieu.
ESTRAGON: Adieu.
Silence.
POZZO: And thank you.
VLADIMIR: Thank *you.*
POZZO: Not at all.
ESTRAGON: Yes yes.
POZZO: No no.
VLADIMIR: Yes yes.
ESTRAGON: No no.
Silence.
POZZO: I don't seem to be able . . . (*long hesitation*) . . . to depart.
ESTRAGON: Such is life.

This is a vaudeville at the edge of the cliff, but vaudeville anyway, so I may be forgiven for being reminded of Jimmy Durante's ditty—"Didja ever get the feelin' that you wanted to go? But still you had the feelin' that you wanted to stay?"

It is a language shorn of metaphor, simile, everything but its instructions, so to speak. The listener hears the theme like a nail drawn across a pane of glass.

So the struggle with what might be called reportorial realism, written "the way people talk," is at least as old as the century. As for myself, my own tendency has been to shift styles according to the nature of my subject. *All My Sons, The Crucible, A View from the Bridge, Death of a Salesman, The Price, The American Clock*, my earliest work, like *The Golden Years*, about the destruction of Mexico by the Spaniards, and the more recent plays, like *The Creation of the World, Some Kind of Love Story*, and *The Last Yankee*, differ very much in their language. This, in order to find speech that springs naturally out of the characters and their backgrounds rather than imposing a general style. If my approach to playwriting is partly literary, I hope it is well hidden. Leroy Hamilton is a native New England carpenter and speaks like one, and not like the New York working men and women in *A Memory of Two Mondays*, or Eddie Carbone, who comes out of a quite different culture.

So the embrace of something called realism is obviously very wide; it can span the distance between a Turgenev and a Becque, between Wedekind and your latest Broadway hit. The main thing I sought in *The Last Yankee* was to make real my sense of the life of such people, the kind of man swinging the hammer through a lifetime, the kind of woman waiting forever for her ship to come in. And second, my view of their present confusion and, if you will, decay and possible recovery. They are bedrock, aspiring not to greatness but to other gratifications— successful parenthood, decent children and a decent house and a decent car and an occasional nice evening with family or friends, and above all, of course, some financial security. Needless to say, they are people who can be inspired to great and noble sacrifice, but also to bitter hatreds. As the world goes I suppose they are the luckiest people, but some of them—a great many, in fact—have grown ill with what would once have been called a sickness of the soul.

And that is the subject of the play, its "matter." For depression is far from being merely a question of an individual's illness, although it appears as that, of course; it is at the same time, most especially in Patricia Hamilton's case, the grip on her of a success mythology which is both naïve and brutal, and which, to her misfortune, she has made her own. And opposing it, quite simply, is her husband Leroy's incredibly enduring love for her, for nature and the world.

A conventionally realistic play would no doubt have attempted to create a "just-like-life" effect, with the sickness gradually rising out of the normal routines of the family's life, and calling up our empathy by virtue of our instant identification with familiar reality. But while Patricia Hamilton, the carpenter's wife, is seen as an individual sufferer, the context of her illness is equally important because, for one thing, she knows, as do many such patients, that more Americans (and West Europeans) are in hospitals for depression than for any other ailment. In life, with such people, a high degree of objectification or distancing exists, and the style of the play had to reflect the fact that they commonly know a great deal about the social setting of the illness even as they are unable to tear themselves free of it. And this affects the play's style.

It opens by directly, even crudely, grasping the core of its central preoccupation—the moral and social myths feeding the disease; and we have a discussion of the hospital's enormous parking lot, a conversation bordering on the absurd. I would call this realism, but it is far from the tape-recorded kind. Frick, like Leroy Hamilton, has arrived for a visit with his wife, and after a moment's silence while the two strangers grope for a conversational opening . . .

FRICK: Tremendous parking space down there. 'They need that for?
LEROY: Well a lot of people visit on weekends. Fills up pretty much.
FRICK: Really? That whole area?
LEROY: Pretty much.
FRICK: 'Doubt that.

The play is made of such direct blows aimed at the thematic center; there is a vast parking space because crowds of stricken citizens converge on this place to visit mothers, fathers, brothers, and sisters. So that the two patients we may be about to meet are not at all unique.

This is in accord with the vision of the play, which is intended to be both close up and wide, psychological and social, subjective and objective, and manifestly so. To be sure, there is a realistic tone to this exchange—people do indeed seem to talk this way—but an inch below is the thematic selectivity which drives the whole tale. Perhaps it needs to be said that this split vision has informed all the plays I have written. I have tried to make things seen in their social context and simultaneously felt as intimate testimony, and that requires a style, but one that draws as little attention to itself as possible, for I would wish a play to be absorbed rather than merely observed.

I have called this play a comedy, a comedy about a tragedy, and I am frankly not sure why. Possibly it is due to the absurdity of people constantly comparing themselves to others—something we all do to one degree or another, but in Patricia's case to the point of illness.

> PATRICIA: There was something else you said. About standing on line.
> LEROY: On line?
> PATRICIA: That you'll always be at the head of the line because . . .
> breaks off.
> LEROY: I'm the only one on it. . . . We're really all on a one-person line, Pat. I learned that in these years.

The play's language, then, has a surface of everyday realism, but its action is overtly stylized rather than "natural."

Finally, a conventionally realistic work about mental illness would be bound to drive to a reverberating climax. But repression is the cultural inheritance of these New Englanders and such theatricality would be a betrayal of *their* style of living and dying. Indeed, short of suicide, the illness, properly speaking, never ends in the sense of tying all the loose strings, nor should the play, which simply sets the boundaries of the possible. For the theme is hope rather than completion or achievement, and hope is tentative always.

A play about them should have a certain amplitude of sound, nothing greater or less, reflecting their tight yet often deeply felt culture. And in a play about them they should recognize themselves— and even possibly what drives them mad—just like the longshoremen who saw themselves in *A View from the Bridge* or the cops in *The*

Price or the salespeople in *Death of a Salesman.* That would be a
satisfactory realism as I saw it.

I suppose the form itself of *The Last Yankee* is as astringently
direct and uncluttered as it is because these people are supremely
the prey of the culture, if only because it is never far from the center
of their minds—the latest film or TV show, the economy's ups and
downs, and above all the endless advertising-encouraged self-
comparisons with others who are more or less successful than they.
This ritualistic preoccupation is at the play's dramatic core and, I
felt, ought not be unclear or misted over, for it is from its grip they
must be freed if they are ever to be free at all. Hence, the repeated
references to ambition, to success and failure, to wealth and poverty, to economic survival, to the kind of car one drives and the suit
one wears. In a word, the play could not be amorphously "realistic" if it was to reflect the obsessiveness of the characters in life. So
if *The Last Yankee* is realism, it is of this kind resulting from an
intense selectivity, which in turn is derived from the way these people live and feel.

But obviously, to make such a strictly thematic play demands
intense condensation and the syncopating of idea and feeling and
language. More than one actor in my plays has told me that it is
surprisingly difficult to memorize the dialogue. It sounds like real,
almost like reported talk, when in fact it is intensely composed,
compressed, "angled" into an inevitability that seems natural but
isn't. For it is always necessary to employ the artificial in order to
arrive at the real. So that the question I bring to a play is not
whether its form and style are new or old, experimental or traditional, but first, whether it brings news, something truly felt by its
author, something thought through to its conclusion and its significance; and second, whether its form is beautiful, or wasteful,
whether it is aberrant for aberrancy's sake, full of surprises that
discover little, and so on.

Something called Realism can land us further from common
reality than the most fantastic caprice. But in the end, if stylization
in theater needs justification—and it does, of course—it is not in its
novelty but in its enhancement of discovery of how life works in
our time. How a thing is said is therefore only as important as what

it is saying. The proof is the deep pile of experimental plays of two, three, five, ten years ago, which can be appreciated now only by the scholar-specialist, a pile, incidentally, no smaller than the one for so many realistic plays of the same era. So finding the truth is no easier now when we are totally free to use any stylistic means at hand than it was a century or half a century ago when a play had to be "real" to even be read, and had to make sense to sensible people.

Call it a question of personal taste rather than principle, but I think that in theater work there is an optimum balance between two kinds of approaches. One is the traditional attempt to fill characters with acknowledged emotion, "as in life." The other is, in effect, to evacuate emotion from characters and merely refer to it rather than acting it out. Brecht, for one, tried to do this and failed, excepting in his most agitprop and forgettable plays. Actually, the strict containment not of emotion but of emotionalism is the hallmark of the Greek tragic plays, of Molière and Racine and the Japanese No plays, while Shakespeare, it seems to me, is the balance, the fusion of idea and feeling. In short, it is by no means the abstracting of emotion I dislike; on the contrary, it is the lack of it and the substitution for it of fashionably alienated ironies.

As I am not a critic and would not do anything to make any writer's life harder, I will desist from naming names, but there has been a plethora of plays in recent years whose claim to modernity is based on indicated rather than felt emotion, on the assumption, I suppose, that this *sec* quality intellectualizes a work and saves it from the banality associated with writing aimed at the audience's belly rather than at its head. The devil to be avoided is, of course, sentimentality—emotion unearned. But emotion can be earned, of course. Yet a play that is not camp and moves people is in danger of dismissal. (Unless it appears in old films, which we allow ourselves to be moved by if at the same instant we can protect our modernity by feeling superior to their time-bound naïveté.) But if the pun can be pardoned, man lives not by head alone, and the balance between the two modes, one aimed at the mind and one at the flesh, as it were, is what will interpret life more fully, rather than headline it with conceptualizations that too often simply clump about on the stilts of dry irony that time and the shifts of cultural politics will make thoroughly disposable. After all, at least part of the aim of a modern play must be to show what life now *feels like*.

Ultimately every assault on the human mystery falls back to the ground, changing little, but the flight of the arrow continues claiming our attention over more time when its direction is toward the castle rather than the wayward air.

On Screenwriting and Language:
Introduction to *Everybody Wins*
1990

A funny thing happens to screenplays on the way to the screen. It isn't simply that they get changed, subtly or otherwise, from their earlier incarnations, but that they become brittle. This is only true for the writer, of course. He misses the lines that were merely shadings of meaning and would probably hold things up in a movie, which, after all, has to *move*. But in the final version of *Everybody Wins*, compared to earlier drafts, surprisingly little of the basic material was altered, although I agreed to cut a few scenes and revise the ending. In general, what I think happened—and this is probably usual in moviemaking—is that suggestion through words became rather more blatant indication through images.

I hasten to add that this is not a gripe, if only because it is, in my view, a generic quality of the form. A description in words tends to inflate, expand, and inflame the imagination, so that in the end the thing or person described is amplified into a larger-than-life figment. But something photographed is lifted out of the imagination and becomes simply what it really is, or less. It is montage, rather than the actual photograph itself, that gives the impression of an imaginary world larger than life. Words, unable to imitate reality, must in their nature serve it up in metaphoric guise, but film gives us the appearance of reality directly.

If a telephone is photographed, isolated on a table, and the camera is left running, it becomes more and more what it is—a telephone in all its detail. Andy Warhol let the camera run on the Empire State Building for maybe an hour or more. I left before the "end" of this picture, so I'm not sure how long it lasted, but in the twenty minutes

I watched, it never to my mind rose to metaphor, simply remaining
what it was—the Empire State Building.

Things go differently on a stage. Set a phone on a table under a
light and raise the curtain, and in complete silence, after a few minutes, something will accrete around it. Questions and anticipations
will begin to emanate from it; we will begin to imagine meanings
in its isolation—in a word, the phone becomes an incipient metaphor. Possibly because we cannot see its detail as sharply as on film
or because it is surrounded by a much greater space, it begins to
animate, to take on suggestive possibilities, very nearly a kind of
self-consciousness. Something of the same is true of words as opposed to images. The word is not and can't be any more than suggestive of an idea or sensation; it *is* nothing in itself.

There is always too much dialogue. And it's true, there is, for one
thing because dialogue cannot be seen. The contradiction, I suppose, is that movies—most of them, anyway—require a writer's
sense of form while inherently rejecting his word-love. And so the
writer, accustomed to forming sentences on which all his effects
rely, ends up with something truncated and not quite his own on
paper; with luck, however, it is paradoxically more his own on the
screen. For it turns out—if he is lucky with director and actors—
that the meaning of his lost lines is actually visible in pictures. I
think that the quality of the final work is rougher and cruder, more
brutally telegraphic, than when it was action described in words.
But again, the word made flesh may *be* more and suggest less. It is
a very mysterious business, and by no means a simple question of
better or worse, but of differences of aesthetic feeling, of timbre
and tissue, that always accompany differences of form. One need
only recall the innumerable fine novels that simply could not be
made to work on the screen because the quality of their language
was removed; their story-essence vanished when their language
was discarded.

Among "real" writers—novelists, playwrights, poets—screenwriting,
when it is not regarded as a cousin of engineering, is seen as an art
on a par with clothing design; the product has no life of its own
until it is occupied by the wearer. I am afraid that this, at least in
my view, is truer than one would wish, but it is necessary to add that
there have been many more significant films over the past 25 years

than plays or, proportionately, even novels. Nevertheless, screen-plays, especially the good ones that work, tend by the nature of the art to be self-effacing, vanishing, as it were, into the total impression of the film, this in contrast to the play, which in the Western tradition has been assimilated to literature as a respectable form apart from performance (something that was not yet the case as late as Elizabethan times, when playscripts were tossed to managers and actors without reaching print). Except among technicians, the screenplay has little or no existence unless filmed, and the few exceptions, like Pinter's unproduced work for the screen, are precisely that—isolated examples that illuminate the rule.

The screenplay is the first element in a collaborative art, but only an element for all that, and not, like a stage play, a thing in itself. It is a sort of libretto for camera, its energies moving outward to serve the other elements in the film and to organize them for a common purpose. The forces in and around the stage play, in contrast, move in the opposite direction, for it is the play that is to be served—by director, actors, designer, costumer. An opera libretto is likewise content not to be noticed by the public, even as the singers and conductor know that it is their vital support, without which the music would fail to fly out to the audience's ear.

The screenplay may do many things, but one thing it must do, and that is give meaning to the pictures. In this sense it is equivalent to the words in a cartoon balloon or the titles sometimes given photographs or paintings. These may orient us as to the time and place a photo was shot or a picture painted, but there can't be many photos or paintings made memorable by their labels and dates. Indeed, the vitality of a screenplay, indispensable as it is to the finished film, springs from the life-giving structure by which the order of the images—the film's most affecting element—is organized.

The very invisibility of the screenplay accounts for the screenwriter's anonymity before the audience and most critics. To be sure, he alone was there when the pages were blank, it was his godlike hand that gave form to dust, but his occasional smart or touching line of dialogue notwithstanding, it isn't really words that people come to hear or long remember; it is actors and their mannerisms, their noses and hair and tones of voice, that really matter to them. And ironically, the more authority the actor has in performing his role, the further from sight the screenwriter recedes; in effect, the actor has eaten him. Indeed, when this happens, the movie is successful, since the actor seems to have originated his lines.

Except for the money, when there is any, screenwriting is a rather thankless profession compared with other forms of writing. The film medium belongs essentially to the director, its attraction for the public will always be the actor, and there will never be a way around that. There cannot be a Eugene O'Neill of the movies. Every element and person in the enterprise exists to serve the director's central purpose, which is to make the actors seem believable.

This may be why the most persuasive film acting is as close to wordless as possible. For a long time the idea that Gary Cooper might be an actor was thought a joke, and the same for Clark Gable, John Wayne, and their numerous heroic-type contemporaries who were "merely" personalities rather than actors. A Spencer Tracy, on the other hand, was certainly an actor because he could speak so well. This mistaken judgment was historically determined by the fact that movies were originally offshoots of the stage, and stage acting was something for which these heroes were indeed unfit. Their way of speaking was either silly and boyish as in Wayne's case, whiny, as with Gable too much of the time, or monotonous, as with Cooper. But the point, which was missed because it was so new, was that all these heroes could show attitudes and feelings— usually simple and fundamental ones like anger or sexual desire, indignation or aggression—much better with their mouths shut than open. And even "show" is too strong a word—it is more accurate to say that they were eminently attributable actors. The mute human, like an animal, keeps all his possibilities intact, gives us nothing to make us doubt his reality while any speech is bound to narrow his plausibility dangerously. Thus, there is a peculiar pressure on words in film to contribute to silent communication rather than monopolizing communication as words do on the stage. Words must above all be utilizable, each one as unadorned a story-mover as possible. The director's first instinct when faced with a multi-sentence speech is to pick it apart with a question for each word: "Why do we need this?" Needless to say, confronted with such a question, no Shakespeare play would last more than an hour.

When an actor talks, he is more vulnerable to disbelief than when he is simply standing there. The very purpose of words in movies is to justify the silences that are the picture's main business. It is silence that creates an infinity of potential meaning that words can only diminish. This, I think, is also why very good prose writers do not usually prosper as screenwriters. Faulkner, Fitzgerald, Tennessee Williams, and a long line of eminent others discovered that their brightest stylistic inventions were precisely what movies reject like excrescences. Language tends to get in the way of the images, and the brighter the language, the more it draws attention to itself, the more it interferes.

The real poetry of a film lies first in its structure of meaning, distinctly a function of the screenplay, and second in the expressiveness of its images, which are realized by the director but have their root, if not more than that, in the writer's work. Language, nevertheless, cannot be more than a servant to the images in the final impression.

Inevitably, especially if one is not accustomed to writing films, the question arises as to exactly why words are in such rivalry with the image as to be nearly self-indulgences. Even the wordy films that come to mind—Huston's *The Dead*, Capra's *Mr. Smith Goes to Washington*, Wilder's *Some Like It Hot* (a brilliantly and eminently *written* film by the late I. A. L. Diamond in collaboration with Wilder)—endure in memory not primarily for their lines but for the snap and marksmanship of their visual moods, their portraits of actors and settings, the things they have let us *see*, and the image-driven story. In the final analysis, dialogue exists at all in film in order to justify images and bridge them to sustain continuity. Dialogue is the musculature of the gestalt, the combination of images whose interactions create meaning. Altogether unlike the novel and even the play, film simply will not stand for writing that is basically commentary, however illuminating or beautiful or telling it may be. The closest one may safely verge on such adornment is in verbal wit, providing it is not convoluted, as it may be on the stage, but pithy and quickly understood. Otherwise, adornment and commentary are left to the director and his cinematographer, who indeed may elaborate through pleasurable explorations of things seen—locales, flesh, fingernails, eyes, all the wonders of the visible that film adores.

The reason or reasons for this image supremacy seem obvious: it is film's replication of dreams, or more precisely, of our relationship to dreams. The film scene, even the apparently legato one, is always secretly in a hurry, much like its unacknowledged matrix, the dream scene, which flashes up in the sleeper and dies away in a matter of seconds. Dreams (if the reader's are anything like mine) are almost never verbal. Sometimes a single emblematic word, or perhaps two, may emerge in a dream scene as a clue (most likely ambiguous) to its intent, but everyone knows the dream in which people are avidly talking, with no words coming from their mouths, thus creating the image of talk rather than talk itself. We all know, too, the dream in which we are shouting a warning or a plea to others, with no sound issuing forth. Yet we know the meaning of what was being said or shouted. The meaning, in short, stems from the situation and not from the words we are trying to say about it. The dreamer is essentially deaf, and this suggests that film's origins, like those of dream, reach back to archaic stages of our evolution, to a period antedating our capacity to understand language, when we communicated in the primitive sign language of infancy. Long before he can understand words, the infant is obviously moved by what he sees, made frightened or happy or curious or anxious by purely visual stimuli. After a mere few months of life he has all the mental capacities required to direct movies or to paint pictures—everything, that is, except a grasp of the coherency of theme that brings relevance and meaning to what he is so pleasurably staring at.

For coherency's sake words—whether spoken or printed on the screen—are indeed necessary, however brief and minimal they may be, and this needs a screenwriter, someone capable of using words efficiently in order to make some sense of pleasure, or, to put it differently, in order to provide a social justification of sensuousness. But coherency in film remains distinctly secondary in importance to the enticing infantile riddle of sheer image itself.

The primitiveness of the image-story, growing as it does primarily from our very earliest months of life, tends to thin out the filmed tale in comparison to the word-driven one. This is admittedly debatable and may be a purely personal reaction brought on by too many years in the theater, but it seems to me the brain needn't work hard before a film; it can coast along in neutral. And perhaps this absence of effort simply makes one's appreciation that much shallower, for dreaming and movie watching are essentially passive activities, something happening *to* us, rather than an active and willful participation in another's imaginary world, as is the case with reading or even watching stage plays built on words instead of pictures.

Before a play we are forced to do the chores of editing, of deciding what is more or less important, of shifting our attention from actor to actor on the stage. In reading any text we have to decide and sometimes puzzle out what the words themselves mean. At the movies we decide nothing, our treasured infantile inertia is barely nudged, for the editor, the director, the lighting, the orchestration, and the overwhelming size of the image itself hand us an unmistakable hierarchy of importance and lay before us the predigested results to wonder at and enjoy. In point of fact, a film is even more primitive than a dream if we consider how far more densely packed with ambiguity and insoluble mystery dreams are. But it is their dream-born primitiveness that accounts for the universal attraction of movies, and it is perhaps the passivity with which they are viewed that supplies the delights of release and escape for people everywhere. A movie is something being done to us, and this is very nice relative to the other forms, which by comparison are work.

So the screenwriter, charged as he is with creating and maintaining coherency in the film, stands in some contradiction to its real nature and fundamental sources of pleasure, which are incoherent, subconscious, sensuous. Indeed, it has long been standard procedure to disinvite screenwriters from the sets and locations of the films they have written (although not this one). They are like a guilty conscience arriving at the scene of a crime, necessary for upholding civilization but not really much fun. Their presence crowds the director, inhibits the actors. In the usual orgy of creative play that filmmaking is, with actors and director and cinematographer seeking to fabricate real feelings and marvellous accidents, the screenwriter—who started it all—represents the principle of good order without which all meaning is likely to escape the enterprise. Naturally, he is suspect.

But he has one final satisfaction. He may, if he so desires, contemplate the amazing fact that from this typewriter clicking away in his lonely room veritable armies of people have sprung forth—actors, makeup artists, food concessionaires, explosives teams, horse wranglers, plane pilots, chauffeurs, bankers, ushers, box office people, ad men and women, sign painters, costumers, hair designers, frogmen, attending physicians, dentists, nurses, truck drivers, mechanics, turbine experts, electricians, and people who know how to stretch shoes quickly or disguise a sudden pimple, plus their spouses and lovers. And all these regiments from the same typewriter ribbon and a few score sheets of paper with words on them. Magic.

Without in the least belittling screenwriting, I would say that it does not require one to write very well. The often agonizing stylistic effort that writing normally demands is obviated, if only because the work is not written to be read. So in this sense screenwriting is easier than other forms. On the other hand, the human relationships, the thematic coherency, and the story in a *good* screenplay are as tough to get right as they are in any other form. I must add my own (probably minority) view, however, that the screenplay requires much more of a shorthand approach to scene writing than the stage play or the novel. It wants things indicated, and as deftly as possible, rather than fleshed out in words, perhaps because the actor's image on the screen is so vast and omnipotent as to be overwhelming in its suggestive power. What in other forms must be written out or spoken may on the screen be achieved with a raised eyebrow, the movement of a mouth or a hand, or a mere mute stare. But the condensation of image demanded by screenwriting is reminiscent of poetry as opposed to the prose of the stage form. In all, then, writing screenplays has its own formidable challenges, not the least of which is the capacity to bear the pleasure and the pain of being a member of the orchestra—in the first section, perhaps, but a member nonetheless—rather than playwright-soloist or novelist-virtuoso. The good part is that if the screenwriter gets less of the credit than he deserves, he may also get less of the blame, so it evens out in the end, and that, one supposes, is fair enough.

ON HIS WORKS

Introduction to *The Golden Years* and *The Man Who Had All the Luck*
1989

Both of these plays came out of the years leading up to World War II, between 1938, my college graduation year, and 1944 when the fighting was raging. For me they are a kind of unadulterated evidence of my reactions to that time and it strikes me oddly that, as up to my neck as I was in the feverish anti-Fascism that swept my generation, the plays I chose to write were so metaphorical. This is especially strange when the only tradition in American theater of which I was aware was realism. I can't imagine what I thought I was doing.

Or, rather, I thought I knew that I was writing against the grain of the Broadway theater of the time, the only theater we had, which as usual was happily wallowing in its traditional sidewalk realism. My primary argument with this form was that I could not connect aspiration with it—it was too much like uninterpreted life. *The Golden Years* looked toward a non-existent poetic theater inspired by the Elizabethan models. Its lavish use of actors was no doubt encouraged by the fact that in the early months of its writing I was on the payroll, at $22.77 a week, of the expiring Playwriting Project of the WPA Theater, and at least in theory could call upon any number of actors for my cast. Unfortunately, before the play was finished, Congress had wiped out the WPA Theater and the play, like any play calling for several immense sets and a cast so large, was doomed as a possible commercial enterprise. It was never produced until the BBC did a radio production in 1987.

Excepting for a revision of three pages at the end of *The Man Who Had All the Luck*, and some mild pruning of both plays, I have left them as they were. *The Man Who Had All the Luck* was given a regular Broadway production and lasted less than a full week after the critics, with one or two interested but puzzled exceptions, could make absolutely nothing of it. I recall at the time being unable to find the slightest connection between the production and the play I imagined I had written, and after watching but one bewildering performance fled back to my desk and began a novel, resolved never to write for the theater again. It was 45 years later, in 1988, that I began to understand the reason for my alienation from my own play, as well, very possibly, for the total incomprehension of the critics.

A staged reading of the play under the direction of Ralph Bell, an old friend who had always had a soft spot in his heart for this play, quickly revealed that it is, indeed, a fable with no relation to realistic theater. A fable, of course, is based on an obsessive grip of a single idea bordering on the supernatural and it is the idea that stands in the forefront, rather than the characters and the verisimilitudes of the tale. The coincidences are arrantly unapologetic in this play and so they should be played, rather than attempts made to rationalize them and dim them down.

I recall the original production lit in reassuring pink and rose, a small-town genre comedy. Given the threatening elements in the story, this atmosphere must indeed have been puzzling. The play is after all attacking the evaluation of people by their success or failure and worse yet, denying the efficacy of property as a shield against psychological catastrophe.

From a distance of half a century I am struck by a certain optimistic undercurrent in both plays, despite one being a tragedy and the other veering pretty close. I must say that, at the time, life at best seemed headed for a bloody showdown with Fascism, or at worst a hapless surrender to it, but while there is plenty of worry in these plays, there is no real despair or defeat of the spirit. This will strike some as perhaps a reflection of a callow Leftism, but in truth it was the way most Americans felt even after a very long decade of

Depression. By the late thirties and early forties we had, of course, known much social violence and all kinds of vileness, but not yet a Holocaust, not yet the bursting of the banks of evil. I can still recall my incredulity at the daylight bombing of Guernica in the Spanish Civil War. As bombings go, it wasn't a very big one. The big ones were still on the way. But I simply could not believe that a European flying low in an airplane on a sunny day over an undefended town, could, whatever his politics, drop live bombs on women out shopping with their baby carriages, on old men sitting before their doorways, on young lovers strolling across the ancient square! It was hard to sleep for weeks afterwards. It was still possible to be shocked. At least within one's mind the lines of some sort of order of permissible human behavior still held.

In the West since the War of 1914–18 every period has known its main menace, some single force threatening life on the planet. For a long time now it has been Communism, and as this menace disintegrates, there are signs that ecological catastrophe is developing into a worldwide substitute. From the mid-thirties to the outbreak of war with the Axis powers it was the Fascist threat—and for some its promise—that pervaded every discussion. An important source of the energy in these plays was my fear that in one form or another Fascism, with its intensely organized energies, might well overwhelm the wayward and self-fixated Democracies. A reader today may find it strange that two such very different works could spring from the same source, or even, perhaps, that they are at all related to contemporaneous political events.

The telltale mark of this preoccupation, as I now see quite clearly, is much the same in both plays, even if one is a tragedy about the Cortés invasion of Montezuma's Mexico in 1522 and the other the tale of a very successful young man in a pastoral Ohio village. They are both struggling against passive acceptance of fate or even of defeat in life, and urge action to control one's future; both see evil as irrational and aggressive, the good as rational, if inactive and benign. Plainly, I was hounded at the time by what seemed the debility of Americans' grasp of democratic values or their awareness of them. And I must recall—to fill out this picture—that these plays were written after a decade of Depression, which had by no means lifted with any certainty as yet, and that the Depression had humbled us, shown us up as helpless before the persistent, ineradicable plague of mass unemployment. Reason had lost a lot of her credentials between 1930 and 1940.

If as the decade ended, the devaluation of the individual—the main lesson of the Depression—was still spiked to the common consciousness, these plays are somewhat surprising testimony to me that I had not lost the belief in the centrality of the individual and the importance of what he thought and did. On this evidence I suppose I might even have been called an individualist—there is nothing like writing a play for unveiling one's illusions! *The Man Who Had All the Luck* tells me that in the midst of the collectivist thirties I believed it decisive what an individual thinks and does about his life, regardless of overwhelming social forces. And likewise, in *The Golden Years*, the fate of all Mexico hung on what an individual—Montezuma—believed about himself and his role in the universe. Indeed, if these plays are to be credited, there is no force so powerful, politically as well as personally, as a man's self-conceptions.

Hearing *The Man Who Had All the Luck* read after four decades, it only then occurred to me that I had written the obverse of the Book of Job. The story of a man who cannot come to terms with the total destruction of his property and all his hopes, when he has done nothing to earn such treatment from God or fate, is very much the same as that of a man who can't seem to make a mistake and whose every move turns out to be profitable and good. What had Job done to deserve such disasters? David Beeves has much the same question in mind, oppressed by his invariably good luck in everything he attempts. And he projects an imminent disaster that will even things up between himself and the rest of humanity. For both these characters the menace is much the same—anarchy in the high command of the universe, a yawning breach between effect and conceivable causation, and they are both an argument with God.

There is mitigation in the Book of Job, of course, since we are shown a purpose behind Job's catastrophe. God starts all the trouble by wagering with the Devil that nothing he can do will shake good Job's faith in Himself. So it is clearly the Evil One who strips Job of his good life in order to destroy his belief in God's justice.

And indeed, it turns out that after much twisting and backsliding Job, despite everything, clings to God—and he is promptly rewarded with the return of all his worldly goods plus God's personal gratitude for his having kept the faith. Of course this won't do in our time if only because most of God's argument with Job consists of reminding the poor man of the incomprehensibility of his obscure powers—"Can you draw out the Leviathan with a fishhook?" and so on. This sort of humiliation is less impressive now when we can press a trigger and destroy whales and might even lift them up with helicopters, and the atom in our hands has the power of a sun. It is the question of justice that we haven't come any closer to clearing up, and indeed the goal of achieving it may be moving further away, so perhaps there is still a little room for *The Man Who Had All the Luck.*

As for the ending of this play—which I am sure I have rewritten twenty times over the past half century, it is as satisfactory as it is possible to be, as complete, let's say, as Job's, which also doesn't quite come down on both feet. The simple fact is that, as moving and imperative as our questioning of our fates may be, there is no possibility of answering the main question—why am I as I am and my life as it is? The more answers one supplies the more new questions arise. David Beeves in this play arrives as close as he can at a workable, conditional faith in the neutrality of the world's intentions toward him. I would emphasize the conditional side of it, but it is better than shooting out your brains in sheer terror of what may happen tomorrow.

The Golden Years, its purplish passages notwithstanding, is a harder if earlier look at passivity and its risks, but here the society as well as an individual is at stake. Montezuma, like the Democracies facing Hitler, was as though hypnotized. Weakened by self-doubt, he looks to Cortés, manifestly a brute and a conqueror, as one who may nevertheless bear within him the seed of the future. Something has ended for Montezuma before Cortés ever arrived in Mexico, the heart-lifting glamor of what men call the future is gone out of his life and he can foresee only deadly and meaningless repetition. There was a metaphorical poetry in this in the late thirties when perfectly intelligent, respectable, even heroic folk like the great flier Charles Lindbergh and his wife Anne could return from a visit to Nazi Germany and call it "The Wave of the Future." I recall feeling myself surrounded in those times by a kind of drifting into cultural suicide and a self-blinded acceptance of murder in high places, and this play was written in alarm. A few years later I did believe that had the Japanese not been deluded enough to attack Pearl Harbor there might well have been sufficient isolationist sentiment in the American people to simply let Hitler have his way with a defeated England and Europe. In a word, our passivity seemed in reality a drift toward an unacknowledged arrangement with Fascism. So—perhaps despite appearances—these are two anti-Fascist plays that were written quite close to the abyss. But perhaps more importantly, they were one very young writer's wrestling with enormous themes.

The Face in the Mirror:
Anti-Semitism Then and Now
1984

Some part of the genesis of this novel, *Focus*, must lie in the Brook-lyn Navy Yard where I worked the night shift in the shipfitting department during World War II, one of some 60,000 men and a few women from every ethnic group in New York. It is no longer possible to decide whether it was my own Hitler-begotten sensitivity or the anti-Semitism itself that so often made me wonder whether, when peace came, we were to be launched into a raw politics of race and religion, and not in the South, but in New York. In any case, whatever the actual level of hostility to Jews that I was witnessing, it was vastly exacerbated in my mind by the threatening existence of Nazism and the near absence among the men I worked with four-teen hours a day of any comprehension of what Nazism meant—we were fighting Germany essentially because she had allied herself with the Japanese who had attacked us at Pearl Harbor.

Moreover, it was by no means an uncommon remark that we had been maneuvered into this war by powerful Jews who secretly controlled the federal government. Not until Allied troops had bro-ken into the German concentration camps and the newspapers published photographs of the mounds of emaciated and sometimes partially burned bodies was Nazism really disgraced among decent people and our own casualties justified. (It is a fiction, in my opin-ion, that national unity around the war reached very deep in a great many people in those times.)

I cannot glance through this novel without once again feeling the sense of emergency that surrounded the writing of it. As far as I knew at the time, anti-Semitism in America was a closed if not forbidden topic for fiction—certainly no novel had taken it as a main theme, let alone the existence within the Catholic priesthood of certain militants whose duty and pleasure was to stoke up Jew-hate. When one is tempted to say that everything in the world has gotten worse, here is one shining exception.

I was reminded of this only recently when, quite by chance, I happened to tune in on a local Connecticut radio station and heard a Catholic priest trying to reason with an obviously anti-Semitic man who was laying the blame for several bombings of Jewish homes and synagogues in the Hartford area on the Jews themselves. There was a widespread search going on for the perpetrators, so the man had called in to the priest's talk program to offer his ideas as to who might have been responsible. He had no doubt it was somebody whom a Jew had mistreated, either one of his employees, or somebody who had bought some defective item from him, or someone he had bilked out of money. Or maybe it was the work of the client of a Jewish lawyer outraged at having been defrauded. There were, he thought, all sorts of interesting possibilities since the Jews, as everyone knew, have a habit of defrauding and exploiting their workers, and in general have no respect for right and wrong and feel responsible only to one another. (The arsonist was caught some weeks later—a mentally disturbed young Jew.)

I had not heard this litany since the 1930s and early '40s. But here it was again, as though freshly minted, brand new discoveries which the caller was supremely confident everyone knew perfectly well but thought it bad manners to talk about in public. And such was the confidence of his manner that he soon had the poor priest on the ropes, and could assert with utmost self-assurance that he was simply being factual and not anti-Semitic.

The differences now, of course, are that no Hitler stands at the head of the greatest armed force in the world vowing the destruction of the Jewish people, and there is an Israel which, notwithstanding all the futility of much of its present vision, is still capable of defending the right of Jews to exist. *Focus*, in short, was written when a sensible person could wonder if such a right had reality at all.

It is inevitable that one should wonder whether anything like the situation in this novel could recur, and it is a question no one can answer. In the Fifties and Sixties I might have persuaded myself that its recrudescence was not likely, and I would have based such reasoning on what had begun to seem a truly profound shift in the world's conception of the Jew. For one thing, anti-Semitism, linked as it was to totalitarianism, was being viewed as one of the keys to the dismantling of democracy and at least in its political forms was no longer an option for people who, whatever their private grievance against Jews, were still committed to the liberal state. By the end of World War II, anti-Semitism was no longer a purely personal matter.

But there was also the shift, however paradoxical, in the perception of the Jew as a consequence of the first successful decades of Israel's life as a state. In a word, the Jew was no longer a shadowy, ghettoized mystery, but a farmer, a pilot, a worker. Throwing off the role of victim, he stood up and was suddenly comprehensible as one of the world's dangerous peoples—dangerous in the conventional military and characterological sense. He was like everybody else now and for a time it would be difficult to imagine the traditional anti-Semitic attitudes feeding themselves on warriors rather than passive victims. For a time, Israeli technical and military missions were spread across Africa and her example seemed about to become an inspiration for any poor country attempting to enter this century.

This exemplary condition was not to last. By an irony so gigantic as to sweep the mind into the explications of mysticism, Israel has turned in the world's perception from a land settled by pastoral socialists and internationalist soldier-farmers into a bellicose armed camp whose adamant tribal defensiveness has inevitably hardened against neighboring peoples to the point of fanaticism. Jewish aloneness is back, but now it is armed. One more impersonation has been added to the long historic list that supplied so many contradictory images; Einstein and Freud and/or Meyer Lansky or another gangster; Karl Marx and/or Rothschild; the Prague communist chief Slansky running Czechoslovakia for Stalin and/or the Jew Slansky hanging by the neck as tribute to Stalin's paranoid anti-Semitism.

Focus is much involved with impersonations. Its central image is the turning lens of the mind of an anti-Semitic man forced by his circumstances to see anew his own relationships to the Jew. To a certain degree, it seems to me that Newman's step toward his human identification with some part of the Jewish situation has indeed occurred, at least in sectors of the democratic world, since the mid-Forties, and so the projection of such a change as occurs in this story was not altogether romantic and unlikely.

But in the four decades since I wrote *Focus*, new perspectives on the Jewish situation have opened up from surprising angles. In particular, the attitudes of some Asian peoples toward certain successful strangers settled in their midst, for example the Chinese in Thailand and the Vietnamese in the Cambodia of Sihanouk before the Vietnamese occupation of that country. It used to amuse me to hear descriptions in Bangkok of the local Chinese which were so exactly similar to what people used to say about Jews, and doubtless still do in the West: "The Chinese really have only one loyalty, to one another. They are very clever, study harder in school, always try to be first in their studies. There are lots of Chinese bankers in Thailand, too many; in fact, it was a real mistake to give Chinese Thai citizenship, because they have secretly taken control of the banking system. Besides, they are spies for China, or would be in time of war. Actually, what they are after is a revolution in Thailand (despite their being bankers and capitalists), so that we would end up as dependents of China."

Many of the same contradictory things were said about Vietnamese who had been settled in Cambodia for generations. The similarities in these two instances were striking—the Chinese in Thailand and the Vietnamese in Cambodia were very frequently visible as merchants, landlords of stores and small houses, peddlers, and an inordinate number of them were teachers and lawyers and intellectuals, enviable in a peasant country. They, so to speak, visibly administered the injustices of life as far as the average Thai or Cambodian could see, since it was to them that one paid the rent or the limitlessly inflated prices of food and other necessities of life, and one could see with one's own eyes how soft a life they led as intellectuals.

It is important also that the host people characterized themselves as somehow more naïve than these strangers, less interested in moneymaking, and more "natural"—that is, less likely to become intellectuals. In the Soviet Union, and the lands ruled by her arms and culture in Eastern Europe, the same sort of accusations are made openly or implicitly. *Focus* is a view of anti-Semitism that is deeply social in this particular sense: the Jew is seen by the anti-Semitic mind as the carrier of that same alienation the indigenous people resent and fear, the same conniving exploitation. I would only add that they fear it because it is an alienation they feel in themselves, a not-belonging, a helplessly antisocial individualism that belies fervent desires to be a serving part of the mythic whole, the sublime national essence. They fear the Jew as they fear the real, it often seems. And perhaps this is why it is too much to expect a true end to anti-Semitic feelings. In the mirror of reality, of the unbeautiful world, it is hardly reassuring and requires much strength of character to look and see oneself.

◌℘◌

Belief in America
(FROM *SITUATION NORMAL . . .*)
1944

Riding away from the camp it became clear for the first time why I had looked so hard for a sign of Belief in the Army. It was, I saw, a personal reason. I had an instinctive fear that millions of men could not be put through the hell of battle and be expected to return to American life as whole men unless they had some basic elementary understanding of why they had had to go through their battle. I had been, I saw now, afraid of what such men would do to America and what their returning to America would do to them. My fear had not been, as I thought all along, that they would not fight well without the Belief, for everything I saw convinced me that our soldiers, for many different and sometimes totally irrelevant reasons, have sufficient faith in their leaders to follow them into battle. Now I saw that the danger lay in the return of the warriors, in the time when they were no longer webbed into the Army organization, no longer under their military leaders commanding them in the pressure of battle and war. Riding away from the camp I wondered for the first time whether I ought not be wandering through St. Paul and Kansas City, New York and Los Angeles, instead of through the camps. For as far as Watson was concerned it was in America as much as in the island where he fought that his wholeness had been wrecked and his mind distracted. It was not only the Japanese who had shaken his wits. We here did our part in that, and with terrible effect.

It is wrong to use a single man as the basis of a statement about

all soldiers, but from what I have been able to learn since speaking
to him I have come to the conclusion that he represents a nearly
classic extreme of a state of mind found in all men who have been
in actual battle, hard battle.

For want of a better word—this one has certain sneering
connotations—Watson was in love, in love with his comrades in
arms. I sensed it as he spoke to me, and I was sure of it when I had
left him. Probably his whole conflict consists of his fear of returning to battle, set against his love for his unit. The feeling of guilt
that such a dilemma would generate in a man needs no defining.
He was not merely letting "the Army" down or his "unit." He was
being forced by fear to forsake a group of men whom he had loved.
His avowal that he would die for any of them was even truer than I
had imagined.

Now what happens to a Watson when he returns to America? It
must be remembered that as far as anyone could tell he returned
whole, sane, and fit for further training. What happened to him
here? What did he see or fail to see here that so shook him?

I can only guess at that. But I am not trying to solve Watson's
problem. In the present state of American affairs I do not know
how his problem can be solved. But Watson is an extreme. Many
hundreds of thousands of men are going to return from terrible
battles, and in some degree they will have shared Watson's feeling
of love and identity with their particular comrades and units. And
in differing degrees they are going to have to transfer that love to
other—civilian—"units" or be forever in that restless, aimless state
of emotional thirst which in other countries at other times has
made veterans the anxious and willing collaborators of any dema-
gogue who joins them together under a common color of shirt, for
a common and often violent social purpose. We will dispense with
the argument against those who still say it can't happen here. It has
begun to happen here too many times for us to argue about it at
this late date. But what about Watson, about the millions of Watsons who are even now coming down the gangplanks in American
ports . . .

They have fought their battle. Carried forward by faith in an
officer, by a feeling of love for their comrades, by an innate sense of
honor, by a plain love of adventure and danger, by whatever drive

obtained in them at the time of battle, they fought their battle, and now they are home. No man has ever felt identity with a group more deeply and intimately than a soldier in battle. But now their uniforms are off. They walk out of the circle of the imperative order, out of the unity of feeling they had known in the Army. They go home.

Home is many things. Home can be a family well loved or a wife longed for whose love is all-sufficing. Home may be the feverish joy of resuming projects left half finished. Home may give Watson—many of them—a satisfying substitute for the close comradeship of the battlefield. The battlefield and its emotions may quickly fade once the fighter is really home.

But maybe not. Home, to many, perhaps to most, means a town or a city cut into a thousand little disjointed pieces, each one an exclusive class in itself. If on returning home, the veteran should find the town in immediate danger of being inundated by a flood, with every sort of person in it working together toward a common goal, the problem might hardly exist for him. With each citizen protecting his neighbor, as he does in time of danger, and all divisions of race, economic and social position melted away in the face of the peril, the veteran would find himself strangely at home among his people. But a flood is a rare thing. The usual veteran returning to his city or town on the usual day finds no common goal at all. He finds every group in town excluding the proximate group. It is rich and poor again, it is white and black again, it is Jew and Gentile again, it is, above all, a mass of little groups each of whose apparent goals in life conflict with the goals of the next group. Watson must return to his former group. He must reassume its little prejudices, its hates, its tiny aims. He must lop off at once that onetime feeling of exhilaration he got from the knowledge that whatever the insignificance of his job, it was helping an enormous mass of men toward a great and worthy goal. Now he must forget that. Now he must live unto himself, for his own selfish welfare. Half of him, in a sense, must die, and with it must pass away half the thrill he knew in being alive. He must, in short, become a civilian again.

There is a great and deep sense of loss in that. A man who has known the thrill of giving himself does not soon forget it. It leaves

him with a thirst. A thirst for a wider life, a more exciting life, a life
that demands all he can give. Civilian life in America is private, it is
always striving for exclusiveness. Our lifelong boast is that we got
ahead of the next guy, excluded him. We have always believed in
the fiction—and often damned our own belief—that if every man
privately takes care of his own interests, the community and the
nation will prosper and be safe. Unless your Watson's attachment
to his family or his wife or his girl is so overwhelming that nothing
can distract him from it, he is going to feel the loss of a social unit,
a group to which he can give himself, a social goal worth his sacrifice. He may find that unit and that goal in his trade union, his
club. But most Americans do not belong to unions, and the goals of
most American clubs will never make up in vitality and largeness
for the goal he left behind. Watson, then, if he has the average
social connections which are slight, is going to wander around his
American town, and he is going to find himself severely lonely a
great and growing part of the time. America, to him, is not moving
in any direction. His life is standing still. And he is alone and dis-
satisfied.

What could civilian America possibly give Watson that it did not
give? There is only one answer to that. The Belief. America tried
everything else imaginable, and nothing satisfied your Watson. It
tried giving him medals, it tried giving him a parade, it tried big
publicity for him, it tried to give him everything within reach of its
well-meaning heart. When people met him they tried being sympathetic, and that did not help. They tried being sorry for him and
they tried being proud, and he did not seem to react fully to any of
it. What did he want from them? They would give him anything he
wanted if only he could tell them what it was that would make him
feel at home in America.

Knowing it or not Watson wanted to find the Belief in America.
It is a very hard concept to nail down; Belief so often means a
dogma of some kind to be memorized and bowed down to, and
that is not a thing that could satisfy Watson. But say it this way. If
when he returned to this shore he walked in the cities and the towns
and all about him he sensed and heard evidence that the people
were unified in one concept—that he, Watson, had gone forth to
rescue something very very precious and that had he not gone forth,

and had that thing been lost, the people would have been left in mourning for it the rest of their lives. What Watson wanted in America is equivalent to what the Russian or British soldier must find when he returns home. In Russia or Britain the broken cities and the maimed children and the many civilian dead and missing say in so many words nearly everything the returning soldier needs to hear. It is very clear, there, why he went; it is superlatively clear what a unity of feeling lay behind him while he was gone, and it is bloody well apparent and understood what it was that he accomplished by going. The force of bombs and the horror of rape and destruction has spawned the quantities of a unified Belief there, and when Tommy and Ivan come marching home their people *know* them through the very arterial link of that commonly held Belief, that rock-like understanding. But here the marks of war are different. Watson found a people without scars and without any commonly held understanding of why he had to go and what he accomplished by going. True, his comrades too were not sure of what, in the end, they were accomplishing by their battles, but for them that kind of understanding, that kind of political Belief was compensated for by an emotional unity born of the common danger and the common military goal—they *knew* each other through that and they were one with each other because of it. What links Watson with the civilians at home though? A parade? Sympathy? Pride in him based on the same kind of understanding required for pride in the hometown football team? The only means by which Watson can rejoin himself with America is by sharing with civilian America a well-understood Belief in the rightness, the justness, the necessity of his fight. That is how he will be made to feel at home. It will by no means dissolve his memories and solve all his problems, but without it nothing can be solved in Watson. He will be wondering why he went and why he is alive for the rest of his days. And what could that Belief be?

Since the war began our most brilliant statesmen and writers have been trying—only in America, as far as I know—to frame a statement, a "name" for this war. They have not found it, and they will not find it, because they are looking for something new. It is pretty late now for this kind of talk, but not too late. From the first day of this war we should have understood that the kind of thing we fight for is a very old thing. We fought for it in 1776 and in 1865, and we found the words for it then, and they are perfectly good words, easy to understand and not at all old-fashioned. They are good words because they recur more times in our ordinary conversation and in the historic conversations of our long tradition than any other words. They represent a concept which, to the vast majority of Americans, must not be offended. The words are not "free enterprise," as the well-known ads of our big industries maintain. Nor are the words, "Keep America the Same," as a certain automobile company insists nearly every week in the national magazines. Neither the people of America nor those of any other nation ever fought a war in order to keep everything the same and certainly never for free enterprise or jobs. No man in his right mind would risk his life to get a job. But we did fight two wars for our Belief. And that Belief says, simply, that we believe all men are equal. We really believe it, most of us, and because a powerful force has arisen in the world dedicated to making the people of the world—us included— unequal, we have therefore decided to fight. We insist upon a state of affairs in which all men will be regarded as equal. There is no nonsense about it. We believe that everything will rot and decline and go backwards if we are forced to live under laws that hold certain nations and peoples to be inferior and without rights. We are thinking primarily of ourselves and our own rights, naturally, but that is perfectly all right, for once our right to be equal is assured we will want nothing better than to see every nation on our level. I believe the majority of Americans agree to this.

Now, if the implications of "all men are equal" were drilled into our men and women, in the Army and out, with at least the assiduousness that the brand names of certain toothpastes are, we would have, I maintain, many fewer Watsons with us now and after the war is over. The concept of equality of man is very easy for a soldier, especially, to take. It is in our tradition quite as firmly as is blueberry pie, for which our radio programs seem to feel most adult Americans are fighting, and sheds considerably more light on the meaning of this war. Its ramifications could be explained in the five-minute orientation periods in the camps quite as easily as the nature of the millimeter. And finally, it happens to be the one idea which Hitler and the Japanese deny most completely and with the heaviest use of force. They, at bottom, demand that this world be fixed into a pattern of inequality of man against man. As Americans we were marked for a secondary status in that world. We refuse to accept it. We are as good as they are, and in time, perhaps, we will help them to be as good as we are. But first we must beat hell out of them until they no longer can dictate our status. Then we will go about making them understand about equality. Again, if this concept of the war, oversimplified as it is, lacking in economic factors as it is, were "sold" across America on even half the advertising budget of our best-selling mouthwash, perhaps—I too am willing to wait and see, but perhaps—the chaos of mind that is America today would be put somewhat in order and many of our returning soldiers made to feel at home.

Watson—the real Watson, the Watson whose story you have just read—is alone in America today. He in particular is alone and lonely because his comrades are not with him, the men he loves. But he is alone and misfitted here also—and more tragically— because America offers him no great social goal. Were we con- scious of our Belief, were we *here in America* acting and working and fighting as civilians for the attainment of that goal, Watson would feel it, he would have a place fighting for it, and it would demand of him that part of his character which requires sharing. As it is, the company is gone and all that the company meant. He must wall himself in from his fellow man, he must live only his own little life and do his own unimportant, unsatisfying job when he gets out of the Army. He must begin again the stale and deadly competition with his fellow men for rewards that now seem color- less, even if necessary to his survival. He is alone. Cut off from mankind and that great movement of mankind he once was part of. And the world is alien, and battle . . . It keeps coming back to me with what apparent suddenness Watson came to fear returning to battle. Is it not possible, as Watson's captain implied, that battle is ten thousand times more horrible to him now than it actually was when he was in it, because he is looking at it now as a man cut off, as a man alone with a lonely man's fears, while at the front he saw it as a joined and united part of the race, as a man who is fight- ing with and for those he loved? Danger breeds understanding, it breeds a growth of common unity among men. And so does Belief.

Not as suddenly, perhaps, and without the bottomless emotional depths that danger plumbs, but understanding and love are bred by a commonality of Belief. We have the Belief. We have always had it, but we have stowed it away like a relic, an heirloom to be taken down from the attic on a Sunday afternoon when visitors come and then hidden away. We need it every day now. For Belief is not a bullet, as has been said. Belief is a shield. When will we start the mills that roll such armament? And who will wither away because he went and returned, unarmed?

Extract from *Timebends: A Life*
1987

Memory inevitably romanticizes, pressing reality to recede like pain. When the escaping Hebrews saw the waters rushing in to cover the God-dried seabed, drowning the pursuing Egyptian army, they sat down on the shore to catch their breaths and promptly forgot all their previous years of miserable argufying and internecine spitefulness.

Now, with only the serene blue sea before them, they were soon telling their children how wonderful life used to be, even under the Egyptians, when at least they were never allowed to forget they were all Jews and therefore had to help one another and be human. Not like now, when everybody's out for himself, etc. . . . The brain heals the past like an injury, things were always better than they are now.

Already in the sixties I was surprised by the common tendency to think of the late forties and early fifties as some sort of renaissance in the New York theater. If that was so, I was unaware of it. I thought the theater a temple being rotted out with commercialized junk, where mostly by accident an occasional good piece of work appeared, usually under some disguise of popular cultural coloration such as a movie star in a leading role.

That said, it now needs correction; it was also a time when the audience was basically the same for musicals and light entertainment as for the ambitious stuff and had not yet been atomized, as it would be by the mid-fifties, into young and old, hip and square, or

even political left and middle and right. So the playwright's challenge was to please not a small sensitized supporting clique but an
audience representing, more or less, all of America. With ticket
prices within reason, this meant that an author was writing for his
peers, and if such was really not the case statistically, it was sufficiently so to support an illusion that had a basis in reality. After all,
it was not thought particularly daring to present T. S. Eliot's *The
Cocktail Party* on Broadway, or Laurence Olivier in a Greek tragedy, or Giraudoux's *The Madwoman of Chaillot*, or any number of
other ambitious works. To be sure, such shows had much shorter
lives than the trash, but that was to be expected, for most people
would much rather laugh than cry, rather watch an actor being hit
on the head by a pig bladder than by some painful truth.

The net of it all was that serious writers could reasonably assume
they were addressing the whole American mix, and so their plays,
whether successfully or not, stretched toward a wholeness of experience that would not require specialists or a coterie to be understood. As alienated a spirit as he was, O'Neill tried for the big
audience, and Clifford Odets no less so, along with every other
writer longing to prophesy to America, from Whitman and Mel-
ville to Dreiser and Hemingway and on.

For Europe's playwrights the situation was profoundly different,
with society already split beyond healing between the working
class and its allies, who were committed to a socialist destiny, and
the bourgeois mentality that sought an art of reassurance and the
pleasures of forgetting what was happening in the streets. (The first
American plays I saw left me wondering where the characters came
from. The people I knew were fanatics about surviving, but onstage
everyone seemed to have mysteriously guaranteed incomes, and
though every play had to have something about "love," there was
nothing about sex, which was all there was in Brooklyn, at least
that I ever noticed.) An American avant-garde, therefore, if only
because the domination of society by the middle class was profoundly unchallenged, could not simply steal from Brecht or even
Shaw and expect its voice to reach beyond the small alienated
minority that had arrived in their seats already converted to its
aims. That was not the way to change the world.

For a play to do that it had to reach precisely those who accepted everything as it was; great drama is great questions or it is nothing but technique. I could not imagine a theater worth my time that did not want to change the world, any more than a creative scientist could wish to prove the validity of everything that is already known. I knew only one other writer with the same approach, even if he surrounded his work with a far different aura. This was Tennessee Williams.

If only because he came up at a time when homosexuality was absolutely unacknowledgeable in a public figure, Williams had to belong to a minority culture and understood in his bones what a brutal menace the majority could be if aroused against him. I lived with much the same sense of alienation, albeit for other reasons. Certainly I never regarded him as the sealed-off aesthete he was thought to be. There is a radical politics of the soul as well as of the ballot box and the picket line. If he was not an activist, it was not for lack of a desire for justice, nor did he consider a theater profoundly involved in society and politics, the venerable tradition reaching back to the Greeks, somehow unaesthetic or beyond his interest.

The real theater—as opposed to the sequestered academic one—is always straining at the inbuilt inertia of a society that always wants to deny change and the pain it necessarily involves. But it is in this effort that the musculature of important work is developed. In a different age, perhaps even only fifteen years later, in the sixties, Williams might have had a more comfortably alienated audience to deal with, one that would have relieved the pressure upon him to extend himself beyond a supportive cult environment, and I think this might well have narrowed the breadth of his work and its intensity. In short, there was no renaissance in the American forties, but there was a certain balance within the audience—a balance, one might call it, between the alienated and the conformists—that gave sufficient support to the naked cry of the heart and, simultaneously, enough resistance to force it into a rhetoric that at one stroke could be broadly understandable and yet faithful to the pain that had pressed the author to speak.

When Kazan invited me up to New Haven to see the new Williams play, A Streetcar Named Desire—it seemed to me a rather too garishly attention-getting title—I was already feeling a certain amount of envious curiosity since I was still unable to commit myself to the salesman play, around which I kept suspiciously circling and sniffing. But at the same time I hoped that *Streetcar* would be good; it was not that I was high-minded but simply that I shared the common assumption of the time that the greater the number of exciting plays there were on Broadway the better for each of us. At least in our minds there was still something approximating a theater culture to which we more or less pridefully belonged, and the higher its achievement the greater the glory we all shared. The playwright then was king of the hill, not the star actor or director, and certainly not the producer or theater owner, as would later be the case. (At a recently televised Tony Awards ceremony, recognizing achievement in the theater, not a single playwright was presented to the public, while two lawyers who operated a chain of theaters were showered with the gratitude of all. It reminded me of Caligula making his horse a senator.)

Streetcar—especially when it was still so fresh and the actors almost as amazed as the audience at the vitality of this theatrical experience—opened one specific door for me. Not the story or characters or the direction, but the words and their liberation, the joy of the writer in writing them, the radiant eloquence of its composition, moved me more than all its pathos. It formed a bridge to Europe for me, to Jouvet's performance in *Ondine*, to the whole tradition of unashamed word-joy that, with the exception of Odets, we had either turned our backs on or, as with Maxwell Anderson, only used archaically, as though eloquence could only be justified by cloaking it in sentimental romanticism.

Returning to New York, I felt speeded up, in motion now. With *Streetcar*, Tennessee had printed a license to speak at full throat, and it helped strengthen me as I turned to Willy Loman, a salesman always full of words, and better yet, a man who could never cease trying, like Adam, to name himself and the world's wonders. I had known all along that this play could not be encompassed by conventional realism, and for one integral reason: in Willy the past was as alive as what was happening at the moment, sometimes even crashing in to completely overwhelm his mind. I wanted precisely the same fluidity in the form, and now it was clear to me that this must be primarily verbal. The language would of course have to be

recognizably his to begin with, but it seemed possible now to infil-
trate it with a kind of superconsciousness. The play, after all,
involved the attempts of his sons and his wife and Willy himself to
understand what was killing him. And to understand meant to lift
the experience into emergency speech of an unashamedly open
kind rather than to proceed by the crabbed dramatic hints and pre-
texts of the "natural." If the structure had to mirror the psychology
as directly as could be done, it was still a psychology hammered
into its strange shape by society, the business life Willy had lived
and believed in. The play could reflect what I had always sensed as
the unbroken tissue that was man and society, a single unit rather
than two.

By April of 1948 I felt I could find such a form, but it would have
to be done, I thought, in a single sitting, in a night or a day, I did
not know why. I stopped making my notes in our Grace Court
house in Brooklyn Heights and drove up alone one morning to the
country house we had bought the previous year. We had spent one
summer there in that old farmhouse, which had been modernized
by its former owner, a greeting card manufacturer named Philip
Jaffe, who as a sideline published a thin magazine for China specialists called *Amerasia*. Mary worked as one of his secretaries and
so had the first news that he wanted to sell the place. In a year or
two he would be on trial for publishing without authorization State
Department reports from John Stewart Service, among a number
of other China experts who recognized a Mao victory as inevitable
and warned of the futility of America continuing to back her favorite, Chiang Kai-Shek. *Amerasia* had been a vanity publication, in
part born of Jaffe's desire for a place in history, but it nevertheless
braved the mounting fury of the China lobby against any opinion
questioning the virtues of the Chiang forces. At his trial the government produced texts of conversations that Jaffe claimed could
only have been picked up by long-range microphone as he and his
friends walked the isolated backcountry roads near this house. Service was one of many who were purged from the State Department,
leaving it blinded to Chinese reality but ideologically pure.

But all that was far from my mind this day; what I was looking
for on my land was a spot for a little shack I wanted to build, where
I could block out the world and bring into focus what was still

stuck in the corners of my eyes. I found a knoll in the nearby woods and returned to the city, where instead of working on the play I drew plans for the framing, of which I really had very vague knowledge and no experience. A pair of carpenters could have put up this ten-by-twelve-foot cabin in two days at most, but for reasons I still do not understand it had to be my own hands that gave it form, on this ground, with a floor that I had made, upon which to sit to begin the risky expedition into myself. In reality, all I had was the first two lines and a death—"Willy!" and "It's all right. I came back." Further than that I dared not, would not, venture until I could sit in the completed studio, four walls, two windows, a floor, a roof, and a door.

"It's all right. I came back" rolled over and over in my head as I tried to figure out how to join the roof rafters in air unaided, until I finally put them together on the ground and swung them into position all nailed together. When I closed in the roof, it was a miracle, as though I had mastered the rain and cooled the sun. And all the while afraid I would never be able to penetrate past those two first lines. I started writing one morning—the tiny studio was still unpainted and smelled of raw wood and sawdust, and the bags of nails were still stashed in a corner with my tools. The sun of April had found my windows to pour through, and the apple buds were moving on the wild trees, showing their first pale blue petals. I wrote all day until dark, and then I had dinner and went back and wrote until some hour in the darkness between midnight and four. I had skipped a few areas that I knew would give me no trouble in the writing and gone for the parts that had to be muscled into position. By the next morning I had done the first half, the first act of two. When I lay down to sleep, I realized I had been weeping—my eyes still burned and my throat was sore from talking it all out and shouting and laughing. I would be stiff when I woke, aching as if I had played four hours of football or tennis and now had to face the start of another game. It would take some six more weeks to complete Act II.

My laughter during the writing came mostly at Willy's contradicting himself so arrantly, and out of the laughter the title came one afternoon. *Death Comes for the Archbishop*, the *Death and the Maiden* Quartet—always austere and elevated was death in

titles. Now it would be claimed by a joker, a bleeding mass of contradictions, a clown, and there was something funny about that,
something like a thumb in the eye, too. Yes, and in some far corner
of my mind possibly something political; there was the smell in the
air of a new American Empire in the making, if only because, as I
had witnessed, Europe was dying or dead, and I wanted to set
before the new captains and the so smugly confident kings the
corpse of a believer. On the play's opening night a woman who
shall not be named was outraged, calling it "a time bomb under
American capitalism"; I hoped it was, or at least under the bullshit
of capitalism, this pseudo life that thought to touch the clouds by
standing on top of a refrigerator, waving a paid-up mortgage at the
moon, victorious at last.

But some 35 years later, the Chinese reaction to my Beijing production of *Salesman* would confirm what had become more and
more obvious over the decades in the play's hundreds of productions throughout the world: Willy was representative everywhere,
in every kind of system, of ourselves in this time. The Chinese
might disapprove of his lies and his self-deluding exaggerations as
well as his immorality with women, but they certainly saw themselves in him. And it was not simply as a type but because of what
he wanted, which was to excel, to win out over anonymity and
meaninglessness, to love and be loved, and above all, perhaps, to
count. When he roared out, "I am not a dime a dozen! *I am Willy
Loman, and you are Biff Loman!*" it came as a nearly revolutionary declaration after what was now 34 years of leveling. (The play
was the same age as the Chinese revolution.) I did not know in
1948 in Connecticut that I was sending a message of resurgent individualism to the China of 1983—especially when the revolution
had signified, it seemed at the time, the long-awaited rule of reason
and the historic ending of chaotic egocentricity and selfish aggrandizement. Ah, yes. I had not reckoned on a young Chinese student
saying to a CBS interviewer in the theater lobby, "We are moved by
it because we also want to be number one, and to be rich and successful." What else is this but human unpredictability, which goes
on escaping the nets of unfreedom?

I did not move far from the phone for two days after sending the
script to Kazan. By the end of the second silent day I would have

accepted his calling to tell me that it was a scrambled egg, an impenetrable, unstageable piece of wreckage. And his tone when he finally did call was alarmingly somber.

"I've read your play." He sounded at a loss as to how to give me the bad news. "My God, it's so sad."

"It's supposed to be."

"I just put it down. I don't know what to say. My father . . ." He broke off, the first of a great many men—and women—who would tell me that Willy was their father. I still thought he was letting me down easy. "It's a great play, Artie. I want to do it in the fall or winter. I'll start thinking about casting." He was talking as though someone we both knew had just died, and it filled me with happiness. Such is art.

For the first time in months, as I hung up the phone, I could see my family clearly again. As was her way, Mary accepted the great news with a quiet pride, as though something more expressive would spoil me, but I too thought I should remain an ordinary citizen, even an anonymous one (although I did have a look at the new Studebaker convertible, the Raymond Lowey design that was the most beautiful American car of the time, and bought one as soon as the play opened). But Mary's mother, who was staying the week with us, was astonished. "*Another* play?" she said, as though the success of *All My Sons* had been enough for one lifetime. She had unknowingly triggered that play when she gossiped about a young girl somewhere in Central Ohio who had turned her father in to the FBI for having manufactured faulty aircraft parts during the war.

But who should produce *Salesman*? Kazan and I walked down Broadway from the park where we had been strolling and talking about the kind of style the production would need. Kazan's partnership with Harold Clurman had recently broken up, and I had no idea about a producer. He mentioned Cheryl Crawford, whom I hardly knew, and then Kermit Bloomgarden, an accountant turned producer, whom I had last seen poring over Herman Shumlin's account books a couple of years before when Shumlin turned down *All My Sons*. I had never seen Bloomgarden smile, but he had worked for the Group Theater and Kazan knew him, and as much because we happened to have come to a halt a few yards from his office building as for any other reason, he said, "Well, let's go up and say hello." When we stood across the desk from him and Kazan said he had a play of mine for him to read, Bloomgarden squeezed up his morose version of a smile, or at least a suggestion of one he planned to have next week.

This whimsical transforming of another person's life reminds me of a similar walk with Kazan uptown from a garage on Twenty-sixth Street where he had left his old Pontiac to be repaired. He began wondering aloud whom he should ask to head a new acting school to be called the Actors Studio, which he and Clurman and Robert Lewis and Cheryl Crawford were organizing. None of these founders was prepared to run the place, Kazan, Clurman, and Lewis being too busy with their flourishing directing careers, and Crawford with her work as a producer. "Lee Strasberg is probably the best guy for it. He'd certainly be able to put in the time." In due course Strasberg became not only the head of the Actors Studio but also its heart and soul, and for the general public its organizer. So his work there was made possible by his having been unemployable at the right moment. But that, come to think of it, is as good a way as any to be catapulted into world fame.

Willy had to be small, I thought, but we soon realized that Roman Bohnen and Ernest Truex and a few other very good actors seemed to lack the size of the character even if they fit the body. The script had been sent to Lee Cobb, an actor I remembered mainly as a mountainous hulk covered with a towel in a Turkish bath in an Irwin Shaw play, with the hilarious *oy vey* delivery of a forever per-secuted businessman. Having flown himself across the country in his own two-engine airplane, he sat facing me in Bloomgarden's office and announced, "This is my part. Nobody else can play this part. I know this man." And he did indeed seem to be the man when a bit later in a coffee shop downstairs he looked up at the young waitress and smiled winsomely as though he had to win her loving embrace before she could be seduced into bringing him his turkey sandwich and coffee—ahead of all the other men's orders, and only after bestowing on his unique slice of pickle her longing kiss.

But while I trusted his and Kazan's experience, I lacked any con-viction of my own about him until one evening in our Grace Court living room Lee looked down at my son, Bob, on the floor and I heard him laugh at something funny the child had said. The sorrow in his laughter flew out at me, touched me; it was deeply depressed and at the same time joyous, all flowing through a baritone voice that was gorgeously reedy. So large and handsome a man pretending to be thoroughly at ease in a world where he obviously did not fit could be moving.

"You know—or do you?—," Lee said to me one day in Bloomgarden's office a week or so before rehearsals were to begin, "that this play is a watershed. The American theater will never be the same." I could only gulp and nod in silence at his portentousness—which I feared might augur a stately performance—and hope that he would make Willy come alive anyway.

But as rehearsals proceeded in the small, periodically abandoned theater on the ratty roof of the New Amsterdam on Forty-second Street, where Ziegfeld in the twenties had staged some intimate revues, Lee seemed to move about in a buffalo's stupefied trance, muttering his lines, plodding with deathly slowness from position to position, and behaving like a man who had been punched in the head. "He's just learning it," Kazan shakily reassured me after three or four days. I waited as a week went by, and then ten days, and all that was emerging from Lee Cobb's throat was a bumpy hum. The other actors were nearing performance levels, but when they had to get a response from Lee all their rhythms slowed to near collapse. Kazan was no longer so sure and kept huddling with Lee, trying to pump him up. Nor did Lee offer any explanation, and I wondered whether he thought to actually play the part like a man with a foot in the grave. Between us, Kazan and I began referring to him as "the Walrus."

On about the twelfth day, in the afternoon, with Eddie Kook, our lighting supplier, and Jimmy Proctor, our pressman, and Kazan and myself in the seats, Lee stood up as usual from the bedroom chair and turned to Mildred Dunnock and bawled, "No, there's more people now. . . . There's more people!" and, gesturing toward the empty upstage where the window was supposed to be, caused a block of apartment house to spring up in my brain, and the air became sour with the smell of kitchens where once there had been only the odors of earth, and he began to move frighteningly, with such ominous reality that my chest felt pressed down by an immense weight. After the scene had gone on for a few minutes, I glanced around to see if the others had my reaction. Jim Proctor had his head bent into his hands and was weeping, Eddie Kook was looking shocked, almost appalled, and tears were pouring over his cheeks, and Kazan behind me was grinning like a fiend, gripping his temples with both hands, and we knew we had it—there was an unmistakable wave of life moving across the air of the empty theater, a wave of Willy's pain and protest. I began to weep myself at some point that was not particularly sad, but it was as much, I think, out of pride in our art, in Lee's magical capacity to imagine, to collect within himself every mote of life since Genesis and to let it pour forth. He stood up there like a giant moving the Rocky Mountains into position.

At the end of the act, Del Hughes, our sweet but hardheaded, absolutely devoted, competent stage manager, came out from a wing and looked out at us. His stunned eyes started us all laughing. I ran up and kissed Lee, who pretended to be surprised. "But what did you expect, Arthur?" he said, his eyes full of his playful vanity. My God, I thought—he really *is* Willy! On the subway going home to Brooklyn I felt once again the aching pain in my muscles that the performance had tensed up so tightly, just as in the writing time. And when I thought of it later, it seemed as though Lee's sniffing around the role for so long recapitulated what I had done in the months before daring to begin to write.

The whole production was, I think, unusual for the openness with which every artist involved sought out his truths. It was all a daily, almost moment-to-moment testing of ideas. There was much about the play that had never been done before, and this gave an uncustomary excitement to our discussions about what would or would not be understood by an audience. The setting I had envisioned was three bare platforms and only the minimum necessary furniture for a kitchen and two bedrooms, with the Boston hotel room as well as Howard's office to be played in open space. Jo Mielziner took those platforms and designed an environment around them that was romantic and dreamlike yet at the same time lower-middle-class. His set, in a word, was an emblem of Willy's intense longing for the promises of the past, with which indeed the present state of his mind is always conflicting, and it was thus both a lyrical design and a dramatic one. The only notable mistake in his early concept was to put the gas hot-water heater in the middle of the kitchen, a symbol of menace that I thought obvious and Kazan finally eliminated as a hazard to his staging. But by balancing on the edges of the ordinary bounds of verisimilitude, Jo was stretching reality in parallel with the script, just as Kazan did by syncopating the speech rhythms of the actors. He made Mildred Dunnock deliver her long first-act speeches to the boys at double her normal speed, then he doubled that, and finally she—until recently a speech teacher—was standing there drumming out words as fast as her very capable tongue could manage. Gradually he slacked her off, but the drill straightened her spine, and her Linda filled up with outrage and protest rather than self-pity and mere perplexity. Similarly, to express the play's inner life, the speech rate in some scenes or sections was unnaturally speeded or slowed.

My one scary hour came with the climactic restaurant fight between Willy and the boys, when it all threatened to come apart. I had written a scene in which Biff resolves to tell Willy that the former boss from whom Biff had planned to borrow money to start a business has refused to so much as see him and does not even remember his working for the firm years ago. But on meeting his brother and father in the restaurant, he realizes that Willy's psychological stress will not permit the whole catastrophic truth to be told, and he begins to trim the bad news. From moment to moment the scene as originally written had so many shadings of veracity that Arthur Kennedy, a very intelligent citizen indeed, had trouble shifting from a truth to a half-truth to a fragment of truth and back to the whole truth, all of it expressed in quickly delivered, very short lines. The three actors, with Kazan standing beside them, must have repeated the scene through a whole working day, and it still wobbled. "I don't see how we can make it happen," Kazan said as we left the theater that evening. "Maybe you ought to try simplifying it for them." I went home and worked through the night and brought in a new scene, which played much better and became the scene as finally performed.

The other changes were very small and a pleasure to make because they involved adding lines rather than cutting or rewriting. In Act

I, Willy is alone in the kitchen muttering to himself, and as his memories overtake him the lighting brightens, the exterior of the house becomes covered with leaf shadows as of old, and in a moment the boys are calling to him in their youthful voices, entering the stage as they were in their teens. There was not sufficient time, however, for them to descend from their beds in the dark on the specially designed elevators and finish stripping out of their pajamas into sweaters and trousers and sneakers, so I had to add time to Willy's monologue. But that was easy since he loved talking to himself about his boys and his vision of them.

The moving in and out of the present had to be not simply indicative but a tactile transformation that the audience could feel as well as comprehend, and indeed come to dread as returning memory threatens to bring Willy closer to his end. Lighting was thus decisively important, and Mielziner, who also lit the show, with Eddie Kook by his side, once worked an entire afternoon lighting a chair.

Willy, in his boss's office, has exploded once too often, and Howard has gone out, leaving him alone. He turns to the office chair, which in the old days was occupied by Frank, Howard's father, who had promised Willy shares in the firm as a reward for all his good work, and as he does so the chair must become alive, quite as though his old boss were in it as he addresses him: "Frank, Frank, don't you remember what you told me? . . ." Rather than being lit, the chair subtly seemed to begin emanating light. But this was not merely an exercise in theatrical magic; it confirmed that we had moved inside Willy's system of loss, that we were seeing the world as he saw it even as we kept a critical distance and saw it for ourselves.

To set the chair off and make the light change work, all surrounding lights had to dim imperceptibly. That was when Eddie Kook, who had become so addicted to the work on this play that his office at his Century Lighting Company had all but ceased operations, turned to me and said, "You've been asking why we need so many lights. [We were using more than most musicals.] The reason is right there in front of you—it takes more lights to make it dark." With fewer lights each one would have to be dimmed more noticeably than if there were many, each only fractionally reduced in intensity to create the change without apparent source or contrivance.

Salesman had its first public performance at the Locust Street Theater in Philadelphia. Across the street the Philadelphia Orchestra was playing Beethoven's Seventh Symphony that afternoon, and Kazan thought Cobb ought to hear some of it, wanting, I suppose, to prime the great hulk on whom all our hopes depended. The three of us were in a conspiracy to make absolutely every moment of every scene cohere to what preceded and followed it; we were now aware that Willy's part was among the longest in dramatic literature, and Lee was showing signs of wearying. We sat on either side of him in a box, inviting him, as it were, to drink of the heroism of that music, to fling himself into his role tonight without holding back. We thought of ourselves, still, as a kind of continuation of a long and undying past.

As sometimes happened later on during the run, there was no applause at the final curtain of the first performance. Strange things began to go on in the audience. With the curtain down, some people stood to put their coats on and then sat again, some, especially men, were bent forward covering their faces, and others were openly weeping. People crossed the theater to stand quietly talking with one another. It seemed forever before someone remembered to applaud, and then there was no end to it. I was standing at the back and saw a distinguished-looking elderly man being led up the aisle; he was talking excitedly into the ear of what seemed to be his male secretary or assistant. This, I learned, was Bernard Gimbel, head of the department store chain, who that night gave an order that no one in his stores was to be fired for being overage.

Now began the parade of the visiting New York theater people to see for themselves, and I remember best Kurt Weill and his wife, Lotte Lenya, who had come with Maxwell Anderson's wife, Mab. We had coffee in a little shop, and Weill kept shaking his head and staring at me, and Mab said, "It's the best play ever written," which I dare repeat because it would be said often in the next months and would begin to change my life.

Of the opening night in New York two things stick to memory. At the back of the lovely Morosco, since destroyed by the greed of real estate men and the city's indifference, Kazan and I were sitting on the stairs leading up to the balcony as Lee was saying, "And by the way he died the death of a salesman . . ." Everything had gone beautifully, but I was near exhaustion since I acted all the parts internally as I watched, and suddenly I heard, ". . . in the smoker of the New York, New Hahven and Hayven." Surely the audience would burst out laughing—but nobody did. And the end created the same spell as it had in Philadelphia, and backstage was the same high euphoria that I had now come to expect. A mob of well-wishers packed the corridors to the dressing rooms. For the first time at a play of mine the movie stars had come out, but my face was still unknown and I could stand in a corner watching them unobserved—Lucille Ball and Desi Arnaz, Fredric and Florence March, and faces and names I have long forgotten, putting me on notice that I was now deep in show business, a paradoxically uncomfortable feeling indeed, for it was too material and real to have much to do with something that was air and whispers.

Finally, edging my way onto the stage, where I hoped to find a place to sit and rest, I saw as in a glorious dream of reward and high success three waiters in rich crimson Louis Sherry jackets arranging plates and silver on an extraordinarily long banquet table stretching almost the entire stage width. On its white linen table-cloth were great silver tureens and platters of beef, fowl, and seafood along with ice-filled buckets of champagne. Whose idea could this have been? What a glorious climax to the triumphant evening! Anticipating the heady shock of cold champagne, I reached for a gleaming glass, when one of the waiters approached me and with polite firmness informed me that the dinner had been ordered by Mr. Dowling for a private party. Robert Dowling, whose City Investing Company owned the Morosco along with other Broadway theaters, was a jovial fellow turning sixty who had swum around Manhattan Island, a feat he seemed to memorialize by standing straight with his chest expanded. I liked his childishness and his enthusiasms. I said that Mr. Dowling would surely not begrudge the play's author a well-earned glass of wine in advance of the celebration, but the waiter, obviously on orders, was adamant. I was dumbfounded, it must be somebody's joke, but a bit later, as Mary and I were leaving with the cast and their friends, we all stopped for a moment at the back of the theater to watch with

half-hysterical incredulity as this rather decorous celebratory dinner proceeded literally inside Willy Loman's dun-colored Brooklyn
house, the ladies in elaborate evening gowns, the men in dinner
jackets, the waiters moving back and forth with the food under a
polite hum of conversation suitable for the Pierre Hotel dining
room, and the diners of course totally oblivious to the crowd of us
looking on, laughing, and cracking jokes. It reminded me of scenes
from Soviet movies of the last insensible days of the czarist court.
Dowling, an otherwise generous fellow, was simply exercising the
charming insensitivity of the proprietor, something Broadway
would begin to see more and more of, but never perhaps on so
grandly elegant and absurd a scale.

Secretly, of course, I was outraged, but sufficient praise was on
the way to put offense to sleep. An hour or so later, at the opening-
night party, Jim Proctor grabbed my arm and pulled me to a phone.
On the other end was the whispered voice of Sam Zolotow, that
generation's theatrical inside dopester and a reporter for the *Times*,
who was actually reading our review directly off Brooks Atkinson's
typewriter as the critic wrote it—I could hear the clacking of the
typewriter on the phone. In his Noo Yawk voice he excitedly whispered word after word as Atkinson composed it under his
nose—"Arthur Miller has written a superb drama. From every
point of view, it is rich and memorable . . ."—and as one encomium
was laid upon another Sam's voice grew more and more amazed
and warm and he seemed to reach out and give me his embrace.
The conspiracy that had begun with me and spread to Kazan, the
cast, Mielziner, and all the others now extended to Zolotow and
Atkinson and the *Times*, until for a moment a community seemed
to have formed of people who cared very much that their common
sense of life in their time had found expression.

Driving homeward down lower Broadway at three in the morning, Mary and I were both silent. The radio had just finished an
extraordinary program, readings of the play's overwhelmingly
glowing reviews in the morning papers. My name repeated again
and again seemed to drift away from me and land on someone else,
perhaps my ghost. It was all a letdown now that the arrow had
been fired and the bow, so long held taut, was slackening again. I
had striven all my life to win this night, and it was here, and I was

this celebrated man who had amazingly little to do with me, or I with him.

In truth, I would have sworn I had not changed, only the public perception of me had, but this is merely fame's first illusion. The fact, as it took much more time to appreciate, is that such an order of recognition imprints its touch of arrogance, quite as though one has control of a new power, a power to make real everything one is capable of imagining. And it can open a voraciousness for life and an impatience with old friends who persist in remaining ineffectual. An artist blindly follows his nose with hands outstretched, and only after he has struck the rock and brought forth the form hidden within it does he theorize and explain what is forever inexplicable, but I had a rationalist tradition behind me and felt I had to account to it for my rise.

I came to wish I had had the sense to say that I had learned what I could from books and study but that I did not know how to do what I had apparently done and that the whole thing might as well have been a form of prayer for all I understood about it. Simply, there is a sense for the dramatic form or there is not, there is stage-worthy dialogue and literary dialogue and no one quite knows why one is not the other, why a dramatic line *lands* in an audience and a literary one sails over its head. Instead, there were weighty interviews and even pronouncements, and worst of all, a newly won rank to defend against the inevitable snipers. The crab who manages to climb up out of the bucket causes a lot of the other crabs to try to pull him back down where he belongs. That's what crabs do.

The fear once more was in me that I would not write again. And as Mary and I drove home, I sensed in our silence some discomfort in my wife and friend over these struggling years. It never occurred to me that she might have felt anxious at being swamped by this rush of my fame, in need of reassurance. I had always thought her clearer and more resolved than I. Some happiness was not with us that I wanted now, I had no idea what it might be, only knew the absence of it, its lack—so soon. In fact, the aphrodisiac of celebrity, still nameless, came and sat between us in the car.

And so inevitably there was a desire to flee from it all, to be blessedly unknown again, and a fear that I had stumbled into a dangerous artillery range. It was all an unnaturalness; fame is the other side of loneliness, of impossible-to-resolve contradictions—to be anonymous and at the same time not lose one's renown, in brief, to be two people who might occasionally visit together and perhaps make a necessary joint public appearance but who would normally live separate lives, the public fellow wasting his time gadding about while the writer stayed at his desk, as morose and anxious as ever, and at work. I did not want the power I wanted. It wasn't "real." What was?

Outlandish as it seemed, the Dowling party in the Lomans' living room came to symbolize one part of the dilemma; the pain and love and protest in my play could be transformed into mere champagne. My dreams of many years had simply become too damned real, and the reality was less than the dream and lacked all dedication.

Preface to *Salesman in Beijing*
1991

Writing a book was the last thought in my mind when I went to China in 1984 to direct a Chinese cast in *Death of A Salesman* at the Beijing People's Art Theatre. There were too many uncertainties to allow for writing anything. Would I manage to communicate with Chinese actors, only one of whom understood English? Would the audience make any sense of the play, whose form, like the society it spoke of, was utterly strange to them? Indeed, one director of the theatre declared on reading the play after rehearsals had begun that "it is impossible to act this thing." And in truth several of the actors would later confess that they could make nothing of it in the beginning.

But it soon turned out that the moon is the moon and actors are actors, the same everywhere. However, what indeed was often very different was their etiquette, what I came to think of as the signals by which Chinese communicate, as well as the assumptions they conventionally make about each other. They are obviously more formal with one another and more deferential to anyone who is older, but—at least in Communist China—the interesting difference was that they rather assumed that anyone expressing a view must be in conformity with whatever social organization he was part of. For instance, it took a lot of persuading for them to believe that Biff, in so stubbornly opposing Willy's belief in money-making, was not speaking for an organization but for himself out of his own experience. More, it was hard for them to imagine that any man would be able to take off and simply float from job to job purely on his own volition. Chinese are attached to society and are directed by it in ways difficult for Westerners to imagine. It was also painfully embarrassing for the actor playing Happy to continue talking to his brother once the latter had closed his eyes and announced that he was going to sleep—this was simply too impolite, and not only for the character but the actor himself.

But beneath these questions of etiquette I found the same basic emotions as we have, the love and pity and false hopes and the rest. The Chinese audience proved this similarity in its reactions to the play whose popularity was such that after a run of many months and much touring through China, as well as television broadcasts, it has recently been mounted again in Beijing with the original cast with two substitutions.

Of course what the Chinese audience makes of this play is another story and no doubt differs from person to person. One woman, an early viewer of our rehearsals, shook her head and referring to Willy said to my wife, Inge Morath—"He's just like my mother." Another, a young man interviewed on CBS TV as he left the lobby of the theatre, thought that Willy's philosophy was absolutely correct. "We all want to be number one man, the boss, this is natural and very good. Biff is wrong." And so Biff would seem to be in post Cultural Revolution China which had just emerged from a period of brutal social levelling, a time when it was immoral for any individual to seek distinction of any kind. (Even keeping goldfish or a pet bird was condemned as perverse anti-social individualism.) To Chinese, Biff sounded a lot like a Red Guard in his refusal to try to excel and personally succeed as Willy was demanding.

This unintended book essentially formed itself partly as the result of the rehearsal schedule. The Chinese rehearse from eight to noon, then break until seven in the evening and work till ten. The hiatus is used for food-shopping and napping. In fear of finding myself separated by language from the day-to-day development of the production, I had brought along a small tape recorder to pick up what I had said during rehearsals, as well as what Ying Ruochang was saying to me. He was Willy, the play's translator, and a fluent English speaker through whom I communicated to the cast. In the afternoons with nothing to do I listened to the morning's transactions, most of which, complicated and onrushing as they were, I had already begun to forget, and typed them out in rough form. What I soon began to realize, now that I could look back even a few days, was that we were all feeling our way rather tentatively into a sort of new and undiscovered country where none of us had been before—they in their imaginary Willy Loman-America and I in a Chinese Brooklyn.

Of course this was all years before the Tiananmen catastrophe, a time, shortly after the end of the Cultural Revolution, when hopes were growing that China had really stepped out on to the road of widening liberties and governmental self-restraint. It seemed impossible, at least to me, that they could ever revert to the violent suppressions of the recent past which they now knew had cost China more than a generation of development. And there seemed a great and growing confidence that a more rational and liberal future was opening up, so much so that they would not even hear of reprisals against those who had persecuted them. No vendetta, the past was the past, they had no need to humiliate former enemies, even those responsible for the deaths and tortures of teachers, writers, artists and workers. I admired their temperance and their resolve to demonstrate tolerance and liberality in order to begin the moderation of civic behavior. Our stage manager, as a matter of fact, had been a militant Red Guard fanatic, one of those who had made the lives of many of the cast miserable in the recent Cultural Revolution period. Worse yet, he was still being a nuisance, rushing at me and jabbing his finger at his watch at the very instant rehearsal time had run out, cutting off a scene or veritably a sentence in order to force conformity with the rules. But now they could smile rather than tremble at his officious antics, and for them this was a big difference. I don't suppose they are smiling any more at such ridiculously meddlesome and often dangerous people.

But China is immortal and will go on winding its way across history, sometimes the world's wise teacher, sometimes its stubbornly ignorant and recalcitrant pupil. This production of *Salesman* happened by sheer chance to occur when the wave of hope was on a steep rise in China. This record of it may be one of a very few candid glimpses inside the minds of quite ordinary Chinese who were actors also in the larger tragedy of our time.

Salesman at Fifty
1999

As far as I know, nobody has figured out time. Not chronological time, of course—that's merely what the calendar tells—but real time, the kind that baffles the human mind when it confronts, as mine does now, the apparent number of months, weeks, and years that have elapsed since 1948, when I sat down to write a play about a salesman. I say "apparent" because I cannot find a means of absorbing the idea of half a century rolling away beneath my feet. Half a century is a very long time, yet I must already have been grown up way back then, indeed I must have been a few years past thirty, if my calculations are correct, and this fact I find indigestible.

A few words about the theatrical era that *Death of a Salesman* emerged from. The only theater available to a playwright in the late Forties was Broadway, the most ruthlessly commercialized theater in the world, with the Off-Broadway evolution still a decade away. That theater had one single audience, not two or three, as is the case today, catering to very different levels of age, culture, education, and intellectual sophistication. Its critics were more than likely to be ex–sports reporters or general journalists rather than scholars or specialists university-trained in criticism. So a play worked or it didn't, made them laugh or cry or left them bored. (It really isn't all that different today except that the reasoning is perhaps more elevated.) That unified audience was the same for musicals, farces, O'Neill's tragedies, or some imported British, French, or Middle European lament. Whatever its limitations, it was an audience that loved theater, and many of its members thought theatergoing not quite a luxury but an absolute necessity for a civilized life.

For playwriting, what I believe was important about that unified audience was that a writer with ambitions reaching beyond realistic, made-for-entertainment plays could not expect the support of a coterie of like-minded folk who would overlook his artistic lapses so long as his philosophical agenda tended to justify their own. That unified audience had come in from the rain to be entertained, and even instructed, if need be, provided the instruction was entertaining. But the writer had to keep in mind that his proofs, so to speak, had to be accessible both to the lawyers in the audience and to the plumbers, to the doctors and the housewives, to the college students and the kids at the Saturday matinee. One result of this mix was the ideal, if not the frequent fulfillment, of a kind of play that would be complete rather than fragmentary, an emotional rather than an intellectual experience, a play basically of heart with its ulterior moral gesture integrated with action rather than rhetoric. In fact, it was a Shakespearean ideal, a theater for anyone with an understanding of English and perhaps some common sense.

Some of the initial readers of the *Death of a Salesman* script were not at all sure that the audience of 1949 was going to follow its manipulations of time, for one thing. Josh Logan, a leading stage and film director of numerous hits, *Mister Roberts* and *South Pacific* among them, had greeted *All My Sons* two years earlier with great warmth, and invested a thousand dollars in *Salesman*, but when he read the script he apologetically withdrew five hundred. No audience, he felt, would follow the story, and no one would ever be sure whether Willy was imagining or really living through one or another scene in the play. Some thirty years later I would hear the same kind of reaction from the theater people in the Beijing People's Art Theater, where I had been invited to stage the play, which, in the view of many there, was not a play at all but a poem. It was only when they saw it played that its real dramatic nature came through.

In the 1949 Broadway audience there was more to worry about than their following the story. In one of his letters O'Neill had referred to that theater as a "showshop," a crude place where a very uncultivated, materialistic public cut off from its own spirituality gathered for a laugh or a tear. Clifford Odets, with his first successes surely the most hotly acclaimed playwright in Broadway history, would also end in bitter alienation from the whole system of Broadway production. The problem, in a word, was seriousness.

There wasn't very much of it in the audience, and it was resented when it threatened to appear on the stage.

So it seemed. But *All My Sons* had all but convinced me that if one totally integrated a play's conceptual life with its emotional one so that there was no perceptible dividing line between the two, such a play could reach such an audience. In short, the play had to move forward not by following a narrow, discrete line, but as a phalanx, all of its elements moving together simultaneously. There was no model I could adapt for this play, no past history for the kind of work I felt it could become. What I had before me was the way the mind—at least my mind—actually worked. One asks a policeman for directions; as one listens, the hairs sticking out of his nose become important, reminding one of a father, brother, son with the same feature, and one's conflicts with him or one's friendship come to mind, and all this over a period of seconds while objectively taking note of how to get to where one wants to go. Initially based, as I explained in *Timebends*, my autobiography, on an uncle of mine, Willy rapidly took over my imagination and became something that has never existed before, a salesman with his feet on the subway stairs and his head in the stars.

His language and that of the Loman family were liberative from any enslavement to "the way people speak." There are some people who simply don't speak the way people speak. The Lomans, like their models in life, are not content with who and what they are, but want to be other, wealthier, more cultivated perhaps, closer to power. "I've been remiss," Biff says to Linda about his neglect of his father, and there would be many who seized on this usage as proof of the playwright's tin ear or of some inauthenticity in the play. But it is in Biff's mouth precisely because it is indeed an echo, a slightly misunderstood signal from above, from the more serious and cultivated part of society, a signal indicating that he is now to be taken with utmost seriousness, even remorseful of his past neglect. "Be liked and you will never want" is also not quite from Brooklyn, but Willy needs aphoristic authority at this point, and again, there is an echo of a—for want of a better word—Victorian authority to back him up. These folk are the innocent receivers of what they imagine as a more elegant past, a time "finer" than theirs. As Jews light-years away from religion or a community that might have fostered Jewish identity, they exist in a spot that probably most Americans feel they inhabit—on the sidewalk side of the glass looking in at a well-lighted place.

As it has turned out, this play seems to have shown that most of the world shares something similar to that condition. Having seen it in five or six countries, and directed it in China and Sweden, neither of whose languages I know, it was both mystifying and gratifying to note that people everywhere react pretty much the same in the same places of the play. When I arrived in China to begin rehearsals the people in the American embassy, with two exceptions, were sure the Chinese were too culturally remote from the play to ever understand it. The American ambassador and the political officer thought otherwise, the first because he had been born and raised in China, and the second, I supposed, because it was his job to understand how Chinese thought about life. And what they were thinking turned out to be more or less what they were thinking in New York or London or Paris, namely that being human—a father, mother, son—is something most of us fail at most of the time, and a little mercy is eminently in order given the societies we live in, which purport to be stable and sound as mountains when in fact they are all trembling in a fast wind blowing mindlessly around the earth.

AN ENEMY OF THE PEOPLE

Preface to Adaptation of Ibsen's
An Enemy of the People
1951

I

At the outset it ought to be said that the word "adaptation" is very distasteful to me. It seems to mean that one writer has ventured into another's chickencoop, or worse, into the sacred chamber of another's personal creations and rearranged things without permission. Most of the time an adaptation is a playwright's excuse for not writing his own plays, and since I am not yet with my back against that particular wall, I think it wise to set down what I have tried to do with *An Enemy of the People*, and why I did it.

There is one quality in Ibsen that no serious writer can afford to overlook. It lies at the very center of his force, and I found in it—as I hope others will—a profound source of strength. It is his insistence, his utter conviction, that he is going to say what he has to say, and that the audience, by God, is going to listen. It is the very same quality that makes a star actor, a great public speaker, and a lunatic. Every Ibsen play begins with the unwritten words: "Now listen here!" And these words have shown me a path through the wall of "entertainment," a path that leads beyond the formulas and dried-up precepts, the pretense and fraud, of the business of the stage. Whatever else Ibsen has to teach, this is his first and greatest contribution.

In recent years Ibsen has fallen into a kind of respectful obscurity that is not only undeserved but really quite disrespectful of culture—and a disservice to the theater besides. I decided to work on *An Enemy of the People* because I had a private wish to demonstrate that Ibsen is really pertinent today, that he is not "old-fashioned," and, implicitly, that those who condemn him are themselves misleading our theater and our playwrights into a blind alley of senseless sensibility, triviality, and the inevitable waste of our dramatic talents; for it has become the fashion for plays to reduce the "thickness" of life to a fragile facsimile, to avoid portraying the complexities of life, the contradictions of character, the fascinating interplay of cause and effect that have long been part of the novel. And I wished also to buttress the idea that the dramatic writer has, and must again demonstrate, the right to entertain with his brains as well as his heart. It is necessary that the public understand again that the stage is *the* place for ideas, for philosophies, for the most intense discussion of man's fate. One of the masters of such a discussion is Henrik Ibsen, and I have presumed to point this out once again.

2

I have attempted to make *An Enemy of the People* as alive to Americans as it undoubtedly was to Norwegians, while keeping it intact. I had no interest in exhuming anything, in asking people to sit respectfully before the work of a celebrated but neglected writer. There are museums for such activities; the theater has no truck with them, and ought not to have.

And I believed this play could be alive for us because its central theme is, in my opinion, the central theme of our social life today. Simply, it is the question of whether the democratic guarantees protecting political minorities ought to be set aside in time of crisis. More personally, it is the question of whether one's vision of the truth ought to be a source of guilt at a time when the mass of men condemn it as a dangerous and devilish lie. It is an enduring theme—in fact, possibly the most enduring of all Ibsen's themes—because there never was, nor will there ever be, an organized society able to countenance calmly the individual who insists that he is right while the vast majority is absolutely wrong.

The play is the story of a scientist who discovers an evil and, innocently believing that he has done a service to humanity, expects that he will at least be thanked. However, the town has a vested interest in the perpetuation of that evil, and his "truth," when confronted with that interest, must be made to conform. The scientist cannot change the truth for any reason disconnected with the evil. He clings to the truth and suffers the social consequences. At rock bottom, then, the play is concerned with the inviolability of objective truth. Or, put more dynamically, that those who attempt to warp the truth for ulterior purposes must inevitably become warped and corrupted themselves. This theme is valid today, just as it will always be, but some of the examples given by Ibsen to prove it may no longer be.

I am told that Ibsen wrote this play as a result of his being practically stoned off the stage for daring to present *Ghosts*. The plot is supposed to have come from a news item which told of a Hungarian scientist who had discovered poisoned water in the town's water supply and had been pilloried for his discovery. If this was the case, my interpretation of the theme is doubly justified, for it then seems beyond doubt that Ibsen meant above and beyond all else to defend his right to stand "at the outpost of society," alone with the truth, and to speak from there to his fellow men.

However, there are a few speeches, and one scene in particular, which have been taken to mean that Ibsen was a fascist. In the original meeting scene in which Dr. Stockmann sets forth his—and Ibsen's—point of view most completely and angrily, Dr. Stockmann makes a speech in which he turns to biology to prove that there are indeed certain individuals "bred" to a superior apprehension of truths and who have the natural right to lead, if not to govern, the mass.

If the entire play is to be understood as the working-out of this speech, then one has no justification for contending that it is other than racist and fascist—certainly it could not be thought of as a defense of any democratic idea. But, structurally speaking, the theme is not wholly contained in the meeting scene alone. In fact, this speech is in some important respects in contradiction to the actual dramatic working-out of the play. But that Ibsen never really believed that idea in the first place is amply proved by a speech he delivered to a workers' club after the production of *An Enemy of the People*. He said then: "Of course I do not mean the aristocracy of birth, or of the purse, or even the aristocracy of the intellect. I mean the aristocracy of character, of will, of mind—that alone can free us."

I have taken as justification for removing those examples which no longer prove the theme—examples I believe Ibsen would have removed were he alive today—the line in the original manuscript that reads: "There is no established truth that can remain true for more than seventeen, eighteen, at most twenty years." In light of genocide, the holocaust that has swept our world on the wings of the black ideology of racism, it is inconceivable that Ibsen would insist today that certain individuals are by breeding, or race, or "innate" qualities superior to others or possessed of the right to dictate to others. The man who wrote *A Doll's House*, the clarion call for the equality of women, cannot be equated with a fascist. The whole cast of his thinking was such that he could not have lived a day under an authoritarian regime of any kind. He was an individualist sometimes to the point of anarchism, and in such a man there is too explosive a need for self-expression to permit him to conform to any rigid ideology. It is impossible, therefore, to set him beside Hitler.

3

On reading the standard translations of Ibsen's work it quickly became obvious that the false impressions that have been connected with the man would seem to be justified were he to be produced in "translated" form. For one thing, his language in English sounds impossibly pedantic. Combine this with the fact that he wore a beard and half-lenses in his eyeglasses, and that his plays have always been set forth with yards of fringe on every tablecloth and drapery, and it was guaranteed that a new production on the traditional basis would truly bury the man for good.

I set out to transform his language into contemporary English. Working from a pidgin-English, word-for-word rendering of the

Norwegian, done by Mr. Lars Nordenson, I was able to gather the meaning of each speech and scene without the obstruction of any kind of English construction.

For instance, Mr. Nordenson, working from the original Norwegian manuscript, set before me speeches such as: "But, dear Thomas, what have you then done to him again?" Or: "The Mayor being your brother, I would not wish to touch it, but you are as convinced as I am that truth goes ahead of all other considerations." Or: "Well, what do you say, Doctor? Don't you think it is high time that we stir a little life into the slackness and sloppiness of halfheartedness and cowardliness?" This last speech now reads: "Well, what do you say to a little hypodermic for these fence-sitting deadheads?"

It was possible to peer into the original play with as clear an eye as one could who knew no Norwegian. There were no English sentences to correct and rewrite, only the bare literalness of the original. This version of the play, then, is really in the nature of a new translation into spoken English.

But it is more too. The original has a tendency to indulge in transitions between scenes that are themselves uninteresting, and although as little as possible of the original construction has been changed and the play is exactly as it was, scene for scene, I have made each act seem of one piece, instead of separate scenes. And my reason for doing this is simply that the tradition of Ibsen's theater allowed the opera-like separation of scenes, while ours demands that the audience never be conscious that a "scene" has taken place at all.

Structurally the largest change is in the third act—Ibsen's fifth. In the original the actual dramatic end comes a little past the middle of the act, but it is followed by a wind-up that keeps winding endlessly to the curtain. I think this overwriting was the result of Ibsen's insistence that his meaning be driven home—and from the front door right through to the back, lest the audience fail to understand him. Generally, in this act, I have brought out the meaning of the play in terms of dramatic action, action which was already there and didn't need to be newly invented, but which was separated by tendentious speeches spoken into the blue.

Throughout the play I have tried to peel away its trappings of the moment, its relatively accidental details which ring the dull green tones of Victorianism, and to show that beneath them there still lives the terrible wrath of Henrik Ibsen, who could make a play as men make watches, precisely, intelligently, and telling not merely the minute and the hour but the age.

Ibsen's Warning
1989

I don't suppose anything has given me more gratification than the success of *An Enemy of the People* in its recent Young Vic production. I have made no secret of my early love for Ibsen's work, and now to have been in some way responsible, along with some very fine young actors and a passionately perceptive director, for a new appreciation of one of his most central ideas, is something that puts a satisfying warmth in my belly.

It is a terrible thing to have to say, but the story of *Enemy* is far more applicable to our nature-despoiling societies than to even turn-of-the-century capitalism, untrammeled and raw as Ibsen knew it to be. The churning up of pristine forests, valleys and fields for minerals and the rights of way of the expanding rail systems is child's play compared to some of our vast depredations, our atomic contamination and oil spills, to say nothing of the tainting of our food supply by carcinogenic chemicals.

It must be remembered, however, that for Ibsen the poisoning of the public water supply by mendacious and greedy interests was only the occasion of *An Enemy of the People* and is not, strictly speaking, its theme. That, of course, concerns the crushing of the dissenting spirit by the majority, and the right and obligation of such a spirit to exist at all. That he thought to link this moral struggle with the preservation of nature is perhaps not accidental. After all, he may well have found enough examples of moral cowardice and selfish antisocial behavior in other areas such as business, science, the ministry, the arts or where you will.

It is many years now since I looked into an Ibsen biography but I seem to recall that the genesis of *Enemy* was usually thought to be a news report of the poisoning of the water supply at a Hungarian spa. If there was a Dr. Stockmann prototype who vainly protested against keeping the public ignorant of the truth, I cannot recall it. But whether or not this was the overt stimulus behind the play the question still remains why Ibsen should have seized upon it so avidly—he wrote this play in a remarkably short time, a few weeks.

Thinking about his choice throws me back to Henry David Thoreau who likewise found in nature's ruin the metaphor of man's self-betrayal. And Thoreau, I think, stood within an intellectual tradition of distrust of progress, one that goes back to the Roman poets, and the concomitant age-old view of the city as inevitably decadent and the unspoiled country as noble. Where it comes to nature even radical artists are likely to be very conservative and suspicious of change; perhaps nature takes on even more of a pure moral value where religion itself has vanished into skepticism. The sky may be empty but to look out on untouched forest or a pristine lake is to see if not God or the gods, then at least their abandoned abode. Ibsen needed an absolute good for evil to work against, an unarguably worthy brightness for dark mendacity to threaten, and perhaps nature alone could offer him that. And, of course, this is even more effective in our time when people have to go to the supermarket to buy clean water.

I am sure that few in the first New York audience of the early Fifties were terribly convinced by the play's warnings of danger to the environment. The anticommunist gale was blowing hard and it was the metaphor that stood in the foreground; moreover, in that time of blind belief in rational, responsible science, any suggestion that, for example, we might be building atomic generating plants that were actually unsafe would have simply been dismissed as dangerous obscurantist nonsense. And given my own identification with the Left, the metaphor was widely suspect as a mere ploy, an attempt to link the Reds, then under heavy attack, with Ibsen's truth-bearer. So neither the story nor the metaphor could carry the credibility that they do now when both have been revalued as alarmingly prophetic instinctual conceptions—it often does indeed take moral courage to stand against commercial and governmental bureaucracies that care nothing for the survival of the real world outside their offices. It is but one more evidence that the artist's powerful desire to penetrate life's chaos, to make it meaningfully cohere, has literally created a truth as substantial as a sword for later generations to wield against their own oppression.

Brewed in *The Crucible*
1958

One afternoon last week I attended a rehearsal of the imminent Off-Broadway production of *The Crucible*. For the first time in the five years since its opening on Broadway, I heard its dialogue, and the experience awakened not merely memories but the desire to fire a discussion among us of certain questions a play like this ought to have raised.

Notoriously, there is what is called a chemistry in the theater, a fusion of play, performance, and audience temper which, if it does not take place, leaves the elements of an explosion cold and to one side of art. For the critics, this seems to be what happened with *The Crucible*. It was not condemned; it was set aside. A cold thing, mainly, it lay to one side of entertainment, to say nothing of art. In a word, I was told that I had not written another *Death of a Salesman*.

It is perhaps beyond my powers to make clear, but I had no desire to write another *Salesman*, and not because I lack love for that play but for some wider, less easily defined reasons that have to do with this whole question of cold and heat and, indeed, with the future of our drama altogether. It is the question of whether we—playwrights and audiences and critics—are to declare that we have reached the end, the last development of dramatic form. More specifically, the play designed to draw a tear; the play designed to "identify" the audience with its characters in the usual sense; the play that takes as its highest challenge the emotional relations of the family, for that, as it turns out, is what it comes to.

I was disappointed in the reaction to *The Crucible* not only for the obvious reasons but because no critic seemed to sense what I was after. In 1953 McCarthyism probably helped to make it appear that the play was bounded on all sides by its arraignment of the witch hunt. The political trajectory was so clear—a fact of which I am a little proud—that what to me were equally if not more important elements were totally ignored. The new production, appearing in a warmer climate, may, I hope, flower, and these inner petals may make their appropriate appearance.

What I say now may appear more technical than a writer has any business talking about in public. But I do not think it merely a question of technique to say that with all its excellences the kind of play we have come to accept without effort or question is standing at a dead end. What "moves" us is coming to be a narrower and narrower aesthetic fragment of life. I have shown, I think, that I am not unaware of psychology or immune to the fascinations of the neurotic hero, but I believe that it is no longer possible to contain the truth of the human situation so totally within a single man's guts as the bulk of our plays presuppose. The documentation of man's loneliness is not in itself and for itself ultimate wisdom, and the form this documentation inevitably assumes in playwriting is not the ultimate dramatic form.

I was drawn to write *The Crucible* not merely as a response to McCarthyism. It is not any more an attempt to cure witch hunts than *Salesman* is a plea for the improvement of conditions for traveling men, *All My Sons* a plea for better inspection of airplane parts, or *A View from the Bridge* an attack upon the Immigration Bureau. *The Crucible* is, internally, *Salesman*'s blood brother. It is examining the questions I was absorbed with before—the conflict between a man's raw deeds and his conception of himself; the question of whether conscience is in fact an organic part of the human being, and what happens when it is handed over not merely to the state or the mores of the time but to one's friend or wife. The big difference, I think, is that *The Crucible* sought to include a higher degree of consciousness than the earlier plays.

I believe that the wider the awareness, the felt knowledge, evoked by a play, the higher it must stand as art. I think our drama is far behind our lives in this respect. There is a lot wrong with the twentieth century, but one thing is right with it—we are aware as no generation was before of the larger units that help make us and destroy us. The city, the nation, the world, and now the universe are never far beyond our most intimate sense of life. The vast majority of us know now—not merely as knowledge but as feeling, feeling capable of expression in art—that we are being formed, that our alternatives in life are not absolutely our own, as the romantic play inevitably must presuppose. But the response of our plays, of our dramatic form itself, is to faint, so to speak, before the intricacies of man's wider relationships and to define him further and redefine him as essentially alone in a world he never made.

The form, the shape, the meaning of *The Crucible* were all compounded out of the faith of those who were hanged. They were asked to be lonely and they refused. They were asked to deny their belief in a God of all men, not merely a god each individual could manipulate to his interests. They were asked to call a phantom real and to deny their touch with reality. It was not good to cast this play, to form it so that the psyche of the hero should emerge so "commonly" as to wipe out of mind the process itself, the spectacle of that faith and the knowing will which these people paid for with their lives.

The "heat" infusing this play is therefore of a different order from that which draws tears and the common identifications. And it was designed to be of a different order. In a sense, I felt, our situation had thrown us willy-nilly into a new classical period. Classical in the sense that the social scheme, as of old, had reached the point of rigidity where it had become implacable as a consciously known force working in us and upon us. Analytical psychology, when so intensely exploited as to reduce the world to the size of a man's abdomen and equate his fate with his neurosis, is a re-emergence of romanticism. It is inclined to deny all outer forces until man is only his complex. It presupposes an autonomy in the human character that, in a word, is false. A neurosis is not a fate but an effect. There is a higher wisdom, and if truly there is not, there is still no aesthetic point in repeating something so utterly known, or in doing better what has been done so well before.

For me *The Crucible* was a new beginning, the beginning of an attempt to embrace a wider field of vision, a field wide enough to contain the whole of our current awareness. It was not so much to move ahead of the audience but to catch up with what it commonly knows about the way things are and how they get that way. In a word, we commonly know so much more than our plays let on. When we can put together what we do know with what we feel, we shall find a new kind of theater in our hands. *The Crucible* was written as it was in order to bring me, and the audience, closer to that theater and what I imagine can be an art more ample than any of us has dared to strive for, the art of Man among men, Man amid his works.

Again They Drink from the
Cup of Suspicion
1989

I did not write *The Crucible* simply to propagandize against McCarthyism, although if justification were needed that would have been enough. There was something else involved. I'll try to explain.

A writer friend was recently telling me about a Moscow theater producer who is interested in putting on a play about the Vietnam War. Why Vietnam? It turns out that what he would really like to illuminate is the Russian defeat in Afghanistan, but with feelings about Afghanistan still running so high he felt he needed a metaphor that would go to the dilemmas underlying such a war, rather than attempting an outright confrontation with the thickets of feeling surrounding Afghanistan itself.

That approach reminded me of my decision to write about the 1692 Salem witch trials, rather than trying to take on Joseph McCarthy and his cohorts directly. In the early fifties McCarthyism, so-called, began as a conservative Republican cavalry charge that in the name of anti-Communism helped scatter the left-liberal coalitions of Democrats and union people who had held together the only recently faded New Deal. But this was no ordinary political campaign. This time the enemy was not merely "The Democrat Party," as McCarthy sneeringly renamed it, but the hidden foreign plot which, naively but often knowingly, it shielded. Thus a certain sublime gloss—national security—was varnished over a very traditional grab for domestic political power.

With amazing speed McCarthy was convincing a lot of not unintelligent people that the incredible was really true, and that, say, General of the Army George Catlett Marshall was a Communist sympathizer, or that Senator Millard E. Tydings of Maryland was a buddy of Earl Browder, head of the American Communist Party. (A photo of both of them standing happily together would only much later be proved to have been a fake manufactured by Roy Cohn, McCarthy's right-hand bandido.)

For a time it began to seem that Senator Joe was heading straight for the White House, the more so when the sheer incredibility of his claims appeared to be part proof that they were real; if the Communists were indeed hidden everywhere, it followed that they would certainly be found where common sense indicated they could not conceivably be.

The case being circular, it was finally all but unarguable. Worse yet, you could not rely on the too-trusting police, the naively legalistic courts, or even the slow-moving F.B.I. to root out the conspiracy. As for the press, it was all but sold to Moscow, secretly, of course. Who then was absolutely reliable? McCarthy, naturally, and those who had his blessing.

This was colorful and fascinating stuff for the stage, but a play takes a year to write and months to see through production, and I could not imagine spending so much time on what seemed to me so obvious a tale. But as the anti-Communist crusade settled in, and showed signs of becoming the permanent derangement of the American psyche, a kind of mystery began to emerge from its melodramas and comedies. We were all behaving differently than we used to; we had drunk from the cup of suspicion of one another; people inevitably were afraid of too close an association with someone who might one day fall afoul of some committee. Even certain words vibrated perilously, words like organize, social, militant, movement, capitalism—it didn't do to be on too familiar terms with such language. We had entered a mysterious pall from which there seemed no exit.

Returning around that time to my alma mater, the University of Michigan, to do a story for *Holiday* magazine, I discovered that students were avoiding living in the co-op rooming houses because the very idea of a nonprofit organization was suspiciously pro-left. The F.B.I. was paying students at Michigan to report secretly on teachers' political remarks, and teachers to report on students.

Why was there so little real opposition to this madness? Of course there was the fear of reprisals, of losing jobs, or perhaps only bad publicity, but there was also guilt, and this seemed to me the main crippler, the internalized cop.

No doubt instinctually, McCarthy and Roy Cohn were handing around full plates of guilt which were promptly licked clean by people who in one way or another had brushed the sleeve of the Communist movement in the thirties—some by joining the party or supporting one of its front organizations, a left-wing union or professional guild, or in whatever manner had at some point in their lives turned to the left. Of course such people were used to being guilty—why else would they have bothered to worry about the poor, the blacks, the lynch victims, the Spanish Republicans, and so on when real Americans were only remotely aware of such inequities around them?

It was a charm, a kind of spell. McCarthy could call the Roosevelt New Deal "20 years of treason" with hardly a rejoinder from the vast multitude of Americans for whom New Deal measures, hardly more than a decade before, had meant the difference between living on the street or in their own homes, between hunger and real starvation. It was a sort of benighted miracle that just about anything that flew out of his mouth, no matter how outrageously and obviously idiotic, could be made to land in an audience and stir people's terrors of being taken over by Communists, their very religion in danger.

I had known the Salem story since college, over a decade earlier, but what kept assaulting my brain now was not the hunt for witches itself; it was the paralysis that had led to more than twenty public hangings of very respectable farmers by their neighbors. There was something "wonderful" in this spectacle, a kind of perverse, malign poetry that had simply swamped the imaginations of these people. I thought I saw something like it around me in the early fifties.

The truth is that the more I worked at this dilemma the less it had to do with Communists and McCarthy and the more it concerned something very fundamental in the human animal: the fear of the unknown, and particularly the dread of social isolation.

Political movements are always trying to position themselves as shields against the unknown—vote for me and you're safe. The difference during witch-hunts is that you are being made safe from a malign, debauched, evil, irreligious, wife-swapping, deceitful, immoral, stinking conspiracy stemming from the very bowels of hell. In Wisconsin in the early fifties a reporter went door to door asking residents if they agreed with certain propositions, ten in number, and discovered that very few people did, and that most thought the first ten amendments to the United States Constitution, unnamed of course in the inquiry, were Communistic. To propose that we should be free to express any idea at all was frightening to a lot of people.

The Colonial government in the 1690s saw itself as protecting Christianity (while unknowingly propagating a thrilling counter-religion of Satan worship) by seizing on the ravings of a klatch of repressed pubescent girls who, fearing punishment for their implicitly sexual revolt, began convincing themselves that they had been perverted by Satan. There were economic and social pressures at work, but the nub of it all as it appeared to the locals at the moment was that the Archfiend had been sneaked into the spotless town by an alien who, even better, was black, the Barbadian slave of the Lord's very own man, the church minister himself. Authority quickly converted the poor girls back to the true religion and made them celebrities for their agonizing bravery in pointing out likely adherents of the Devil.

But were there not really Communists, whereas there never were any witches? Of course. And there are also paranoids who are really being followed. There was a very real military face-off in the fifties between America and the Soviet Union, and we had only recently "lost" China, but were these grounds for blacklisting actors and writers in Hollywood, or destroying professionals in many other fields, and for turning the country into a whispering gallery? What research showed me, and what I hoped the play would show the country and the world, was the continuity through time of human delusion, and the only safeguard, fragile though it may be, against it—namely, the law and the courageous few whose sacrifice illuminates delusion.

In the 35 years since the play was written it has become my most produced work by far. I doubt a week has gone by when it has not been on some stage somewhere in the world. It seems to be produced, especially in Latin America, when a dictatorship is in the offing, or when one has just been overthrown.

There is so often a telltale social sidelight connected to its production. Years ago in South Africa, black Tituba had to be played by a white woman in blackface, but the director, Barney Simon, terrified though he was of attack, wanted the white audience to contemplate the story. Last year I happened to meet Nien Cheng, the seventy-year-old author of *Life and Death in Shanghai*, an account of her six-year imprisonment during the Cultural Revolution. Tears formed in her eyes when she shook my hand, tears, as it surprisingly turned out, of gratitude.

Released from prison, she had spent months recuperating when a director friend, Huang Tsolin, invited her to see his production of *The Crucible* in a Shanghai theater. She said she was astounded: "I could not believe the play was not written by a Chinese because the questions of the court were exactly the same ones the Cultural Revolutionaries had put to me!"

I saw the play in Tbilisi, Soviet Georgia, where John Proctor wore seventeenth-century Turkish pantaloons and a gorgeous wide moustache and was chased through a forest by a crowd waving scimitars. At Olivier's fabulous 1965 National Theatre production, with Colin Blakely and Joyce Redman, I overheard a young woman in front of me whispering to her escort, "Didn't this have something to do with that American Senator—what was his name?" I have to admit that it felt marvelous that McCarthy was what's-his-name while *The Crucible* was *The Crucible* still.

Simone Signoret and Yves Montand did a stirring French film, a version of their Paris stage performance, with a screenplay by Jean-Paul Sartre in which the New England farmers were, inexplicably, Roman Catholic. The Long Wharf Theater in New Haven is about to open it under Arvin Brown's direction—it was Long Wharf's first production 25 years ago—and the Roundabout Theater will be doing it later this season. An HBO film of it is to be made this winter for both television and theatrical distribution. In Glasgow recently two productions were running at the same time, one by a young Soviet company. The Schiller Theater in Berlin will have it on in a few months.

I have wondered if one of the reasons the play continues like this is its symbolic unleashing of the specter of order's fragility. When certainties evaporate with each dawn, the unknowable is always around the corner. We know how much depends on mere trust and good faith and a certain respect for the human person, and how easily breached these are. And we know as well how close to the edge we live and how weak we really are and how quickly swept by fear the mass of us can become when our panic button is pushed. It is also, I suppose, that the play reaffirms the ultimate power of courage and clarity of mind whose ultimate fruit is liberty.

It Could Happen Here—And Did
1967

I keep no file of reviews, but if memory serves, *The Crucible* was generally dismissed as a cold, anti-McCarthy tract, more an outburst than a play. A relatively small band of rooters kept it on the Broadway stage for six months or so.

It is certain that a reading now of those reviews would leave unexplained, to say the least, why the play has continued to be produced here and around the world these fifteen years, or why it should have run through several seasons in France and remains in many permanent repertories, including Olivier's National Theatre in Britain. There have been years when it was more often performed than *Death of a Salesman*. Something living must thrive in the play which, I was told on its opening, was a dead husk.

Perhaps its victory over adversities has made me prouder of it than of anything else I have written, and perhaps it is permissible to say why I think it has refused to be dismissed.

The prime point at issue in 1953 when it opened was whether the analogy was a sound one between the Massachusetts witch hunt and the then-current hysteria about Communists boring from within the government, labor, education, entertainment and the intellectual community. After all, there never were any witches while there certainly were Communists, so that *The Crucible* appeared to some as a misreading of the problem at best—a "naïveté," or at worst a specious and even sinister attempt to whitewash the guilt of the Communists with the noble heroism of those in 1692 who had rather be hanged than confess to nonexistent crimes. Indeed, the critic Eric Bentley wrote that one never knew what a Miller play was about.

I believe that life does provide some sound analogies now and again, but I don't think they are any good on the stage. Before a play can be "about" something else, it has to be about itself. If *The Crucible* is still alive, it can hardly be due to any analogy with McCarthyism. It is received in the same way in countries that have never known such a wave of terror as those that have. The bulk of the audiences, for example, in the British National Theatre, are too young to have known McCarthyism, and England is not a hysterical country. Nor, quite rightly, is it for them a play about a "problem" to be "solved."

The truth is that as caught up as I was in opposition to McCarthyism, the playwriting part of me was drawn to what I felt was a tragic process underlying the political manifestation. It is a process as much a part of humanity as walls and food and death, and no play will make it go away. When irrational terror takes to itself the fiat of moral goodness, somebody has to die. I thought then that in terms of this process the witch hunts had something to say to the anti-Communist hysteria. No man lives who has not got a panic button and when it is pressed by the clean white hand of moral duty, a certain murderous train is set in motion. Socially speaking this is what the play is and was "about," and it is this which I believe makes it survive long after the political circumstances of its birth have evaporated in the public mind.

Is it a political play? It is, I think, but in a particular sense. It is very often done in Latin America just before a dictatorship is about to take over—as a warning—and just after one has been overthrown, as a reminder. It was one of the first foreign works to be done after Stalin's death, and I will wager that it will be done soon after Franco goes to his reward. As I say, it is very popular in England, where hysteria is not one of the national vices. I think it is a political play but not in terms of Left and Right. Its underlying reference is to political paranoia, whichever side makes use of that source of power.

But paranoid politics is not easy to discuss for the reason that *our* fears are always based on something quite palpable and real, while *theirs* are illusory. I realize now that it was probably impossible to have expected an audience and critics in 1953 to feel the heat of a play which so much as implied that a state of deep fear was not entirely new in the world, let alone that the evil plotters might just be worth some dispassionate examination. On top of this, to have treated this fear as a tragic thing rather than a necessary and realistic and highly moral sort of patriotism, was more than could be borne by liberals and conservatives alike.

We customarily think of paranoia as a craziness, a diseased delusionary state in which fears are obviously out of proportion to any conceivable stimulus. But if this were all, we should never be endangered by it. Paranoia has a power and it rises not basically from ravings about plots and hidden conspiracies, but from the grain of recognizable fact around which the fantasies are woven.

The paranoid feels endangered by some person or group mysteriously controlling his actions despite his will. His violence is therefore always defensive, trained against oppressors who mean to kill him before he can kill them. His job is therefore to unmask and disarm, to find the seemingly innocent traces of the pervading malevolence, and he comes to recognize hostility even in the way a person folds his hands or turns his head. His only hope is power, power to neutralize the dangers around him. Naturally, since those dangers can be anywhere, his power must also be total in order to work.

And of course it is true that to one degree or another we are, in fact, hostile to each other, and when we are accused of holding that hostility, we do indeed hate the accusation and the accuser. So that the paranoid creates the reality which proves him right. And this is why the paranoid, who in normal times might merely end in an institution, can rise to the leadership of a society which is really insecure and at a loss as to the causes of its spiritual debility. Nothing is as frightening as to not know why one is frightened. Given the "cause" we can act, and thus keep ourselves from flying apart altogether.

Paranoid politics is seductive, too, because all politics requires that we symbolize people, until individuals cease to exist and there are only compliant supporters or the opposition. The paranoid discovers the murderous potential in the opposition, which it therefore must destroy. When, during World War II, for example, we ripped 100,000 Japanese-Americans out of their California farms and shops and confined them to Midwestern camps, we were indulging the paranoid side of our realistic fears of Japan. But was it really probable that *all* these men, women and children were secret agents? The grain of truth was that some, or perhaps one of them, was. Their non-"whiteness" enhanced our irrationality; we never rounded up German-Americans even though crowds of them, unlike the Japanese, had been marching around with Nazi flags in Jersey right up to the day we declared war.

A few years after its original production, *The Crucible* opened again in New York, Off-Broadway, and the script was now judged by many of the same critics as an impassioned play rather than a cold tract, and it ran two years. It is true that the original production was formalized and rather ballet-like, but not by that much. It was simply that in 1958 nobody was afraid any more. Nor do I imagine that I can convince many people that this is basically what was changed and for good reason. Great fear, like great pain, is not easily recalled, it is self-healing, and the more of it we have felt the less of it we can really get ourselves to remember. And this forgetfulness is part of the tragedy.

But no amount of paranoids walking around has very great political significance unless a partner appears who, naturally, is Interest. Hitler without the support of German big business would have merged with the legions of the mentally lost. Stalin in his last years slept in a different bed every night, employed food-tasters, and ordered the executions of people whose names he merely heard in conversation, but if the Revolution had created a healthy, ongoing society, it could not have tolerated such a chief. Had the witch-crying girls started their shenanigans in a stable community certain of itself and its future, they would have been soaked in cold water and put to bed.

But land titles were in dispute in Salem due to edicts from Boston and London; the repressions of the Puritan code no longer seemed holy to people born after the early deprivations of the militant pioneers. A host of socially disruptive pressures were upon Salem which seemed to threaten a disorder beyond the power of the mind to analyze. The girls lifted up a cause for it all out of the morass. Americans in the late forties and fifties felt paralyzed before a power of darkness expanding its reign; we had "lost" China (which we had never "had") and Eastern Europe. Enormous Communist parties existed in France and Italy. McCarthy solved the problem of our helplessness with a stroke—we were infiltrated by the enemy. Twenty years of conservative frustration with contemporary America was unleashed until, like the girls, McCarthy was in a position of such incredible authority that the greatest people in the land shuddered at the thought that their names might fall from his sniggering lips.

The fantasy of the fifties has rich documentation, but the Rosenberg case, because it ended in death, provides one insight which may throw some light on paranoid fear. In the final speech of the presiding judge is the statement that the defendants committed one of the gravest crimes in all history in giving the atom-bomb secret to Russia. Yet, no expert competent to make such a judgment had been called, and even more instructive—the defense attorney was so eager to prove *his* adherence to the reigning fear that he moved to impound the diagram of the bomb lens allegedly transmitted by the Rosenbergs, so that nobody in the future could steal it again—or, by the way, examine its validity. Recently, however, it was examined by a group of physicists who had actually worked on the lens, and their verdict was that it was scientifically a farce. I am reasonably sure that the passion of the judge's speech was real, and certainly he was not crazy. He was, however, afraid.

Can it all happen again? I believe it can. Will it?

The opposite of paranoid politics is Law and good faith. An example, the best I know, is the American Constitution, and the Bill of Rights, which de-symbolize the individual and consider him as the sum of his acts rather than his hidden thoughts and propensities for plotting evil.

And there are signs that somehow, someway, people in responsible positions have learned at least part of the lesson. Despite our being in a war, despite the immense opposition to it, the draft-card burning and demonstrations, the President and the leadership of the country as a whole have not rallied the unwashed to go hunting for people whose bad thoughts are cheating us of victory.

But what will happen if the American becomes more desperately frustrated, if this war goes on for years, if a sense of national powerlessness prepares the ground for cries of "Betrayal!"—the old paranoid cry to which the highly moral mad respond by seeing where others are blind?

Laws, as we know, are made of bendable stuff; panic systematized around a grain of fact waits forever in the human brain. The tragic reply, John Proctor's, is unfortunately no defense against this kind of social dissolution, but spoken in good time it is perhaps our only safety: "A fire, a fire is burning. I hear the boot of Lucifer, I see his filthy face. And it is my face, and yours, Danforth. For them that quail to bring men out of ignorance as I have quailed, and as you do now when you know in all your black hearts that this be fraud—God damns our kind especially. . . ." A foisted analogy? Only if we are certain that the slide into darkness is far, far behind us. As things stand, Proctor's passion has its own life intact and will until Power is guaranteed against the temptations of the irrational. The surgeons say they work to make their job unnecessary. *The Crucible* was written in that spirit—that the coiled thing in the public heart might die of light. A reasonable thought, but an unreasonable hope which against all reason never disappears.

The Crucible in History
1999

It would probably never have occurred to me to write a play about the Salem witch trials of 1692 had I not seen some astonishing correspondences with that calamity in the America of the late Forties and early Fifties. There were other enticements for me in the Salem period, however; most especially the chance it offered to write in what was for me a practically new language, one that would require new muscles.

I was never a scholar or an historian, of course; my basic need was somehow to respond to a phenomenon which, with only small exaggeration, one could say was paralyzing a whole generation and in an amazingly short time was drying up the habits of trust and toleration in public discourse. I refer, of course, to the anticommunist rage that threatened to reach hysterical proportions and sometimes did. I can't remember anyone calling it an ideological war, but I think now that that is what it amounted to. Looking back at the period, I suppose we very rapidly passed over anything like a discussion or debate and into something quite different, a hunt not alone for subversive people but ideas and even a suspect language. The object, a shock at the time, was to destroy the least credibility of any and all ideas associated with socialism and communism, whose proponents had to be either knowing or unwitting agents of Soviet subversion. An ideological war is like guerrilla war, since the enemy is first of all an idea whose proponents are not in uniform but are disguised as ordinary citizens, a situation that can scare a lot of people to death.

I am not really equipped to deliver a history of Cold War America, which like any other period is packed with passionately held illusions and ideas distorted on all sides by fear. Suffice to say it was a time of great, no doubt unprecedented fear, but fear, like love, is mostly incommunicable once it has passed. So I shall try to limit myself, as far as possible, to speak of events as they struck me personally, for those are what finally created *The Crucible*.

One knew that congressional investigations of subversion had been going on since the Thirties. The Dies committee, beginning with Nazi subversion in America, ended up with a neverending and often silly investigation of communists. But the country in the Thirties was not under external threat, and nobody seemed to take seriously any menace from an American Communist Party that could hardly elect a dogcatcher. From my perspective, what changed everything was the victory of the Chinese communists in 1949. Inevitably, the Chinese Reds were seen as all but an arm of the expansionist post–World War II Soviet machine, and a look at the map would indeed show that an enormous new part of the planet had turned red.

"Who Lost China!" almost instantly became the Republican mantra. Who were the traitors inside the Democratic administrations, going back to Roosevelt, that had sold out our favorite Chinese, Chiang Kai-shek? This, I think, was the first notable injection of the idea of treason and foreign agents into domestic political discourse. To me the simplicity of it all was breathtaking. There had to be left-wing traitors in government, otherwise how could the Chinese—who, as everyone knew, loved Americans more than anybody—have turned against the pro-American Chiang Kai-shek in favor of a Soviet agent like Mao Tse-tung?

All I knew about China in 1949 was what I had read by Edgar Snow and Jack Belden and Teddy White and other American reporters. What it amounted to was that the Nationalist regime was feudal and thoroughly corrupt and that the Reds were basically a miserably exploited peasantry that at long last had risen up and thrown their exploiters into the sea. I thought it was a great idea. In any event, the idea of our "losing" China seemed the equivalent of a flea losing an elephant. Nevertheless, there was a growing uproar in and out of Congress. One read that the China Lobby, a wealthy support group backing Chiang Kai-shek's hopes to return to Beijing from Taiwan, was reportedly paying a lot of the bills and that Senator McCarthy was one of their most effective champions.

The partisan political manipulation of a real issue was so patent that President Truman could dismiss the Republican scare as a "red herring." But it is an indication of its impact on the public mind that he soon had to retreat and institute a loyalty board of his own to investigate the allegiance of government employees.

To call the ensuing atmosphere paranoid is not to say that there was nothing real in the American–Soviet standoff. To be sure, I am far more willing than I was then, due to some experiences of my own with both sides, to credit both the American and Soviet leadership with enough ignorance of each other to have ignited a third world war. But there was something of the inauthentic, the spurious, and the invented in the conflict, if only because of the swiftness with which all values were being forced in a matter of months to literally reverse themselves. I recall some examples.

Death of a Salesman opened in February of 1949 and was hailed by nearly every newspaper and magazine; parenthetically, I should add that two exceptions come to mind, one Marxist, the other ex-Marxist. The Marxist was the *Daily Worker*, which found the play defeatist and lacking militant protest; the ex-Marxist, Mary McCarthy, who seemed outraged by the idea of elevating it to the status of tragedy and just hated it in general, particularly, I thought, because it was so popular. Real tragedy would have to close in two weeks. Anyway, several movie studios wanted it, and it was finally Columbia Pictures that bought it and engaged a great star, Fredric March, to play Willy.

In something like two years or less, as I recall, with the picture finished, I was asked by a terrified Columbia to sign an anticommunist declaration in order to ward off picket lines which apparently the American Legion was threatening to throw across the entrances of theaters showing the film. In the numerous phone calls that followed, the air of terror was heavy. It was the first intimation of what would soon follow. I declined to make any such statement, which, frankly, I found demeaning; what right had any organization to demand anyone's pledge of loyalty? I was sure the whole thing would soon go away, it was just too outrageous.

But instead of disappearing, the studio, it now developed, had actually made another film, a short which was to be shown with *Salesman*. This was called *The Life of a Salesman* and consisted of several lectures by City College School of Business professors. What they boiled down to was that selling was basically a joy, one of the most gratifying and useful of professions, and that Willy was simply a nut. Never in show business history has a studio spent so much good money to prove that its feature film was pointless. I threatened to sue (on what basis I had no idea), but of course the short could not be shown lest it bore the audience blind. But in less than two years *Death of a Salesman* had gone from a masterpiece to a pariah that was basically fraudulent.

In 1948, '49, '50, '51, I had the sensation of being trapped inside a perverse work of art, one of those Escher constructs in which it is impossible to know whether a stairway is going up or down. Practically everyone I knew, all survivors of the Great Depression of course as well as World War II, was somewhere within the conventions of the political left of center; one or two were Communist Party members, some were sort of fellow travelers, as I suppose I was, and most had had one or another brush with Marxist ideas or organizations. I have never been able to believe in the reality of these people being actual or putative traitors any more than *I* could be, yet others like them were being fired from teaching or other jobs in government or large corporations. The unreality of it all never left me. We were living in an art form, a metaphor that had no long history but, incredibly enough, suddenly gripped the country. So I suppose that in one sense *The Crucible* was an attempt to make life real again, palpable and structured—a work of art created in order to interpret an anterior work of art that was called reality but was not.

Again—it was the very swiftness of the change that lent it this unreality. Only three or four years earlier an American movie audience, on seeing a newsreel of—let's say—a Russian solider or even Stalin saluting the Red Army, would have applauded, for that army had taken the brunt of the Nazi onslaught, as most people were aware. Now they would have looked on with fear or at least bewilderment, for the Russians had become the enemy of mankind, a menace to all that was good. It was the Germans who, with amazing rapidity, were turning good. Could this be real? And how to mentally deal with, for example, American authorities removing from German schoolbooks all mention of the Hitler decade?

In the unions, communists and their allies, who had been known as intrepid organizers, were now to be shorn of union membership and turned out as seditious, in effect. Harry Bridges, for example, the idol of West Coast longshoremen, whom he had all but single-handedly organized, would be subjected to court trial after court trail to drive him out of the country and back to his native Australia as an unadmitted communist. Academics, some of them prominent in their fields, were especially targeted, many forced to retire or simply fired for disloyalty; some of them communists, some fellow travelers, and inevitably, a certain number who were simply unaffiliated liberals who refused to sign one of the dozens of anti-communist pledges being required by college administrations.

The sweep went not only very wide but deep. By 1950 or thereabouts there were subjects one would do better to avoid and even words that were best left unspoken. The Spanish Civil War, for example, had quickly become a hot button. That war, as some of you may not recall, resulted from an attack in 1936 by the Spanish army upon the democratically elected Spanish government. After almost three years of terrible fighting, in which Nazi air force planes and Mussolini's troops helped him, the fascist Generalissimo Franco took power. Spain would become the very symbol of the struggle against fascism; but more and more one heard, after about 1950, that Franco's victory was actually a not unworthy triumph of anticommunists. This despite the common belief through the Thirties and Forties that had Franco been thrown back, opening Hitler's Atlantic flank to hostile democrats rather than allied fascists, his war against Europe might well have had to be postponed if not aborted.

Again, it was the swiftness of this change that made it so fictional to me. Occasionally these quick changes were rather comical, which didn't help one's sense of reality.

One day in 1950 or thereabouts a stranger called, asking to come and see me about some matter he would prefer not to talk about on the phone and dropping as one of his bona fides that he had fought in Spain. I figured he was in trouble politically and must be really desperate if he imagined that I could help him. (A few ill-informed people still imagined I had some clout of this kind.) He arrived at my Brooklyn Heights house, a bright, youngish fellow carrying a briefcase. We chatted for a few minutes and then got down to business. Opening his briefcase, he took out a large map of a Texas oil field, rolled it out on my desk, and pointing at various black dots explained that these were oil wells in which he was selling stock. When I confessed surprise that an idealistic antifascist fighter should be ending up as an oil stock salesman, he asked, "Why not?" and with a touch of noble sincerity added, "Once the workers take over they're going to need oil!" This was a harbinger of the wondrous rationalizations that I would have cause to recall as our future arrived.

I should add that my uneasy fictional view of things turned out not to be entirely unwarranted; some six or seven years later, I would be cited for contempt of Congress for refusing to identify writers I had met at one of the two communist writers' meetings I had attended many years before. Normally, these citations resulted in a trial in federal court that took half an hour to lead to inevitable convictions. But my lawyer, Joseph Rauh Jr., brought in a former senator, Harry M. Cain, who had been head of the loyalty board under Eisenhower, to testify as an expert witness that my plays showed no signs of having been written under communist discipline. Cain had a curious history; a decorated Korean War veteran and fierce anticommunist, he had been a sidekick of McCarthy's and a weekly poker partner of his. But disillusionment had worn him down when, as head of the loyalty board, he had had to deal with the hundreds of letters a week from people suspecting neighbors, friends, and relatives of communist sympathies. The idea of the whole country spying on itself began to depress him, and he came to feel that from his Washington window he was looking out at a terrified nation and worse—some substantial fraction of it was quite literally crazed. The climax for him came with a series of relentlessly persistent letters from a Baltimore postman complaining of having been fired for disloyalty. What bothered him was the handwriting, which was barely literate. Communists were bad people, but they were rarely illiterate. Finally Cain invited the man to his office and realized that the accusations were not credible; this led him to wonder about the hundreds of other accusations he had with little or no examination been regularly forwarding to the FBI. At last he went directly to Eisenhower and told him he was convinced that the loyalty board itself was incompatible with political liberty. The next morning he found that he himself had been fired.

But that was still six or seven years on. My brushes with the fictional world in which I lived went back to 1947, when *All My Sons*, as the result of protests by the Catholic War Veterans, was removed from the Army's theatrical repertoire in Europe as a threat to soldiers' morale—since it told the story of a manufacturer selling defective parts to the Air Force. In a few years a former officer in that theatrical troop wrote to inform me that not only had *All My Sons* been banned but an order was given that no other play written by me was to be produced by the Army. As far as the Army was concerned, I had simply disappeared as an American writer. But this would be a useful experience when, in the late Sixties, as president of International PEN, I would find myself commiserating with Soviet writers and those in other communist countries who had seen their names obliterated from the rosters of living authors.

But it is impossible, certainly not in this short time, to properly convey the fears that mark the period. Nobody was being shot, to be sure, although some were going to jail, where at least one, a man named William Remington, was murdered, by an inmate hoping to shorten his sentence for having killed a communist. Rather than physical fear it was the sense of impotence, which seemed to deepen with each passing week, of being unable to speak simply and accurately of the very recent past when being Left in America, and for that matter in Europe, was simply to be alive to the dilemmas of the day. To be sure, I had counted myself a radical since my years in college and had tried and failed to read *Das Kapital*; but the Marxist formulations had certainly given shape to my views of politics— which in fact meant that to understand a political phenomenon you had to look for the money. It also meant that you believed capitalism was quite possibly doomed, but between 1929 and around 1936 there were moments when *not* to believe that would put you in a political minority. I may have dreamed of a socialism where people no longer lived off another's labor, but I had never met a spy. As for the very idea of willingly subjecting my work not only to some party's discipline but to anyone's control, my repugnance was such that as a very young and indigent writer I had turned down fairly lucrative offers to work for Hollywood studios because of a helpless revulsion at the thought of someone other than myself literally owning the paper I was typing on. It would not be long, perhaps four or five years, before the fraudulence of Soviet cultural claims was as clear to me as they should have been earlier, but I would never find it believable, either in the Fifties or later, that with their thuggish self-righteousness and callous contempt for artists' freedoms, the unabashed Soviet way of controlling culture could be successfully exported to America, except, perhaps, in Madison Avenue advertising agencies. In any case, to believe in that danger I would have to share a bed with the Republican Right.

Which is not to say that there was not much sincerity in the fears people felt in the Fifties, and, as in most things human, much cynicism as well, if not corruption. The moral high ground, as in most things human, was wreathed in fog. But the fact remained that some greatly talented people were being driven out of the country to live and work in England, screenwriters like Carl Foreman and Donald Ogden Stewart, actors like Charlie Chaplin and Sam Wanamaker (who, incidentally, in his last years, led the campaign to build a copy of Shakespeare's theater on the Thames). I no longer recall the number of our political exiles, but there were more than too many.

My subpoena before the House committee came some four years after The Crucible was produced, but I had been shot at more than once as a result of that play. Shortly after its production, the renewal of my outdated passport had been denied when I applied in order to go to Belgium, at the invitation of the Belgo-American Association, to attend the first European performance of the play. The stated grounds for confiscating my passport were that my presence abroad was not in the best interests of the United States. A rather farcical situation soon developed—and I should say that farce was always a step away from all the tragedies of the period. Since the play was the first and practically the only artistic evidence Europe had of resistance to what was considered a fascistic McCarthyism, the applause at the final curtain was intense and insistent, and since the newspapers had announced that I had accepted the invitation to be present, there were calls for the author. These went on and on until the American ambassador felt compelled to stand

and take a bow. A species of insanity was spreading everywhere. Here was the ambassador, an officer of the State Department, acknowledging the applause for someone deemed by that department too dangerous to be present. It must surely have struck some of the audience as strange, however, that an author would be wearing a wide diplomatic sash diagonally across his chest; and the next morning's papers had loads of fun with the scene, which, of course, could hardly have advanced the best interests of the United States.

I should explain what I meant by the cynicism and corruption of the Red hunt. By 1956, when HUAC subpoenaed me, the tide was going out, and the committee was finding it difficult to make the front pages anymore. However, the news of my forthcoming marriage to Marilyn Monroe was too tempting to be passed up. That it had some connections with my being subpoenaed was confirmed when Chairman Walter of HUAC sent word to Joseph Rauh, my lawyer, that he would be inclined to cancel my hearing altogether if Miss Monroe would consent to have a picture taken with him. The offer having been declined, the good chairman, as my hearing came to an end, proceeded to entreat me to write less tragically about our country. This lecture cost me some $40,000 in lawyer's fees, a year's suspended sentence for contempt of Congress, and a five-hundred-dollar fine. Not to mention about a year of inanition in my creative life.

But back to the late Forties and early Fifties; my fictional view of the period, my sense of its unreality was, like any impotence, a psychologically painful experience. A very similar paralysis at a certain point descended on Salem.

A new cautionary diction was swiftly ensconced in our way of talking to one another. In a country that a bit more than a quarter of a century earlier had given three million votes to Eugene Debs, the Socialist presidential candidate, the very word "socialism" was all but taboo. Words had gotten fearsome. As I would learn directly from students and faculty in Ann Arbor on a 1953 reporting visit for *Holiday* magazine, students were actually avoiding renting rooms in the houses run by the housing cooperative for fear of being labeled communist, so darkly suggestive was the word "cooperative." On hearing this, even I was amazed. But there was more— the head of orientation at the university told me that the FBI had enlisted professors to report on students voicing left-wing opinions and—some more comedy—they had also engaged students to report on professors with the same views. When I published these facts in *Holiday*, the Pontiac division of General Motors threatened to withdraw all advertising from the magazine if I ever appeared in it again; Ted Patrick, its editor, promptly badgered me for another piece, but I didn't know the reason why for some years.

It was a time—as I would learn only decades later from my FBI record, obtained under the Freedom of Information Act—when the FBI shadowed a guest of mine from a dinner party in my Brooklyn Heights house. The guest's name was blacked out, and I have been puzzling ever since about his identity. The point is that reading my FBI record in the Seventies I was not really surprised to learn this. In the Fifties everybody over forty believed that his phone was being tapped by the FBI, and they were probably right.

What is important here is that none of this was secret; everybody had a good idea of what was happening but, like me, felt helpless to reverse it. And to this moment I don't think I can adequately communicate the sheer density of the atmosphere of the time, for the outrageous had so suddenly become the accepted norm.

In the early Fifties, for example, with Elia Kazan, who had directed *All My Sons* and *Death of a Salesman*, I submitted a film script to Harry Cohn, the head of Columbia Pictures. It described the murderous corruption in the gangster-ridden Brooklyn longshoremen's union, whose leadership a group of rebel workers was trying to overthrow. Cohn read the script and called us to Hollywood, where he simply and casually informed us that, incredibly enough, he had first had the script vetted by the FBI and that they had seen nothing subversive in it; on the other hand, however, the head of the AFL motion picture unions in Hollywood, Roy Brewer, had condemned it outright as totally untrue communist propaganda, since, quite simply, there were no gangsters on the Brooklyn waterfront. Cohn, no stranger to the ways of gangsterism, having survived an upbringing in the tough, famously crime-ridden Five Points area of Manhattan, opined that Brewer was quite naturally only trying to protect Joe Ryan, his brother AFL union leader, the head of the AFL Brooklyn longshoremen. Brewer also threatened to call a strike of projectionists in any theater daring to show the

film, no idle threat since he controlled *their* union. (Ryan, incidentally, would shortly go to Sing Sing prison for gangsterism. But that
was not yet.) Meanwhile Cohn offered his solution to our problem
with Brewer; he would produce the film if I would agree to make
one simple change—the gangsters in the union were to be changed
to communists. This would not be easy; for one thing, I knew all
the communists on the waterfront; there was a total of two of them
(both of whom, incidentally, in the following decade became mil-
lionaire businessmen).

And so I had to withdraw the script, which prompted an indignant telegram from Cohn: "As soon as we try to make the script
pro-American you pull out." One understood not only the threat in
those words but the cynicism; he certainly knew that it was the
Mafia that controlled waterfront labor. Nevertheless, had I been a
screenwriter in Hollywood, my career would have ended with this
refusal to perform this patriotic idiocy. I have to say that there were
days when I wondered if we would end in an unacknowledged, perhaps even comfortable American fascism.

But the theater had no such complications, no blacklist, not yet
anyway; and I longed to respond to this climate of fear if only to
protect my sanity. But where to find a transcendent concept? As I
saw it, the difficulty was that we had grown so detached from any
hard reality I knew about. It had become a world of signals, gestures, loaded symbolic words, and of rites and rituals. After all, the
accusations of Party membership of film writers, actors, and directors never mentioned treasonous acts of any sort; what was in their
brains was the question, and this created a kind of gestural phantom land. I did not yet think of it this way at the time, but looking
back I think we had entered an ideological war, as I have said, and
in such wars it was ideas and not necessarily actions that arouse
anger and fear. And this was the heart of the darkness—that it had
come rather quickly to be believed that a massive, profoundly organized conspiracy was in place and being carried forward mainly by
a concealed phalanx of intellectuals, including labor people, teachers, professionals of all sorts, sworn to undermine the American
government. And it was precisely the invisibility of ideas that was
helping to frighten so many people. How could a play deal with
this mirage world?

There was a fundamental absurdity in the Salem witch-hunt, of course, since witches don't exist, but this only helped relate it more to what we were going through. I can't recall the date anymore, but to one of the Un-American Activities Committee hearings, several Hollywood writers brought piles of their film scripts for the committee to parse for any sign of Marxist propaganda. Of course there would hardly be anything that provocative in a Hollywood movie of the time, but in any case the committee refused to read the scripts, which I imagined was a further humiliation for the writers. But what a cruel irony, that these terribly serious Party members or sympathizers, in the attempt to prove themselves patriotic Americans, should feel compelled to demonstrate that their work was totally innocuous!

Paranoia breeds paranoia, of course, but below paranoia there lies a bristling, unwelcome truth, a truth so repugnant as to produce fantasies of persecution in order to conceal its existence. For example, the unwelcome truth denied by the Right was that the Hollywood writers accused of subversion were not a menace to the country or even the bearers of meaningful change. They wrote not propaganda but entertainment, some of it of a mildly liberal cast, to be sure, but most of it mindless; or when it was political, as with Preston Sturges or Frank Capra, entirely un-Marxist. In any real assessment, the worst they could do was contribute some money to Party coffers. But most Hollywood writers were only occasionally employed, and one doubted that their contributions could have made any difference to a party so completely disregarded by the American public and, in the bargain, so thoroughly impregnated by the FBI. Yet they had to be portrayed as an imminent danger to the republic.

As for the Left, its unacknowledged truth was more important for me. If nobody was being shot in our ideological war but merely vivisected by a headline or two, it struck me as odd, if understandable, that the accused were largely unable to passionately cry out their faith in the ideals of socialism. Attacks on the committees' right to demand that a citizen reveal his political beliefs, yes; but as for the idealistic canon of their own convictions, the accused were largely mute. It was a silence, incidentally, that in the public mind probably tended to confirm the committees' characterization of them as conspirators wrapping themselves in darkness. In their defense, the committees instantly shut down as irrelevant any attempts to explicate their ideas, any idealistic displays; but even outside, in public statements beyond the hearings, they relied almost wholly on legalistic defenses rather than the articles of the faith in which they unquestionably believed. The rare exception, like Paul Robeson's forthright declaration of faith in socialism as a cure for racism, was a rocket that momentarily lit up the sky, but even this, it must be said, was dimmed by his adamant refusal to recognize, at least publicly, what he knew to be the murder of two Soviet Jewish artists, his good friends, under Stalin's anti-Semitic decrees. It was one of the cruel twists of the time that while he would not in Washington display his outrage at the murders of his friends, he could in Moscow choose to sing a song in Yiddish that the whole public knew was his protest against Soviet anti-Semitism.

In a word, the disciplined avoidances of the Left bespoke a guilt that the Right found a way to exploit. A similar guilt seems to reside in all sorts of American dissidents, from Jehovah's Witnesses to homosexuals, no doubt because there is indeed an unacknowledged hostility in them toward the majority for whose cherished norms they feel contempt. It may be that guilt, perhaps, helped to account to some degree for the absence in our theater of plays that in any meaningful way confronted the deepening hysteria, which after all was the main event in our culture. Here was a significant part of a whole generation being forced to the wall, with hardly a word about it written for the stage. But it may simply have been the difficulty of finding a dramatic locution, a working symbolization that might illuminate the complex fog of the unspoken in which we were living.

To put it differently, stuffed in the pockets of both sides was a hidden agenda. On the Right it was, quite simply, their zeal to finally disgrace and wipe out what remained of New Deal attitudes, particularly that dreadful tendency in Americans to use government to help the helpless and to set limits around the more flagrant excesses of unbridled capitalism. Instead, their advertised goal was the defense of liberty against communism.

What the Left was not saying was that they were in truth dedicated to replacing capitalism with a society based on Marxist principles, and this could well mean the suppression of non-Marxists for the good of mankind. Instead, they were simply espousing constitutional protections against self-incrimination. Thus the fresh wind of a debate of any real content was not blowing through these hearings or these terrible years. The result was miasma, and on the Left, the guilt of the wholly or partially insincere. The Right, of course, convinced as it always is of its persecution, is certain that it represents the incoherent and stifled but genuine wishes of the majority and is thus a stranger to guilt.

How to express all this, and much more, on a stage? I began to despair of my own paralysis. I was a fisherman without a hook, a seaman without a sail.

On a lucky afternoon I happened upon a book, *The Devil in Massachusetts*, by Marion Starkey, a narrative of the Salem witch-hunt of 1692. I knew this story from my college reading more than a decade earlier, but now in this changed and darkened America it turned a wholly new aspect toward me, namely, the poetry of the hunt. Poetry may seem an odd word for a witch-hunt, but I saw now that there was something of the marvelous in the spectacle of a whole village, if not an entire province, whose imagination was literally captured by a vision of something that wasn't there.

In time to come the very notion of equating the Red hunt with the witch-hunt would be condemned by some as a deception. There certainly were communists, and there never were witches. But the deeper I moved into the 1690s, the further away drifted the America of the 1950s, and rather than the appeal of analogy I found something somewhat different to draw my curiosity and excitement.

First of all, anyone standing up in the Salem of 1692 who denied that witches existed would have faced immediate arrest, the hardest interrogation, and quite possibly the rope. Every authority—the church in New England, the kings of England and Europe, legal scholars like Lord Coke—not only confirmed their existence but never questioned the necessity of executing them when discovered. And of course, there was the authority of the Bible itself [Exodus 22:18]: "Thou shalt not suffer a witch to live." To deny witches was to deny the existence of the Devil's age-old war against God, and this, in effect, left God without an opposite and stripped him of his first purpose—which was to protect the Christian religion and good order in the world. Without evil, what need was there for the good? Without the Devil's ceaseless plotting, who needed God? The existence of witches actually went to prove the existence of God's war with evil. Indeed, it became obvious that to dismiss witchcraft was to forgo any understanding of how it came to pass that tens of thousands had been murdered as witches in Europe, from Scandinavia across to England, down through France and Spain. And to dismiss any relation to the hunt for subversives was to shut down an insight into not only the remarkably similar emotions but literally the numerous identical practices, both by officials and victims, in both outbreaks.

Of course there were witches, if not to most of us then certainly to everyone in Salem; and of course there were communists, but what was the content of their menace? That to me became the issue. Having been deeply influenced as a student by a Marxist approach to society (if less so as I grew older) and having known any number of Marxists and numerous sympathizers, I could simply not accept that these people were spies or even prepared to do the will of the Soviets in some future crisis. That such people had thought to find some hope of a higher ethic in the Soviets was not simply an American but a worldwide irony of catastrophic moral proportions, for their like could be found all over Europe and Asia. But as the Fifties dawned, they were stuck with the past they had chosen or been led into. Part of the unreality of the great anti-Left sweep of the Fifties was that it picked up a lot of people to expose and disgrace who had already in their hearts turned away from a pro-Soviet past but had no stomach for naming others who had merely shared their illusions. In short, then, the whole business for me remained what Truman had initially called it, not a moral crusade but a political red herring.

Nevertheless, the hunt captured some significant part of the American imagination, and its power demanded respect. And turning to Salem was like looking into a petri dish, a sort of embalmed stasis with its principal moving forces caught in stillness. One had to wonder what the human imagination fed on that could inspire neighbors and old friends to suddenly emerge overnight as hell's own furies secretly bent on the torture and destruction of

Christians. More than a political metaphor, more than a moral tale, *The Crucible*, as it developed for me over the period of more than a year, became the awesome evidence of the power of the inflamed human imagination, the poetry of suggestion, and finally the tragedy of heroic resistance to a society possessed to the point of ruin.

As I stood in the stillness of the Salem courthouse, surrounded by the miasmic swirl of the images of the 1950s but with my head in 1692, what the two eras had in common was gradually gaining definition. In both was the menace of concealed plots, but most startling were the similarities in the rituals of defense and the investigative routines. Three hundred years apart, both prosecutions were alleging membership in a secret, disloyal group; should the accused confess, his honesty could be proved only in precisely the same way—by naming former confederates, nothing less. Thus the informer became the very proof of the plot and the investigation's necessity.

Finally, in both eras, since the enemy was first and foremost an idea, normal evidentiary proof of disloyal actions was either deemphasized, left in limbo, or not required at all; and indeed, actions finally became completely irrelevant; in the end, the charge itself, suspicion itself, all but became the evidence of disloyalty.

And, most interestingly, in the absence of provable disloyal actions both societies reached for very similar remedies. Something called the Attorney General's List was promulgated, a list of communist-front organizations, membership in which was declared not so much illegal as reason to suspect subversive conduct or intentions. If membership in an organization could not be called illegal, it could at least be made disgusting enough to lose you your job and reputation.

One might wonder whether many spies would be likely to be joining communist fronts, but liberals very possibly might and indeed had done so at various turns in the road, frequently making common cause with the Left and with communists during the New Deal period a decade earlier. The witch-hunt in 1692 had a not dissimilar evidentiary problem but a far more poetic solution. Most suspected people named by others as members of the Devil's conspiracy had not been shown to have actually *done* anything—not poisoning wells, setting barns on fire, sickening cattle, aborting babies or calves, nor somehow undermining the virtue of wives (the Devil having a double, phenomenally active penis, as everybody knew). Rather than acts, these suspect folk needed only to have had the bad luck to have been "seen" by witnesses consorting with the Devil. The witnesses might be dismally addled hysterics, but they might also be sober citizens who'd somehow gotten themselves suspected of practicing witchcraft and could clear themselves only by confessing and naming coconspirators. But, as in the Fifties, there was a supply of nonhysterical lawyers in and around the witch-hunt, as well as Harvard-educated ministers, and as accusations piled up one obvious fact was more and more irritating to them; as they well knew, the normal fulcrum of any criminal prosecution, namely, acts, deeds, crimes, and witnesses thereto, was simply missing. As for ordinary people, as devout as they might be and strictly literal about Biblical injunctions, they still clung to the old habit of expecting some sort of proof that an accused was guilty, in this case, of being an accomplice of the Devil.

To the rescue came not an Attorney General's List but a piece of poetry smacking of both legalistic and religious validity; it was called "spectral evidence." Spectral evidence, in normal jurisprudence, had been carefully winnowed out of the prosecutorial armory by judges and lawyers as being too manifestly open to fabrication. But now, with society under this hellish attack, the fateful decision was made to bring it back in, and the effect was like the bursting of a dam. Suddenly all the prosecution needed do was produce a witness who claimed to have seen not an accused person but what was called his familiar spirit, his living ghost, as it were, in the act of poisoning a pig or throwing a burning brand into a barn full of hay. You could be at home asleep in your bed, but your spirit could be crawling through your neighbor's bedroom window to feel up his wife. The owner of that wandering spirit was thereupon obliged to account to the court for its crime. With the entrance of spectral evidence, the air was quickly filled with the malign spirits of those identified by good Christians as confederates of the Beast, and with this, of course, the Devil himself really did dance happily into Salem village and proceeded to take the place apart.

And in no time at all, people in Salem began *looking* at each other with new eyes and *hearing* sounds from neighbors' throats that they had never heard before and *thinking* about each other with new insights far deeper than their former blind innocence toward one another could have given them. And now, naturally, a lot of things that had been bewildering before suddenly made sense. Why, for instance, had London annulled all property deeds, causing everybody to be fighting with everybody else over boundary lines? Why was the congregation forever turning in on itself in fierce doctrinal fights and bitter arguments with ministers who one after another had had to flee the contentiousness of Salemites? Clearly, it was the Devil who had been muddling people's brains to set them against each other. But now, now at last, with the Lord's help, they had the gift of sight; the afflicted children had opened up their eyes to the plot in which, unknowingly, like innocent birds in a net, they were all caught. Now, with the admission of spectral evidence, they could turn to the traitors among them and run them to their deaths.

I spent some ten days in the Salem courthouse reading the crudely recorded trials of the 1692 outbreak, and it was striking how totally absent was the least sense of irony, let alone humor. I can't recall whether it was the provincial governor's nephew or son who with a college friend had come from Boston to watch the strange proceedings; at one point both boys burst out laughing at some absurd testimony. They were promptly jailed and were saved only by friends galloping down from Boston with a bribe for a guard, who let them escape from a very possible hanging.

Irony and humor were not exactly at a premium in the Fifties either. I was in my lawyer's office one afternoon to sign some contract, and a lawyer in the next office was asked to come in and notarize my signature. While this man was stamping the pages, I continued a discussion with my lawyer about the Broadway theater, which at one point I said was corrupt, that the art of theater had been totally displaced by the bottom line, that being all that really mattered anymore. Looking up at me, the notarizing lawyer said, "That's a communist position, you know." I started to laugh until I saw the constraint in my lawyer's face, and despite myself I quickly sobered up.

I am glad, of course, that I managed to write *The Crucible*, but looking back I have often wished I'd had the temperament to have done an absurd comedy, since that is what the situation often deserved. There is something funny in the two sophisticated young Bostonians deciding to trot down to Salem to look in on the uproar among the provincials, failing to realize that they had entered a new age, a new kind of consciousness. I made a not dissimilar mistake as the Fifties dawned, and I continued to make it. A young film producer I didn't know asked me to write a script for a film about what was then called juvenile delinquency. A mystifying, unprecedented outbreak of gang violence had exploded all over New York. The city, in return for a good percentage of the profits, had contracted with this producer to open police stations, schools, and so on to his camera. I spent the summer of 1955 on Brooklyn streets, wrote an outline, which, incidentally, was much praised by the Catholic Youth Organization's leadership, and was ready to proceed with the script when an attack on me as a disloyal leftist was opened in the *New York World-Telegram and Sun*. The cry went up that so long as I was the screenwriter the city must cancel its contract with the producer. A hearing was arranged, attended by some twenty-two city commissioners, including those of the police, fire, welfare, and not least the sanitation departments, as well as two judges. At the long conference table there also sat a lady in sneakers and a sweater who produced a thick folder of petitions and statements I had signed, going back to my college years, provided to her, she said, by the House Un-American Activities Committee. I defended myself; I thought I was making some sense when the lady began literally screaming that I was killing the boys in Korea. She meant that I *personally* was doing it, as I could tell from the froth at the corners of her mouth, the fury in her eyes, and her finger pointing straight into my face. The vote was taken and came up one short of continuing the city's collaboration, and the film was killed that afternoon. As we were filing out, the two judges came up and offered their sympathy. I always wondered whether the crucial vote against me came from the sanitation department. But it was not a total loss; it would soon help with the writing of *The Crucible*, the suffocating sensation of helplessness before the spectacle of the impossible coming to pass.

Since you, or some of you, are historians, I have emphasized history in these remarks, but I doubt if I'd have written the play had the question of language not so powerfully drawn me on. The trial record in the Salem courthouse, of which I was allowed to borrow a photocopy, was written by ministers in a primitive shorthand. This condensation gave emphasis to a gnarled, densely packed language that suggested the country accents of a hard people. (A few years on, when Laurence Olivier staged his London production, he used the gruff Northumberland accent.) In any event, to lose oneself day after day in that record of human delusion was to know a fear, not perhaps for one's safety precisely but of the spectacle of perfectly intelligent people giving themselves over to a rapture of such murderous credulity. It was as though the absence of real evidence was itself a release from the burdens of this world; in love with the invisible, they moved behind their priests closer to that mystical communion that is anarchy and is called God. Evidence, in contrast, is effort; leaping to conclusions is a wonderful pleasure; and for a while there was a highly charged joy in Salem, for now that they could see through everything to the frightful plot being daily laid bare in court sessions, their days, formerly so eventless and long, were swallowed up in hourly revelations, news, surprises. *The Crucible*, I think, is less a polemic than it might have been had it not been filled with wonder at the protean imagination of man.

As a commercial entertainment, the play failed, of course. To start with, the title: Nobody knew what a crucible was. Most of the critics, as sometimes does happen, never caught on to the play's ironical substructure, and the ones who did were nervous about validating a work that was so unkind to the same basic principles as underlay the current hunt for Reds, sanctified as it was. On opening night, old acquaintances shunned me in the theater lobby, and even without air-conditioning the house was noticeably cool. But the problem was also with the temperature of the production. The director, a great name in the theater of the Twenties, Thirties, and into the Forties, had decided that the play, which he believed a classic, should be staged like what he called a Dutch painting. In Dutch paintings of groups, everyone is always looking front. We knew this from the picture on the wooden boxes of Dutch Masters cigars. Unfortunately, on a stage such rigidity only propels an audience to the exits. It would be several years before a gang of young actors, setting up chairs in the ballroom of the McAlpin Hotel, set fire to the audience and convinced the critics; and the play at last took off and soon found its place in the world. There were cheering critics this time, but now of course McCarthy was dead, and the fever on whose waves of heat he had spread his wings had cooled, and more and more people found it possible to face the dying embers and read the terrible message in them.

It is said that no one would buy land in Salem for a hundred years. The very ground was accursed. Salem's people, in the language of the time, had broke charity with one another.

But the Devil, as he usually does after such paroxysms, had the last laugh. Salem refuses to fade into history. A few years ago the foundation of an old colonial-era church in a town near Salem began to sag. The contractor engaged to make repairs dug out some of the loose stones and crawled underneath to inspect matters. There he discovered what looked like barely buried human skeletons. Harvard scientists were called in and confirmed that the remains of some twenty-two people were under the church. Now no one has ever known exactly where in Salem the gibbet was located, but the bodies of the twenty-two people hanged there for practicing witchcraft had never been found. Moreover, according to one legend, as their ultimate punishment they were denied Christian burial.

The scientists wanted to remove the skeletons and try to identify them. But some quite aged parishioners, descendants not only of the witchcraft victims but no doubt of their persecutors as well, were adamantly opposed. The younger church members were all for it but decided to wait until the elders had passed away rather than start a ruckus about the matter. In short, even after three centuries, the thing, it seems, cannot find its serene, uncomplicated end.

And, indeed, something very similar occurred in Salem three hundred years ago. After the hunt had blown itself out, after Cotton Mather, having whipped up the hysteria to and beyond the point of murder, finally conceded that demanding the admission of spectral evidence had been his dreadful mistake, the legislature awarded to some, though not all, of the victims' families a few pounds' damages along with a mild apology: "Sorry we hanged your mother," and so forth. But in the true Salem style of solemn bewilderment, this gesture apparently lacked a certain requisite disorder, so they also included reparations to some informers whose false accusations had hanged people. Victims and victimizers, it was all the same in the end, I suppose it was just the good old American habit of trying to keep everybody happy.

The Crucible is my most-produced play, here and abroad. It seems to be one of the few shards of the so-called McCarthy period that survives. And it is part of the play's history, I think, that to people in so many parts of the world its story seems so like their own. I think it was in the mid-Seventies—dates at my age take on the viscosity of poached eggs—but in any case, I happened to be at my publishers when another Grove Press author came in. Her eyes filled with tears at our introduction, and she hastened to explain: She was Yuen Cheng, author of *Life and Death in Shanghai*, the story of her six-year solitary confinement during the Cultural Revolution. It seems that on her release, an old friend, a theater director, took her to see a new production of his in Shanghai, *The Crucible*, a play and author she had never heard of. As she listened to it, the interrogations sounded so precisely the same as the ones she and others had been subject to by the Cultural Revolutionaries that she couldn't believe a non-Chinese had written it. And picking up the English text, she was amazed, she said, not least by the publication date, which of course was more than a decade before the Cultural Revolution. A highly educated woman, she had been living with the conviction that such a perversion of just procedure could happen only in the China of a debauched revolution! I have had similar reactions from Russians, South Africans, Latin Americans and others who have endured dictatorships, so universal is the methodology of terror portrayed in *The Crucible*. In fact, I used to think, half seriously—although it was not far from the truth—that you could tell when a dictator was about to take power in a Latin American country or when one had just been overthrown, by whether *The Crucible* was suddenly being produced there.

The net of it all, I suppose, is that I have come, rather reluctantly, to respect delusion, not least of all my own. There are no passions quite as hot and pleasurable as those of the deluded. Compared with the bliss of delusion—its vivid colors, blazing lights, explosions, whistles, and sheer liberating joys—the dull search for evidence is a deadly bore. In *Timebends*, my autobiography, I have written at some length about my dealings with Soviet cultural controllers and writers when as president of International PEN I would attempt to impress its democratic values upon them in their treatment of writers. Moving about there and in East Germany, Hungary, and Czechoslovakia in communist times, it was only by main force that I could dredge up memories of my old idealism, which I had attached to what in reality had turned out to be little more than a half-feudal society led by an unelected elite. How could this possibly be? I can only think that a man in a rushing river will grasp at any floating thing passing by. History, or whatever piece of its debris one happens to connect with, is a great part of the answer. For me it was my particular relation to the collapse of key institutions in the Great Depression, the sometimes scary anti-Semitism I kept running into and the Left's thankful condemnation of it, the Spanish Civil War and the all-but-declared pro-fascist sympathies of the British, and Roosevelt's unacknowledged collaboration with their arms blockade of the republic (the so-called Non-Intervention Policy). Indeed, on Franco's victory, Roosevelt told Secretary of the Interior Harold Ickes, according to Ickes's autobiography, that his Spanish policy was "the worst mistake I ever made." In a word, out of the Great Crash of 1929, America and the world seemed to awaken to a new sense of social responsibility, something which to the young seemed very much like love. My heart was with the Left if only because the Right hated me enough to want to kill me, as the Germans amply proved. And now, of course, the most blatant and foulest anti-Semitism is in Russia, leaving people like me filled not so much with surprise as a kind of wonder at the incredible amount of hope there once was and how it disappeared and whether in time it will ever come again, attached to some new illusion.

And so there is hardly a week that passes when I don't ask the unanswerable—what am I now convinced of that will turn out to be ridiculous? And yet one can't forever stand on the shore; at some point, even if filled with indecision, skepticism, reservation and doubt, you either jump in or concede that life is forever elsewhere.

Which I daresay was one of the major impulses behind the decision to attempt *The Crucible*. Salem village, that pious, devout settlement at the very edge of white civilization, had taught me—three centuries before the Russo-American rivalry and the issues it raised—that a kind of built-in pestilence was nestled in the human mind, a fatality forever awaiting the right conditions for its always unique, forever unprecedented outbreak of alarm, suspicion, and murder. And to people wherever the play is performed, on any of the six continents, there is always a certain amazement that the same terror that had happened to them had happened before to others. It is all very strange. On the other hand, the Devil is known to lure people into forgetting precisely what it is vital for them to remember—how else could his endless reappearances always come with such marvelous surprise?

Introduction to
A View from the Bridge
(TWO-ACT VERSION)
1960

A play is rarely given a second chance. Unlike a novel, which may be received initially with less than enthusiasm, and then as time goes by hailed by a large public, a play usually makes its mark right off or it vanishes into oblivion. Two of mine, *The Crucible* and *A View from the Bridge*, failed to find large audiences with their original Broadway productions. Both were regarded as rather cold plays at first. However, after a couple of years *The Crucible* was produced again Off-Broadway and ran two years, without a line being changed from the original. With McCarthy dead it was once again possible to feel warmly toward the play, whereas during his time of power it was suspected of being a special plea, a concoction and unaesthetic. On its second time around its humanity emerged and it could be enjoyed as drama.

At this writing I have not yet permitted a second New York production of *A View from the Bridge* principally because I have not had the desire to see it through the mill a second time. However, a year or so after its first production it was done with great success in London and then in Paris, where it ran two years. It is done everywhere in this country without any apparent difficulty in reaching the emotions of the audience. This play, however, unlike *The Crucible*, I have revised, and it was the revision which London and

Paris saw. The nature of the revisions bears directly upon the questions of form and style which interest students and theater workers. The original play produced on Broadway (Viking, 1955) was in one act. It was a hard, telegraphic, unadorned drama. Nothing was permitted which did not advance the progress of Eddie's catastrophe in a most direct way. In a Note to the published play, I wrote:

> What struck me first about this tale when I heard it one night in my neighborhood was how directly, with what breathtaking simplicity, it did evolve. It seemed to me, finally, that its very bareness, its absolutely unswerving path, its exposed skeleton, so to speak, was its wisdom and even its charm and must not be tampered with. . . . These *qualities* of the events themselves, their texture, seemed to me more psychologically telling than a conventional investigation in width which would necessarily relax that clear, clean line of his catastrophe.

The explanation for this point of view lies in great part in the atmosphere of the time in which the play was written. It seemed to me then that the theater was retreating into an area of psycho-sexual romanticism, and this at the very moment when great events both at home and abroad cried out for recognition and analytic inspection. In a word, I was tired of mere sympathy in the theater. The spectacle of still another misunderstood victim left me impatient. The tender emotions, I felt, were being overworked. I wanted to write in a way that would call up the faculties of knowing as well as feeling. To bathe the audience in tears, to grip people by the age-old methods of suspense, to theatricalize life, in a word, seemed faintly absurd to me if not disgusting.

In *The Crucible* I had taken a step, I felt, toward a more self-aware drama. The Puritan not only felt, but constantly referred his feelings to concepts, to codes and ideas of social and ethical importance. Feeling, it seemed to me, had to be made of importance; the dramatic victory had to be more than a triumph over the audience's indifference. It must call up a concept, a new awareness.

I had known the story of *A View from the Bridge* for a long time. A waterfront worker who had known Eddie's prototype told it to me. I had never thought to make a play of it because it was too complete, there was nothing I could add. And then a time came when its very completeness became appealing. It suddenly seemed to me that I ought to deliver it onto the stage as fact; that interpretation was inherent in the very existence of the tale in the first place. I saw that the reason I had not written it was that as a whole its meaning escaped me. I could not fit it into myself. It existed apart from me and seemed not to express anything within me. Yet it refused to disappear.

I wrote it in a mood of experiment—to see what it might mean. I kept to the *tale*, trying not to change its original shape. I wanted the audience to feel toward it as I had on hearing it for the first time— not so much with heart-wringing sympathy as with wonder. For when it was told to me I knew its ending a few minutes after the teller had begun to speak. I wanted to create suspense but not by withholding information. It must be suspenseful because one knew too well how it would come out, so that the basic feeling would be the desire to stop this man and tell him what he was really doing to his life. Thus, by knowing more than the hero, the audience would rather automatically see his life through conceptualized feelings.

As a consequence of this viewpoint, the characters were not permitted to talk about this and that before getting down to their functions in the tale; when a character entered he proceeded directly to serve the catastrophe. Thus, normal naturalistic acting techniques had to be modified. Excessive and arbitrary gestures were eliminated; the set itself was shorn of every adornment. An atmosphere was attempted in which nothing existed but the purpose of the tale.

The trouble was that neither the director, the actors, nor I had had any experience with this kind of staging. It was difficult to know how far to go. We were all aware that a strange style was called for which we were unsure how to provide.

About a year later in London new conditions created new solutions. Seemingly inconsequential details suggested these solutions at times. For one, the British actors could not reproduce the Brooklyn argot and had to create one that was never heard on heaven or earth. Already naturalism was evaporated by this much: the characters were slightly strange beings in a world of their own. Also, the pay scales of the London theater made it possible to do what I could not do in New York—hire a crowd.

These seemingly mundane facts had important consequences. The mind of Eddie Carbone is not comprehensible apart from its

relation to his neighborhood, his fellow workers, his social situation. His self-esteem depends upon their estimate of him, and his
value is created largely by his fidelity to the code of his culture. In
New York we could have only four strategically placed actors to
represent the community. In London there were at least twenty
men and women surrounding the main action. Peter Brook, the
British director, could then proceed to design a set which soared to
the roof with fire escapes, passageways, suggested apartments, so
that one sensed that Eddie was living out his horror in the midst
of a certain normality, and that, invisibly and without having to
speak of it, he was getting ready to invoke upon himself the wrath
of his tribe. A certain size accrued to him as a result. The importance of his interior psychological dilemma was magnified to the
size it would have in life. What had seemed like a mere aberration had now risen to a fatal violation of an ancient law. By the
presence of his neighbors alone the play and Eddie were made more
humanly understandable and moving. There was also the fact that
the British cast, accustomed to playing Shakespeare, could incorporate into a seemingly realistic style the conception of the play—
they moved easily into the larger-than-life attitude which the play
demanded, and without the self-conscious awkwardness, the uncertain stylishness which hounds many actors without classic
training.

As a consequence of not having to work at making the play seem
as factual, as bare as I had conceived it, I felt now that it could
afford to include elements of simple human motivation which I had
rigorously excluded before—specifically, the viewpoint of Eddie's
wife, and *her* dilemma in relation to him. This, in fact, accounts for
almost all the added material which made it necessary to break the
play in the middle for an intermission. In other words, once Eddie
had been placed squarely in his social context, among his people,
the mythlike feeling of the story emerged of itself, and he could be
made more human and less a figure, a force. It thus seemed quite in
keeping that certain details of realism should be allowed; a Christ-
mas tree and decorations in the living room, for one, and a realistic
make-up, which had been avoided in New York, where the actor
was always much cleaner than a longshoreman ever is. In a word,
the nature of the British actor and of the production there made it

possible to concentrate more upon realistic characterization while the universality of Eddie's type was strengthened at the same time.

But it was not only external additions, such as a new kind of actor, sets, and so forth, which led to the expansion of the play. As I have said, the original was written in the hope that I would understand what it meant to me. It was only during the latter part of its run in New York that, while watching a performance one afternoon, I saw my own involvement in this story. Quite suddenly the play seemed to be "mine" and not merely a story I had heard. The revisions subsequently made were in part the result of that new awareness.

In general, then, I think it can be said that by the addition of significant psychological and behavioral detail the play became not only more human, warmer and less remote, but also a clearer statement. Eddie is still not a man to weep over; the play does not attempt to swamp an audience in tears. But it is more possible now to relate his actions to our own and thus to understand ourselves a little better not only as isolated psychological entities, but as we connect to our fellows and our long past together.

❧

Foreword to *After the Fall*
1964

This play is not "about" something; hopefully, it is something. And primarily it is a way of looking at man and his human nature as the only source of the violence which has come closer and closer to destroying the race. It is a view which does not look toward social or political ideas as the creators of violence, but into the nature of the human being himself. It should be clear now that no people or political system has a monopoly on violence. It is also clear that the one common denominator in all violent acts is the human being.

The first real "story" in the Bible is the murder of Abel. Before this drama there is only a featureless Paradise. But in that Eden there was peace because man had no consciousness of himself nor any knowledge of sex or his separateness from plants or other animals. Presumably we are being told that the human being becomes "himself" in the act of becoming aware of his sinfulness. He "is" what he is ashamed of.

After all, the infraction of Eve is that she opened up the knowledge of good and evil. She presented Adam with a choice. So that where choice begins, Paradise ends, Innocence ends, for what is Paradise but the absence of any need to choose this action? And two alternatives open out of Eden. One is Cain's alternative—or, if you will, Oswald's; to express without limit one's unbridled inner compulsion, in this case to murder, and to plead unawareness as a virtue and a defense. The other course is what roars through the rest of the Bible and all history—the struggle of the human race through the millennia to pacify the destructive impulses of man, to express his wishes for greatness, for wealth, for accomplishment, for love, but without turning law and peace into chaos.

The question which finally comes into the open in this play is, how is that pacification to be attained? Quentin, the central character, arrives on the scene weighed down with a sense of his own pointlessness and the world's. His success as an attorney has crumbled in his hands as he sees only his own egotism in it and no wider goal beyond himself. He has lived through two wrecked marriages. His desperation is too serious, too deadly to permit him to blame others for it. He is desperate for a clear view of his own responsibility for his life, and this because he has recently found a woman he feels he can love, and who loves him; he cannot take another life into his hands hounded as he is by self-doubt. He is faced, in short, with what Eve brought to Adam—the terrifying fact of choice. And to choose, one must know oneself, but no man knows himself who cannot face the murder in him, the sly and everlasting complicity with the forces of destruction. The apple cannot be stuck back on the Tree of Knowledge; once we begin to see, we are doomed and challenged to seek the strength to see more, not less. When Cain was questioned, he stood amazed and asked, "Am I my brother's keeper?" Oswald's first words on being taken were, "I didn't do anything." And what country has ever gone into war proclaiming anything but injured innocence? Murder and violence require Innocence, whether real or cultivated. And through Quentin's agony in this play there runs the everlasting temptation of Innocence, that deep desire to return to when, it seems, he was in fact without blame. To that elusive time, which persists in all our minds, when somehow everything was part of us and we so pleasurably at one with others, and everything merely "happened" to us. But the closer he examines those seemingly unified years the clearer it becomes that his Paradise keeps slipping back and back. For there was always his awareness, always the choice, always the conflict between his own needs and desires and the impediments others put in his way. Always, and from the beginning, the panorama of human beings raising up in him and in each other the temptation of the final solution to the problem of being a self at all—the solution of obliterating whatever stands in the way, thus destroying what is loved as well.

This play, then, is a trial; the trial of a man by his own conscience, his own values, his own deeds. The "Listener," who to some will be a psychoanalyst, to others God, is Quentin himself turned at the edge of the abyss to look at his experience, his nature and his time in order to bring to light, to seize and—innocent no more—to forever guard against his own complicity with Cain, and the world's.

But a work of fiction, like an accident witnessed in the street, inevitably gives rise to many differing accounts. Some will call it a play "about" Puritanism, or "about" incest, or "about" the transformation of guilt into responsibility, or whatever. For me it is as much a fact in itself as a new bridge. And in saying this I only dare to express what so many American writers are trying to bring to pass—the day when our novels, plays, pictures and poems will indeed enter into the business of the day, the mindless flight from our own actual experience, a flight which empties out the soul.

Guilt and *Incident at Vichy*
1965

About ten years ago a European friend of mine told me a story. In 1942, said he, a man he knew was picked up on the street in Vichy, France, during a sudden roundup of Jews, taken to a police station, and simply told to wait. Refugees of all sorts had been living in Vichy since the invasion of France because the relatively milder regime of Marshal Pétain had fended off some of the more brutal aspects of German occupation. With false papers, which were not hard to buy, a Jew or a politically suspect person could stay alive in the so-called Unoccupied Zone, which covered the southern half of the country. The racial laws, for one thing, had not been applied by Pétain.

In the police station the arrested man found others waiting to be questioned, and he took his place on line. A door at the front of the line would open, a Vichy policeman would beckon, a suspect would go in. Some soon came out again and walked free into the street. Most did not reappear. The rumor moved down the line that this was a Gestapo operation and that the circumcised would have to produce immaculate proof of their Gentileness, while the uncircumcised would of course go free.

The friend of my friend was a Jew. As he got closer and closer to the fatal door he became more and more certain that his death was near. Finally, there was only one man between him and that door. Presently, this last man was ordered into the office. Nothing stood between the Jew and a meaningless, abrupt slaughter.

The door opened. The man who had been the last to go in came out. My friend's friend stood paralyzed, waiting for the policeman to appear and beckon him into the office. But instead of walking past him with his pass to freedom, the Gentile who had just come out stopped in front of my friend's friend, thrust his pass into his hand, and whispered for him to go. He went.

He had never before laid eyes on his saviour. He never saw him again.

In the ten years after hearing it, the story kept changing its meaning for me. It never occurred to me that it could be a play until this spring when *Incident at Vichy* suddenly burst open complete in almost all its details. Before that it had been simply a fact, a feature of existence which sometimes brought exhilaration with it, sometimes a vacant wonder, and sometimes even resentment. In any case, I realize that it was a counterpoint to many happenings around me in this past decade.

That faceless, unknown man would pop up in my mind when I read about the people in Queens refusing to call the police while a woman was being stabbed to death on the street outside their windows. He would form himself in the air when I listened to delinquent boys whose many different distortions of character seemed to spring from a common want of human solidarity. Friends troubled by having to do things they disapproved of brought him to mind, people for whom the very concept of choosing their actions was a long forgotten thing. Wherever I felt the seemingly implacable tide of human drift and the withering of will in myself and in others, this faceless person came to mind. And he appears most clearly and imperatively amid the jumble of emotions surrounding the Negro in this country and the whole unsettled moral problem of the destruction of the Jews in Europe.

At this point I must say that I think most people seeing this play are quite aware it is not "about Nazism" or a wartime horror tale; they do understand that the underlying issue concerns us now and that it has to do with our individual relationships with injustice and violence. But since a few critics persist in their inability to differentiate between a play's story and its theme, it is just as well to make those differences plain.

The story as I heard it never presented a "problem": everyone believes that there are some few heroes among us at all times. In the words of Hermann Broch, "And even if all that is created in this world were to be annihilated, if all its aesthetic values were abolished . . . dissolved in skepticism of all law . . . there would yet survive untouched the unity of thought, the ethical postulate." In short, the birth of each man is the rebirth of a claim to justice and requires neither drama nor proof to make it known to us.

What is dark if not unknown is the relationship between those who side with justice and their implication in the evils they oppose. So unknown is it that today in Germany it is still truly incomprehensible to many people how the crude horrors of the Nazi regime could have come to pass, let alone have been tolerated by what had for generations been regarded as one of the genuinely cultured nations of the world. So unknown that here in America, where violent crime rises at incredible rates—and, for example, the United Nations has to provide escorts for people leaving the building after dark in the world's greatest city—few people even begin to imagine that they might have some symbolic or even personal connection with this violence.

Without for an instant intending to lift the weight of condemnation Nazism must bear, does its power not become more comprehensible when we see our own helplessness toward the violence in our own streets? How many of us have looked into ourselves for even a grain of its cause? Is it not for us—as it is for the Germans—the others who are doing evil?

The other day on a news broadcast I heard that Edward R. Murrow had been operated on for lung cancer. The fact was hardly announced when the commercial came on—"Kent satisfies best!" We smile, even laugh; we must, lest we scream. And in the laughter, in the smile, we dissolve by that much. Is it possible to say convincingly that this destruction of an ethic also destroys my will to oppose violence in the streets? We do not have many wills, but only one: it cannot be continuously compromised without atrophy setting in altogether.

The first problem is not what to do about it but to discover our own relationship to evil, its reflection of ourselves. Is it too much to say that those who do not suffer injustice have a vested interest in injustice?

Does any of us know how much of his savings-bank interest is coming from investments in Harlem and Bedford-Stuyvesant real estate, those hovels from which super profits are made by jamming human beings together as no brute animals could be jammed without their dying? Does anyone know how much of his church's income is derived from such sources?

Let the South alone for a moment—who among us has asked himself how much of his own sense of personal value, how much of his pride in himself is there by virtue of his not being black? And how much of our fear of the Negro comes from the subterranean knowledge that his lowliness has found our consent and that he is demanding from us what we have taken from him and keep taking from him through our pride?

It was not to set forth a hero, either as a fact of history or as an example for us now, that I wrote this play but to throw some light on evil. The good and the evil are not compartments but two elements of a transaction. The hero of the play, Prince Von Berg, is mistakenly arrested by a Nazi race "expert." He comes into the detention room with his pride of being on the humane side, the right side, for he has fled his Austria and his rank and privilege rather than be part of a class which oppresses people.

None of the horrors he witnesses are really surprising to him here, nothing is forbidden any more, as he has long known. What he discovers in this place is his own complicity with the force he despises, his own inherited love for a cousin who, in fact, is a Nazi and an oppressor, the material cause, in short, for what before was a general sense of guilt, namely, his own secret joy and relief that, after all, he is not a Jew and will not be destroyed.

Much is made of guilt these days, even some good jokes. Liberalism is seen now as a response to guilt; much of psychiatry has made a business of evaporating guilt; the churches are no longer sure if their age-old insistence on man's guilt is not an unwitting spur to neurosis and even the acting-out of violence; the Roman Catholic church has only recently decided to lift the Crucifixion guilt from the Jews alone and to spread it evenly over mankind.

I have no "solution" to human guilt in this play, only a kind of remark, no more. I cannot conceive of guilt as having an existence without the existence of injustice. And injustice, like death itself, creates two opposing interests—one more or less profits from it, the other more or less is diminished by it. Those who profit, either psychically or materially, seek to even out the scales by the weight of guilt. A "moral" ounce is taken up to weigh down the otherwise too-light heart which contemplates uneasily its relative freedom from injustice's penalty, the guilt of having been spared.

In my play, the hero is that man whose guilt is no longer general but suddenly a clear transaction—he has been, he sees, not so much an opponent of Nazism but a vessel of guilt for its brutalities. As a man of intense sympathy for others he will survive but at a price too great for him to pay—the authenticity of his own self-image and his pride. And here I stop; I do not know why any man actually sacrifices himself any more than I know why people commit suicide. The explanation will always be on the other side of the grave, and even that is doubtful.

If they could speak, could the three boys who were murdered in Mississippi really explain why they had to go to the end? More—if each of them could discover for us in his personal history his motives and the last and most obscure corner of his psychology, would we really be any closer to the mystery of why we first require human sacrifices before our guilt can be transformed into responsibility? Is it not an absurdity that the deaths of three young men should make any difference when hundreds have been lynched and beaten to death before them, and tens of thousands humiliated?

The difference, I think, is that these, including Chaney, the young Negro, were not inevitable victims of Mississippi but volunteers. They had transformed guilt into responsibility and in so doing opened the way to a vision that leaped the pit of remorse and helplessness. And it is no accident that the people of Mississippi at first refused to concede they had been murdered, for they have done everything in their power to deny responsibility for the "character" of the Negro they paternalistically "protect," and here in these three young bodies was the return with interest for their investment in the guilt that does not act.

At the end of *Incident at Vichy*, the Prince suddenly hands his pass to a Jew, a psychiatrist, who accepts it in astonishment, in awe and wonder, and walks out to freedom. With that freedom he must accept the guilt of surviving his benefactor. Is he a "good" man for accepting his life this way or a "bad" one? That will depend on what he makes of his guilt, of his having survived.

In any case, death, when it takes those we have loved, always hands us a pass. From this transaction with the earth the living take this survivor's reproach; consoling it and at turns denying its existence in us, we constantly regenerate Broch's "unity of thought, the ethical postulate"—the debt, in short, which we owe for living, the debt to the wronged.

It is necessary to say something more about Germany in this context of guilt. I cannot read anyone's mind, let alone a nation's, but one can read the drift of things. About a year ago I wrote some thoughts about the current Frankfurt trials of Nazi war criminals, which were published in Germany, among other countries. There was much German mail in response and a good lot of it furious, in part because I asked the question whether a recrudescence of Nazism was possible again in the future. The significant thing in many letters was a resentment based on the idea that the Nazis and the regime were something apart from the German people. In general, I was giving Germany a "bad name."

Apart from the unintended humor, I think this reaction is to be faced by the world and especially by the Germans. It is, in fact, no good telling people they are guilty. A nation, any more than an individual, helps nobody by going about beating its chest. I believe, in truth, that blame and emotional charges of a generalized guilt can only help to energize new frustrations in the Germans and send them striving for dignity through a new, strident, and dangerous nationalism. Again, guilt can become a "morality" in itself if no active path is opened before it, if it is not transformed into responsibility. The fact, unfortunately, is that for too many the destruction of the Jews by Germans has become one of Orwell's non-actions, an event self-propelled and therefore incomprehensible.

But if the darkness that persists over human guilt were to be examined not as an exceptional condition or as illness but as a concomitant of human nature, perhaps some practical good could come of it instead of endless polemic. If the hostility and aggression which lie hidden in every human being could be accepted as a fact rather than as reprehensible sin, perhaps the race could begin to guard against its ravages, which always take us "unawares," as something from "outside," from the hands of "others."

The reader has probably been nodding in agreement with what I have just said about Germany, but who among us knew enough to be shocked, let alone to protest, at the photographs of the Vietnamese torturing Vietcong prisoners, which our press has published? The Vietnamese are wearing United States equipment, are paid by us, and could not torture without us. There is no way around this— the prisoner crying out in agony is *our prisoner.*

It is simply no good saying that the other side probably does the same thing; it is the German's frequent answer when you raise the subject of Nazi atrocities—he begins talking about Mississippi. And more, if he is intelligent he will remind you that the schoolbooks sent to Germany by the United States immediately after the war included the truth about Nazism, but that they were withdrawn soon after when the Cold War began, so that a generation has grown up which has been taught nothing about the bloodiest decade in its country's history.

What is the lesson? It is immensely difficult to be human precisely because we cannot detect our own hostility in our own actions. It is tragic, fatal blindness, so old in us, so ingrained, that it underlies the first story in the Bible, the first personage in that book who can be called human. The rabbis who collected the Old Testament set Cain at its beginning not out of some interest in criminology but because they understood that the sight of his own crimes is the highest agony a man can know and the hardest to relate himself to.

Incident at Vichy has been called a play whose theme is "Am I my brother's keeper?" Not so. "Am I my own keeper?" is more correct.

Guilt, then, is not a featureless mist but the soul's remorse for its own hostility. We punish ourselves to keep from being punished and to keep from having to take part in regenerating that "unity of thought, that ethical postulate," which nevertheless is reborn with every child, again and again forever.

℘

The Price—The Power of the Past
1999

The sources of a play are both obvious and mysterious. *The Price* is first of all about a group of people recollected, as it were, in tranquillity. The central figures, the New York cop Victor Franz and his elder brother, Walter, are not precise portraits of people I knew long, long ago but close enough, and Gregory Solomon, the old furniture dealer, is as close as I could get to reproducing a dealer's Russian-Yiddish accent that still tickles me whenever I hear it in memory.

First, the bare bones of the play's story: the Great Crash of 1929 left Victor and Walter to care for their widowed father, who had been ruined in the stock market collapse and was helpless to cope with life. While Victor, loyal to the father, dropped out of college to earn a living for them both and ended up on the police force, Walter went on to become a wealthy surgeon.

The play begins decades later on the attic floor of the decrepit brownstone where the cop and his father had lived, surrounded by piles of furniture from their old apartment that the father had clung to. Now the building, owned by the father's brother, is to be torn down, so the furniture must be sold.

The conflict of how to divide the proceeds cuts open the long-buried lives of both men, as well as that of Victor's wife, Esther, and reveals the choices each has made and the price each has paid. Through it all weaves the antic ninety-year-old furniture dealer Gregory Solomon, who is yards ahead of them as he tries to shepherd them away from the abyss toward which he knows they are heading.

Behind the play—almost any play—are more or less secret responses to other works of the time, and these may emerge as disguised imitation or as outright rejection of the dominating forms of the hour. *The Price* was written in 1967, and since nobody is going to care anymore, it may as well be admitted that in some part it was a reaction to two big events that had come to overshadow all others in that decade. One was the seemingly permanent and morally agonizing Vietnam War, the other a surge of avant-garde plays that to one or another degree fit the absurd styles. I was moved to write a play that might confront and confound both.

I enjoyed watching some of the absurd plays—my first theater experiences were with vaudeville in the Twenties, after all, and absurdist comics like Bert Williams and Willie Howard, with their delicious proto–shaggy-dog stories and skits, were favorites. More, for a while in the Thirties our own William Saroyan, who with all his failings was an authentic American inventor of a domestic absurdist attitude, had held the stage. One would not soon forget his *Time* magazine subscription salesman reading—not without passion—the entire page-long list of names of *Time*'s reporters, editors, subeditors, fact checkers, department heads and dozens of lesser employees, to a pair of Ozark hillbillies dressed in their rags, seated on their rotting porch and listening with rapt incomprehension.

But the Sixties was a time when a play with recognizable characters, a beginning, middle and end was routinely condemned as "well made" or ludicrously old-fashioned. (That plays with no characters, beginning or end were not called "badly made" was inevitable when the detonation of despised rules in all things was a requisite for recognition as modern. That beginnings, middles, and ends might not be mere rules but a replication of the rise and fall of human life did not frequently come up.)

Often against my will, however, I found myself enjoying the new abstract theater; for one thing, it was moving us closer to a state of dream, and for dreams I had nothing but respect. But as the dying continued in Vietnam with no adequate resistance to it in the country, the theater, so it seemed to me, risked trivialization by failing to confront the bleeding, at least in a way that could reach most people. In its way, *Hair* had done so by offering a laid-back lifestyle opposed to the aggressive military-corporate one. But one had to feel the absence—not only in theater but everywhere—of any interest in what had surely given birth to Vietnam, namely, its roots in the past.

Indeed, the very idea of an operating continuity between past and present in any human behavior was démodé and close to a laughably old-fashioned irrelevancy. My impression, in fact, was that playwrights were either uninterested in or incapable of presenting antecedent material altogether. Like the movies, plays seemed to exist entirely in the now; characters had either no past or none that could somehow be directing present actions. It was as though the culture had decreed amnesia as the ultimate mark of reality.

As the corpses piled up, it became cruelly impolite if not unpatriotic to suggest the obvious, that we were fighting the past; our rigid anticommunist theology, born of another time two decades earlier, made it a sin to consider Vietnamese Reds as nationalists rather than Moscow's and Beijing's yapping dogs. We were fighting in a state of forgetfulness, quite as though we had not aborted a national election in Vietnam and divided the country into separate halves when it became clear that Ho Chi Minh would be the overwhelming favorite for the presidency. This was the reality on the ground, but unfortunately it had to be recalled in order to matter. And so fifty thousand Americans, not to mention millions of Vietnamese, paid with their lives to support a myth and a bellicose denial.

As always, it was the young who paid. I was fifty-three in 1968, and if the war would cost me nothing materially, it wore away at the confidence that in the end Reason had to return lest all be lost. I was not sure of that anymore. Reason itself had become unaesthetic, something art must at any cost avoid.

The Price grew out of a need to reconfirm the power of the past, the seedbed of current reality, and the way to possibly reaffirm cause and effect in an insane world. It seemed to me that if, through the mists of denial, the bow of the ancient ship of reality could emerge, the spectacle might once again hold some beauty for an audience. If the play does not utter the word Vietnam, it speaks to a spirit of unearthing the real that seemed to have very nearly gone from our lives.

Which is not to deny that the primary force driving *The Price* was a tangle of memories of people. Still, these things move together, idea feeding characters and characters deepening idea.

Nineteen sixty-eight, when the play is set, was already nearly forty years since the Great Crash, the onset of the transformed America of the Depression decade. It was then that the people in this play had made the choices whose consequences they had now to confront. The Thirties had been a time when we learned the fear of doom and had stopped being kids for a while; the time, in short, when, as I once noted about the era, the birds came home to roost and the past became present. And that Depression cataclysm, incidentally, seemed to teach that life indeed had beginnings, middles and a consequential end.

Plays leave a wake behind them as they pass into history, with odd objects bobbing about in it. Many of these, in the case of *The Price*, are oddly funny for such a serious work. I had just finished writing it and with my wife, Inge Morath, went to the Caribbean for a week's vacation. Hurrying onto the beach in our first hour there, we noticed a man standing ankle-deep in the water, dressed in shorts and a wide-brimmed plantation hat, who looked a lot like Mel Brooks. In fact, he *was* Mel Brooks. After a few minutes' chat I asked if there was any fishing here. "Oh, God, yes," he said, "yesterday there was one came in right there," and he pointed a yard away in the shallow water. "Must have been three feet long. He was dead. But he may be over there today," he added, pointing down the beach.

He wanted to know if I was writing, and I said we were casting a new play called *The Price*, and he asked what it was about. "Well," I said, "there are these two brothers . . . "

"Stop, I'm crying!" he yelled, frightening all the Protestants lying on the beach.

Then there was the letter from the Turkish translator, who assured me that he had made only one change in the text. At the very end, he wrote, after the two brothers nearly come to blows and part forever, unreconciled and angry, there follows a quiet, rather elegiac moment with the old furniture dealer, the cop, and his wife.

Just as they are leaving the stage, the translator explained, he had to bring back the elder brother, Walter, to fall tearfully into the cop's arms. This, because the audience would fear that *the actors themselves* would have had to have a vendetta that could only end in a killing if they parted as unreconciled as the script required. And so, out of the depths, rose the Turkish past . . .

Conditions of Freedom:
Two Plays of the Seventies
1989

I

It is pointless any longer to speak of a period as being one of transition—what period isn't?—but the seventies, when both these plays were written, seemed to resist any definition even at the time. *The Archbishop's Ceiling* in some part was a response to this indefinition I sensed around me. Early in the decade the Kent State massacre took place, and while the anti–Vietnam War movement could still mobilize tens of thousands, the freshness had gone out of the wonderful sixties mixture of idealism and bitterness that had sought to project a new unaggressive society based on human connection rather than the values of the market economy. There was a common awareness of exhaustion, to the point where politics and social thought themselves seemed ludicrously out of date and naively ineffectual except as subjects of black comedy. Power everywhere seemed to have transformed itself from a forbidding line of troops into an ectoplasmic lump that simply swallowed up the righteous sword as it struck. Power was also doing its own, often surprising thing.

At least as an atmosphere, there was a not dissimilar disillusion in Eastern Europe and, for different reasons, in France too. As president of International P.E.N., I had the opportunity to move about in Eastern Europe, as well as in the Soviet Union, and I felt that local differences aside, intellectual life in the whole developed world had been stunned by a common failure to penetrate Power with a more humane and rational point of view. It may have been that the immense sense of relief and the high expectations that rushed in with the defeat of Hitler and Mussolini's fascism had to end in a letdown, but whatever the causes, by the seventies the rational seemed bankrupt as an ultimate sanction, a bar to which to appeal. And with it went a sense of history, even of the evolution of ideas and attitudes.

The ups and downs of disillusionment varied with time and place, however. It was possible to sit with Hungarian writers, for example, while they talked of a new liberalizing trend in their country, at the very moment that in Prague the depths of a merciless repression were being plumbed. There, with the Soviet ousting of Dubček and the crushing of all hope for an egalitarian socialist economy wedded to liberal freedoms of speech and artistic expression, the crash of expectations was especially terrible, for it was in Prague that this novel fusion seemed actually to have begun to function.

The seventies was also the era of the listening device, government's hidden bugs set in place to police the private conversations of its citizens—and not in Soviet areas alone. The White House was bugged, businesses were bugging competitors to defeat their strategies, and Watergate and the publication of the Pentagon Papers (which polls showed a majority of Americans disapproved) demonstrated that the Soviets had little to teach American presidents about domestic espionage. The burgling of psychiatrists' offices to spy out a government official's private life, the widespread bugging by political parties of each other's offices, all testified to the fact that the visible motions of political life were too often merely distractions, while the reality was what was happening in the dark.

Thus, when I found myself in Eastern European living rooms where it was all but absolutely certain that the walls or ceilings were bugged by the regime, it was not, disturbingly enough, an absolutely unfamiliar sensation for me. Of course there were very important differences—basically that an Eastern writer accused of seditious thoughts would have no appeal from his government's decision to hound him into silence, or worse. But the more I reflected on my experiences under bugged ceilings, the more the real issue changed from a purely political one to the question of what effect this surveillance was having on the minds of people who had to live under such ceilings, on whichever side of the Cold War line they happened to be.

Vaclav Havel, the Czech playwright who was later to serve a long term in prison, one day discovered a bug in his chandelier when house painters lowered it to paint the ceiling; deciding to deliver it to the local police, he said that it was government property that he did not think rightfully belonged to a private person. But the joke was as unappreciated as the eavesdropping itself was undenied. Very recently, in the home of a star Soviet writer, I began to convey the best wishes of a mutual friend, an émigré Russian novelist living in Europe, and the star motioned to me not to continue. Once outside, I asked if he wasn't depressed by having to live in a tapped house. He thought a moment, then shrugged—"I really don't know how I feel. I guess we figure the thing doesn't work!"—and burst out laughing at this jibe at Soviet inefficiency. Was he really all that unaffected by the presence of the unbidden guest? Perhaps so, but even if he had come to accept or at least abide it fatalistically, the bug's presence had changed him nonetheless. In my view it had perhaps dulled some resistance in him to Power's fingers ransacking his pockets every now and then. One learns to *include the bug* in the baggage of one's mind, in the calculus of one's plans and expectations, and this is not without effect.

The occasion, then, of *The Archbishop's Ceiling* is the bug and how people live with it, but the theme is something different. There are a number of adaptations to such a life: one man rails furiously at the ceiling, another questions that a bug is even up there, a third has changes of opinion from day to day; but man is so adaptable—and anyway the bug doesn't seem to be reacting much of the time and may simply be one more nuisance—that resistance to its presence is finally worn down to nothing. And that is when things become interesting, for something like the naked soul begins to loom, some essence in man that is simply unadaptable, ultimate, immutable as the horizon.

What, for instance, becomes of the idea of sincerity, the unmitigated expression of one's feelings and views, when one knows that Power's ear is most probably overhead? Is sincerity shaken by the sheer fact that one has so much as *taken the bug into consideration*? Under such pressure who can resist trying to some degree, however discreet and slight, to characterize himself for the benefit of the ceiling, whether as obedient conformist or even as resistant? And what, in that case, has been done to one's very identity? Does this process not overturn the very notion of an "I" in this kind of world? It would seem that "I" must be singular, not plural, but the art of bureaucracy is to change the "I" of its subjects to "we" at every moment of conscious life. What happens, in short, when people know that they are—at least most probably, if not certainly—at all times talking to Power, whether through a bug or a friend who is really an informer? Is it not something akin to accounting for oneself to a god? After all, most ideas of God see him as omnipresent, invisible, and condign in his judgments; the bug lacks only mercy and love to qualify, it is conscience shorn of moral distinctions.

In this play the most unreconcilable of the writers is clearly the most talented. Sigmund really has no permanent allegiance except to the love of creating art. Sigmund is also the most difficult to get along with, and has perhaps more than his share of cynicism and bitterness, narcissism and contempt for others. He is also choking with rage and love. In short, he is most alive, something that by itself would fuel his refusal—or constitutional incapacity—to accept the state's arrogant treatment. But with all his vitality, even he in the end must desperately call up a sanction, a sublime force beyond his ego, to sustain him in his opposition to that arrogance; for him it is the sublimity of art, in whose life-giving, creative essence he partakes and shares with other artists whose works he bows to, and in the act transcends the tyranny.

In a sense *Archbishop* begs the question of the existence of the sacred in the political life of man. But it begins to seem now that some kind of charmed circle has to be drawn around each person, across which the state may intrude only at its very real economic and political peril.

Glasnost, which did not exist in the seventies, is to the point here, for it is at bottom a Soviet attempt, born of economic crisis, to break up the perfection of its own social controls in order to open the channels of expression through which the creativity, the initiatives, and the improvisations of individual people may begin to flow and enrich the country. The problem, of course, is how to make this happen in a one-party state that in principle illegalizes opposition. But the wish is as plain as the desperate need of the economy itself, indeed of the regime, for the wisdom of the many and the release of their energies. Finally, the question arises whether, after so many generations of training in submission, the habits of open-minded inquiry and independence can be evoked in a sufficient number of people to make such a policy work.

Late in 1986, when glasnost was a brand-new idea scarcely taken seriously as the main thrust of the new administration, a Russian writer expressing the pre-glasnost view said to me, "What you people in the West don't understand is that we are not a competitive society and we don't wish to be. We want the government to protect us, that is what the government is for. When two Western writers meet, one of them most likely asks the other what he is writing now. Our writers never ask such a question. They are not competing. You have been in our Writers Union and seen those hundreds of writers going in and out, having their lunches, reading newspapers, writing letters, and so on. A big number of those people haven't written anything in years! Some perhaps wrote a few short stories or a novel some years ago—and that was it! They were made members of the Union, got the apartment and the vacation in the south, and it is not so different in any other field. But this is not such a terrible thing to us!"

But, I countered, there were surely some highly talented people who produced a good deal of work.

"Of course! But most are not so talented, so it's just as well they don't write too much anyway. But is it right that they should be thrown out in the streets to starve because they are not talented? We don't think so!"

What he had chosen to omit, of course, was that the mediocrities, of which he was all but admittedly one, usually run things in the Writers Union, something the gifted writers are usually too prickly and independent to be trusted to do. And so the system practically polices itself, stifling creativity and unpalatable truth-telling, and extolling the mediocre. But its main object, to contain any real attempts at change, is effectively secured. The only problem is that unless the system moves faster it may be permanently consigned to an inferior rank among the competing societies.

And so it may well have come to pass that the sanctity of the individual, his right to express his unique sense of reality freely and in public, has become an economic necessity and not alone a political or aesthetic or moral question. If that turns out to be the case, we will have been saved by a kind of economic morality based on necessity, the safest morality of all.

II

The American Clock was begun in the early seventies and did not reach final form until its production at the Mark Taper Forum in Los Angeles in 1984, a version that in turn was movingly and sometimes hilariously interpreted in the Peter Wood production two years later at the British National Theatre. The seemingly endless changes it went through reflected my own search for something like a dramatic resolution to what, after all, was one of the vaster social calamities in history—the Great Depression of the thirties. I have no hesitation in saying that as it now stands, the work is simply as close to such a resolution as I am able to bring it, just as the experience itself remains only partially resolved in the hands of historians. For the humiliating truth about any "period" is its essential chaos, about which any generalization can be no more than just that, a statement to which many exceptions may be taken.

With all its variety, however, there were certain features of the Depression era that set it apart, for they had not existed before in such force and over such a long time. One of the most important of these to me, both as a person living through those years and as a writer contemplating them three decades afterwards, was the introduction into the American psyche of a certain unprecedented *suspense*. Through the twenties the country, for me—and I believe I was typical—floated in a reassuring state of nature that merged boundlessly with the sea and the sky; I had never thought of it as even having a system. But the Crash forced us all to enter history willy-nilly, and everyone soon understood that there were other ways of conducting the nation's business—there simply had to be, because the one we had was so persistently not working. It was not only the radicals who were looking at the historical clock and asking how long our system could last, but people of every viewpoint. After all, they were hardly radicals who went to Washington to ask the newly inaugurated President Roosevelt to nationalize the banks, but bankers themselves who had finally confessed their inability to control their own system. The objective situation, in a word, had surfaced; people had taken on a new consciousness that had been rare in more prosperous times, and the alternatives of fascism or socialism were suddenly in the air.

Looking back at it all from the vantage of the early seventies, we seemed to have reinserted the old tabula rasa, the empty slate, into our heads again. Once more we were in a state of nature where no alternatives existed and nothing had grown out of anything else. Conservatism was still damning the liberal New Deal, yearning to dismantle its remaining prestige, but at the same time the Social Security system, unemployment and bank insurance, the regulatory agencies in the stock market—the whole web of rational protections that the nation relied on—were products of the New Deal. We seemed to have lost awareness of community, of what we rightfully owe each other and what we owe ourselves. There seemed a want of any historical sense. America seems constantly in flight to the future; and it is a future made much like the past, a primeval paradise with really no government at all, in which the pioneer heads alone into the unknown forest to carve out his career. The suddenness of the '29 Crash and the chaos that followed offered a pure instance of the impotence of individualist solutions to so vast a crisis. As a society we learned all over again that we are in fact dependent and vulnerable, and that mass social organization does not necessarily weaken moral fiber but may set the stage for great displays of heroism and self-sacrifice and endurance. It may also unleash, as it did in the thirties, a flood of humor and optimism that was far less apparent in seemingly happier years.

When Studs Terkel's *Hard Times* appeared in 1970, the American economy was booming, and it would be another seventeen years before the stock market collapsed to anything like the degree it had in 1929. In any case, in considering his collection of interviews with survivors of the Depression as a partial basis for a play (I would mix my own memories into it as well), I had no prophecy of doom in mind, although in sheer principle it seemed impossible that the market could keep on rising indefinitely. At bottom, quite simply, I wanted to try to show how it was and where we had come from. I wanted to give some sense of life as we lived it when the clock was ticking every day.

The idea was not, strictly speaking, my invention but a common notion of the thirties. And it was a concept that also extended outward to Europe and the Far East; Hitler was clearly preparing to destroy parliamentary governments as soon as he organized his armies, just as Franco had destroyed the Spanish Republic, and Japan was manifestly creating a new empire that must one day collide with the interests of Britain and the United States. The clock was ticking everywhere.

Difficulties with the play had to do almost totally with finding a balance between the epic elements and the intimate psychological lives of individuals and families like the Baums. My impulse is usually toward integration of meaning through significant individual action, but the striking new fact of life in the Depression era—unlike the self-sufficient, prosperous seventies—was the swift rise in the common consciousness of the social system. Uncharacteristically, Americans were looking for answers far beyond the bedroom and purely personal relationships, and so the very form of the play should ideally reflect this wider awareness. But how to unify the two elements, objective and subjective, epic and psychological? The sudden and novel impact of the Depression made people in the cities, for example, painfully conscious that thousands of farm families were being forced off their lands in the West by a combination of a collapsed market for farm goods and the unprecedented drought and dust storms. The farmers who remained operating were aware—and openly resentful—that in the cities people could not afford to buy the milk for which they could not get commercially viable prices. The social paradoxes of the collapse were so glaring that it would be false to the era to try to convey its spirit through the life of any one family. Nevertheless the feeling of a unified theatrical event evaded me until the revision for the 1984 Mark

Taper production, which I believe came close to striking the balance. But it was in the British National Theatre production two years later that the play's theatrical life was finally achieved. The secret was vaudeville.

Of course the period had much tragedy and was fundamentally a trial and a frustration for those who lived through it, but no time ever created so many comedians and upbeat songs. Jack Benny, Fred Allen, W. C. Fields, Jimmy Durante, Eddie Cantor, Burns and Allen, and Ed Wynn were some of the headliners who came up in that time, and the song lyrics were most often exhilaratingly optimistic: "Love Is Sweeping the Country," "Life Is Just a Bowl of Cherries," "April in Paris," "I'm Getting Sentimental over You," "Who's Afraid of the Big Bad Wolf?" It was, in the pop culture, a romantic time and not at all realistically harsh. The serious writers were putting out books like Nathanael West's *Miss Lonelyhearts*, Erskine Caldwell's *God's Little Acre*, Jack Conroy's *The Disinherited*, André Malraux's *Man's Fate*, Hemingway's *Winner Take Nothing*, and Steinbeck's *In Dubious Battle*, and Edward Hopper was brooding over his stark street scenes, and Reginald Marsh was painting vagrants asleep in the subways, but Broadway had O'Neill's first comedy, *Ah, Wilderness!*, and another comical version of the hard life, *Tobacco Road*, Noel Coward's *Design for Living*, the Gershwins' *Let 'Em Eat Cake*, and some of the best American farces ever written—*Room Service*, *Three Men on a Horse*, and *Brother Rat* among them.

In the Mark Taper production I found myself allowing the material to move through me as it wished—I had dozens of scenes by this time and was shifting them about in search of their hidden emotional as well as ideational linkages. At one point the experience brought to mind a sort of vaudeville where the contiguity of sublime and ridiculous is perfectly acceptable; in vaudeville an imitation of Lincoln doing the Gettysburg Address could easily be followed by Chinese acrobats. So when subsequently Peter Wood asked for my feeling about the style, I could call the play a vaudeville with an assurance born of over a decade of experimentation. He took the hint and ran with it, tossing up the last shreds of a realistic approach, announcing from the opening image that the performance was to be epic and declarative.

Out of darkness, in a brash music hall spotlight, a baseball pitcher appears and tosses a ball from hand to glove as he gets ready on the mound. The other characters saunter on singing snatches of songs of the thirties, and from somewhere in the balcony a man in a boater and striped shirt, bow tie and gartered sleeves—Ted Quinn—whistles "I Found a Million-Dollar Baby in a Five-and-Ten-Cent Store." At one side of the open stage, a five-piece jazz band plays in full view of the audience (impossible in the penurious New York theater), and the sheer festivity of the occasion is already established.

The most startling, and I think wonderful, invention of all was the treatment of the character of Theodore K. Quinn. This was the actual name of a neighbor of mine, son of a Chicago railroad labor organizer, who had worked himself up from a poor Chicago law student to the vice-presidency of General Electric. The president of GE, Quinn's boss through most of the twenties, was Gerard Swope, a world-famous capitalist and much quoted social thinker, who decided as the thirties dawned that Quinn was to succeed him on his retirement. Quinn, in charge of the consumer products division of the company, had frequently bought up promising smaller manufacturers for Swope, incorporating their plants into the GE giant, but had developed a great fear that this process of cartelization must end in the destruction of democracy itself. Over the years his rationalization had been that he was only taking orders—although in fact it was on his judgment that Swope depended as to which companies to pick up. Then the excuses were threatened by his elevation to the presidency, an office with dictatorial powers at the time. As he would tell me, "Above the president of General Electric stood only God."

The real Ted Quinn had actually been president of GE for a single day, at the end of which he put in his resignation. "I just couldn't stand being the Lord High Executioner himself," he once said to me. He went on to open an advisory service for small businesses and made a good fortune at it. During World War II he was a dollar-a-year head of the Small Business Administration in Washington, seeing to it that the giant concerns did not gobble up all the available steel. Particularly close to his heart was the Amana company, a cooperative.

Quinn also published several books, including *Giant Business,
Threat to Democracy,* and *Unconscious Public Enemies,* his case
against GE-type monopolies. These, along with his anti-monopoly
testimony before congressional committees, got him obliterated
from the roster of former GE executives, and the company actually
denied—to journalist Matthew Josephson, who at my behest made
an inquiry in 1972—that he had ever so much as worked for GE.
However, in the course of time a film director friend of mine who
loved to browse in flea markets and old bookstores came on a
leather-covered daily diary put out by GE as a gift for its distribu-
tors, circa 1930, in which the company directors are listed, and
Theodore K. Quinn is right there as vice-president for consumer
sales. The fact is that it was he who, among a number of other
innovations, conceived of the compact electric refrigerator as a
common consumer product, at a time when electric refrigeration
was regarded as a purely commercial item, the behemoth used in
restaurants, hotels, and the kitchens of wealthy estates.

From the big business viewpoint Quinn's central heresy was that
democracy basically depended on a large class of independent entre-
preneurs who would keep the market competitive. His fear was
that monopoly, which he saw spreading in the American economy
despite superficial appearances of competition, would end by crippling the system's former ingenuity and its capacity to produce high-
quality goods at reasonable prices. A monopoly has little need to
improve its product when it has little need to compete. (First Communist China and then Gorbachev's Russia would be grappling
with a very similar dilemma in the years to come.) He loved to reel
off a long list of inventions, from the jet engine to the zipper, that
were devised by independent inventors rather than corporations and
their much advertised laboratories: "The basic things we use and
are famous for were conceived in the back of a garage." I knew him
in the fifties, when his populist vision was totally out of fashion,
and maybe, I feared, an out-of-date relic of a bygone America. But I
would hear it again in the seventies and even more loudly in the
eighties as a muscle-bound American industrial machine, wallowing for generations in a continental market beyond the reach of foreign competition, was caught flat-footed by German and Japanese
competitors. Quinn was a successful businessman interested in

money and production, but his vision transcended the market to embrace the nature of the democratic system for which he had a passion, and which he thought doomed if Americans did not understand the real threats to it. He put it starkly once: "It may be all over, I don't know—but I don't want to have to choose between fascism and socialism, because neither one can match a really free, competitive economy and the political liberties it makes possible. If I do have to choose, it'll be socialism, because it harms the people less. But neither one is the way I'd want to go."

Perhaps it was because the style of the National Theatre production was so unashamed in its presentational declarativeness that the Ted Quinn role was given to David Schofield, a tap dancer with a brash Irish mug, for Quinn was forever bragging about—and mocking—his mad love of soft-shoe dancing. And so we had long speeches about the dire consequences of business monopoly delivered by a dancer uncorking a most ebullient soft-shoe all over the stage, supported by some witty jazz played openly before our eyes by a deft band. As Quinn agonizes over whether to accept the presidency of GE, a phone rings at the edge of the stage; plainly, it is as the new president that he must answer it. He taps his way over to it, lifts the receiver, and simply places it gently on the floor and dances joyously away.

It was in the National Theatre that I at last heard the right kind of straightforward epic expressiveness, joyful and celebratory rather than abashed and veiled, as economic and political—which is to say epic—subjects were in the mouths of the characters. In this antic yet thematically precise spirit, accompanied by some forty songs out of the period, the show managed to convey the *seriousness* of the disaster that the Great Depression was, and at the same time its human heart.

There was one more invention that I particularly prized. Alone in her Brooklyn house, Rose Baum sits at the piano, bewildered and discouraged by the endless Depression, and plays some of the popular ballads of the day, breaking off now and then to muse to herself about the neighborhood, the country, her family, her fading hopes. The actress sat at a piano whose keyboard faced the audience, and simply held her hands suspended over the keys while the band pianist a few yards away played the romantic thirties tunes.

Gradually a triple reality formed such as I have rarely witnessed in the theater: first, the objective stage reality of the band pianist playing, but somehow magically directed by Rose's motionless hands over her keyboard; and simultaneously, *the play's memory* of this lost past that we are now discovering again; and finally, the middle-aged actress herself seeming, by virtue of her motionless hands suspended over the keys, to be recalling this moment from her very own life. The style, in short, had fused emotion and conscious awareness, overt intention and subjective feeling—the aim in view from the beginning, more than a decade before.

Preface to *Mr. Peters' Connections*
1998

A play ought to explain—or not explain—itself, but a play with both living and dead characters interacting may justifiably ask for a word or two of explanation.

Mr. Peters is in that suspended state of consciousness which can come upon a man taking a nap, when the mind, still close to consciousness and self-awareness, is freed to roam from real memories to conjectures, from trivialities to tragic insights, from terror of death to glorying in one's being alive. The play, in short, is taking place inside Mr. Peters' mind, or at least on its threshold, from where it is still possible to glance back toward daylight life or forward into the misty depths.

Mr. Peters is, of course, alive. So is his wife, as well as Rose, who turns out to be their daughter, and Leonard, her boyfriend. Adele, the black bag lady, is neither dead nor alive, but simply Peters' construct, the to-him incomprehensible black presence on the dim borders of his city life.

Cathy-May is long dead, but the dead in memory do not quite die and often live more vividly than in life. Cathy-May's husband is Peters' conjecture as to what kind of man she might have married, given her nature as he knew it when they were lovers. And Calvin, a.k.a. Charley, who turns out to be Peters' brother, is also long dead, even if the competition between them is very much alive in Peters' mind along with its fraternal absurdities.

As for the set, it should look like whatever the reader or producer imagines as a space where the living and the dead may meet, the gray or blue or blazing red terrain of the sleeping mind where imagination runs free. Fragments of jazz and sheer-sound should also rise and fall. The stage may be ablaze with light at times or steeped in cavernous darkness at others. It may threaten or reassure, for the action of the play is the procession of Mr. Peters' moods, each of them summoning up the next, all of them strung upon the line of his anxiety, his fear, if you will, that he has not found the secret, the pulsing center of energy—what he calls the subject—that will make his life cohere.

ON SOCIETY AND
POLITICS

JUVENILE DELINQUENCY

Bridge to a Savage World
1958

Before taking up the film itself I should like to say a few words about conditions surrounding the writing of this memorandum.

For a period of two months I lived with various gangs, in effect, being present during periods of violence, attending secret mediation sessions, questioning every sort of person having any connection with or knowledge of the enormous and complex drama called Juvenile Delinquency. I have before me a mountain of notes and documents, personal stories, anecdotes and so forth. It would be vain to attempt at this stage anything approaching an organized, continuous scenario. The material is still in the process of incubation; I have many questions whose answers no one yet knows.

At this time, therefore, I can only set forth the raw materials of the film, and then only in part. It would be perfectly simple to set a "story" down here, but while it might engage the reader it would be fruitless for me, since I am withholding my inner commitment until I am certain that the story of this film is the story of Juvenile Delinquency and not merely a persuasive fraction thereof.

Nevertheless, it is possible in these few pages to open up a chink in the façade which has thus far shielded the Delinquency problem from intelligent inspection. If I speak of a problem instead of a drama I mean to include both terms in one, for the reality I have seen on the streets is the drama itself. In short, I am endeavoring to keep myself out of this material, to let it form before me as though I were merely an observing and, I hope, understanding eye.

As a consequence of this hands-off attitude I have restrained myself thus far from pressing to completion the several story elements that have already occurred to me. In the following pages the reader will be quickly aware that I am jumping about, so to speak; a character is taken up, spoken of and then dropped, only to appear again a few pages later. A theme is announced and then left to fall by the wayside, but soon retrieved in a later paragraph. All this makes for less than easy reading, but I do not want to knit it all together yet. It is not my way of working. I will be ready to write when the tapestry begins to weave itself into a piece. I am not ready now.

A word, perhaps, is necessary about the New York City Youth Board, a direct arm of the Mayor's Office. It is now about eleven years old. It began as an experimental project, one of the first of its kind. Its novelty consists of its methods and philosophy which go counter to much previous social-work procedure. The main feature of its method is that instead of sitting in an office, its men go out into the streets, the pool rooms, the dance halls, the homes and hangouts of the very worst gangs, prepared to spend years with them, giving them every kind of leadership and aid in order to relate their members to the values of civilized society. Youth Board workers, one of whom is the hero of this film, have suffered every kind of psychological indignity. But in a few neighborhoods a handful of men has sometimes held back slaughter and in many individual cases raised up seemingly incorrigible young men to decency.

This picture will end in a victory, a victory whose magnitude I can barely suggest in these summary pages. I do not mean to suggest that the Youth Board has solved the problem of delinquency. What it has done, however, is to develop a spirit and a technique which do work. In this picture we shall meet boys who, before they are reached, could fit comfortably into the behavior patterns of the early hordes that roamed the virgin forests. There are elements in the gang codes today which are more primitive than those that governed the earliest clan societies. When a Youth Board worker descends into the streets he is going back into human history a distance of thousands of years. Thus, it is fruitless merely to say that the delinquent must be given love and care—or the birch rod. What is involved here is a profound conflict of man's most subtle values. The deeper into their lives the Youth Board worker goes, the more apparent it becomes that they are essentially boys who have never made contact with civilized values; boys without a concept of the father, as the father is normally conceived, boys without an inkling of the idea of social obligation, personal duty or even rudimentary honor. To save one of these is obviously a great piece of work and it has been done time after time.

But it has been done in a way that does not conform to the stereotyped notions of social work. What is involved is a deep spiritual transformation which, among other things, makes for the highest drama. The Youth Board worker in this picture is a faithful portrait of actual workers I have met. He is a kind of man not many people realize exists in this world and he is creating boys in his image. The saved boy, in a word, becomes not merely a "good citizen," or "just like anybody else" after having been an outlaw. Having seen society from the very bottom, the insight he gains is remorselessly honest when he does gain insight. He cannot be "conned"; he is immune to the easy solutions that bemuse the rest of us who are less tightly bound to reality; he is pragmatic and breathtakingly idealistic at the same time. The saved boy in this picture, Paul Martense, will be the second most important character after Jerry Bone, the Youth Board worker.

What follows, then, is a patchwork. I warn again that there will be no attempt to develop characters fully, only to suggest their nature; nor will I try to arrive at any climax. This is purely and simply a glimpse into what is at stake in this film.

Jerry Bone is one pole of the story. He is the Youth Board worker. The other pole consists of the South Bay Rangers, a neighborhood street gang. This sector of the picture is made of Bone's struggle to save the members of this gang from their inevitable disaster. About Bone now. . . .

To the naked eye Jerry Bone would be hard to connect with social work. His skin is tanned—he spends as much of his scarce free time on the beach at Coney Island where, in an energetic moment, he might be found tumbling and doing acrobatics. He has the fisty walk of an athlete, the sloping shoulders of one who spent a lot of time at the heavy punching bag in his youth. A close look will discern bridgework where his teeth have been knocked out.

But there the resemblance to a pug stops. It is true that he has the extroverted laugh, the body-readiness of the physical man, and when he walks down a South Bay street there is nothing much to contrast him with the tone of that slum. When he stands on a street corner gabbing with the boys, an unknowing observer would take him for one of them grown to manhood (which, in a way, he is, having been in a gang in his youth). Here, one would say, is an off-duty lifeguard, or perhaps—yes, even a slightly affluent small-time racket guy.

Given the appearance of a worker who has acquired some slight middle-class standing, one is then more deeply struck by what comes out of his mouth. He can sling the jive with any of them: "I'm down for that, man." "You cats are really steamin', man." These fall effortlessly from his tongue. But mixed in will be terms like "maturing," "escape," "inhibition."

Bone taught judo in the Army; for a while, most recently, he was a substitute physical-education teacher in a high school. He can fell a man twice his size and has had to do it more than once. But we are not going to create here the hard-fisted man with the heart of gold and the tear in his eye. Bone is too busy trying to see to let tears blur his vision. Too busy trying to understand the vast book knowledge of which he has only a smattering—but for whose wisdom he has a fierce instinctive understanding.

Bone is boyish. He loves boys because he is still boyish himself. He still wears a kind of Ivy League style of clothes, and his hair is cut crew-style. His need for that kind of clothes, very good clothes, expresses the yearning of his boyhood when he was the youngest son in a large family of boys, and never until he was in his late teens had his first crack at a new suit. He is always shaved, his hair is combed, he looks as if he just got out of a shower.

Bone is just the man for the Youth Board project. He will use the most unorthodox methods, never take no for an answer, break through red tape and official apathy with the single-minded verve of the street boy crashing the movie house. None of which, I hope, implies that he is the anti-intellectual sneering at the sheltered, middle-class, social worker. Bone is college-trained, but at night. He respects theory, but reads it with the pragmatic sense of one who is dedicated to saving boys, not proving a theory.

Bone is in a strange position, as are all Youth Board workers, in relation to the Law. He has the right* not to divulge information to the police if, in his judgment, it would save a boy to keep it to himself. He is thus between two dynamic and relentless forces. On the one hand he is trying to be an example of responsible citizenship to the boys, teaching them to obey and respect the law; on the other hand there will be situations in which he must make the terrible decision to keep his mouth shut on the bet—and it is always a bet—that in the long run he will have brought a boy closer to decency by not divulging his crime. For Bone is not a sentimentalist in action. There will be times when, despite his efforts, a boy appears beyond reach. Then he will "waste" him, and when he does we will know the agency of that decision because it always involves predicting the future, and we will know by the time this decision is made in the picture that many a boy who seemed hopeless regained his decency, given the right chance at the right time.

Thus, the police suspect Bone and regard him as at best a nuisance and at worst a sapper of their authority. He is trying to make the boys respect the police, but he must bring them to it in many subtle ways, and during that process there will be times when he must stand up against the police in defense of the boys, even as he, in his mind, is cursing the necessity of alienating, for the moment, the boys from the police.

There will be two sides of Bone's life in this film. One relates to his work with the Rangers, his street life. The other, equally important, is his home life. He is married, has two children. Put baldly in summary fashion it is difficult to set the tone of his relation with his family, but it will have to suffice here to say that his home-life story follows, roughly, this outline: he begins the picture with his new job, and his wife, Helen, is gratified at the excitement he feels for it as well as the fact that the salary will be steady and higher than he had before. Bone is our bridge, our entryway into this subworld, and he is that for his wife as well. He often brings his boys home so that they may see how a good family lives. But like most of the audience, Helen soon notices that among his boys are dangerous

---

* Note: This is no longer completely true. The sanctity of the delinquent's confidences concerning crimes has been rather successfully broken down by the Police Department.

characters. The love she is willing to put out at first, the kind of love Jerry has, is gradually being shriveled by certain acts of ingratitude on the part of certain boys; she, like the audience, will turn against individual boys when they trick Jerry, when they deceive and harm him. In contrast, we shall see the continuing conflict in Jerry as to whether he is being an idiot for having his faith in these characters, and we shall ultimately come to see on the screen a kind of love in him which most men never approach for their fellow human beings.

But Helen has more to struggle against than a recurring suspicion and even distaste for some of these boys whom her husband must accept and spiritually embrace in his work. She knows, at a certain point, that he is in danger, that he has, in fact, been attacked and never told her. And as the years wear on and Jerry goes deeper and deeper into the South Bay jungle, he is home less and less of the time; she is sick of having him awakened at three and four in the morning to run out in any weather to bring back some—to her—worthless kid from the edge of the abyss.

And finally, Jerry's own kids, having lived a life of waiting for him, having lived, in fact, without his supervision, begin to show the dreadful signs of delinquency themselves. The thematic principle of this story, barely suggested here, is that we have time for everything but our children; but more, that sometimes it is beyond good and evil. Our world with its remorseless disciplinary demands—the machines must be tended, the mail opened, the phone answered—our world is organized without any reference to a family life. And this is one—only one—cause for the bewilderment of our kids. As well, this home-life side of Bone's life will reinforce a central theme of the picture which is the measure of love which we must bring to our lives if we are not to slide back into a life of violence, such as Juvenile Delinquency presents. Jerry Bone is a carrier of love, and this picture will be a kind of love story—his profound respect and affection for the young human being. But it is our tragic circumstance that we have only so much love for strangers, and because we have not enough, those strangers are striking back at the loveless world we have made.

Jerry Bone will end this story by resigning from the Youth Board. He will have had it. But in a way that will, through its frank facing of the problem, throw light upon what truly must be done in the future. He has spent nearly five years tramping the streets day and night, winter and summer. He is scarred, and he is tired, and he is no longer the thirty-year-old athlete we saw at the beginning. Now he must be a father to his own. But he has changed a neighborhood, as we shall witness, and above all he has made a few confused boys into knowing men. To one of them. Paul Martense, he will pass on the torch. For Paul Martense will have become a new Youth Board worker himself, Paul whom we first saw in this picture leading a gang in street-fighting with an iron bar in his right hand. We will end with Paul Martense walking into a strange neighborhood, as we began with Jerry moving into South Bay looking for the lost boys.

The proud exhaustion of Jerry Bone will emblazon the fact I believe must be placed before the people. This work is hard beyond belief; it wears out people, it makes those who engage in it face every one of their own failings. For to do this work truly, to do it well, it is not enough to "know" or to be "good." One must be open to knowledge, and above all one must learn how to set fear aside. Here, in rough summary, is the beginning of the picture as I see it now. Perhaps it will help to create a sense of the picture's tone.

Jerry Bone is walking down a South Bay street. It is night. Bone is obviously on a quest; as unobtrusively as he can he watches any passerby, but makes no advance toward the few people he sees. The neighborhood is one of decaying brick and brownstone four-story tenements, small factories, and a few boarded-up buildings.

He sees a loudly dressed, grey-haired, handsome man standing on a corner, stops and asks, "Any of the boys around?" The man looks him over with humorous suspicion. "What boys?" he asks, uncommunicatively. "Oh," Jerry begins in a desultory way, "Jouncey Barnes, Joe Meister, Paul Martense. . . ."

"You know those guys?" the handsome man asks.

"No, but I'd like to meet them," says Bone.

The man just smiles as though he can see through Bone. Bone knows what the man thinks, thanks him and moves on. Two kids playing stickball hit the ball accidentally toward him; he makes the catch, tosses it back, tries to talk to them, but they look at him suspiciously and obviously want him gone. He goes.

He comes on ten boys standing on a street corner. He tries to

move in on their conversation. In this group are Joe Meister and
Jouncey. The subject is baseball. They tolerate Bone for a moment.
Then without ado they break up in two's and three's, leaving him
with Jouncey and Meister. These two advise him that nobody likes
cops around here. Bone says he is not a cop. They imply that if he is
not a cop he is pushing dope, and if not, he is a fag from uptown
looking for thrills. They can't get over his clothes, his crew
haircut—he's a square. He starts to tell them he is here to help
them, and they turn their backs and walk into a bar, with a kind of
warning that he is a stranger here and had better watch his step.

Bone moves on. He comes on another group (all these boys are
between fifteen and twenty, with a few "stompers" thrown in—the
stompers being under fifteen). This second group is drinking beer
in parked cars and on the corner. As he approaches, two boys begin
sparring. One is Livertrouble, the other is Rabbit Lewis, both
skinny kids. Livertrouble quickly wants to quit because of his
liver—a doctor's chance remark about his liver has been his excuse
for quitting school and remaining an illiterate. Rabbit is a bright
little guy who has never slept anywhere but in hallways or parked
cars. Bone watches as the group eggs on the two. He is being
noticed, but in the excitement he is not being confronted. Rabbit is
now seriously beating Livertrouble, who is hard put. Bone now
steps in and coaches Livertrouble, standing behind him and helping
to move Livertrouble's arms to parry Rabbit's blows.

Suddenly Livertrouble becomes aware of Jerry, this stranger
guiding his arms, and disengages himself. Once again the coldness
rises in the group. The older boys demand to know why Bone is
stopping the fight. Bone says he merely wanted to show Livertrouble a few pointers; he used to teach boxing, he says. To the cops?—
they ask. No, says Bone, he's got nothing to do with the cops; he
taught in Beekman High School. Suddenly one boy steps forward
and says he recognizes Bone. Bone asks if he went to Beekman
High and they all laugh, for few of them have seen a high school
inside. Bone is moving closer to them now as he places himself—he
also coached a Golden Gloves boxing team from Saint Mark's Par-
ish, and this is how the boy remembered him. But they keep assuming he is some new kind of cop, a plainclothesman come to do
undercover work among them. Worse, he is being openly razzed by

Jouncey, Joe Meister—both of whom have now joined this group—and Paul Martense, among others. But Paul is interested in Bone's way of speaking; when he says a word that Paul does not understand he asks Bone what it means. They are now arguing about the meanings of words, astronomy, engineering—in which one boy is interested in a rudimentary way—and other disconnected subjects. But the cold suspicion is there and we are constantly brought up short by it.

As he seems to be making a slight headway, a squad car stops at the curb, cops get out, line up the whole gang, including Jerry Bone, frisk them all and they are taken to jail. In the precinct house Jerry speaks up for the boys, defending their right to stand peacefully on the street corner. The captain of police believes Jerry is a dope pusher, and finally Jerry takes out a card, explains he is a worker with the New York City Youth Board. The captain, never having heard of the Youth Board, questions Jerry suspiciously. Jerry explains that it is a new, experimental project trying to straighten out the gangs by going down into the streets with the boys.

The captain regards Jerry as a social worker now, the worst nuisance some cops can think of. Through their argument we learn that this is the worst neighborhood in the city, three boys have been killed in the past two months; nobody is safe on the streets because of these hoodlums. Jerry continues to defend the boys, attempting to placate the captain at the same time. The captain, to prove their viciousness, points out the major characters among the boys—(and of the film)—calling off the frightful record of each one in turn.

Thus we are introduced to the five leaders of the South Bay Rangers—among others: Jouncey, Joe Meister, Paul Martense, Houseroof McCall, Blitz Capolino. Their offenses go from burglary to mugging, to statutory rape to gang fighting, car theft, vandalism and assorted mayhem. As we spot each boy we see before us what anyone would call a grizzly crew of hoodlums, their hair long in the zoot style, their lips set in a sneer—the usual image of the captured gang-busting kid.

The captain now picks out three boys who are on parole and intends to lock them up because they are not supposed to be out on the streets at night. Jerry argues him out of it, promising to convince them to stay home from now on. The captain lets them all go with the warning that he is going to crack heads the next time they are found gathered together anywhere at night.

Out on the street the boys are overjoyed at Jerry's ability to "psyche up" the cops. Throughout the scene in the precinct house they were bewildered, then astonished, and finally wondrous—this is the first human being who had shown the slightest concern for them without lecturing them or demanding anything in return.

As they walk, the questioning begins. Who pays Jerry Bone? What is he doing here? Why does he bother? How much does he make? Will he be coming back again? The answers to each question amazes them even more. He will be here for years; he makes thirty-three hundred a year; he will come in the day and in the night; the city pays him; and most importantly—and it is said under a lamppost in the hush of a slum night in spring—Jerry likes boys. He himself was brought up in such a slum. He wants to see them get a break; he will try to help in getting jobs. . . .

Immediately he is swamped with requests. One boy wants him to tell his parole officer that he is sick so that tomorrow he won't have to report in. Jerry, however, refuses; explains he will never lie for them. Suspicion descends again. Another boy wants a job at sixty-five a week. Jerry says he might arrange one for thirty-two.

Once it is clear he is not Santa Claus, Jouncey and Joe Meister insist the whole scene in the precinct was staged—that Bone is here to find who murdered the victims of their last gang fight with the Golden Moguls. Jouncey looks as though he is going to challenge Jerry right there. Jerry says he never fights unless nothing else is possible. Jouncey takes this for weakness and baits him. There is a deep difference of opinion among the gang, an uneasiness. But Paul Martense is taken with Jerry. He tries to draw Jouncey off. . . .

Suddenly a boy comes running into the group. (I ought to add that one of the big subjects Jerry throws at the boys after leaving the precinct house is gang-fighting. He is here essentially to stop further wars but is getting nowhere.) The new arrival announces that the Moguls have just invaded Ranger turf. Instantly the boys take off. Jerry is bewildered. A moment ago they were lounging around the lamppost, full of curiosity, some hostility, but a lot of humor and amusement—now they are all business. He follows them and finds they have disappeared around a corner. Suddenly

Jouncey, Joe Meister, and Paul Martense come scaling over a six-foot board fence which shields an empty lot—the arsenal; they land on the sidewalk with iron bars in their hands, behind them scrambling over the fence come ten, twenty, forty—about seventy-five boys, all armed with the ugliest weapons. They sweep past Jerry who can't find one of them to answer him. He follows them on the run, trying to get anybody to tell him where they are going and why. They now begin splitting up—and to be brief, confront the enemy gang; the war flares, vicious fighting ensues, Jerry can't bear the sight of it and turns away, as he shields himself in a doorway, and in three minutes it is over. But not before both sides promise further revenge, and a half-dozen boys are left unconscious and bleeding.

WHY DID THEY FIGHT?

Now, when he tries to help, Jouncey and Joe Meister and Paul Martense and others flare up at him. For he wants to know why they fought, what good it did— Their honor was at stake, their dignity, their neighborhood. For a moment Jerry sees that for them this fighting represents a kind of knighthood, an opportunity for bravery, for conquest, for courage, against an enemy that can be seen and felt and hurt. They want compliments on their bravery now, not questions. He helps them carry away their wounded.

The *process* of the story—aside from Bone's relation to his wife and family—is a process of identification of the boys with Bone. When Bone refuses to lie for them; quietly, stubbornly helps them only so long as they will face their obligations to authority; when he will not trade punches with them short of the last extremity of self-protection—and then fells them quickly; when, in short, they try and fail to degrade him and he survives with his values intact and is still not a "square" or a YMCA guy, they begin not only to respect him but to identify themselves with him as one does with one's father. But this has its costs too, for while there are some who are raised up to a new standard of personal values through such identification, there are others who spiritually faint, so to speak, before the terrific climb they will have to make in order to be "like Jerry."

Some of these become even worse than they were before, and Bone himself will become aware as he sets forth these values (but, of course, always through behavior, example, and sometimes at terrible risk to himself) he will become aware that what he is teaching them he must first teach himself. Thus, we shall witness the maturation of Jerry Bone even as he is helping these dangerous boys to grow up. The picture will span a period of four years.

Bone, as I have said, will be our bridge, our entryway into this subworld that has come to terrify us in this age. I intend to work this story so that its two poles interact upon each other toward a climax that will illuminate not only how a boy—or boys—is saved, but how, in his effort to save them, Bone himself has had to face and transform his own private life.

Of the boys, five of whom will be major in size, one, Paul Martense—along with his girl—will be the leading character second to Bone. Of the others, their fates will each be unique, even while their beginnings were the same—that is, we shall meet them all as hoodlums, with the defiant zoot haircuts (which slowly become Jerry's crew-cut as they come to identify themselves with him), the zoot pegged pants, and the cold, brutal sneer. The body of the picture will be a kind of mining operation—we will move deeper and deeper into their souls with Jerry Bone.

Outwardly, the suspense, the progression of the story will be generated by two impending possibilities. Having drawn them away from gang-fighting and marauding, Bone can never know when, without a moment's notice to him, they will resume it—and it will threaten many times and in the most brutal forms. The overhanging question will be, quite simply, whether and how each of these boys, with whom we shall have sympathy, will "make it."

SALVATION IS A MATTER OF MATERIAL THINGS

The bare fact will be borne in upon us that in many, many cases salvation is a matter of material things. Jouncey, for instance, who is one of the most violent of the boys, who kicks Jerry's teeth in one night when Jerry seems to be playing basketball so expertly as to menace Jouncey's leadership—Jouncey who has already cut his hair short in tacit admission that he is trying to be like Jerry—Jouncey later that night is brought down to a weeping hulk not by Jerry calling him an ungrateful mutt, but by his own confusions. For, in fact, Jerry has come back, after their fight, to apologize to him for his own stupidity; he never should have shown up Jouncey on the basketball court and he asks now to be pardoned. But he presses Jouncey to face certain facts of his (Jouncey's) behavior, mainly, that time and again Jouncey, who loves Jerry in an unadmitted way, is suddenly and crazily moved to kill him—as he was moved to try to kill an inoffensive man the other night who asked him a street number.

I will not attempt to detail this scene here, except to say that Jouncey is an illegitimate boy whose mother feels her guilt whenever she lays eyes on him, and yet wants to help him; a boy looking endlessly for his father; a brawny boy who wants Jerry's love, yet cannot accept it; a boy who is moving toward dope addiction as a way out, and yet is strong enough to break the habit when he wants to.

I realize as I give these bare facts that he is repugnant; he is. But he will be a striving, groping, oftentimes sweet and gallant and winning boy. He will know his greatest triumph when Jerry arranges for him to call up the Army General in charge of recruiting—and he convinces the General to forget his police record and let him join the Army. But he will return AWOL, lost, ready for vengeance against himself, and he will commit his great crime in order to bring himself over the edge of his abyss.

But before he does, Jouncey will come to Jerry and ask—finally plead—to be taken to somebody who will help him out of his confusion. (I repeat, on the surface this will be a hoodlum, somebody to frighten any man on any street.) Jerry will try to get a psychiatrist to take him on free of charge—and there will be none in the whole city, for the facilities are jammed.

In another instance, Rabbit will finally be brought by Jerry to the point where he is ready to face the consequences of his actions, a victory for him and for Jerry. But the prisons have no facilities for curing junkies; Jerry tries everywhere but every place is full. He finally gets Rabbit into Kings County on a ruse and he is put out in a few days. He wants help, he is ready to be helped and there is no place he can get it. He surrenders himself to the police in the hope that more isolation in itself, combined with his now fierce will to survive, will cure him. But, ironically, they do not put him in jail. They parole him to his one surviving relative—an aunt in a country town—the condition being that he never come back to his neighborhood. He tries, he works, but he's lonely for the companionship of the streets. Rabbit is a boy who never had a family, was put on the streets at seven when his parents died. In this rural family he finds not companionship but commands, discipline, and the attitude that he might do wicked things at any time. In South Bay he is accepted, left alone. . . . Rabbit ends a junky, the ultimate image of the boy whom nobody gave a damn for; a boy to whom Jerry came too late.

But there will be Joe Meister, a shy bruiser of no intellect who learns where his true dignity lies; who finds in Jerry the good father he never had—although his father is alive and always tried to help him, but never had any dignity himself. His father, a longshoreman with seven kids, works hard, spends his evenings in the congenial bar, addresses everybody as "Cuz," challenges all newcomers to a footrace around the block—but hasn't a clue to the fact that in all this he has reduced himself in Joe's eyes to a clown, and Joe is ashamed of him even as he shields him from strangers who might laugh at him. Joe Meister will end, as I have said, a steady working man who still gets drunk on Saturday night but is paying his way and is learning that you don't have to slap a girl across the face in order to show you're a man. And he learned it from Jerry one night when in a hallway they sat on a step, and Joe asked Jerry if he ever hit his wife, and why not, and why would she obey if he didn't hit her, and a world is opened up to him of people who are faithful to one another because they love one another.

There will be a moment when, without Jerry ever suggesting it. Joe Meister and Paul and Jouncey himself will turn this gang toward the dope pushers and run them out. This will be one of the new "dignities" to which they attach their old, destructive *esprit de corps*.

They will have stopped gang warfare in stages. Most of these stages are outwardly more hilarious than grave. Briefly, Jerry finally convinces them that it is absolutely stupid for a hundred or two hundred guys to risk arrest, jail, or being hurt or killed, just because two members of rival gangs gave each other a dirty look, interfered with each other's girls, and so forth. He arranges the first "fair fight." A member from each gang is chosen, they get into Jerry's car, and he drives them around the water front looking for a battle ground. He lengthens out the ride, subtly trying to get them to know one another. Each of them is growing more and more scared of the other one, now that they are alone together, and both are getting angry, therefore, at Jerry for not letting them go at it. He finally has to let them out. They circle each other endlessly, for the will to fight is not quite there any more; they finally join, fight for five minutes, the agreed-on time, get back in the car and Jerry drops them on their respective corners where their gangs await the results.

We will shoot each of the gladiators reporting how he very nearly killed the other. We will hear a report, in effect, of some Louis-Schmeling fight—and we will see how both sides "won"—and how Jerry tells each boy what a great contribution he made to the good name of the neighborhood (the neighborhood being like a nation), and he will enlist these gladiators in keeping the peace. I ought to add that if the cops caught them fighting they'd have pulled them in, and Jerry with them, thus the secrecy of the ride.

We will see the varied development of the cops. I wish to mirror reality, and it is real to say that some cops love to bat these boys around, and some learn from Jerry, and more importantly from the gradual change in the neighborhood, that something new has entered their lives. *They* begin imitating Jerry's methods—sometimes with idiotic results. But it will come to pass where they know that Jerry knows more about crime here than they can hope to, because he has the confidence of the boys. They will come to respect that confidence. There will also be cops who mistrust him to the end, for the wedding to force is not quickly broken.

There will be Jerry's attempt to transform the gang into a social club devoted to constructive ends like holding dances. We will see that these boys do not know how to dance, that they have not been able to get girls because the girls have been afraid of them. We will see their first lesson in democratic debating procedure and the riot that results the first time Jerry tries it with them. Their first dance when suddenly members of the Moguls entered—and Jerry managed to get them to let the Moguls dance with their girls, for a minute or so. And how they nearly fainted when Paul Martense suggested they ask the precinct to send a cop over to police the dance. They only agree when Paul says this will make the cops work for *them*.

We will see how Livertrouble conceived the idea, on a very hot night, of making a swimming pool out of the water tank on the roof of the housing project, and the lesson in physics that resulted.

And one of the greatest days of their lives (and mine) when they finally agreed to go on a camping trip. Throughout the picture their boredom will be like an insistent counterpoint to every moment, every act. They simply have nothing to do. The great city is building and rebuilding, the traffic is endlessly flowing, the phones by the millions are ringing, the lights are blinking on a thousand marquees, but they are afraid to leave their corner, especially alone, and they live without an inkling that people are supposed to occupy themselves, that their lives are supposed to be meaningful. Thus, the idea of a camping trip is outlandish at first. What's to be gained? Girls? Free whiskey? What? No, Jerry says, you just have fun together. The simple fact is these boys never learned how to play.

Doubtfully they prepare. The first thing is to steal camping supplies. Jerry makes them return them because he won't go with stolen goods. (This motif flows through everything; he does not lecture them, but simply will not commit an immoral act. Thus, as they grow to identify themselves with him, they cease to suggest immoral acts to him, ultimately police one another. The time comes when individuals in the gang call down others for "disappointing Jerry." They are tougher with their defaults than Jerry is.)

I will not detail the camping trip lest I lengthen out this report beyond measure. We will see the slum confronting nature. Livertrouble catching a fish, the first live one he ever saw, tying a string around it and walking along the shore with "my fish," which he is heartbroken to leave when they have to return home. ("I'm commutin' with nature," he said to me.) We will see the "Y" director at first refusing Jerry the use of the camp; the "Y" to be sure does want underprivileged kids, but the Rangers are too tough for them. He accedes on Jerry's promise that they won't destroy the camp.

The terror of the camp's overseer when he first sees the boys arriving in two jalopies and Jerry's car; his joyous farewell after they have left the place cleaner than it ever was before (because they wouldn't let Jerry down). But the chaos of trying to organize meals, the hilarious competition—suddenly four guys have got to be cook. The baseball game, when Jerry discovers that nobody wants to play the outfield. Why? Because if a guy is way out there all alone and misses the ball the indignity will be too much for him. They end by playing the outfield in droves—ten guys running for the ball so that no individual will have to take umbrage if he misses an easy fly.

Their sudden, and unprepared, confrontation with some middle-class kids. The Rangers are tough, they have seen or committed almost every crime—but these sissies, as they appear, can really play baseball, swim better, run further, because they have learned to cooperate, because they've had a chance to play, because they didn't start smoking and drinking at the age of nine. The Rangers watch the sissies play, but in a somber, introspective mood. Some of the most beautiful insights into their lives will come in this sequence. We will see two worlds meet here.

THE QUEST FOR GIRLS

We will see the transformation, in some boys, of their attitudes towards girls. When Jerry came on the scene the common thing was to take a girl—one you respect, that is—to the movies, then come out and back to the neighborhood, and when you meet the guys on the corner you say, "Ah right, get lost. Go on home." If she stops to talk to another guy you rap her across the mouth.

The first to openly question this is Paul Martense. Jerry brings his wife, Helen, down to the neighborhood to meet the boys. They are stupefyingly respectful toward her; are set back when she, a most respectable woman if she is Jerry's wife, addresses them in plain talk, as an equal who rather admires them. When she leaves they are full of questions for Jerry about her, questions that leave out no detail. It is Paul, first, who sees the difference—Jerry really *respects* his wife. Paul has been trying to go with a girl—the sister of Joe Meister. But—and we shall follow them on a date—he doesn't know what, quite, he ought to do. Instinctively he wants to be tender with her; but his code requires brutality. It is through Jerry's example, as well as his open answers to Paul's tortured questions, that he comes to face the fact that it's all right to be sweet to a girl, that even if he made love to her sometime he might still want to marry her without being a fool.

With Joe Meister the process is reduced to a comic-pathetic level, for he is so much more mawkish than Paul, less perceptive—he will stop himself from hitting a girl, but then not know what to talk about, and tell her to get the hell home or he *will* rap her.

If it is possible—and I believe I have a way to do it inoffensively— I would want to show how this gang showed for the first time that it had accepted Jerry Bone. I will not detail the scene here except to say that Jerry is offered a great honor—first chance at a slut the gang is lining up. I understand the shock with which this will be read, but in any case, the moment when Jerry is accepted by the gang will mark a high moment in the first third of the film, be it through this means or another.

So then, another element in the development of this tale will be the quest for girls, and the maturation of their attitudes toward girls—as well as the failure of many of them to make that leap. This theme will move us into parked cars and the arguments therein, the roller-skating rink which is a hunting ground, and will move side-by-side with the more melodramatic elements toward the conclusion. As an instance, we will note how gradually girls do appear among the boys; at the second dance nearly every boy has a girl with him.

We will hang around with the gang on a summer night, hear them singing the latest jazz under the lamppost or in a parked car, go with them as they get bored with this, one to a bar where a holdup is discussed; another to a junky's apartment, there to obliterate his fears; another to his own house where he studies a book on astronomy in order to confound Jerry and the boys with his knowledge; another to write a letter to a pal in jail.

We will discover the subtle means by which the gang as a group moves to save Rabbit from destruction as an addict—even as they themselves are no paragons in other respects. We will see the gang in conflict with itself. not knowing what to do, when they are confronted with a threat that formerly was always answered with a murderous fight. But now they turn to Jerry for a lead, and he makes them look into themselves for a course of action.

How Joe Meister wanted Jerry to go with him to a church one night to pray for Rabbit, who is dying. And how Joe feared to walk into the church because on his entry "the joint might fall down."

We will be privy to the dreams they tell Jerry.

And the conflict that runs through the picture between Gook, the professional dope pusher, the very symbol of ultimate disaster, the man who waits for all the boys at the end of the road and will appear like a threatening spirit around corners, in the night, in the dawn, and where he has been we know there is now a broken kid. The threat to Jerry's life and how he—who could destroy Gook with his fists—eliminated Gook and even lived to hear Gook begging him for help in curing himself.

How Jerry finally had to "waste" Rabbit, and brought himself to make the phone call to the cops, telling them where he could be found. How he forces himself to be present, so that he can take the responsibility before Rabbit; how they chase Rabbit across the rooftops and when they catch him—nearly drowning in the tank where he is hiding—he slumps into their arms and says, "Thank God."

And the many reversions: their amazing callousness toward a buddy whose sister has died; their vicious cruelties toward Jerry.

The struggles by some boys to prevent the gang from going with girls; the sometimes hilarious measures these characters will take to prevent the gang from "softening" and "punking out."

The bewilderment of the parents who unknowingly teach their kids delinquent patterns—the father who buys off a cop and gets his son freed, and the son who comes to wish he had been made to serve his time instead.

The crazy solutions—the overprotective mother who has saved and saved, and desperately, to stop her son from stealing and mugging, buys him a brand-new car—with which he steals more efficiently. And how Jerry made her see what it was she should have been doing with her son all her life. . . .

The threads are all there—I could go on for fifty pages in this vein—but the tapestry remains to be woven. I would add only one element here because it will be thematic.

We read about gangs, we see pictures of them, and the image is one of fierceness. They are certainly fierce in battle—but that is only one part of what they are. A gang fight rarely if ever lasts more than three or four minutes. That fact is a key to many others with which I intend to infuse this film. The truth is that they are scared kids underneath it all, so scared that, as I have said, a gang war can be quickly mediated—if one is adept and knowing. What they must have in exchange for peace, however, is a shred of dignity. These are children who have never known life excepting as a worthless thing; they have been told from birth that they are nothing, that their parents are nothing, that their hopes are nothing. The group in this picture will end, by and large, with a discovery of their innate worth. And Jerry Bone will have been the carrier of that cargo. That is what the picture is about.

The Bored and the Violent
1962

If my own small experience is any guide, the main difficulty in approaching the problem of juvenile delinquency is that there is very little evidence about it and very many opinions as to how to deal with it. By evidence I do not mean the news stories telling of gang fights and teenage murders—there are plenty of those. But it is unknown, for instance, what the actual effects are on the delinquent of prison sentences, psychotherapy, slum-clearance projects, settlement-house programs, tougher or more lenient police attitudes, the general employment situation, and so on. Statistics are few and not generally reliable. The narcotics problem alone is an almost closed mystery.

Not that statistical information in itself can solve anything, but it might at least outline the extent of the disease. I have it, for instance, from an old and deservedly respected official—it is his opinion anyway—that there is really no great increase in delinquent acts but a very great intensification of our awareness of them. He feels we are more nervous now about infractions of the social mores than our ancestors, and he likes to point out that Shakespeare, Boccaccio, and other writers never brought on stage a man of wealth or station without his bravos, who were simply his private police force, necessary to him when he ventured out of his house, especially at night. He would have us read *Great Expectations, Oliver Twist, Huckleberry Finn*, and other classics, not in a romantic mood but in the way we read about our own abandoned kids and their depredations. The difference lies mainly in the way we look at the same behavior.

The experts have only a little more to go on than we have. Like the surgeon whose hands are bloody a good part of the day, the

social worker is likely to come to accept the permanent existence of
the delinquency disease without the shock of the amateur who first
encounters it.

A new book on the subject [by Vincent Riccio and Bill Slocum],
All the Way Down, reports the experience of a social worker—of
sorts—who never got used to the experience, and does not accept
its inevitability. It is an easy book to attack on superficial grounds
because it has no evident sociological method, it rambles and jumps
and shouts and curses. But it has a virtue, a very great and rare one,
I think, in that it does convey the endless, leaden, mind-destroying
boredom of the delinquent life. Its sex is without romance or sexuality, its violence is without release or gratification—exactly like
the streets—movies and plays about delinquency notwithstanding.

Unlike most problems which sociology takes up, delinquency
seems to be immune to the usual sociological analyses or cures. For
instance, it appears in all technological societies, whether Latin or
Anglo-Saxon or Russian or Japanese. It has a very slippery correla-
tion with unemployment and the presence or absence of housing
projects. It exists among the rich in Westchester and the poor in
Brooklyn and Chicago. It has spread quickly into the rural areas and
the small towns. Now, according to Harrison Salisbury, it is the big
problem in the Soviet Union. So that any single key to its causation is
nowhere visible. If one wants to believe it to be essentially a symptom
of unequal opportunity—and certainly this factor operates—one
must wonder about the Russian problem, for the Soviet youngster
can, in fact, go right up through the whole school system on his ability alone, as many of ours cannot. Yet the gangs are roaming the
Russian streets, just as they do in our relatively permissive society.

So no one knows what "causes" delinquency. Having spent some
months in the streets with boys of an American gang, I came away
with certain impressions, all of which stemmed from a single, overwhelming conviction—that the problem underneath is boredom.
And it is not strange, after all, that this should be so. It is the theme
of so many of our novels, our plays, and especially our movies in
the past twenty years and is the hallmark of society as a whole. The
outcry of Britain's so-called Angry Young Men was against precisely this seemingly universal sense of life's pointlessness, the
absence of any apparent aim to it all. So many American books and

articles attest to the same awareness here. The stereotype of the man coming home from work and staring dumbly at a television set is an expression of it, and the "New Wave" of movies in France and Italy propound the same fundamental theme. People no longer seem to know why they are alive; existence is simply a string of near experiences marked off by periods of stupefying spiritual and psychological stasis, and the good life is basically an amused one.

Among the delinquents the same kind of mindlessness prevails, but without the style—or stylishness—which art in our time has attempted to give it. The boredom of the delinquent is remarkable mainly because it is so little compensated for, as it may be among the middle classes and the rich who can fly down to the Caribbean or to Europe, or refurnish the house, or have an affair, or at least go shopping. The delinquent is stuck with his boredom, stuck inside it, stuck to it, until for two or three minutes he "lives"; he goes on a raid around the corner and feels the thrill of risking his skin or his life as he smashes a bottle filled with gasoline on some other kid's head. In a sense, it is his trip to Miami. It makes his day. It is his shopping tour. It gives him something to talk about for a week. It is *life*. Standing around with nothing coming up is as close to dying as you can get. Unless one grasps the power of boredom, the threat of it to one's existence, it is impossible to "place" the delinquent as a member of the human race.

With boredom in the forefront, one may find some perspective in the mélange of views which are repeated endlessly about the delinquent. He is a rebel without a cause, or a victim of poverty, or a victim of undue privilege, or an unloved child, or an overloved child, or a child looking for a father, or a child trying to avenge himself on an uncaring society, or whatnot. But face to face with one of them, one finds these criteria useless, if only because no two delinquents are any more alike than other people are. They do share one mood, however. They are drowning in boredom. School bores them, preaching bores them, even television bores them. The word rebel is inexact for them because it must inevitably imply a purpose, an end.

Other people, of course, have known boredom. To get out of it, they go to the movies, or to a bar, or read a book, or go to sleep, or turn on TV or a girl, or make a resolution, or quit a job. Younger persons who are not delinquents may go to their room and weep, or write a poem, or call up a friend until they get tired talking. But note that each of these escapes can only work if the victim is sure somewhere in his mind, or reasonably hopeful, that by so doing he will overthrow his boredom and with luck may come out on the other side where something hopeful or interesting waits. But the delinquent has no such sense of an imminent improvement. Most of the kids in the Riccio and Slocum book have never known a single good day. How can they be expected to project one and restrain themselves in order to experience such joy once more?

The word rebel is wrong, too, in that it implies some sort of social criticism in the delinquent. But that would confuse him with the bourgeois beatnik. The delinquent has only respect, even reverence, for certain allegedly bourgeois values. He implicitly believes that there are good girls and bad girls, for instance. Sex and marriage are two entirely separate things. He is, in my experience anyway, deeply patriotic. Which is simply to say that he respects those values he never experienced, like money and good girls and the Army and Navy. What he has experienced has left him with absolute contempt, or more accurately, an active indifference. Once he does experience decency—as he does sometimes in a wife—he reacts decently to it. For to this date the only known cure for delinquency is marriage.

The delinquent, far from being the rebel, is the conformist par excellence. He is actually incapable of doing anything alone, and a story may indicate how incapable he is. I went along with Riccio and the gang in his book to a YMCA camp outside New York City for an overnight outing. In the afternoon we started a baseball game, and everything proceeded normally until somebody hit a ball to the outfield. I turned to watch the play and saw ten or twelve kids running for the catch. It turned out that not one of them was willing to play the outfield by himself, insisting that the entire group hang around out there together. The reason was that a boy alone might drop a catch and would not be able to bear the humiliation. So they ran around out there in a drove all afternoon, creating a stampede every time a ball was hit.

They are frightened kids, and that is why they are so dangerous. But again, it will not do to say—it is simply not true—that they are

therefore unrelated to the rest of the population's frame of mind.
Like most of us, the delinquent is simply doing as he was taught.
This is often said but rarely understood. Only recently a boy was
about to be executed for murder in New York state. Only after he
had been in jail for more than a year after sentencing did a campaign develop to persuade the governor to commute his sentence to
life imprisonment, for only then was it discovered that he had been
deserted by his father in Puerto Rico, left behind when his mother
went to New York, wandered about homeless throughout his childhood, and so on. The sentencing judge learned his background only
a week or two before he was to be officially murdered. And then
what shock, what pity! I have to ask why the simple facts of his
deprivation were not brought out in court, if not before. I am afraid
I know the answer. Like most people, it was probably beyond the
judge's imagination that small children sometimes can be treated
much worse than kittens or puppies in our cities.

It is only in theory that the solution seems purely physical—
better housing, enlightened institutions for deserted kids, psychotherapy, and the rest. The visible surfaces of the problem are easy to
survey—although we have hardly begun even to do that.

More difficult is the subterranean moral question which every
kind of delinquency poses. Not long ago a gang was arrested in a
middle-class section of Brooklyn, whose tack was to rob homes
and sell the stuff to professional fences. Many of these boys were
top students, and all of them were from good, middle-class backgrounds. Their parents were floored by the news of their secret depredations, and their common cry was that they had always given
their sons plenty of money, that the boys were secure at home, that
there was no conceivable reason for this kind of aberration. The
boys were remorseful and evidently as bewildered as their parents.

Greenwich, Connecticut, is said to be the wealthiest community
in the United States. A friend of mine who lives there let his sons
throw a party for their friends. In the middle of the festivities a
gang of boys arrived—their own acquaintances, who attend the
same high school. They tore the house apart, destroyed the furniture, pulled parts off the automobile and left them on the lawn,
and split the skulls of two of the guests with beer cans.

Now if it is true that the slum delinquent does as he is taught, it must be true that the Greenwich delinquent does the same. But obviously the lines of force from example to imitation are subtler and less easily traced here. It is doubtful that the parents of this marauding gang rip up the furniture in the homes to which they have been invited. So that once again it is necessary to withhold one's cherished theories. Rich delinquency is delinquency, but it is not the same as slum delinquency. But there is one clear common denominator, I think. They do not know how to live when alone. Most boys in Greenwich do not roam in gangs, but a significant fraction in both places find that counterfeit sense of existence which the gang life provides.

Again, I think it necessary to raise and reject the idea of rebellion, if one means by that word a thrust of any sort. For perspective's sake it may be wise to remember another kind of youthful reaction to a failed society in a different era. In the Thirties, for instance, we were also contemptuous of the given order. We had been brought up to believe that if you worked hard, saved your money, studied, kept your nose clean, you would end up made. We found ourselves in the Depression, when you could not get a job, when all the studying you might do would get you a chance, at best, to sell ties in Macy's. Our delinquency consisted in joining demonstrations of the unemployed, pouring onto campuses to scream against some injustice by college administrations, and adopting to one degree or another a socialist ideology. This, in fact, was a more dangerous kind of delinquency than the gangs imply, for it was directed against the social structure of capitalism itself. But, curiously, it was at the same time immeasurably more constructive, for the radical youth of the Thirties, contemptuous as he was of the social values he had rejected, was still bent upon instituting human values in their place. He was therefore a conserver, he believed in *some* society.

Gide wrote a story about a man who wanted to get on a train and shoot a passenger. Any train, any passenger. It would be a totally gratuitous act, an act devoid of any purpose whatever, an act of "freedom" from purpose. To kill an unknown man without even anger, without unrequited love, without love at all, with nothing in his heart but the sheerly physical contemplation of the gun barrel and the target. In doing this one would partake of death's

irreproachable identity and commit an act in revolt against meaning itself, just as death is, in the last analysis, beyond analysis.

To think of contemporary delinquency in the vein of the Thirties, as a rebellion toward something, is to add a value to it which it
does not have. To give it even the dignity of cynicism run rampant
is also overelaborate. For the essence is not the individual at all; it
is the gang, the herd, and we should be able to understand its
attractions ourselves. It is not the thrust toward individual expression but a flight from self in any defined form. Therefore, to see it
simply as a protest against conformism is to stand it on its head; it
is profoundly conformist but without the mottoes, the entablature
of recognizable, "safe" conformism and its liturgy of religious,
patriotic, socially conservative credos.

The Greenwich gang, therefore, is also doing as it was taught,
just as the slum gang does, but more subtly. The Greenwich gang is
conforming to the hidden inhumanity of conformism, to the herd
quality in conformism; it is acting out the terror-fury that lies hidden under Father's acceptable conformism. It is simply conformity
sincere, conformity revealing its true content, which is hatred of
others, a stunted wish for omnipotence, and the conformist's secret
belief that nothing outside his skin is real or true. For which reason
he must redouble his obeisance to institutions lest, if the acts of
obeisance be withheld, the whole external world will vanish, leaving him alone. And to be left alone when you do not sense any existence in yourself is the ultimate terror. But this loneliness is not the
poet's, not the thinker's, not the loneliness that is filled with incommunicable feeling, insufficiently formed thought. It is nonexistence
and must not be romanticized, as it has been in movies and some of
the wishful Beat literature. It is a withdrawal not from the world
but from oneself. It is boredom, the subsidence of inner impulse,
and it threatens true death unless it is overthrown.

All of which is said in order to indicate that delinquency is not the
kind of "social problem" it is generally thought to be. That is, it
transcends even as it includes the need for better housing, medical
care, and the rest. It is our most notable and violent manifestation
of social nihilism. In saying this, however, it is necessary to short-
circuit any notion that it is an attempt by the youth to live "sincerely." The air of "sincerity" which so many writers have given the

delinquent is not to be mistaken as his "purpose." This is romanticism and solves nothing except to sentimentalize brutality. The gang kid can be sincere; he can extend himself for a buddy and risk himself for others; but he is just as liable, if not more so than others, to desert his buddies in need and to treat his friends disloyally. Gang boys rarely go to visit a buddy in jail excepting in the movies. They forget about him. The cult of sincerity, of true human relations uncontaminated by money and the social rat race, is not the hallmark of the gang. The only moment of truth comes when the war starts. Then the brave show themselves, but few of these boys know how to fight alone and hardly any without a knife or a gun. They are not to be equated with matadors or boxers or Hemingway heroes. They are dangerous pack hounds who will not even expose themselves singly in the outfield.

If, then, one begins to put together all the elements, this "social problem" takes on not merely its superficial welfare aspects but its philosophical depths, which I think are the controlling ones. It is not a problem of big cities alone but of rural areas too; not of capitalism alone but of socialism as well; not restricted to the physically deprived but shared by the affluent; not a racial problem alone or a problem of recent immigrants, or a purely American problem. I believe it is in its present form the product of technology destroying the very concept of man as a value in himself.

I hesitate to say what I think the cure might be, if only because I cannot prove it. But I have heard most of the solutions men have offered, and they are spiritless, they do not assume that the wrong is deep and terrible and general among us all. There is, in a word, a spirit gone. Perhaps two world wars, brutality immeasurable, have blown it off the earth; perhaps the very processes of technology have sucked it out of man's soul; but it is gone. Many men rarely relate to one another excepting as customer to seller, worker to boss, the affluent to the deprived and vice versa—in short, as factors to be somehow manipulated and not as intrinsically valuable persons.

Power was always in the world, to be sure, and its evils, but with us now it is strangely, surrealistically masked and distorted. Time was, for example, when the wealthy and the politically powerful flaunted themselves, used power openly as power, and were often cruel. But this openness had the advantage for man of clarity; it created a certain reality in the world, an environment that was defined, with hard but touchable barriers. Today power would have us believe—everywhere—that it is purely beneficent. The bank is not a place which makes more money with your deposits than it returns to you in the form of interest; it is not a sheer economic necessity, it is not a business at all. It is "Your Friendly Bank," a kind of welfare institution whose one prayer, day and night, is to serve your whims or needs. A school is no longer a place of mental discipline but a kind of day-care center, a social gathering where you go through a ritual of games and entertainments which insinuate knowledge and the crafts of the outside world. Business is not the practice of buying low and selling high, it is a species of public service. The good life itself is not the life of struggle for meaning, not the quest for union with the past, with God, with man that it traditionally was. The good life is the life of ceaseless entertainment, effortless joys, the air-conditioned, dust-free languor beyond the Mussulman's most supine dream. Freedom is, after all, comfort; sexuality is a photograph. The enemy of it all is the real. The enemy is conflict. The enemy, in a word, is life.

My own view is that delinquency is related to this dreamworld from two opposing sides. There are the deprived who cannot take part in the dream; poverty bars them. There are the oversated who are caught in its indefiniteness, its unreality, its boring hum, and strike for the real now and then—they rob, they hurt, they kill. In flight from the nothingness of this comfort they have inherited, they butt against its rubber walls in order to feel a real pain, a genuine consequence. For the world in which comfort rules is a delusion, whether one is within it or deprived of it.

There are a few social theorists who look beyond poverty and wealth, beyond the time when men will orient themselves to the world as breadwinners, as accruers of money-power. They look to the triumph of technology, when at least in some countries the physical struggle to survive will no longer be the spine of existence. Then, they say, men will define themselves through varying "styles of life." With struggles solved, nature tamed and abundant, all that will be left to do will be the adornment of existence, a novel-shaped swimming pool, I take it, or an outburst of artistic work.

It is not impossible, I suppose. Certainly a lot of people are already living that way—when they are not at their psychiatrists'. But there is still a distance to go before life's style matters very much to most of humanity in comparison with next month's rent. I do not know how we ought to reach for the spirit again, but it seems to me we must flounder without it. It is the spirit which does not accept injustice complacently and yet does not betray the poor with sentimentality. It is the spirit which seeks not to flee the tragedy which life must always be but seeks to enter into it, thereby to be strengthened by the fullest awareness of its pain, its ultimate non sequitur. It is the spirit which does not mask but unmasks the true function of a thing, be it business, unionism, architecture, or love.

Riccio and Slocum's book, with all its ugliness, its crudeness, its lack of polish and design, is good because it delivers up the real. It is only as hopeless as the situation is. Its implied solutions are good ones: reform of idiotic narcotics laws, a real attempt to put trained people at the service of bewildered, desperate families, job-training programs, medical care, reading clinics—all of it is necessary, and none of it would so much as strain this economy. But none of it will matter, none of it will reach further than the spirit in which it is done. Not the spirit of fear with which so many face delinquency, nor the spirit of sentimentality which sees in it some virtue of rebellion against a false and lying society. The spirit has to be that of those people who know that delinquents are a living expression of our universal ignorance of what life ought to be, even of what it is, and of what it truly means to live. Bad pupils they surely are. But who from his own life, from his personal thought, has come up with the good teaching, the way of life that is joy? This book shows how difficult it is to reach these boys; what the country has to decide is what it is going to say if these kids should decide to listen.

Many Writers: Few Plays
1952

It is impossible for anyone living in the midst of a cultural period to say with certainty why it is languishing in its produce and general vitality. This is especially true of the theater, where we tend to compare our usually vapid present with "Chekhov's period," or "Ibsen's," or our own previous decades, much to our disadvantage, forgetting that the giants usually stood alone in their time. Nevertheless, even optimists now confess that our theater has struck a seemingly endless low by any standard. I cannot hope to try to explain the reasons for this but certain clues keep recurring to me when thinking on the matter.

We can find no solace in the fact that there never have been more than a handful of first-class playwrights in any one country at any one time, for we have more than the usual number in America now, but few plays from them, and fewer still of any weight. A lizardic dormancy seems to be upon us; the creative mind seems to have lost its heat. Why?

I think the answers will be found in the nature of the creative act. A good play is a good thought; a great play is a great thought. A great thought is a thrust outward, a daring act. Daring is of the essence. Its very nature is incompatible with an undue affection for moderation, respectability, even fairness and responsibleness. Those qualities are proper for the inside of the telephone company, not for creative art.

I may be wrong, but I sense that the playwrights have become more timid with experience and maturity, timid in ethical and social idea, theatrical method, and stylistic means. Because they are unproduced, no firm generalization can be made about the younger playwrights, but from my personal impressions of scripts sent me from time to time, as well as from talks I have had with a few groups of them, I have been struck and dismayed by the strangely high place they give to inoffensiveness.

I find them old without having been young. Like young executives, they seem proudest of their sensibleness—what they call being practical. Illusion is out; it is foolish. What illusion? The illusion that the writer can save the world. The fashion is that the world cannot be saved. Between the determinism of economics and the iron laws of psychiatrics they can only appear ridiculous, they think, by roaring out a credo, a cry of pain, a point of view. Perhaps they really have no point of view, or pain either. It is incomprehensible to me.

Recently a young Chilean director, who has put on more than thirty plays in his own country, and spent the past three years studying theater on a fellowship in France, in Britain, and in two of our leading universities, told me this: "Your students and teachers seem to have no interest at all in the meanings of the ideas in the plays they study. Everything is technique. Your productions and physical apparatus are the best in the world, but among all the university people I came to know, as well as the professionals, scarcely any want to talk about the authors' ethical, moral, or philosophical intentions. They seem to see the theater almost as an engineering project, the purpose being to study successful models of form in order, somehow, to reproduce them with other words."

All this means to me, if true, is that this generation is turning Japanese. The Japanese are said to admire infinite repetitions of time-hallowed stories, characters, and themes. It is the triumph of the practical in art. The most practical thing to do is to repeat what has been done and thought before. But the very liquor of our art has always been originality, uniqueness. The East is older. Perhaps this sterile lull is therefore the sign of our aging. Perhaps we are observing several seasons of hush and silence to mark the passage through our youth. Our youth that was Shaw and Ibsen and O'Neill and all the great ones who kept turning and turning the central question of all great art—how may man govern himself so that he may live more humanly, more alive?

Japanism, so to speak, took over Hollywood long ago, and now the movie is ritual thinly veiled. The practical took command. The "showman" won. High finance took sterility by the hand, and together they rolled the product smooth, stripped off all its offensive edges, its individuality, and created the perfect circle—namely, zero.

I think the same grinding mill is at work in the theater, but more deceptively because we have no big companies enforcing compliance to any stated rules. But we have an atmosphere of dread just the same, an unconsciously—or consciously—accepted party line, a sanctified complex of moods and attitudes, proper and improper. If nothing else comes of it, one thing surely has: it has made it dangerous to dare, and, worse still, impractical. I am not speaking merely of political thought. Journalists have recently made studies of college students now in school and have been struck by the absence among them of any ferment, either religious, political, literary, or whatever. Wealthy, powerful, envied all about, it seems the American people stand mute.

We always had with us the "showman," but we also had a group of rebels insisting on thrusting their private view of the world on others. Where are they? Or is everybody really happy now? Do Americans really believe they have solved the problems of living for all time? If not, where are the plays that reflect the soul-racking, deeply unseating questions that are being inwardly asked on the street, in the living room, on the subways?

Either the playwrights are deaf to them, which I cannot believe, or they are somehow shy of bringing them onto the stage. If the last is true we are unlikely to have even the "straight" theater again—the melodramas, the farces, the "small" plays. It is hard to convince you of this, perhaps, but little thoughts feed off big thoughts; an exciting theater cannot come without there being a ferment, a ferment in the colleges, in the press, in the air. For years now I seem to have heard not expressions of thought from people but a sort of oblong blur, a reflection in distance of the newspapers' opinions.

Is the knuckleheadedness of McCarthyism behind it all? The Congressional investigations of political unorthodoxy? Yes. But is that all? Can an artist be paralyzed except he be somewhat willing?

You may pardon me for quoting from myself, but must one always be not merely liked but well liked? Is it not honorable to have powerful enemies? Guardedness, suspicion, aloof circumspection—these are the strongest traits I see around me, and what have they ever had to do with the creative act?

Is it quixotic to say that a time comes for an artist—and for all those who want and love theater—when the world must be left behind? When, like some pilgrim, he must consult only his own heart and cleave to the truth it utters? For out of the hectoring of columnists, the compulsions of patriotic gangs, the suspicions of the honest and the corrupt alike, art never will and never has found soil.

I think of a night last week when a storm knocked out my lights in the country, and it being only nine o'clock it was unthinkable to go to bed. I sat a long time in the blacked-out living room, wide awake, a manuscript unfinished on the table. The idea of lying in bed with one's eyes open, one's brain alive, seemed improper, even degrading. And so, like some primitive man discovering the blessings of fire, I lit two candles and experimentally set them beside my papers. Lo! I could read and work again.

Let a storm come, even from God, and yet it leaves a choice with the man in the dark. He may sit eyeless, waiting for some unknown force to return him his light, or he may seek his private flame. But the choice, the choice is there. We cannot yet be tired. There is work to be done. This is no time to go to sleep.

The Night Ed Murrow Struck Back
1983

Fear, like love, is difficult to explain after it has subsided, probably because it draws away the veils of illusion as it disappears. The illusion of an unstoppable force surrounded Senator Joseph McCarthy of Wisconsin at the height of his influence, in the years from 1950 to 1954. He had paralyzed the State Department, cowed President Eisenhower, and mesmerized almost the entire American press, which would in all seriousness report his most hallucinatory spitballs as hard front-page news. His very name struck terror not only in the hearts of the several million Americans who in the previous decades of the Forties or Thirties had had a brush with any branch or leaf of the Left, but also those who had ever expressed themselves with something less than a violent hatred of the Soviets, Marx, or for that matter cooperatives—or even certain kinds of poetry. At my own hearing before the House Un-American Activities Committee, a flank of the McCarthy movement, a congressman from Cincinnati asked me with wild incredulity, "You mean you believe that a man has the right to write a poem about *anything*?" When I confirmed this opinion, he turned to his fellow committeemen and simply threw up his hands.

How this vaudevillelike absurdity could have been taken in dead seriousness by vast numbers of Americans is hard to explain in retrospect. The Fifties' Red hunt not only terrified people but drove some few to suicide. It is not easy to conceive of Harry Truman, ex-artilleryman and quintessential small-town American, being labeled a traitor to his country, yet Senator Joe McCarthy and his fellow Republican leaders blithely went about pronouncing Truman's and Roosevelt's administrations "twenty years of treason." Never was this greeted with scorn or laughter. How to explain it?

Of course, an outrageous mixture of viciousness and naïve provincialism is endemic to the political extremes. Stalin awoke one morning and decided that all the Jewish doctors were in a plot to poison the party leadership, and nobody laughed then either. I had known an outlandish tap dancer who in desperation was touring Europe in the Thirties with his little troupe; in Berlin he found himself to his amazement the idol of the newly risen Nazi establishment, and soon of Hitler himself. Tap dancing so delighted Hitler that he spoke of ordaining it the *echt* German dance, which all the *Volk* must begin learning at once—a veritable nation of tap dancers was to spring forth, with my friend to be the head teacher. One morning a uniformed "race expert" showed up at his hotel prepared to measure his cranium, nose, mouth, and the spatial relationships of his face to make sure he was the Aryan type. My friend, a Jew, explained that he had an urgent appointment and took the next train out of the country.

By 1953 it was common talk in Europe that America had at last met her own native dictator in Joe McCarthy; but if a great many Americans agreed, they were in no position to say so safely, especially if they worked in government, or as teachers, or in the larger corporations. Another dreamlike element, moreover, was that McCarthy's Senate investigating subcommittee, whose claimed intent was the rooting out of communists hidden in the government, never seemed to find any actual Reds, let alone one who might be guilty of betraying the United States. To his critics, however, McCarthy would reply, "It isn't the number of communists that is important; it's the general effect on our government," one of his more candid statements.

He rose like a rocket to his power in a matter of weeks once he had stood on a podium waving a piece of paper and declaring, "I hold in my hand the names of . . ." I have since forgotten whether it was sixty-two or thirty-nine "card-carrying communists" inside the State Department, but it hardly matters because in subsequent months he himself kept changing the count and of course could never produce one name of an actual person. Yet his fraudulence, which had perhaps seemed so obvious to me because I had uncles like him who shot off their mouths in argument and said anything that came into their heads, was frighteningly persuasive to a lot of

Americans, including some important newsmen. One half understood why the country was still in shock at having "lost" China to Mao, whose revolution had swept into Peking in 1949. How could this mucky peasant horde have won fairly and squarely against a real general like Chiang Kai-shek, whose wife, moreover, was the graduate of an American college and so beautiful besides? It could only be that worming their ways through our State Department were concealed traitors who had "given" the country to the Reds. In the light of Vietnam, we have perhaps come to understand the limits of our power, but in the early Fifties any such concept was unimaginable. Henry Luce, for example, was confidently propagating "the American century," when we would lead the grateful human race into baseball, private enterprise, eight-cylinder Buicks, and, of course, Christianity; and for a fact, the Swiss franc aside, the American dollar was truly the only nonfunny money in the world. Before he had finished, Joe McCarthy would have "named" the revered ex-general of the U.S. Army, George Catlett Marshall, as a communist.

McCarthy had struck gold with the point of a syllogism; since he was totally and furiously against communism, anyone who opposed him had therefore to be in favor of communism, *if only by that much.* This simply numbed the opposition or backed them into futile defensive postures. For example, when Senator Millard Tydings, having investigated McCarthy's charges that the State Department was full of Reds, reported that they were "a fraud and a hoax perpetrated on the Senate of the United States and on the American people," McCarthy, for revenge, then went into Maryland and, charging Tydings with being "soft" on communism, helped defeat him for reelection! His was a power blessed by Cardinal Spellman, a power that the young John F. Kennedy would not bring himself to oppose any more than did Eisenhower until 1954, near the end of McCarthy's career. For myself, I believed McCarthy might well be on his way to the presidency, and if that happened an awful lot of Americans would literally have to take to the boats.

When it was announced in 1953 that Edward R. Murrow would be devoting the entire half hour of his prestigious weekly TV commentary to an analysis of McCarthy, my own joy was great but it was mixed with some skepticism. Murrow had been the brightest star at CBS for more than a decade and remains to this day the patron saint of anchormen for his judiciousness and devotion to the truth. It was during the London blitz that he had seared our minds with the unique sound of his voice, a gravelly baritone that had rolled out to us across the Atlantic each night from the fog and blast of London under bombardment, his quiet toughness a reassurance that the great beleaguered city was still alive.

But all that anti-Nazi wartime gemütlichkeit was long gone now; indeed, CBS in the past couple of years had cooperated with the unacknowledged blacklisting of radio and TV writers, actors, and directors who had or were accused of having too much enthusiasm for the Left by newly sprouted self-appointed guardians of the airwaves like *Red Channels*, a broadsheet listing the names of purported subversives. In true private-enterprise style they were always ready to "clear" you for a fee plus your signed anticommunist declaration, or preferably an ad in *Variety*, which you paid for, with some similarly edifying and spontaneous patriotic locution. Still, it would be fascinating to see how far Murrow and CBS would want to go against the snarling senator from Wisconsin whose totally missing scruples had made him murderously effective as a debater. I was not at all sure it would be far enough.

There was such a widespread feeling of helpless paralysis before the McCarthy movement by this time that one questioned whether any mere journalist, whatever his wit and courage, could stay on his feet with him.

In such apocalyptic gloom, very nearly convinced that my days as an American playwright were numbered even as I was generally thought to be a great success, I adapted Ibsen's *An Enemy of the People* with the hope of illuminating what can happen when a righteous mob starts marching. But despite a brilliant performance by Fredric March as Dr. Stockmann, the critics batted the play right back at my feet. For one thing, it was a post-Odets and pre-Brecht time, when things artistic were supposed to deal with sentiments and aspirations, but never with society.

The failure of that production only deepened the sense of a mass mythic shadow dance, a ritualized, endlessly repeated consent to a primitive anticommunism that could end only with demagogues in power over the country. In the Salem witch hunts of 1692, a story I had known since college, I thought I saw nakedly unveiled something like the immemorial psychic principles of what we were once again living through. There too people had been at odds with a reality that indeed was sawing straight across their conception of themselves and nullifying the omnipotent powers of their society. There too men had been seized with paranoid terrors of dark forces ranged against them. It is hardly accidental that apart from *The Crucible* our theater would mount no other reply to a movement that surely meant to destroy its freedom. So feverish, so angry, so fearful had people become that any mention of the senator's name on a stage, or even an allusion to his antics, would have generated an impacted silence in the majority, and open rage in his partisans.

In *The Crucible* a public hysteria, based upon economic, sexual, and personal frustrations, gathers the folds of the sublime about itself and destroys more than twenty lives in the village of Salem, Massachusetts, in 1692. Between its heroes and villains stands a timeless hunger for mythic solutions to intractable moral and social dilemmas—particularly the myth of a hidden plot by subterranean evil forces to overwhelm the good. But *The Crucible*, too, would fail; either mistrusted as a "false analogy"—there had never been witches but there certainly were Reds, quite as though McCarthy had really uncovered a Soviet plot utilizing highly placed Americans—or regarded as a "cold" play, a charge partially justified by its direction as a disinterred classic. Interestingly, within two years, a new Off-Broadway production would succeed, judged hot stuff now by many of the same critics who theorized that I had more warmly revised the script. But the only revision had been the relaxation of society after McCarthy's quick decline and death—which, I suppose, permitted a longer view of the issues raised in the drama.

Shortly before Murrow's broadcast was announced, I had had my own personal little brush with a McCarthyite State Department. The Belgo-American Association, a business group, had invited me to come over to Brussels for the European premiere of *The Crucible* in the National Theatre, and I applied for a renewal of my outdated passport. A new passport was quickly denied me. "Not in the best interests of the United States," they said. So at the end of the opening performance, the audience, believing I was in the house, the papers having reported I had accepted to attend, began calling for the author, who, of course, was still in Brooklyn. The roar of the audience would not cease—to Europeans *The Crucible* at the time was reassurance that fascism had not yet overwhelmed Americans—and the United States ambassador had finally to stand and take my bow for me, a scandal in the papers the next morning when the imposture was revealed. (But who knows if he had stood up in sympathy for me or in silent protest at his department's stupidity in denying me a passport?)

All in all, by the time of Murrow's broadcast, I had only a small capacity left to believe that he would really do more than remonstratively tap McCarthy's shoulder. The broadcast was coming somewhat late in the game, now that an occasional soft murmuring of common sense was being heard in the press—although that, too, was still in danger of being suppressed once the senator got around to blasting its authors. For me, there was little reason anymore to expect a meaningful resistance to McCarthyism when I knew that, myself not altogether excepted, people were learning to keep a politic silence toward idiocies that a few short years before they'd have derided or laughed at.

An unsettling experience at a cocktail party shortly before the broadcast had stayed with me. I had overheard a TV producer assuring a circle of guests that he was free to hire any actor or produce any script he chose to and that no blacklist ever existed. Since I had friends who had not been hired in over a year despite long careers in TV and radio, and two or three who had suffered mental illness as a result, and I knew of at least two suicides attributable to the despair generated by blacklisting, I walked over to the producer and offered him the television rights to *The Crucible*. He laughed, assuring me and his listeners that he would of course be honored but his budget would never stand for what such rights would doubtless cost. So I offered them to him for a dollar. He went on laughing and I went on persisting, growing aware, however, that our little audience, many of them in television and the theater, was turning against me for a display of bad manners.

Leaving that party, I exchanged glances with people who I was certain shared my knowledge and views but who showed nothing in their faces. It was an experience that would be useful to me in future years when writing about the life of the artist in the Soviet Union, China, and Eastern Europe, where what might be called a permanent state of McCarthyism reigns, at times more virulently than others, but always warning artists—who, after all, are the eyes and voices of the society—that their souls ultimately belong to Daddy.

Edward R. Murrow appeared on the screen that night of the much-anticipated broadcast, as usual a picture of classy Bogartian straightforwardness, the cigarette between the fingers with the lethal smoke coiling up around the peaked eyebrows and the straight black hair, unsmiling as ever, his voice nasal and direct. I did not yet own a set, so I was watching this at my poet-friend Leroy's house a couple of blocks from my own in Brooklyn Heights. Leroy believed he was blacklisted in TV and radio, but a few producers occasionally gave him scriptwriting work because they loved him. People also gave him old but usable cars, trips to Florida, and more or less shared a mystic belief that Leroy must not die of want, with which Leroy agreed. He had once found a new can of anchovies on the sidewalk and a month later, on a different street, the key. Leroy had even graver doubts than I about what Murrow would be able to do.

Murrow could often affect an airy confidence and even sentimentality, rather like Cronkite talking about Vermont farmers, but not tonight; tonight he had his chin tucked in like a boxer and apprehension tightened the corners of his eyes with the knowledge, no doubt, that if some back talk against McCarthy had squeaked up recently in the press, his partisans were still passionate, religiously devoted to him, and numerous. Watching Murrow appear on the tube we were all aware of those millions out there who must hate him now for spoiling their god, or trying to; and even in that poet's snug and remote living room with its in-laws' cast-off furniture, the American violence charged the air. Tina, Leroy's wide-cheekboned blonde wife, who usually could never see a TV set switched on without turning away and launching a new topic of conversation, now stared in silence at Murrow's familiar face blossoming on the black and white tube.

To her and Leroy this broadcast was of far more than academic or abstract interest. Two of Leroy's closest relatives had gained some fame as American volunteers fighting for the Spanish loyalists against Franco. This, combined with his having the usual Left views of a Thirties survivor, was enough of a taint on Leroy to damage his right to sign his own name on the occasional radio script he was able to sell. On the slim proceeds of such fitful commerce he pressed on with writing his poems. And Tina pressed on with her winsome complaints that Leroy was stubbornly immune to the American Dream of wealth and fame. Thus she stared at Murrow like a woman in love with a fighter climbing into a ring.

I think it only dawned on us as he started to speak that Murrow was the first man to challenge McCarthy out in public rather than into his sleeve, and I think we were scared for him now, although we were still pretty sure that establishment politesse would gentle his confrontation with the senator. And indeed, Murrow's introduction was not at all belligerent. But this was television, not print, and it quickly became clear what his strategy was going to be— McCarthy was going to hang himself before the whole country by reruns of his own filmed performances. And there now unwound pictures of him hectoring witnesses before his Senate subcommittee, railing against a bespectacled author of an obscure college textbook with the accusation that this man was a member of the American Civil Liberties Union, "listed as a front doing the work of the Communist party." But the stinger was the speech before a mass rally during the recent Eisenhower–Adlai Stevenson contention for the presidency.

A cold and windy day, and McCarthy behind the podium, hatless, a burly and handsome man in a saturnine way, quick to laugh through a clamped jaw—more of a tight-assed snicker really, as though not to overly warm his icy ironies. Watching him again in these reruns was even scarier than seeing him the first time, in the previous months, for now somehow he was there to be studied and he was indeed villainous, almost laughably so. Now one saw that his great wish was for a high style, his models might well have been Oscar Wilde or Bernard Shaw, epigrammatists of the cutting Irish persuasion who could lay the opponent low with a jibe impossible ever to erase. Oddly, though, it was hardly ten minutes into the program when one knew it was the end of McCarthy, not altogether for reasons of content but more because he was so obviously handling subjects of great moment with mere quips, empty-sounding jibes, lumpy witticisms; it had not seemed quite as flat and ill-acted before.

At one point, as the applause of his audience died down he gave them his little knowing grin and said, "Strangely, Alger . . . I mean Adlai . . ." and a sweep of appreciative roaring laughter sent him into a helpless giggling spell and redoubled his audience's big-decibeled recognition for this association of Adlai Stevenson with Alger Hiss, an accused communist with whom Stevenson had no connection whatsoever. Now, with the election over and settled and its passions gone, the sheer vileness of this man and his crummy tactic was abstracted from its original moment and there he stood in all his mendacity, appearing joyfully immune to all moral censure or the most minimal claims of decency.

The Murrow broadcast was a deep, if not mortal, wound for McCarthy. At least it seemed so to me at the time. By the end of the half hour all our debt to Murrow came clear and my skepticism toward him had gone. But McCarthy was given his own half-hour rebuttal period three weeks later, and we gathered again to hear what he would have to say. Now live in the studio, a subdued McCarthy seemed to know he had been badly hurt by the Murrow broadcast. A plaintive tenor line lifted his voice into the doubtlessly authentic plaint of a persecuted man. "If there had been no communists in our government, we would not have given China to the communists!" This was one of his standards, but under attack now he knew he had to get more specific, and so maps appeared on the screen, showing how the dark stain of communism had spread from Russia over China, engineered by a tiny secret group of schemers, their agents, and their dupes like—yes, like Edward R. Murrow. In his rebuttal, McCarthy, left to himself, undid himself. Unaccustomed to anyone confronting him with his lies, he seemed unable to use elementary caution. Murrow, he blithely said, was a member of the terrorist organization the Industrial Workers of the World; Harold Laski, "the greatest communist propagandist in England," had dedicated his last book to Murrow. Now snarling, he attempted the ultimate unmasking of Murrow with his by-then familiar horror words: "Edward R. Murrow, the cleverest of the jackal pack which is always found at the throat of anyone who dares to expose individual communists and traitors; Murrow, who served the communist cause as part of the transmission belt from the Russian secret police into the American home." McCarthy's desperate appeal ended something like "The Communist Party opposes me; Murrow opposes me; Murrow is a transmission belt of communist propaganda." Such was his counterattack.

But Murrow, unlike others, had a network to allow him the last word. And he had easy pickings: the ACLU had never been "listed" by any agency as a front; Murrow had simply never belonged to the IWW; and Laski, a rather confused on-and-off-again Marxist professor, had dedicated his book to Murrow for his valiant broadcasts from bombed London in the late war. As for the communists supporting Murrow, this consisted of a notice in the *Daily Worker* that his upcoming McCarthy telecast was a "Best Bet."

Oddly, one lacked the urge to applaud Murrow at the end. He had been so persuasive because he had said what everyone had always known, that Joe McCarthy had merely been the master of the rhetorical style of lawyer-talk, an actor in love with the sound of his voice and his capacity to hold an audience in astonishment.

What ultimately undid McCarthy was hubris, his attacks on the patriotism of the leadership of the Army, on General George Marshall and Eisenhower himself. He may have gone mad with his power and too much booze. But Murrow's broadcast had cut the bag open and it was empty. How could one applaud our having striven so long after wind? Still, there was no doubt that night that Murrow's was the voice of decency, and if he and CBS had not struck at McCarthy until his decline had begun—if it was less a dragon slaying than a coup de grace—it still demonstrated, and would continue for years to come, the persistence of scruple as a living principle, one that had for so long been defied and doubtless would be again, and yet would live.

Murrow, in his summing up, said, "We are not a nation of fearful men," and one knew that there are things that do have to be repeated as fact even when they are only hopes. But for that kind of hope this nation is in Murrow's eternal debt.

1956 and All This
1956

I obviously can have no special competence in the field of foreign policy. I only know what I read in the papers, and the fact that I am a creative writer does not make my opinions either wiser or more persuasive than those of any other man. But it seems to me that there might be some good purpose in one of my profession expressing himself on this kind of problem. A certain awareness of attitudes outside our borders has been forced on me over the past ten years. My plays are regularly produced on the stages of Europe, Asia, Australia, and other areas. I have not traveled extensively abroad for some seven years now, but I do receive a steady mail from artists, producers, and audiences in foreign countries; there are visits and a steady correspondence with them and frequent newspaper reviews and articles concerning my work.

From all these sources I have a certain group of impressions, especially of Europe, which have at least one rather unusual basis, namely, the comparative foreign reaction to works written for the American audience.

Through these varying reactions to the same object, national attitudes can be examined in a perspective less turbulent and possibly of more lasting truth than purely political studies will elicit. In a theater, people are themselves; they come of their own volition; they accept or reject, are moved or left cold not by virtue of reason alone or of emotion alone, but as whole human beings.

A communion through art is therefore unusually complete; it can be a most reliable indication of a fundamental unity; and an inability to commune through art is, I think, a stern indication that cultures have not yet arrived at a genuine common ground. Had there been no Flaubert, no Zola, no Proust, de Maupassant, Stendhal,

Balzac, Dumas; had there been no Mark Twain, or Poe, Haw-
thorne, Emerson, Hemingway, Steinbeck, Faulkner, or the numerous other American artists of the first rank, our conviction of
essential union with France and of France with us would rest upon
the assurances of the two Departments of State and the impressions
of tourists. I think that had there been no Tolstoy, no Gogol, no
Turgenev, no Chekhov or Dostoyevsky, we should have no assurance at all nor any faint hope that the Russian heart was even ultimately comprehensible to us. Just recently the new government of
Ceylon, which has just replaced the avowedly pro-British, pro-
American regime, was and is still thought to be anti-American. The
program is to nationalize foreign-owned plantations, and for the
first time in history they will exchange Ambassadors with Moscow
and Peking. The Prime Minister, an Oxford graduate, took pains
to correct the idea he was anti-Western. He said, "How could I be
against a country that produced Mark Twain?"

There is more than a literary appreciation behind this remark, I
think. Literature of the first rank is a kind of international signal-
ing service, telling all who can read that wherever that distant
blinker is shining live men of a common civilization.

Now, at the outset, I want to make clear that I disagree with
those who believe the United States has entirely failed in its foreign
policy since the close of World War II. But I think that the values
this country has stood for in the past, more than in the present,
have helped to keep alive a promise of a democratic future for the
world. I do not believe, however, that our policy has stopped communism. I think that our armament has been a deterrent. But that
is all. A policy of merely deterring anything is negative. I believe the
time is upon us, and has been for some time now, when an entirely
new approach has to be taken to the whole problem of what the
future is to be. I base this upon the assumption that the atomic and
armament statement is a historic fact which will remain for an
indefinite period. In short, the policy was justified, if it was at all,
on the basis of an imminence of war. I am proceeding on the
ground that there will not be a war and cannot be. I summarize
these conclusions at the outset so that the criticisms I may level now
will be taken as they are intended—as guides to a positive foreign
policy, and not an exercise in sarcasm. For good or ill, what the

government has done in the world we have done; equally, what it will do in the future must represent, more than ever before, the real feelings and the judgments of the people. My quarrel, in fact, is that our policy has ceased to reflect the positive quality of the American people, and rests basically on their fears, both real and imaginary. We are much more than our fears, but the world does not often know that. And now to certain observations from my experience as a dramatist.

To begin with, I have often been struck, in foreign reviews of my plays, by the distinct difference in the foreign critic's attitudes toward meaning in a play, toward the theater as an institution. Here, our critics and most of the people in our audiences are pragmatists. As in our scientific tradition, our industrial tradition, in most of the things we do, we are almost wholly absorbed by the immediate impact of an idea or an invention. A thing is judged almost exclusively by whether it works, or pays, or is popular. In the scientific fields, my understanding is that this has been both an advantage and a liability, because our traditionally meager interest in theoretical, pure science has held back our scientific advance. At the same time, of course, our concentration upon practical, applied science has helped to give us a highly developed industry and a profusion of consumers' goods. The roster of those scientists who developed the atomic bomb is, as we know, very heavily weighted with foreign names, for this was a child of pure research. The opposing emphasis here and abroad is probably accounted for by the smallness of the European market for the products of applied science, for one thing. From this lack they have in this case made a virtue. But the irony remains that despite our enormous scientific establishment and our admitted superiority in many applied fields, there is evidently an impression abroad, founded until recently on fact, that we have little intellectual interest in science. I believe there is now a consciousness here of that need which is long past due.

In the field of the drama the same sort of irony prevails, and I think its operating principle has a certain effect upon a rather wide sector of European opinion. On the one hand, one feels the European writer, the critic, and from my mail the audience too are more interested in the philosophic, moral and principled values of the play than we are. One senses that they rather look askance at our lack of interest in these matters, and I often think that for this among other reasons they so often regard us as essentially a people without seriousness. The truth is that while our plays move much more rapidly than theirs do, are less likely to dwell on long conversations woven around piquant paradox and observation for its own sake, and while they strive more to be actions than thoughts, it is often admitted that if there is a leadership in the contemporary play since the Second World War, at least in terms of international public appeal, America has it. Put simply, we write plays for people and not for professors or philosophers; the people abroad accept and love many of our plays, and in some cases, even the philosophers do too. The point I would make here is that without any special consciousness of the attempt, we have created in the past few decades a kind of American dramatic style. We have also created an American movie style, an American style of dress, and probably architecture, and a style of shopping, and a style of comic books, and a style of novel writing and popular music—in a word, we have spontaneously created methods of reaching the great mass of the people whose effectiveness and exportability, if one may use an ugly word, are not equaled anywhere else.

This has had a multiple effect and it is not easy to separate the good from the bad. But I know, for instance, that there is great resentment among thinking people in Europe at the inroads made by *Reader's Digest* and comic books. One finds Dick Tracy all over the place. As a result of this particular kind of export, we are unwittingly feeding the idea that we incline ever so slightly to the moronic. The idea, for instance, of publishing an abridged novel is barbaric to them, and I'm not sure they're wrong. At the same time, however, our best writers are in many cases their secret or admitted models.

It is time to interject here some word about the importance of what is vaguely called culture in our foreign relations, a matter to which our government, to put it gently, is stupendously indifferent. In 1950, I was interviewed by the press in Copenhagen. It was an entirely literary interview. But when the reporters had left, one man stayed behind. Unlike the others who were of an intellectual sort, he wanted to know where I lived, what sort of a house, whether I played with my children, owned a car, dressed for dinner, and so forth. He turned out to have been from a tabloid paper which was read mainly by what he termed shopgirls. Now, I have yet to be interviewed by the New York *Daily News,* for instance, so I asked him what interest his readers could have in a person who wrote such morose and dreary plays. "It is very important for them to know that there are writers in America," he said. I could hardly believe they doubted that. "Oh yes," he said, "they will be very surprised to read about you, that you exist." But if they were that ignorant, I said, what difference would it make to them whether writers exist in America? What importance could the whole question have for them? "Very important," he said. "They are not intellectuals, but they think anyway that it is necessary for a country to have intellectuals. It will make them more sympathetic to America."

This is but one of many similar incidents which have made me wonder whether we are struggling, unknowingly, with a difference in cultural attitudes which may even warp and change purely political communication at any particular moment.

It is not that we are a people without seriousness. It is that we measure seriousness in an entirely different way than they do. They are the inheritors of a culture which was established, and I believe still exists, on an essentially aristocratic concept, which is to say, out of societies whose majority was nearly illiterate, education was for the few and the artist a kind of adornment to the political state, a measure of its glory and its worth. The artist for us, even as we may pay him much better than they do and cheat him much less, is more of an odd duck, and even among his fellow artists here he does not really exist except when he gains a great popular following. Again, our pragmatism is at work. I think that more Americans than not concede an artist his importance in proportion to his ability to make money with what he creates, for our measure of value is closely attuned to its acceptance by the majority. The artistic product has traditionally had little if any intrinsic justification for most of us. And this has presented our artists with a very lonely and frustrating life on the one hand, but on the other with a worthy if nearly impossible challenge. We regard it as our plain duty to make high art, if we are able, but to make it for all the people. More often than not, however, the art that *is* made sacrifices art for popularity partly because popularity pays fabulously among us. But the challenge is the right one anyway, I believe. The thing of importance now, however, is that even as we have produced some of the best works of literature of this era, we yet stand accused with perfect sobriety of being a mindless country. In this area the Russians have an inherited advantage over us. Despite all their differences from the Western tradition, their inherited attitude toward the artist and the intellectual has essentially the same sort of consciousness as that of the European. I think, for instance, of the time Dostoyevsky died. The entire Russian nation went into mourning for a novelist. I think of the endless lines of people who came to sit at Tolstoy's feet in his later years. I think too of the time a few years ago when I visited the Royal Dramatic Theater in Stockholm and saw an announcement of a forthcoming cycle of Strindberg's plays. I asked the director whether Strindberg was a popular writer in his native Sweden, and the director said he was not. Still for at least one period in each season, Strindberg's plays are regularly produced. "But why do you do this if he is not very popular?" I asked. "That isn't the point," he said. "He was our greatest dramatist and one of the best in the world; it is up to us to keep his plays alive and before the public." Later, we walked through the vast dressing room area of the theater, and there was one which, he said, is not often used. It belonged to a great actor who was now too aged to play. Yet they kept his dressing room solely for his use just in case he might drop in to rest of an afternoon. They needed dressing rooms badly, but it was inconceivable to take this once-great actor's name off his door until he had died.

This is not the occasion to examine the right and wrong of that system; I only wish to say that there is in Europe at least the strong remnant of the idea that the artist is the vessel of his country's selfhood, the speaker who has arisen among his countrymen to articulate if not to immortalize their age. I believe, as well, that because this reverence remains, it leads them to believe that they care more for art than we do, and that it follows we have no real life of the spirit but only a preoccupation with commodities. I would go even further and say that often our immense material wealth is the cue for them to believe that we care less for people than for things. I will not comment here on how much we care for people or how little; I am trying to avoid the question of the civilizing value of this kind of reverence for art. I will only say that at least in one country, Germany, its alleged pride in its artists did not seem to mitigate its ferocity in two world wars. But this is not the whole story either, and I leave it to go on with my observations.

In the different attitudes toward art can be detected attitudes which may be of significance politically. The reviews and comments upon my own play, *Death of a Salesman*, are of interest in this connection. When the play opened in New York it was taken for granted that its hero, the Salesman, and the story itself, were so American as to be quite strange if not incomprehensible to people of other nations; in some countries there is, for instance, no word that really conveys the idea of the salesman in our sense. Yet, wherever it has been shown there seems to have been no difficulty at all in understanding and identifying with the characters, nor was there any particular notice taken of the hero's unusual occupation. It seems to me that if this instantaneous familiarity is any guide, we have made too much of our superficial differences from other peoples. In Catholic Spain, where feudalism is still not a closed era; among fishermen in Norway at the edge of the Arctic Circle; in Rome, Athens, Tokyo—there has been an almost disappointing similarity of reaction to this and other plays of mine in one respect at least. They all seem to feel the anxieties we do; they are none of them certain of how to dissolve the questions put by the play, questions like—what ultimate point can there be for a human life? What satisfaction really exists in the ideal of a comfortable life surrounded by the gadgets we strive so hard to buy? What ought to be the aim for a man in this kind of a world? How can he achieve for himself a sense of genuine fulfillment and an identity? Where, in all the profusion of materiality we have created around us, is the cup where the spirit may reside? In short, what is the most human way to live?

I have put these questions because the commentators around the world have put them, but also because they do inform the play and I meant them to. Yet, no American reviewer actually brought up any of these questions. A play is rarely discussed here as to its philosophic meanings, excepting in a most cursory way; yet the basic effect upon us and the effect upon foreign audiences is evidently very similar. What I am trying to point out, again, is that it is less often the fact itself, the object itself about which we differ, than our unwillingness to rationalize how we feel. I sense that even as we do create the things of the spirit it seems to them rather an accident, rather a contradiction of our real character. I would add that had my plays not worked in Europe, which is to say that had they really been only philosophical works and not infused with the American pragmatic need for scenes to move with a pace and with characters made clear and familiar, the European would not be likely to be interested in them either.

I think it is true to say that for the most part as a nation we do not understand, we do not see that art, our culture itself, is a very sinew of the life we lead. Truly, we have no consciousness of art even as it has changed our tastes in furniture, in the houses we buy, in the cars we want. Only as it is transformed into things of daily use have we the least awareness of its vital functioning among us, and then it is only as its by-products appear in the most plain aspects of usefulness. As an example, even while abstract art is gazed at without comprehension, if not with hatred, its impact upon our linoleum designs, our upholsteries, our drapes, our women's dresses, our buildings, our packages, our advertising—these uses or misuses are quickly accepted without a thought. We have made in real life a most modern environment in many cases and have little conscious awareness of modernity; they have kept an outmoded environment in many cases and have a heightened awareness of what is modern.

This whole antipathy for theorizing, of knowing intellectually what we are doing, has very often crippled our ability to appraise reality. We so often become drowned in our own actions. For instance, it seems to me that this government has acted time and again as though its reasons would be automatically accepted without question or suspicion. In recent months we have armed Pakistan, a nation imbedded in the Indian nation, and one with which India has some potentially explosive disagreements. The reason given for arming Pakistan was security against Russia and China. For the Indian government, however, there could only be one result of this arming and it would be to strengthen Pakistan against India. To defend our act by claiming naïveté will simply not do under the circumstances. We intended the arms for defense against Russia and China, therefore that is all they will be used for. To rise above our immediate action and interest, to see beyond the moment and through the eyes of another country   this requires a kind of imagination which, to be sure, is not very difficult to achieve, but one must be accustomed to using it. In general, it seems to me, speaking as an artist and not a politician, this government has proceeded at times quite as though individual actions could have no larger meaning; quite as though, in dramatic terms, each moment of the play we are writing were to be judged for itself and separately from the play as a whole.

This evident inability to see a context behind an action does not stop at Politics. I think it is part of our method of seeing life. Again, I will use the theater as an example. Our critics will be inclined to see the hero of a play as a psychological figure, as an individual, a special case always, and their interest flags beyond that point. It is even said that, strictly speaking, it is not their business as to the larger significance of a character portrayed on the stage. They are present to discern whether he is interesting, logically formed, persuasive as a fiction, and so forth. The European, however, while interested in the character's manifest surface, is equally intent upon discovering what generality he represents. It is not the business of our critics to decide or most often to even discuss whether a play is built upon a tattered and outworn idea; if an old and worn idea is made to work on the stage once again in terms of effects and suspense and so forth, it is enough. In the European review one will inevitably find some estimate of the value of the concept behind the play. In other words, it is assumed to begin with that a thing is always made with an intention and that the intention is as important to evaluate as the effects it manages to create.

Thus it is that we find ourselves unable to meet the suspicions of Europeans in many situations, and find ourselves puzzled and even angered as a result. For instance, it is no secret to anyone in Europe that our borders are, in effect, sealed. And when, as happened recently, a writer of the eminence of Graham Greene is denied entry here for a visit in transit to the Far East, I am sure that most Americans cannot find the slightest patriotic interest in the situation. It happens that for a short time some decades ago, Mr. Greene, a converted Catholic, belonged to the Communist Party and has been an anti-Communist ever since. More importantly, his works are known around the world, and they are regarded by tens of thousands of people as sincere attempts to wrestle with some of the most serious moral and religious and ethical problems of this age. I can only ascribe his exclusion to a complete unwillingness, perhaps even an inability, to admit that Mr. Grcene is not any Greene but a very particular Greene existing in a definite Red context; that being a writer of his stature is not a fact of any consequence but a politically important consideration; that for millions of people in the world his profession and the high seriousness with which he has practiced it lend him a certain dispensation, the dispensation of the truth-seeker; and finally, that to refuse him entry into this country implied that this country feared what he might see here. I am sure that given these considerations, our officials would reply that the law is the law; that a writer is only another name to them. Yet it is impossible not to conclude that the real interests of the United States, to say nothing of its dignity, are transgressed by such an action.

I believe that this attitude toward culture is a disservice to us all because it lays us open to extremely dangerous suspicions which can spread out to stain our whole effort to preserve the democratic idea in the world, especially when we have had to create so large a military machine. A display of force is always a generator of fear in others, whether it be in private or public, local or international affairs. We consent to the policeman's carrying a gun not because we have lost our fear of the bullet but because we have agreed to suspend that fear on the assurance that the policeman carrying it is acculturated with us, that he shares our values, that he holds high what we hold high. But at the same time he must be willing to use that gun, he must be psychologically able to commit violence if we are to believe in his protection, and his willingness to slay, if it is not securely hedged about by his very clearly displayed respect for our values, quickly becomes a fearful thing. It is no different with a nation which would convince the world of its peaceful intentions even as it is heavily armed and its troops are stationed around the world. In the final analysis a reliance on force is always a confession of moral defeat, but in the affairs of nations it is tragically necessary sometimes to confess that defeat and to gather and rely on force. But to forget even for a moment that only the most persuasively demonstrated belief in civilized values can keep the image of

force from being distorted into a menacing image—to forget this is
to invite the easy demolition of our efforts for peace.

To prove an assertion whose implications are so vast is impossible, yet I must say that in a very profound way the differences I
have indicated in our attitudes toward culture itself have often
made it possible for Russian propaganda to raise fear of us in foreign peoples.

In passing, I should like to touch for a moment on a minor but I
think indicative paradox inherent here. A recent article in *The New
York Times Magazine* on Russian education and another group of
photographs in *Life* described the high seriousness of the Russian
college students, their evident dedication to their work, a picture so
intense as to throw up in the mind the counter-image of so many
American students for whom college is quite another thing. Unless
I am entirely mistaken, the same article and the same photographs
would not appear extraordinary to the European. What would be
strange to him and cause him to wonder on his community with us,
would be pictures of some of the shenanigans indulged in by some
of our students. What I am trying to indicate here again is that
there are superficial differences in our attitudes to culture in this
particular area which show us to be less intimately connected to
the European than the Russian is. The same is true of our kind of
theater as contrasted with the German, let us say, and the Russian.
I emphasize that the official attitude toward these manifestations of
culture is extremely weighty outside this country. Yet the fact
remains, and I believe it to be a demonstrable fact, that with all our
absence of apparent awe, we have produced more than a decent
quota of cultural works in the past two decades. The crucial importance of the image we cast in the world is not appreciated among us
and, in my opinion, is one of the wounds through which the blood
of our influence and our dignity is constantly seeping out. I go back
once again to the image of our force. If our enormous power to
destroy—and whatever else it is, military force is a destructive
force—if we are content to allow it to appear in the hands of a people who make nothing of culture, who are content to appear solely
as businessmen, technicians, and money-makers, we are handing to
the Russian, who appears to make so much of culture, an advantage of regiments. And the further irony is that the serious Russian,

both student and artist, has been so hamstrung by the tyrannical strictures on thought in his country, that his intellectual production has in recent years been brought to nearly a standstill, excepting in those scientific pursuits connected with militarily valuable science. It is, in their case, an irony which does not escape the notice of the world, in fact, it is precisely their tyranny that has kept nations out of their grasp. I believe, in short, that if we could only recognize and admit to our successes in culture, if the policy of our government and our people toward the things of the mind and the spirit were especially conscious and made serious, we have at hand a means of coming into closer harmony with other peoples who at bottom share our basic values.

But lest I seem to advocate a new advertising campaign, let me quickly correct the impression. To be sure, the object of a business or a nation in its relations with the world outside is to show its best qualities. More precisely, the obvious thing to do is to exhibit to the world whatever the world will most easily take to its heart for its own, those things which will make other peoples fear us less and love us more, those things with which they can identify themselves. For it is easier to misunderstand and hate that which seems alien and strange.

Our most popular, most widely seen cultural export is the American movie. It is a powerful convincer because hardly anybody in the world doesn't like to go to the movies. More important, however, it is spontaneously made, it appears without an ulterior political motive. So the man who sees it does so voluntarily and with his resistance down.

The trouble with the movies, however, is the same sort of trouble which Americans themselves often create when they go to Europe. Our movies draw the affections of people, their admiration, and envy for the opulence they generally portray, and also their disgust—as for instance, when a woman douses a cigarette in a perfectly good, uneaten, fried egg. At the same time, the movie star is beloved, his private life is followed with the interest long ago reserved for the minor gods. As such, we can only be glad so many foreigners like to see our pictures.

But even as we gain by them, we lose something of tremendous importance. Most movies are admittedly and even proudly brainless. When you have as much destructive power as we do, it is of the first importance that the world be continuously made aware not merely of how silly we can be, and at times how vulgar, but of how deep an attachment the American people have for the nicest cultivation of humane values.

It is in our novels, our poems, our dance, our music, and some of our plays, primarily, that we can and do reveal a better preoccupation. Yet, I can say from personal experience and from the experiences of other writers, that the work of art in which we really examine ourselves, or which is critical of society, is not what this government regards as good propaganda. I am not aware, for instance, that the export of any comic book has been interfered with, but only recently a nonfiction book was refused a congressional appropriation for inclusion in our overseas libraries because it showed a dust storm and a picture of an old-time country schoolhouse. In my opinion, it is not only not bad to show such things, nor bad to send our critical works around the world, but a necessity. For it is clearly one of our handicaps that we somehow insist, at least officially, that we have no inkling of a tragic sense of life. We posture before the world at times as though we had broken with the entire human race and had hold of a solution to the enigma of existence that was beyond questioning. As a dramatist I know that until the audience can identify itself with the people and the situations presented on the stage, it cannot be convinced of anything at all; it sits before an utterly uncomprehensible play of shadows against an unseeable wall. Thus, when a work or an action or a speech or a declaration of the world is presented without a trace of decent humility before the unsolved problems of life, it is not only that we do not really reflect our real selves, but that we must inevitably alienate others. For the truth is that we have not discovered how to be happy and at one with ourselves, we have only gone far in abolishing physical poverty, which is but one single element in the solution. And by harping only on that, we in effect declare a want of spirituality, a want of human feeling, a want of sympathy in the end. I believe we have solutions for poverty which the world must eventually come to adopt or adapt to other conditions, and we are obligated to demonstrate always what we have accomplished, obligated not only to ourselves but to humanity, which hungers for ways to organize production and create material wealth. But along with our success we have created a body of art, a body of literature which is markedly critical, which persists in asking certain human questions of the patterns we have created, and they are questions whose ultimate answers will prove or disprove our claims to having built a genuine civilization and not merely a collection of dominating inventions and bodily comforts. We are too often known abroad as dangerous children with toys that can explode the planet for us to go on pretending that we are not conscious of our underlying ethical and moral dilemmas.

It is no disgrace to search one's soul, nor the sign of fear. It is rather the first mark of honesty and the pool from which all righteousness flows. The strength of a Lincoln as he appeared in the eye of the world was not compounded of a time-bound mastery of military force alone, nor of an image monolithic and beyond the long reach of doubt. That man could lead and in our best moments leads us yet because he seemed to harbor in his soul an ever-renewing tear for his enemies and an indestructible desire to embrace them all. He commanded armies in the cruelest kind of war between brothers, yet his image is of a peaceful man. For even as history cast him as a destroyer of men, as every leader in war must always be, he seemed never to have lost that far-off gaze which cannot obliterate the tragic incompleteness of all wisdom and must fill with sympathy the space between what we know and what we have to do. For me, it is a reassuring thing that so much attention and appreciation is shown our novels and plays of high seriousness, for it signifies, I think, that others wish to see us more humanly and that the world is not as satisfied as we sometimes wish to appear that we have come to the end of all philosophy and wonderment about the meaning of life. It is dangerous to be rich in a world full of poverty. It is dangerous in obvious ways and in ways not so obvious.

During the war I worked for some time in the Brooklyn Navy Yard repairing and building ships for our fleet. The ships of many allied nations were often repaired there and we got to know many of the foreign crews. I remember one afternoon standing on the deck of a British destroyer with a British sailor at my side, when alongside us an American destroyer was passing out into the harbor. It was a boiling hot summer day. As the American ship moved slowly beside us a sailor appeared on her deck and walked over to a

1956 AND ALL THIS

water cooler on the deck and drank. On British destroyers a thirsty man went below to a tap and drank lukewarm water; when he bathed it was out of a portable basin, the same one he washed his clothes in. I glanced at the British seaman sweating on the deck beside me and I said, "That's what you guys ought to have, eh?" "Oh," he said, with an attempt at a sneer, "your ships are built for comfort." It was not that he couldn't bear the idea of ice water on a hot day. I feel reasonably sure he would not have joined a demonstration against the British Admiralty had a water cooler been installed on his deck. But the mere fact that we had coolers on our decks did not at once overwhelm him with a reverence for our superiority. The essential emotion in his mind was a defense of his own dignity and the dignity of his country in the face of what ought to have been a promising hope for himself but was taken as a challenge, if not a kind of injury to his own pride. I am not saying we ought not to have water coolers, either in our ideas or on our ships, but a foreign policy based solely on water coolers and water coolers alone may create as much envy, distrust, and even hatred as anything else. As a matter of fact, his deprivation he made into a positive virtue. It was common to hear Britishers say that their fleet was made to fight, unlike ours, that they had no comforts, no shower baths, plenty of cockroaches, and what to us would be miserable food, because they had no time and ought to have no time for anything but their guns, and because a ship of the fleet had no right to be anything but a floating gun platform. And finally, they convinced themselves that we couldn't hit anything anyway.

It is important for us to recall that there was a time not long ago when the positions were almost exactly reversed. It was the time of our frontier, the time when for the European, America was an uncomfortable place, without the amenities of his civilization. And at that time a stock situation in our plays and novels and our folklore was the conflict between the elegant but effete European or Englishman being outwitted or mocked or in some other way overcome morally by the inelegant, poor, roughhewn Yankee the mark of whose superiority was his relative poverty, an inability to spell, and a rugged, even primitive jealousy of his own independence. I was reminded of this irony by the latest novel of the aforementioned Graham Greene called *The Quiet American*. This is the story of an

American working in Asia for a cloak and dagger bureau in Washington, and his friendship and conflict with a British newspaperman. One is struck time and again by the Britisher's resentment of the American's precautions again disease or dirt—a veritable phobia of contamination—quite like the old literature in which the Englishman appears in tweeds and cap to shoot buffalo in the West, his sandwich hamper neat and ready, the napkin included. It is not merely the resentment which is important, but Greene's evident conviction that the American's relative wealth insulates him from any interest or insight into the realities around him, particularly the stubborn problem of the meanings of existence, meanings which transcend the victory over material want. And Greene reflects as well a kind of grudging admiration for the Asiatic Communists compared to the smooth-faced, naïve American, for the Communist, he says, knows how to talk to his fellow poor. In contrast, the Americans are prosperous and spiritually blank-eyed; they walk with the best of intentions in the impenetrable delusion that theirs is the only civilized way to live; in this book they walk in a closed circle outside of which the alien millions of the world, especially the poor, lead a life unknown and unknowable to them, and they are forced, the Americans are in this book, finally to rely upon devious policies of political opportunism and terroristic force. I will add that there is a pronounced quality of the caricature in this book, a caricature which quite astounded me coming from the pen of Graham Greene. It is easy to cast a stone at him and walk away, but there it is, a book which evidently appears quite accurate to the British and presumably to the European, whose reviewers took no note of the caricature in it; the work of a man who has not shown himself to be a fool in the past and is surely not against democracy.

It is time, I think, for us to step back and with open eyes, and a dignified humility, to look at where we are. How does it come to pass that so successful a system and so free should so steadily lose its hold upon the hearts of men over a single decade, when its competition is a tyranny whose people live in comparative poverty and under the rule of men instead of law? Is it truly possible that everything can be laid to the success of Communist propaganda? If that is true, then I think the jig is up, for then history is truly made of words, and words that lie. But it is demonstrably untrue, for there has never been a Communist revolution in a country with parliamentary government, except for Czechoslovakia, which was a revolution under Russian bayonets. Nevertheless, there is a sense in the world that somehow we are helpless, except for our armament, against a positive ideology which moves forward as we stand still or move backward. The conviction grows, it seems, that we have nothing really to say that we haven't said, and nothing to do except to stand by our guns.

I would make certain simple and self-evident observations and leave the largest conclusions to you. There is a revolution going on every single day in this era. Sometimes it erupts only in North Africa, sometimes in Iran, sometimes in a less obvious way in Greece, sometimes in the heart of Africa itself. By and large the foreign policy of the United States has gone on the assumption that things ought to remain as they are. By and large we have adopted a posture of resistance to change and have linked our fate and our dignity and our idea of safety to those regimes and forces which are holding things down. It is as though the misery of most of the world would not exist had the Communists not given it a name. We have, in more ways than one, made them into magicians. We had a Point Four program. We were going to buy the friendship of peoples with a few hundred million dollars. But the basic conditions of misery, the basic setup under which this misery is perpetuated and will continue to be perpetuated—for this we have no official word. The deepest hope, and we must come to admit it, was that they would take our aid and stop shouting. As a consequence, even by our own admission, enormous amounts of our aid have made the rich richer, as in Greece, and the poor no better off. Nor is this entirely our fault in a technical sense. It is not our fault that thieves steal for themselves, but there is a possibility which lies in another direction, a possibility which costs money to realize, but in my view presents our one great hope. One, but only one element in it, involves our resolution as a people and as a government that abject poverty and human freedom cannot coexist in the world. It is the desperation born of poverty that makes freedom a luxury in men's minds. Were this country to place as the first object in its foreign policy a resolution, a call, a new dedication to the war on poverty, a new wind would, I think, begin to blow through the stifled atmosphere of international relations.

I believe such a program set at the very forefront of our work in the world would have not economic consequences alone, but ultimately political and institutional changes would occur. There ought to be in training here technicians and experts for loan wherever they are needed, an army of them ready to move into any land asking for them. We ought to be building as many atomic power reactors as we can build, and we ought to be offering them to any nation asking for them. And above all, we ought to make clear that there are no strings attached.

The objection will be that we have already tried this and what have we got in return? I say that we have not tried it unpolitically. In India, in Italy, in Greece and other places, we have given aid on conditions of political fealty, and there is no blinking that fact. We have said, in effect, your misery does not move our hearts if you do not believe as we do. I say that it is the peoples of the world more than their governments who must be reached and raised up, and if that is the aim, if the love of the American people and their sympathy is permitted to surround this aid, instead of the fear of the American people turning all help into a species of bribery, we shall have reason for hope. Nehru is not suspicious of America because we have given India help in the past but because we have withheld it at times and threatened to at others when he says something we don't like. We ought to make it absolutely clear to the world that we are precisely what has never been before, a nation devoting itself now to the international onslaught on poverty, a nation eager for change, not in fear of it. Certainly we shall be greeted with cynicism, but if we adopt cynicism we are falling into the trap set for us, as we so often have over the past ten years.

But along with economic and technical aid on a scale far beyond that of the past, our entire attitude toward cultural matters must be revolutionized. There ought to be an army of teachers in training here for foreign service, people who can teach languages, mathematics, science, and literature. We ought to appear in the world as the source and pool from which the nations may draw for the new age that is to come. Our own gates must be thrown open to the musicians, the players, the writers, the literature of these countries, and our own artists must be invited to perform wherever there is an audience for them. And what do we get in return? Nothing.

Nothing but the slow, but I believe inevitable, understanding of the peoples of the world, nothing but the gradual awakening to the fact that we are not a fearful country, nor a country that knows all the answers, but a country with an understanding for the poor, a country which has such an abundance of materials and talents that it wishes to reach out its hand to others less favored.

But whatever the technical aspects of this approach, however difficult they may be to put into force, they are simple compared to the change in spirit required of us. I think the single most important alteration that has occurred among us since the Second World War is an insidious infusion of cynicism. No more were we going to be naïve, not again taken in by large visions and giveaways and the whole social-worker, Rooseveltian panorama of idealism. We were dealing now with sharks, and we must know how.

Yet, when was it that we held our undisputed moral leadership in the world? When did we start to lose it? It is simply no good laying the blame on communist propaganda because it was no more wily after the war than before. We have lost sight of the context in which we are living. We have come to imagine that because there are two major powers there can only be one of two ways the social and economic organization of the world can materialize. But already there are three. There is Tito's Yugoslavia, striving to remain independent, trying to establish a kind of socialism and at the same time to put forth at least a root from which may grow a tradition of civil liberty. And there are four. There is India, insistent upon social planning and a high degree of government supervision of economic life, yet tolerant of private property and private business, but rejecting the American system of unrestricted private enterprise. And there are five, with Israel mixing completely socialized villages and farms with a private economy developing in the cities. And there will probably be six, seven, eight, or a dozen different combinations of social and economic forces in as many areas before the next decade is finished. Only one rule can guide us if we are to be wise, and it is, again, that misery does not breed freedom but tyranny.

We have long since departed from any attempt to befriend only democratic nations and not others. The police states included by us in what we call the Free World are too numerous to mention. The Middle East and certain states in South America are not noteworthy for their respect for civil rights, nor is Franco Spain or the Union of South Africa. All these states promise only one thing in common—an allegiance to the West. But if we are not to be taken in by our own propaganda we shall have to see that they have other less amiable traits in common. They are economically backward and their regimes have vested interests in backwardness. Why then do we include them in the Free World? Because they claim in common a hatred of socialism and a willingness to fight with our side in case of war. But what if there is not to be war in our generation? Then we have only collected deserts that might have been watered but were not.

This brings me to my final point and it is the most vital and the most debatable of all. I believe that the world has now arrived, not at a moment of decision, but two minutes later. When Russia exploded her atom bomb the decision of history was made, and it was that diplomacy based either on the fear or the confidence that the final decision would be made by war, is no longer feasible. I believe the arms stalemate is with us for an indefinite time to come, and that to base a foreign policy upon an ingathering of states willing to side with us in war is to defeat ourselves in the other contest, the main contest, the crucial contest. I believe that the recent shift of Russian emphasis to economic, social, and cultural penetration rather than revolutionary tactics issuing in ultimate war, is based on this new situation. I believe that literally the hands, or more precisely, the fists, of the nations are tied if they only knew it, and that it is their hearts and minds which are left with the struggle. I believe that in its own devious way history has placed the nations squarely in a moral arena from which there is no escape.

But the implications go even further. The whole concept of Russian-type socialism and American capitalism competing for the allegiance of mankind is going to fall apart. There will be no pure issue from this struggle. There will be so many mutations and permutations of both systems, that it will be impossible to untangle them and call them one or the other.

The danger, I believe, is that the Communist idea will, in fact, be able to accommodate itself to the new complexity, but that we shall not, because we shall have refused to see that great social changes can be anything but threats to us. The danger is that without our participation in the reorganization of the backward sections of the world, our central value, the dignity of the human being based upon a rule of law and civil liberty, will never become part of the movement of peoples striving to live better at any cost.

For that and that alone ought to be our mission in this world. There are many mansions not only in heaven but on earth. We have or ought to have but one interest, if only for our safety's sake, and it is to preserve the rights of man. That ought to be our star and none other. Our sole aim in the past ten years was the gathering in of states allied against the Soviet Union, preparing for an attack from that source. As from some fortress town of the Middle Ages, we have seen the world. But now as then history is making fortresses ridiculous, for the movement of man is outside and his fate is being made outside. It is being made on his farm, in his hut, in the streets of his cities, and in his factories.

In the period of her so-called naïveté, America held the allegiance of people precisely because she was not cynical, because her name implied love and faith in people, and because she was the common man's country. In later years we have gone about forgetting our simplicity while a new ideology has risen to call for justice, however cynically, and imparting the idea that Russia stood for the working man. Meanwhile in a small voice we have spoken of justice and in a big voice of arms and armaments, wars and the rumors of wars. Now we must face ourselves and ask—what if there is to be no more war? What is in us that the world must know of? When we find this, the essence of America, we shall be able to forge a foreign policy capable of arousing the hopes and the love of the only force that matters any more, the force that is neither in governments nor armies nor banks nor institutions, the force that rests in the heart of man. When we come to address ourselves to this vessel of eternal unrest and eternal hope, we shall once again be on our way.

Concerning Jews Who Write
1948

There is a great deal of talk going on about attempting to create a Jewish literary movement. In this time when Jews have become so highly aware of their identity as Jews, when a new national feeling has taken hold of so many of us, the argument is heard that the Jewish artists and writers have it as their duty to address themselves in their works to Jewish themes, Jewish history and contemporary Jewish life.

There are possibly several hundred Jewish writers in America of whom a handful write in Yiddish. Very few have written more than one work about Jews or Jewish problems. Why is this so?

In the first place, few of us have ever felt any binding tie to what could be called Jewish life. We have graduated out of it, so to speak, in the same way that second and third generation Americans of every nationality have tended to adopt the customs and habits and attitudes of the American nation as a whole. And of course, the Jewish writer is not alone in having broken his ethnic ties, for Jews who are businessmen, professionals of every kind, workers of every kind, have done the same thing. In other words, the cords which bind any people together to the degree that warrants their being called a homogeneous nation or people, have been so loosened and cut as to leave the Jewish writer with no other identity than his American identity.

This alienation is not in any way reprehensible, as some people seem to imply. Western culture, western art and literature are much more highly developed, much more varied, and much more at home in America than are Hebrew culture, art and literature, if only because the latter have been enchained for two thousand years and more. Further, it is not as though the Jewish writer were deserting a highly unified culture of his own to adopt a rival culture through which his fame could spread around the world, instead of being confined to a few million dispersed Jews. It was not a unified culture that we left behind. Indeed, in my own experience it could hardly have been called a culture at all. I know that during my first 15 years I was brought up in a religious home, my grandfather was the president of his synagogue, and I read enough Hebrew to understand about 20 per cent of what I read. My parents hardly ever spoke Yiddish, and any concept of a Jewish culture, in the sense of a British or French culture, was until quite recently utterly unknown to me.

THE INNOCENT GENERATION

Unless I am quite mistaken, unless I am a remarkable exception, my experience tells me that my generation in America was Jewish only in a very peculiar and particular sense. We did not think in Yiddish or Hebrew, we thought in English. We did not yearn for some national home outside of America; we felt no ties with Europe that really had any operative effect upon our psychology; and we had no personal ambitions that could distinguish us from any other American family. Significantly, although I knew of course that I was Jewish, that I was forbidden to go to a Christian church both by my Christian friends and by my family, I did not feel myself in any way set apart, in any way a minority, in any way a traditional Jew, until I left high school and went to work. Without the slightest trepidation I sailed into a firm that had never hired a Jew, got a job, and then was slowly brought to realize by means of the usual methods, that I was not of the same strain as my idol Abraham Lincoln, that my grandfather, whom I had come to identify somehow with Herbert because he loved Hoover so well, was in reality somehow different from Herbert Hoover, and that, in sum, I was not being regarded by my fellow workers as an ordinary American but as a kind of second-hand American.

I can't tell you how strange it felt not to be what I thought I was. I remember coming home after about a week on the job. I was a stock and shipping clerk in a large auto parts warehouse. We had about a hundred thousand different items in the place, from 1911 Packard manifolds to Chevrolet piston pins. I didn't know the stock, naturally, so one night I stayed an hour after quitting time to go over some of the bins in order to familiarize myself with the locations of things. I was into the fan pulleys when the manager of the warehouse came down the aisle and stopped beside me. He was smiling, and said, "You're going to own the place pretty soon, heh." The point is that I thought it a compliment. I still didn't know I was a "Jew" and that for a Jew to be conscientious was a conspiracy. As a matter of fact, when I related the incident to my parents, such was the friendliness they felt in America that they too saw nothing unfriendly in it. That was the year they all voted for Hoover.

UNCONSCIOUS JEWISH CULTURE

The point is that my Jewishness was not in any positive way dramatized to me, but by the cut of a discriminatory remark. I had always known, of course, that we were not Christians, that there was a kind of antipathy between our God and their God, but it was all in the family, so to speak. I never remember having chosen my friends on the basis of their race or religion, and I was brought up in Harlem where Negroes, Puerto Ricans, Italians and Jews crowded into the schools. Where then, was our Jewish culture? Now that I look back on it I can find its traces, but it must be remembered that all this is a rationalization after the fact. Until I had to fight competitively in the economic world, I had about the same idea of myself as any other American boy had.

The outcroppings of a Jewish culture that I can perceive from this distance were on the order of the sabbath ceremony on Friday night. This was really the closest I ever got to God, but my God was not, in my mind anyway, opposed or truly delimited from any other God. It was not a ceremony that was protecting me from any-thing outside. It was simply, in my youthful unawareness, the way any well-behaved family ate dinner on Friday night. It was an hour in my week when I felt the warmth of closeness with my family, and especially an hour when I sensed the full force of my grandfa-ther's dignity, inasmuch as he wrapped himself in the quiet aura of a certain sanctity. He, I felt, was speaking to God; he knew what he was doing; when he blessed the bread I felt instinctively that he had learned the manner of blessing and the words directly from Moses. Inasmuch as I was not afraid of being a Jew, the whole ceremony had no protective significance. It was similar to saluting the flag. In a long period of peace one salutes the flag mumbo-jumbo and that's the end of it. In a war, when danger threatens, the ritual takes on combative proportions.

The same is true of Jewishness, in my opinion. I feel that had even the relative calm and prosperity of the twenties continued for two or three more decades, Jewishness as a state of mind and anti-Semitism would have very largely disappeared. The former may shock some Jews to whom Jewish history was taught in an intelli-gent way, to whom the ethic of Judaism was handed on for what it is, the very fountainhead of the highest Christian ethic. But for them the identity of Judaism and of Jewishness would have had to be maintained on a cultural level, on a non-combative level, on a level of philosophy and morality. Judaism would then appear for what it actually is, a religion, and in less devout hands, a moral philosophy. And it would have to stand or fall on its relevancy for the day.

Unhappily, anti-Semitism has confused my generation on the matter of the Hebrew religion as separate from Jewish culture. To my mind the Hebrew religion is a matter of option to the Jewish writer as to all Jews, but Jewish culture is his to defend whether he is religious or not. For if he does not defend it, he may die of its destruction. In the last analysis, the minimum of what we mean by Jewish culture today, and in this present world context, is the sim-ple right to have been descended from Jews. Jewish culture is the sum and total of what history has made us. It is what the enemy wishes to burn. It is us, expressed in any form.

JEWS WITHOUT STIGMA

But let me go on with some personal history which I believe impinges upon the question of a new Jewish cultural revival. After working two years I finally had enough money for tuition, and I enrolled in a midwestern university. Now I was a little less, but not much less, innocent about the Jewish situation. For instance, my first friend there was the boy who sat next to me in the English class. He was tapped by a well-known fraternity. Naturally he wanted me with him. I hadn't the money or inclination for fraternity life so I declined. He was a very rich boy and very affable. Our friendship continued throughout the year. In my sophomore year I wrote a play and it was all about Jewish people. It won the literary prize of the year and was produced on the campus. I ran into him again after the play was produced. He pretended not to notice me. I think that was when I knew I was a Jew.

The important thing, however, was the fact that I wrote my first play about Jews, and that I never regarded them, while writing, as Jews but as people. The creative act was completely innocent, it was absolutely clear of any pleading, or any sense of difference. I wrote as though the whole world were Jewish. At the same time, there were explicit references to the Jewish religion, there was a scene, the best scene, of a Friday night sabbath. There was a Jewish villain manipulating people to his own advantage, and a Jewish hero opposing him. There was good and evil in the most delightfully true proportions, with never a qualm about "revealing" anything about Jews. The play was a great success.

INNOCENCE IS SHATTERED

Why didn't I go on writing about Jews?

I think a psychological shock did it. It was a shock that flew over two thousand miles of ocean, over the mountains of Eastern America, and right into my room in a little midwestern college town. It was Hitler. It was what he was saying about Jews and doing to Jews. And worse, it was the difference between my own indignation, my own anger, and the absolute calm, the indifference of the people around me. I felt for the first time in my life that I was in danger.

And most important, my first play was optioned three times by three different Broadway producers. All of them wanted to do it, and all finally gave up for the stated reason that it was not a time to come forward with a play about Jews, especially a play in which a villain was Jewish. Really he wasn't a very bad villain, in fact a rather likeable villain, probably because I loved everybody in those days. Nevertheless I think I gave up the Jews as literary material because I was afraid that even an innocent allusion to the individual wrong-doing of an individual Jew would be inflamed by the atmosphere, ignited by the hatred I suddenly was aware of, and my love would be twisted into a weapon of persecution against Jews. No good writer can approach material in that atmosphere. I cannot censor myself without thwarting my passion for writing itself. I turned away from the Jews as material for my work.

I take my story no further because I believe that what I have told you is sufficient to raise the discussion of a new Jewish literary movement onto a realistic plane. If, in the midst of writing my first play, in the midst of my innocence, when being Jewish seemed merely to be a person—if then someone had said, write more about Jews, bring out of the half darkness the whole truth about life among Jews as you know it, I would have had not the slightest conflict, I would have pitched into the task with joy. And my work, I think, would have been positive, full of humor and the optimism that comes from knowing the Jews well. But today I am no longer innocent. I have been insulted, I have been scorned, I have been threatened. I have heard of violence against Jews, and I have seen it. I have seen insanity in the streets and I have heard it dropping from the mouths of people I had thought were decent people. Instantly, therefore, and inevitably, when I confront the prospect of writing about Jewish life my mood is defensive, and combative. There is hardly a story or play I could write which would not have to contain justifications for behavior that in any other people need not be justified.

ART IN DEFENSE OF OUR PEOPLE

It is a similar dilemma to that of the writers in the thirties. In those days they could not conceive of being socially significant unless everything they wrote had a strike in it. So today, at first blush, many of us cannot see a Jewish theme excepting in direct relation to anti-Semitism. And unfortunately, the same is true of the audience, which seems to approach every work about Jews as though it must be inevitably a plea for relief from oppression, and therefore somehow spurious as art.

If my history parallels that of other Jewish authors, then I think the solution lies in a direction but dimly seen at present. Assuming, for one, that most of us want to be of help in protecting ourselves and our people by means of our art, it seems to me that we must do a very difficult thing with our minds. We must lift ourselves out of the present. That, in order to see the Jewish present. We must move into the area of Jewish life with a new vision, a vision that excludes defensiveness, a point of view which assumes at once that the Jew need not be "sold" to the American people. It is Sholom Aleichem's attitude which excluded no part of Jewish life or psychology, which made excuses for nothing but never hesitated to arraign society where society was at fault. It is the attitude of the total truth. I think that with so many of them possessed of profound talents, we ought to be able to create a gallery of Jewish characters so powerful in their reality, so hearty in their depictions, so deeply felt in their emotional lives, that the audience or the reader, by the pure force of the characters themselves will be brought to that state of love and innocence in which I once so briefly lived, when all men are wondrous again and basically good, when all the Gods are friendly and in the family, and when Jews are Jews again in literature and art—in other words, when they are what they were to me—people trying to make some sense out of life, people out of the common pool of humanity, people lazy, people ambitious, people in love, people in jail, people running away, and people dying bravely on some military mountain.

For us the issue is not whether we are Jews who write, or Jewish writers. It is merely that we know something that no one else can know as well; something that the world needs desperately to know. It is the peculiar and happy quality of art that it carries understanding with it. To face away from Jewish life when one has a story to tell is not to be more universal and less parochial; it is to refuse to do best what no one else can do at all; and equally important, to draw upon Jews for our works is to bring into the family of people—our people, our beloved and creative people, who have been edged away from the table to wait in the shadows like ghosts or pariahs. I am not asking Jews who write to confine themselves to any material any more than I would lay the same rule upon myself. I say only that we wrong ourselves and our own art, as well as our people, by drawing a curtain upon them. In short, I speak not of duty but really of opportunity, and it seems to me that those who understand me ought ponder the relation of their art to the condition of Jewish man.

Miracles
1973

Sometime back in the Fifties, *Life* sent out a questionnaire asking opinions on the new revolution then taking place, allegedly. I sent mine back unanswered, with the note that there was no revolution. It seems to me now that I was right and wrong.

The only moment of near revolution I know about, at least in my lifetime, was in the winter of 1932 when the leading bankers went to Washington and seriously discussed with the Treasury Department the idea of the Government taking over all the banks. That, and a few days in Flint, Michigan, during the sit-down strikes. These events—along with the widespread talk in business circles and among the people, that the system was actually at an end and some form of socialist ownership had to be the next step lest total chaos overwhelm the United States—had the look of the real thing. In the ensuing one hundred days, the Roosevelt Administration devised a flood of legislation that saved capitalism by laying down what essentially were limits to how crooked you were allowed to be, or how rapacious, without going to jail. And direct money payments to desperate people was made public policy. It was a revolutionary moment, and it lasted for perhaps four or five years, primarily, I think, because the Establishment had lost its nerve, did not really have a clue to solving mass unemployment. Inevitably, to stand in the avant-garde meant espousing socialism; it meant being political.

The turmoil of the Fifties and Sixties came to a head in a booming economy, just after the Establishment had retrieved its poise to the point where it had cleaned out—through McCarthyism—the universities, the arts, of the last of the people who had a social, let alone a socialist, vision. If there were one concept that might stand for the Thirties avant-garde, it was the solidarity of humanity, and if the Fifties had an emblem, it was loneliness. The Thirties radical, of whatever stripe, saw a pattern of deliquescence in the American system; the Fifties youth was bereft of any such comfort. When the new struggle came, it was inevitably a personal and not a political one—because American politics had its strength back and was at least working again.

But if the Sixties was not a revolution in any classic sense—a transfer of power between classes—it did partake of the revolutionary process by overturning certain attitudes toward what a human being is and what he might be. More, the latter-day revolt has offered a new pattern, just as the one in the Thirties attempted to do, to account for the human condition, a hidden matrix which guided us all. So, in the psychological sense, there is a continuity between both generations, and there are others too.

It is commonplace to say that the Thirties revolt was one of the mind while the latest is one of the gut, a contrast between rationalism and mysticism. This distinction is too neat to be true. Of course a lot of people, probably the majority who became radical in the Thirties, were inspired by unfilled bellies and narrowed-down chances to make a buck. Which is natural and legitimate. As natural and legitimate as the number of Fifties and Sixties revolutionaries whose new vision was limited to the idea of getting laid without the etiquette of courting and bullshit.

I was about fourteen when the Depression hit, and like a lot of others who were more or less my age, the first sign of a new age was borne into the house by my father. It was a bad time for fathers who were suddenly no longer leaders, confident family heads, but instead men at a loss as to what to do with themselves tomorrow. The money had stopped, and these men were trained by American individualism to take the guilt on themselves for their failures, just as they had taken the credit for their successes. Under the streetlamp at the corner drugstore the talk was suddenly shifting from whether you were going to be a doctor, lawyer, businessman, or scientist, to what the hell you were going to do after the dreaded day you were graduated from high school. There were suicides in the neighborhood. We had all been sailing this proud and powerful ship, and right there in the middle of the ocean it was beached, stuck on some invisible reef.

It seems easy to tell how it was to live in those years, but I have made several attempts to tell it, and when I do try I know I cannot quite touch that mysterious underwater thing. A catastrophe of such magnitude cannot be delivered up by facts, for it was not merely facts whose impact one felt, not merely the changes in family and friends but a sense that we were in the grip of a mystery deeper and broader and more interior than an economic disaster. The image I have of the Depression is of a blazing sun that never sets, burning down on a dazed, parched people, dust hanging over the streets, the furniture, the kitchen table. It wasn't only that so many high-class men, leaders, august personages, were turning out to be empty barrels—or common crooks, like the head of the stock exchange. It was that absolutely nothing one had believed was true, and the entire older generation was a horse's ass.

So I went back to the synagogue—an Orthodox synagogue. And there I found three old men playing pinochle in the entrance corridor of that ugly building. I drew up a chair and sat with them. I had no idea what I wanted there. I could read Hebrew but understand little of what I had been saying. I walked inside and looked at the altar. I thought something would speak to me, but nothing did. I went home and came back a few more times. But the sun stood as still in the heavens as it ever had, and nothing spoke. I even joined the little choir, but still nothing happened to me, nothing moved within me.

The mute threat underlying unemployment is that you will never cease being a child. I was favored—I had gotten a job delivering rolls and bread from four to seven every morning, for four dollars a week. Freezing cats followed my bike from house to house, crying in pain. The summer dawns were lovely over the sleeping one-family houses, but they were spoiled by my fear of time bringing me closer to graduation. A man was not wanted anywhere, and the job ads in the *New York Times* specified "White," or "Christian," although there were never more than a dozen openings, anyway. A man, let alone a boy, wasn't worth anything. There was no way at all to touch the world.

One afternoon on a windy street corner, while I was waiting my turn to play handball against the pharmacist's brick wall, a guy who was already in college started talking about capitalism. I had never heard of capitalism. I didn't know we lived under a system. I thought it had always been this way. He said that the history of the world (what history?) was the history of the class struggle (what is a class?). He was incomprehensible but a hell of a handball player, so I respected him. He was unique, the only one I knew who stayed on the same subject every time I met him. He kept pouring this stuff over my head, but none of it was sticking; what he was saying didn't seem to have anything to do with me. I was listening only for what I wanted to know—how to restore my family. How to be their benefactor. How to bring the good times back. How to fix it so my father would again stand there as the leader, instead of coming home at night exhausted, guilty.

This guy kicked the trip wire one afternoon. We were on the beach at Coney Island. In those days families were living under the boardwalk in scrap-metal or wood-slat shacks. We could smell feces and cooking there in the sun. And this guy said, "You are part of the declassed bourgeoisie."

Life quickened, insane as it sounds, because . . .

My father was no longer to blame. It wasn't he who had failed; it was that we were all in a drama, determined by history, whose plot was the gradual impoverishment of the middle class, the enrichment of the upper, and the joining of the middle with the workers to set up a socialist economy. I had gotten what the synagogue had not given me—the ennobling overview. It was possible again to think that people were important, that a pattern lay hidden beneath the despair and the hysteria of the mothers, that the fathers would again be in their places. Life suddenly had a transcendent purpose, to spread this news, to lift consciousness. For the day would arrive when conflict would end. Things would no longer have value, the machines would provide. We would all live, like people in a park on Sunday, quietly, smiling, dignified. The age of Things was over. All that remained was for people to know it.

They usually call this the experience of materialist religion, but it had little materialism for me. I wasn't looking to it for anything like money or a better job but for a place, literally, in the universe. Through Marxism you extended your affection to the human race.

The emptiness of days filled with a maturing purpose—the deepening crisis of capitalism, bursting into the new age, the inexorable approach of nirvana.

It was the last of the forgoing philosophies. The deeds of the present, the moment, had no intrinsic importance, but only counted insofar as they brought closer or held back the coming of the new. Man-as-sacrifice was its essence; heroism was what matterèd. We were in the Last Days, all signs pointed to Apocalypse. Self was anathema, a throwback; individual people were dematerialized. A Russian, Ostrovsky, wrote *An Optimistic Tragedy*, and the title signified the mood, I think, wherever Marx's vision had taken root. Joy was coming—no matter what.

The Thirties has never been rendered in literature, because the emotions reported are all coiled around political and economic events, when in truth a religious sweep was central to everything one felt, an utter renewal of mankind, nothing less. The mystic element was usually elided, I imagine, because to share Marx was to feel contempt for all irrationality. It was capitalism that was irrational, religious, obscure in the head, and Hitler was its screaming archangel. Pride lay not in what one felt but what one was capable of analyzing into its class components. The story went around that Wall Street stockbrokers were calling Earl Browder, head of the Communist Party, for his analysis of the economy. A communist *knew*, had glimpsed the inevitable.

Similarly, the movement in the Sixties was hermetic and, like its ancestor, was unable to penetrate the national mind with anything more than its crude, materialist side. To the man on the street, it was merely a generation lying across the road of Progress, crying out F—— Work. And its worst proponents so defined it, too. In the case of both "revolutions," a redemptive thrust, without which such movements are never propelled, could not be transmitted beyond the ranks, and both revolutions appeared to the outsider as contemptuous of man's higher ideals, spirituality, and innate goodness. To most supporters of the Spanish loyalists, their struggle was far more profound than any politics could embrace; the Spanish civil war was a battle of angels as well as the lowly poor against the murderous rich. When the dark spirit won, it was not only a factional victory but the shaking of Inevitability, human future itself had been overwhelmed. While Picasso painted *Guernica*, the State Department, business and religious leaders, and most of the press were oddly hesitant about saying unkind words about Hitler and Mussolini, the law-and-order boys behind Franco. Of the minority of Americans who even knew a war was going on in Spain, probably half were on the side of the Church and fascism. To these people, the republic stood for license, atheism, radicalism, and—yes, even the socialization of women, whatever that meant. So for me the commonly held attitude toward Sixties youth had echoes. The country was fixated on the body of the new revolt while its spirit went either unnoticed or was mangled by the media or the movement's own confused reporters.

The Thirties and Sixties "revolutions," for want of a better word, show certain stylistic similarities and differences. The earlier radical took on a new—for the middle class—proletarian speech, often stopped shaving and wore the worker's brogans and the lumberjack's mackinaw: his tailor, too, was the Army-Navy surplus store. He found black jazz more real than the big band's arranged sentimentality, found Woody Guthrie and Ledbetter and folk music authentic because they were not creations of the merchandiser but a cry of pain. He turned his back, or tried to, on the bounds of family, to embrace instead all humankind, and was compromised— when he found himself lifted up the economic ladder—in his effort to keep his alienation intact. When he married he vowed never to reconstruct the burdensome household he had left behind, the pots and pans, the life of things. The goal was the unillusioned life, the opposite of the American Way in nearly all respects. The people were under a pall of materialism, whipped on unto death in a pursuit of rust. The list of similarities is longer than this, but the differences are the point.

Once nipped by Marx, the Thirties radical felt he was leading a conditional life. He might contribute money, or himself, to help organize a new union, but important as the union was, it paled before its real, its secret, meaning—which was that it taught the worker his strength and was a step toward taking state power away from the capitalist class. If the Thirties radical viewed a work of art or a friend, the measure of value came to be whether socialism was being brought closer or pushed farther away by that art or that friend. And so his life moved into a path of symbols, initially ways to locate himself in history and in society, but ultimately that which ruled his mind while reality escaped.

The Thirties radical soon settled into living for the future, and in this he shared the room of his mind with the bourgeoisie. It could not have been otherwise. Capitalism and socialism are forgoing systems; and you cannot tend the machine, on which both systems are based, whenever the spirit moves you, but *on time*, even when you would rather be making love or getting drunk. Remember the radical of the Thirties came out of a system that had stopped, and the prime job was to organize new production relations that would start it up again. The Sixties radical opened his eyes to a system pouring its junk over everybody, or nearly everybody, and the problem was to stop just that, to escape being overwhelmed by the mindless, goalless flood that marooned each person on his island of commodities.

The Sixties people would stop time, money time, production time, and its concomitant futurism. Their Marxist ancestors had also wanted man as the measure of all things but sought to center man again by empowering the then-powerless. What came of it was Russia and, at home, the pork-chop trade-union leaders and their cigars. So power itself was now the spook, and the only alternative, if humankind was to show a human face again, was to break the engagement with the future, with even sublimation itself. You lived now, lied now, loved now, died now. And the Thirties people, radical or bourgeois, were horrified and threatened by this reversal because they possessed the same inner relation to the future, the self-abnegating masochism that living for any future entails.

Dope stops time. More accurately, money time and production time and social time. In the head is created a more or less amiable society, with one member—and a religion, with a single believer. The pulsing of your heart is the clock, and the future is measured by prospective trips or interior discoveries yet to come. Kesey, who found his voice in the Sixties, once saw America saved by LSD, the chemical exploding the future forever and opening the mind and heart to the now, to the precious life being traded away for a handful of dust. Which leads to another big difference between the two generations and something that I think informs the antic jokiness in the Sixties radical style.

The Thirties radical never dreamed the world could really explode. In fact, as Clausewitz had said and Marx would have agreed, war was merely politics by other means. If we hated fascism, it too was merely politics, even the clubbing of radicals and Jews. That even fascists could burn up people in ovens was unthinkable. What the Holocaust did was posit a new enemy who indeed was beyond the dialectic, beyond political definition. It was man.

So that Apocalypse, as inherited by the Sixties generation, was not what it used to be, the orderly consequence of a dying system, but an already-visual scene in Hiroshima and Auschwitz whose authors were, in one case, parliamentary politicians. Oppenheimer-like humanists quoting the Upanishads, decent fellows all and, in the other, their tyrant enemies. Political differences and principles guaranteed nothing at all. What had to be projected instead was a human nowness, Leary's turning on and dropping out, lest the whole dark quackery of political side-taking burn us all in our noble motives. The very notion of thinking, conceptualizing, theorizing—the mind itself—went up the flue; and many bourgeois governments, for a little while, backed up in fear not of an ideology but of a lifestyle—a mass refusal to forgo.

For myself, I knew this had no hope and not because it eschewed a political vision but because its idea of man was wrong. Because a man cries "Brother!" doesn't make him one, any more than when his father muttered "Comrade." The struggle with evil doesn't cancel out that easily, as the fate of Marxists had shown. More, from where I sat, the religious accents of Sixties radicalism were not entirely apart from those of Thirties radicalism. Like the Christians, Marx had projected a Judgment Day on the barricades, an Armageddon out of which the last would rise to be first, then to direct the withering away of the state itself once socialism came to pass, the veritable kingdom where conflict is no more and money itself vanished in an abounding surplus of goods. You wanted a car, you just picked one up and left it when you didn't need it anymore—a sort of celestial Hertz. If the last thing Jesus or Marx had in mind was a new fatalism, that was nevertheless what most human beings made of the stringent and muscular admonitions these prophets pronounced, and what most of the voyagers into the Age of Aquarius were making, I thought, of the punishing, disciplined yoga that had evolved this new vision. Once you have thought yourself into an alignment with Fate, you are a sort of Saving Remnant for whom mere reality is but an evolution of symbolic events, until finally you are no longer really anything at all except a knower—and thus your deeds cannot be judged by mortal judgment, so anything goes. Differences there are, of course, but Manson, Stalin and that long line of Christian crusaders join hands in this particular dance. How often have I heard survivors of the Thirties astonished that they could have said the things they said, believed what they had believed. A faith had been running underneath that newfound pride in objective social analysis, that sense of merging with the long line into the Inevitable, and a faith exploded is as unrecoverable to the heart in its original intensity as a lost love.

The latter-day Edenism of the Sixties had a sour flavor, for me at least: it was repeating another first act of another disillusioned play. I saw the love-girls, free at last, but what would happen when the babies came?

Most girls with babies are funny. They like to know exactly *where they are*. If only because babies reintroduce linear time and long-term obligation, high-flying anarchy must come to earth.

Kesey's new book *Garage Sale*, a mélange of his own and his friends' writing, is a sort of geologic section of some thirteen years in the wilderness. But his screenplay, which appears in this book, is the real surprise, a hail and farewell to the era. From the height of its final pages you can look down and begin to sense a form at last in the whole insane pageant. For Kesey had not merely taken a dive into his bloodstream and glimpsed, as it were, the interior of his eyes, but emerged into the ring where the Others are, the brothers and sisters toward whom a newfound responsibility flows, and toward the world itself. The time-honored way to make that discovery was the Hebrew-Christian self-torture—the near-dissolution of the body inviting God. Here it is otherwise, the enhancing of the senses and pleasure, the blending of the physicality of Eastern mysticism with the Mosaic injunction to serve the People, whose well-being is the measure of all truth. If responsibility can be reached through pleasure, then something new is on the earth.

Skeptic that I am, I could believe in this. My zodiacal friends tell me that in terms of an individual, the Great Wheel says the human

race is now thirty-five years of age, and that's when human beings
are most creative, when Jesus gathered together all that he was and
died. So Love is coming toward us, the Age of Aquarius. Scorched
by an earlier Inevitable, I shy from this one, and I warn whoever
will listen that the tension with evil has no end, or, when it does, the
man within has died. Nevertheless, when I think back to what life
was like in the Thirties and see from that long-ago vantage what is
happening now, I stand in the glistening presence of miracles.

Radical or conservative, we worshipped the big and the smoke
from the chimney, and the earth was only there to chew up and
drill holes in, the air a bottomless garbage pail. Now my ten-year-
old daughter turns the key off when I am parked and waiting
for someone. How miraculous. We got out of Vietnam because
the Army wouldn't fight it anymore. That's the simple truth and
how miraculous. Nixon—Billy Graham and prayer breakfasts
notwithstanding—has revealed himself—and, really, by himself.
As though the earth had squeezed up his roots and he rotted where
he stood, this lawless man of disorder. How miraculous. The seed
of the visionless has spent itself in him. How miraculous. In the
early Fifties a Catholic university survey asked me why I thought
there were so few of the faith in the arts or in the contentions of
social debate. I wrote back that Irish Catholicism and Yankee Puritanism had combined in this country to sink the inquiring mind
without a trace. Now? The spectacle of a Catholic priest demonstrating, leading the poor, is miraculous. Reporters stand up and
yell at a presidential press officer, accusing him of having told them
lies, and this in the White House, with the flag on the platform.
How miraculous. The power company wants to run a high-tension
line across my countryside and my neighbors, many of them having
voted for Nixon, descend on what used to be routine, company-
dominated "hearings," and invoke beauty and demand their aesthetic rights as though they were poets. How miraculous. Notre
Dame University invites me to read. How miraculous. The stock
market drops at rumors of war and soars with signs of peace.
Incredible. I speak at West Point. Not believable. And tell them, a
week after Nixon's invasion of Cambodia, from where I had just
returned, that it is a disaster, a disgrace, and will surely bomb the
Cambodians into the communist camp. A sixty-year-old colonel,

with a horizontal Guards moustache, ramrod fellow beribboned up to his chin, stands and says he was U.S. Military Attaché in Phnom Penh for nine years and that Mr. Miller has spoken the truth. How miraculous. Only one cadet stands to ask why I choose to undermine their morale, and he is the son of the union chief in Chicago. How miraculous. And afterward, on the porch of an officer's house with a dozen colonels, all Vietnam vets, close-cropped and loose on scotch, they confide their mourning—for the Corps, the country, and a dwindling sense of honor. They talk of resigning, of being ashamed to wear the uniform into New York and, longingly, of Eisenhower's Order of the Day to the legions about to storm the Normandy beaches because that order spoke of mankind, of lifting the yoke of tyranny, and one man exclaims: "Imagine those words in an order anymore!" Would they ever know a rightful cause again, in or out of war? They were acolytes in a sullied church, and if these men blamed the politicians for defeat, they were also no longer sure we had deserved to win. That ancient scorn for human circumstances was faltering, even here, in the cannon's heart. Something is changing.

I suppose that in part I have been looking at Sixties radicalism from the Left Bank, from Prague and Red Square, as well as from my own home. It is always disappointing to American radicals to hear that things are worse abroad. Sounds like liberal smuggery. But I don't mean conditions, only the spirit. Especially is this difficult to swallow right now when the tide has played out here, the revolution eddying, and indifference again prevails. Who has gained from it all except MGM Records and the department stores with their new lines of eighty-dollar jeans? What came of the love-ins but fatherless children? And heavier contracts for the stars? And the sharp-eyed managers of perfidious guitars? What comfort that the cop looking for hash under the mattress has curls sticking out behind his helmet? The truth is that the fundamental demand of the French students in the 1968 revolution was that their universities be changed into the utilitarian American kind.

In 1968 I met with some thirty writers and editors and other hairy types in the office of *Listy*, the Prague literary magazine. They wanted someone from outside to know they were about to be jailed by the Russian toadies running the government. They asked me to come because I am an American, and only the Americans *might* respond to their disaster. These fellows had little hope, but it was all they did have. The Vietnam war was raging then, and they could read the *New York Times* and know we were imperialists and racists and lacked anything you could call culture, and yet the hope, what there was of it, pointed toward us. A few of them had been here and knew the score, had seen Harlem and Bedford-Stuyvesant and our wrecked cities—compared to their Prague, barbaric, corrupt, incredibly hard places, and merciless to the unsuccessful. Yet it was as though from this insane country were the impossible help possible—from this armed place that was at the moment killing another struggling people.

Under the Kremlin wall one day I remarked to my Soviet interpreter, a bright chap, that there must have been some fast footwork in that palace. . . . To my surprise the fellow was offended and said, "It is not our business." And the few who try to make it their business keep a bag packed with clean underwear, for jail. Those few, to my amazement, look to Americans as the free-swinging opposites of what their countrymen are. Not really to the American radical but to what they see as a man-centered idea still alive among us.

One of the owners of a German automobile company, this man naturalized now and based in New York, tells me he had to bring over the company's engineers and make them attend Senate hearings on auto emissions to convince them that they must take seriously the problem of auto pollution—because the Americans meant business, something these engineers had refused to believe because nobody in Europe meant business. A swim in the Mediterranean off Nice, a sail in the Sea of Japan, or a water-ski off the Italian west coast makes Coney Island look as pristine as Thoreau's pond.

But no listing of hopeful improvements can really alter the despair with modern life which is shared everywhere; the difference, if there is one, is a residual eagerness in Americans to believe despair is not life's fixed condition but only another frontier to be crossed. Perhaps only the black man can know the more universal despair—which changes only to remain forever the same—yet he has certainly evolved out of his passivity toward it.

In the central square of Wilmington, North Carolina, in the twilight of a fall 1940 evening, about a thousand blacks spread out along the storefronts and sat down or lounged among their jalopies and busted trucks. I happened to be there, temporarily employed by the Library of Congress to record speech patterns, no less, in that state. Quite accidentally I came upon this strange display. Eerie— for I knew instantly that they were not there to no purpose, and in 1940 you simply did not connect black people with assertion, let alone protest. (Blacks had stood apart from the whole radical Thirties, except for a handful who had never succeeded in rousing their own people.) I used the excuse of my microphone to find out what was going on, and I collected a crowd of men who were somewhat reassured by the Great Seal of the U.S. painted in gold on my truck—in those days the Federal Government was Roosevelt, whom white racists hated.

They were diffident country people, shy and suspicious, but pieced out for me the fact that they had been recruited from backwoods farms and hamlets to build the new Wilmington shipyard in the swamps nearby, a mucky, mosquito-tormented job. Now that the yard was finished, they had all been summarily fired to make way for white workers to come in and take the clean shipbuilding jobs. Only one of the men so much as raised his voice, a large fellow with powerful arms and a heavy bass voice. He stepped out of the polite shyness and roared, "Captain, we just about tripped! We got *no place to go!*" Then they dispersed. No police came to ride them down. By nine that night these people had all vanished, presumably into the woods from which they came. White Wilmington had barely taken notice of the occupation of the square, and in fact these black people had hardly raised their voices. Next day I interviewed the chief of Bethlehem's operation there and he was bewildered that there could even be an issue. Blacks hired in a shipyard to work alongside *whites?* That level of awareness is not possible anymore, even if so many blacks still live as though in an occupied country, a territory the Depression never left.

If only because the good news of Aquarius never touched our racism, it left an uneasiness; but there is another disquiet as well. Like the Thirties, the Sixties did not know quite what to do with evil. In the fever of the newfound Marxism, evil was seen evaporating with the disappearance of the private owner and his exploitation of people, but the snob T. S. Eliot said it better—"They are trying to make a world where no one will have to be good." Now again, by means of drugs or prayer or sex, we'll merge all impulses into a morally undifferentiated receptivity to life, and evil will shrivel once exposed to the sun. It is as though evil were merely fear, fear of what we conceal within, and by letting it all hang out we leap across the categories of good and bad. To both "revolutions," good and bad were inventions of the Establishment, mere social norms, and so it seemed that Stalin was liquidating not people but the dying past. Just as Manson, to many, is an ambiguous villain—the faces of his victims fade beside his victory over self-repression. There was something strangely pure in his massacre, since he did not even know his victims. André Gide wrote this story long ago—of a man who fires his gun in a railroad car and kills a man he never saw before—this in order to spring free of the ultimate repression through a totally gratuitous act, to find the irreducible self. Nihilism may save pride but it leaves its casualties and no fewer than does the moral code it sought to squash. Embittered now and defeated, the Sixties people find themselves no longer trained for nirvana but, yet again, in the United States. Still, they changed it forever, if this is a comfort.

By 1949, a Thirties man would never know there had ever existed, only a few years before, a movement for social justice, loud and pervasive. By 1949 the word "society" had become suspect again. But ten years later, justice was once more the issue. It was simply that the inventions of the Thirties had been absorbed, just as now the nation has both rejected and digested the Sixties idea. And this may be why, in my case anyway, a return from abroad always yields a faintly surprising experience of hope. It does keep changing here, it does go on: the blind, blundering search—which is not the case in more completed places. Evidently we are not fated to be wise, to be still in a contemplation of our cyclical repetitiousness, but must spawn new generations that refuse the past absolutely and set out yet again for that space where evil and conflict are no more.

It will not come—and it is coming.

The Battle of Chicago: From the Delegates' Side
1968

There was violence inside the International Amphitheater before violence broke out in the Chicago streets. One knew from the sight of the barbed wire topping the cyclone fence around the vast parking lot, from the emanations of hostility in the credential-inspecting police that something had to happen, but once inside the hall it was not the hippies one thought about anymore, it was the delegates.

Violence in a social system is the sure sign of its incapacity to express formally certain irrepressible needs. The violent have sprung loose from the norms available for that expression. The hippies, the police, the delegates themselves were all sharers in the common breakdown of the form which traditionally has been flexible enough to allow conflicting interests to intermingle and stage meaningful debates and victories. The violence inside the amphitheater, which everyone knew was there and quickly showed itself in the arrests of delegates, the beatings of newsmen on the floor, was the result of the suppression, planned and executed, of any person or viewpoint which conflicted with the president's.

There had to be violence for many reasons, but one fundamental cause was the two opposite ideas of politics in this Democratic party. The professionals—the ordinary senator, congressman, state committeeman, mayor, officeholder—see politics as a sort of game in which you win sometimes and sometimes you lose. Issues are not something you feel, like morality, like good and evil, but something you succeed or fail to make use of. To these men an issue is a segment of public opinion which you either capitalize on or attempt to assuage according to the present interests of the party. To the amateurs—the McCarthy people and some of the Kennedy adherents—an issue is first of all moral and embodies a vision of the country, even of man, and is not a counter in a game. The great majority of the men and women at the convention were delegates from the party to the party.

Nothing else can explain their docility during the speeches of the first two days, speeches of a skull-flattening boredom impossible to endure except by people whose purpose is to demonstrate team spirit. "Vision" is always "forward," "freedom" is always a "burning flame," and "our inheritance," "freedom," "progress," "sacrifices," "long line of great Democratic presidents" fall like drops of water on the head of a tortured Chinese. And nobody listens; few even know who the speaker is. Every once in a while a cheer goes up from some quarter of the hall, and everyone asks his neighbor what was said. For most delegates just to be here is enough, to see Mayor Daley in the life even as the TV cameras are showing him to the folks back home. Just being here is the high point, the honor their fealty has earned them. They are among the chosen, and the boredom of the speeches is in itself a reassurance, their deepening insensibility is proof of their faithfulness and a token of their common suffering and sacrifice for the team. Dinner has been a frankfurter, the hotels are expensive, and on top of everything they have had to chip in around a hundred dollars per man for their delegation's hospitality room.

The tingling sense of aggressive hostility was in the hall from the first moment. There were no Chicago plainclothes men around the Connecticut delegation; we sat freely under the benign smile of John Bailey, the Democratic National Chairman and our own state chairman, who glanced down at us from the platform from time to time. But around the New York delegation there was always a squad of huskies ready to keep order—and indeed they arrested New Yorkers and even got in a couple of shoves against Paul O'Dwyer when he tried to keep them from slugging one of the members. Connecticut, of course, was safely machine, but New York had great McCarthy strength.

The McCarthy people had been warned not to bring posters into the hall, but at the first mention from the platform of Hubert Humphrey's name hundreds of three-by-five-foot Humphrey color photos broke out all over the place. By the third day I could not converse

with anybody except by sitting down; a standing conversation
would bring inspectors, sometimes every fifteen seconds, asking for
my credentials and those of anyone talking to me. We were forbidden to hand out any propaganda on the resolutions, but a nicely
printed brochure selling the Administration's majority Vietnam
report was on every seat. And the ultimate mockery of the credentials themselves was the flooding of the balconies by Daley ward
heelers who carried press passes. On the morning before the convention began, John Bailey had held up twenty-two visitors' tickets,
the maximum, he said, allowed any delegation, as precious as gold.

The old-time humor of it all began to sour when one realized that
of 7.5 million Democrats who voted in the primaries, eighty percent
preferred McCarthy's and/or Robert Kennedy's Vietnam positions.
The violence in the hall, let alone on the streets, was the result of
this mockery of a vast majority who had so little representation on
the floor and on the platform of the great convention. Had there
never been a riot on Michigan Avenue the meeting in the amphitheater would still have been the closest thing to a session of the All-
Union Soviet that ever took place outside of Russia. And it was not
merely the heavy-handed discipline imposed from above but the
passionate consent from below that makes the comparison apt.

On the record, some six hundred of these men were selected by
state machines and another six hundred elected two years ago, long
before the American people had turned against the Vietnam war. If
they represent anything it is the America of two years past or the
party machine's everlasting resolve to perpetuate the organization.
As one professional said to me, "I used to be an idealist, but I
learned fast. If you want to play ball you got to come into the park."
Still, another of them came over to me during the speech of Senator
Pell, who was favoring the bombing halt, and said, "I'd love to vote
for that but I can't. I just want to tell you." And he walked away.

Connecticut caucused before casting its vote for the administration plank. We all, forty-four of us, sat in a caucus room outside
the great hall itself and listened to Senator Benton defending the
bombing position and Paul Newman and Joseph Duffey attacking
it. The debate was subdued, routine. The nine McCarthy people
and the thirty-five machine people were merely being patient with
one another. One McCarthy man, a teacher, stood up and with a

THE BATTLE OF CHICAGO

cry of outrage in his voice called the war immoral and promised revolution on the campuses if the majority plank was passed. Angels may have nodded, but the caucus remained immovable. Perhaps a few were angry at being called immoral, in effect, but they said nothing to this nut.

But when the roll was called, one machine man voted for the minority plank. I exchanged an astonished look with Joe Duffey. Another followed. Was the incredible about to happen?

We next began voting on the majority plank, the Johnson position. The machine people who had voted "Yes" on the minority plank also voted "Yes" on the majority plank. The greatness of the Democratic party is its ability to embrace conflicting viewpoints, even in the same individuals.

Having disposed of Vietnam, Mr. Bailey then suggested the delegation take this opportunity to poll itself on its preference for a presidential candidate, although nominations had not yet been made on the floor of the convention. This, I said, was premature since President Johnson, for one, might be nominated by some enthusiast and we would then have to poll ourselves all over again. In fact, I knew privately that William vanden Heuvel, among others, was seriously considering putting up the president's name on the grounds that the Vietnam plank was really a rephrasing of his program and that he should be given full credit as its author rather than Humphrey, who was merely standing in for him. But Mr. Bailey merely smiled at me in the rather witty way he has when his opponent is being harmlessly stupid, and Governor Dempsey, standing beside him behind the long table at the front of the room, assured all that as head of the delegation he would see to it that in the event of a nomination on the floor of any candidate other than Humphrey, McCarthy, and McGovern, we would certainly be allowed to change our votes. Immediately a small man leaped to his feet and shouted, "I nominate Governor Dempsey!" The governor instantly pointed at him and yelled, "Good morning, Judge!" This automatic reward of a seat on the bench, especially to a man obviously of no distinction, exploded most of the delegation— excepting the indignant teacher—into a burst of laughter and the governor and his nominator swatted at each other in locker-room style for a moment. Then seriousness returned, and resuming his official mien of gravity, the governor ordered the polling to begin. The nine McCarthy delegates voted for McCarthy and the rest for Humphrey, and there was no doubt of an honest count. It may be a measure of the tragedy in which both factions were caught that when, later on, the governor was handed teletyped reports of the Michigan Avenue riots, his face went white, and he sat with his head in his hands even as it became clearer by the minute that Humphrey and the administration would be victorious.

After two nights on the floor, whatever trends and tides the TV commentators might have been reporting, one felt like a fish floating about in still water. Nothing had been said on either side that aroused the slightest enthusiasm. The water above was dark, and whatever winds might be raising waves on the surface did not disturb the formless chaos, really the interior leaderlessness of the individual delegates. We were the crowd in an opera waiting for our cue to shout in unison when the time for it came. First depression and then anger began moving into the faces of the McCarthy people as the speeches ground on. Some of us had campaigned all over the state and the nation to rouse people to the issues of the war, and in many places we had succeeded. There was no trace of it here and clearly there never could have been. The machine had nailed down the nomination months before. We had not been able even to temper the administration's Vietnam plank, not in the slightest. The team belonged to the president, and the team owned the Democratic party.

As I sat there on the gray steel chair, it was obvious that we could hardly have expected to win. Behind Connecticut sat two rows of Hawaiians. Middle-aged, kindly looking, very polite, eager to return a friendly glance, they never spoke at all. When it came time for any vote, their aisle man picked up his phone, listened, hung up, stood, and turned thumbs up or down. The brown faces watched his hands. So much for deliberation. It was not quite that crude among the others, except for Illinois, but Illinois did not need thumbs. Illinois had somehow located the fact that we McCarthy people of Connecticut were occupying nine seats in the same row, and Illinois stared at us from time to time with open, almost comical, ferocity. Every time I turned to my left, I found the face of a man who might have been a retired hockey player. He sat staring at me through close-set eyes over a strong, broken nose, his powerful hands drooping between his knees, his pointy shoes worn at the heels, his immense neck bound to bursting by a tiny knot in his striped tie. Once I tried to give him a smile of greeting, a recognition of his interest. He gave nothing, like a watchdog trained to move only on signal.

There was this discipline but there was no leadership. None of the Humphrey people ever argued with me when I said they were sinking the party by hanging the Johnson position on the war around Humphrey's neck. None ever had a positive word to say about Humphrey himself. They were beyond—or beneath—discourse, and if by some miracle Humphrey had let it be known he was now in favor of an unconditional halt in the bombing they would have been as perfectly happy to applaud that stand as the opposite. They were lemminglike, clinging to one another in a mass that was moving toward where the leaders had pointed. And then, suddenly, there was a passion.

Representative Wayne Hays of Ohio got to the podium and began, like the others, in a rhetorical vein. Something to the effect that his teacher in school had taught him that history was a revelation of the past, a guide to the present, and a warning of the future. The delegates resumed their private conversations. But suddenly he was talking about hippies in paired contraries. Not long hair, he said, but long thought; not screaming in the streets but cleaning the streets; not . . .

Leadership, quite unannounced, had arrived. All around me men were turning to this clear voice on the platform. His list of mockeries of the errant generation mounted and grew more pointed, more vicious, more mocking, and applause was breaking out all over the floor, men were getting to their feet and yelling encouragement, and for the first time in two days there was electricity in the crowd, a vibrant union of mind, a will to act, a yea-saying from the heart. Men were hitting each other on the back with elation, fists were raised in encouragement, bull roars sounded out, and an ovation swept over Hays as he closed his papers and walked off. It was a congregation of the aged, men locked into a kind of political senility that was roaring its challenge across the six miles of superhighway to the ten thousand children just then gathering for the slaughter

opposite the Conrad Hilton Hotel. The old bulls against the young
bulls under the overhanging branches of the forest.

Then it struck me that there was no issue cleaving the convention; there was only a split in the attitude toward power, two mutually hostile ways of being human. The Humphrey men were
supporting him not basically because he was right but because he
was vice president and the candidate of the president. In any ten of
them there will only be two or three at most who are themselves
convinced that we should be in Vietnam, that if necessary we must
fight on for years, that lamentable as the civilian casualties are they
are justified by the need to protect democracy and the Thieu–Ky
Government, and so on. This minority is passionate, it is deeply
afraid that the communist powers, if they win in Vietnam, will
flood over into Hawaii and ultimately California. But the others
are supporting authority which happens at the moment to be fighting the war. Congressman Don Irwin of Norwalk, for example, is
a principled supporter of the war and for him it is righteous, to the
point where he openly says his position will probably defeat him
the next time he runs. He is a man in his forties who smiles constantly and in a group quickly loses his voice from laughing so
much, a common vocal problem with professionals, the accepted
social greeting being laughter. They shake hands and laugh. It is
not unnecessary, it is not merely a tic but a working out of conflict,
for many of them have had terrible political battles against one
another and have come close to insulting one another in various log
jams, and the quick laugh is a signal of mutual disarmament, a
warding-off of violence, for many are physical men quick to take
umbrage, like their forefathers who more than once beat each other
senseless in the halls of Congress.

There were two Americas in Chicago, but there always are. One is
passionately loyal to the present, whatever the present happens to be;
the other is in love with what is not yet. Oppressed by the team spirit
all around me, I thought of a morning in Moscow when I was passing under the walls of the Kremlin with a young interpreter. I said
that there must have been some terrific battles in those offices the
day they decided to get rid of Khrushchev. The young man refused to
join this idle speculation: "We don't think about what goes on in
there. It is not our business. They know what they are doing."

But everywhere I went I also met young—and not so young—Russians who knew it was up to them to make the future of the country, men and women who wanted a hand on the tiller. But there they have no legal means of putting new ideas forward; here we do. Or did. The underlying fright in the Democratic convention, and the basic reason for the violence on Michigan Avenue, was that perhaps the social compact had fallen apart. As one TV correspondent said to me as we stood watching the line of troops facing the hippies across the boulevard from the Hilton, "It lasted two hundred years. What law says it may not be over? Maybe we've come to the end of the string. Those kids," he went on, "are not bohemians. Most of them aren't what you'd call hippies, even. There are a lot of graduate students in that crowd, medical students, too. They haven't dropped out at all. Somebody upstairs had better start asking himself what they're trying to tell the country."

To me, standing there at four in the morning with the arc lights blasting the street and no one knowing when the police and the troops would again go berserk, the strangest irony was that the leader they had come to hate, the president, had months ago removed himself as being too divisive. And yet all the force of the state was in play to give that president what he wanted in the convention. The whole thing might have been understandable if the country were in love with its leader. What, I wondered, was being so stoutly defended on this avenue?

The question itself only added to the general surrealism. In the main CBS workroom behind the auditorium, I watched a row of five TV sets. NBC was showing the attack by the club-swinging police, the swarming squads of helmeted cops, and one heard the appalling screaming. Next to it, CBS was showing the platform speaker inside the auditorium and the applauding delegates. Next to CBS was ABC, with close-ups of bleeding demonstrators being bandaged. Then a local station showing a commercial, Mister Clean having his moustache rubbed off. The last was another local station whose screen showed some sort of ballet.

In one of the corridors a young man stopped me, holding the microphone of a portable tape recorder up to my mouth. He came from the University of Chicago's radio station. We quickly agreed the whole spectacle was a horror. "How can you have anything to do with this?" he asked. My answer, which I found embarrassing at that moment, was that I had hoped to change it and that it might be changed if people like me tried to move into the party in a serious way rather than only during presidential campaigns.

"But how can you have any faith now in this kind of democratic politics?"

He was intelligent and eager and angry, and I thought I had misunderstood him. "What would you put in its place?" I asked.

"Well, I don't know. But not this."

"But what, then? One way or another people have to delegate powers to run the country, don't they? This is one way of delegating them. Right?"

"You mean you believe in this?" he asked, incredulously.

"Not this. Not this gang, no. But. . . ." I broke off, aware now that it was not merely the antics of the convention we were talking about. "Do you mean that the more intelligent should rule? The more idealistic? Is that it?"

"Well, not this," he repeated, his anger mounting.

"But what are you going to substitute for this?" The crowds were pushing us to one side and then another. The announcer on a nearby TV set was yelling a description of the battle on Michigan Avenue. "Are you just going to substitute intelligent people telling the others what to do instead of the others telling the intelligent? Isn't that the same kind of violence we're going through right here? What are you going to put in place of this?"

The look in his eyes amazed me. He seemed never to have considered the problem. It was unbelievable. He was ready, it seemed, for some kind of benevolent dictatorship. If this, this hall full of middle-aged men who had yelled their pleasure at the condemnation of the young—if this was democracy, he hated it, and that hatred was enough for him. We were being torn apart now by the crowd. I called to him as he moved away, "That's the problem, don't you see? What do you want? It's not enough to hate all this!" But he was gone.

Life is always more perfect than art. The endings and codas it provides to experience always tell more of the truth than any construction on the stage or in a book. At about two in the morning, after the fighting on Michigan Avenue had quieted, about five hundred delegates under the impromptu chairmanship of New York's Paul O'Dwyer decided to hold a march past the scene of the carnage. We gathered a few blocks from the Hilton, many of us holding lighted candles, and moved in near silence, some singing softly, toward the battleground. Police, who had been alerted to our plan, sat in squad cars on the avenue, none getting out, for we were official delegates and not to be pushed around, or not yet anyway. The night was lovely; all the stars were out. Chicago looked beautiful. A block from the Hilton we were stopped by a police captain. He was six-and-a-half-feet tall, wearing the blue crash helmet whose edges were lined with gray rubber, a hinged Plexiglas face shield pushed up. I have never seen such eyes or a smile so fixed and hard. The procession halted, and O'Dwyer stepped forward to parley.

"Now, what is it you want to do, gentlemen?" the officer asked.

O'Dwyer said that we intended to walk past the hippies, who were still congregated in the little park across the street from the hotel, past them and the line of soldiers and police facing them.

"I see," said the officer. "All right, then. Just keep it orderly and quiet. We are here to protect lives and property. Keep it orderly and keep moving."

We moved, and as we approached the hippies who had crowded to the edge of the park to see this strange, apparitional procession, they began whistling, and some said, "It's a wake, a funeral for the Democratic party." We kept coming, and some of them began to get the point. Cheers went up. We exchanged the V-for-victory sign. There was laughter and someone began to sing "We Shall Overcome." The line of soldiers stood expressionless, holding their rifles up to bar us from the hotel across the street, some of them looking at our candles as though they were in a hallucination. Nothing happened. In a while, the silence returned to the avenue again. The conversation between us and these kids was neither more nor less interesting than any such conversation on any street anywhere.

Next afternoon, I went to a TV studio to join a telecast being beamed by Telstar to England. I had been told to get there no later than three o'clock because the program was being sent live and the Telstar time was open only from 3:30 to 4. I had had to commandeer a taxi with a Time-Life sticker on the windshield, there being no free taxis or buses because of strikes. Breathless, I ran in at 3:10 to find that the other participants had not arrived. But the moderator, Bryan Magee, told me to take it easy. "We are going to tape it and send it by plane to London, so there's time now. You see," he said, raising one eyebrow, "the United States Government has preempted the Telstar, due to the Czech crisis. No one believes it, of course."

In a few minutes, Pierre Salinger and former ambassador to Poland John Gronouski arrived. They knew nothing of the preemption. Once again Bryan Magee said he did not believe the excuse for the preemption. Gronouski had no opinion, but he did not look happy. We proceeded to discuss the convention, the riots and Chicago, but someone had turned out our star just as someone had made it impossible for the TV people to shoot outside the International Amphitheater on simultaneous hookups.

Checking into this scandalous censorship, this heavenly blackout, I discovered later that it was not true. According to BBC in London, there had been no interruption in Telstar's availability. How and why Bryan Magee had been misinformed I do not know, but the interesting fact remains that he, Salinger, Ambassador Gronouski and I never questioned that the government had indeed tried to block this telecast. The point is, that I remember quite clearly a time when something like this would not have been credible. Now everything is possible, anything at all, and that is where we're at.

I left Chicago while the final session was going on. What the new candidate might or might not say seemed the last thing in the world to concern oneself about. And this, because the authority, the leadership was not in him. It was not in anyone whose face was visible in Chicago. It was in the president, and he was only an unseen presence whom no majority man on that platform dared contradict or too openly obey. I wondered who would eat the president's birthday cake, now that he had decided it was too dangerous to appear— in one of his own cities, and in his own convention. I stood in the airport with thirty or so other passengers waiting to board the plane, which, quite symbolically, had had to be replaced with another because of a faulty oil warning light. We waited an hour.

A long line of draftees appeared, kids in shirtsleeves, carrying valises, chattering like campers, walking five abreast down the corridor. A few Negro boys were scattered in among them, and as one Negro passed he turned to the watching passengers and called out, "We're off to defend your country. Your country!" And another Negro boy just behind him held out his hand: "Got some pennies, anybody?" The passengers said nothing, their faces registered nothing.

During our telecast, Ambassador Gronouski had said that Hubert Humphrey could not be blamed for what had happened in Chicago. Pierre Salinger said he could be, that he was the leader and could at least have dissociated himself from a riot of police. Ambassador Gronouski said Hubert Humphrey had a good rapport with youngsters. I said it was time to stop talking like this. Mrs. Humphrey had announced she was going to visit all the new youth-aid projects, including the Junior Chamber of Commerce. Where had these people been living? What had to happen before the powers realized they were not living in this time and in this place?

On the wide lawn behind my house at five o'clock in the morning the stars hung as bright and orderly as they had over Michigan Avenue. The sun rose on time. The morning paper said that a poll showed that the majority of Americans sympathized with the police. It was not a surprise. Not in the least. The voice that might have spoken both with authority, respectability, and confidence about the honest despair of a generation of Americans had never been heard in Chicago. Within a day I was being asked from London to organize a protest against the jailing of writers by the Russians in Prague. Prague, perhaps the freest city, the most hopeful and experimental in Eastern Europe, was being cleansed of the enemies of the people.

The Limited Hang-Out: The Dialogues
of Richard Nixon as a Drama
of the Antihero
1974

Let us begin with a few meaningless statements. The president is the chief law-enforcement officer of the United States. He also represents what is best in the American people, if not in his every action then certainly in his aims. These assertions were violated by Lyndon Johnson, John Kennedy, Dwight Eisenhower, and Franklin Roosevelt, not once but many times in each case. Johnson fabricated the Tonkin Gulf hysteria. Kennedy set the country on the rails into Vietnam even as he espoused humanistic idealism. Eisenhower lacked the stomach to scuttle Nixon despite his distaste, if not contempt, for Nixon's unprincipled behavior. Roosevelt tried to pack the Supreme Court when it opposed him and stood by watching the destruction of the Spanish republic by fascism because he feared the outrage of the Catholic hierarchy if he supported a sister democracy. And so on and on.

When necessity dictates, our laws are as bendable as licorice to our presidents, and if their private conversations had been taped an awful lot of history would be different now.

Yet Nixon stands alone, for he alone is without a touch of grace. It is gracelessness which gives his mendacity its shine of putrescence, a want of that magnanimity and joy in being alive that animated his predecessors. Reading the presidential transcripts, one is confronted with the decay of a language, of a legal system; in these pages what was possibly the world's best hope is reduced to a vaudeville, a laugh riot. We are in the presence of three gangsters who moralize and a swarming legion of their closely shaved underlings.

Let us, as the saying goes, be clear about it—more than forty appointed cohorts of Richard Nixon are already either in jail, under indictment, or on the threshold of jail for crimes which, as these transcripts demonstrate, the president tried by might and main to keep from being discovered. The chief law-enforcement officer could not find it in his heart to demand the resignation of even one of them for betraying the public trust. Those whom public clamor forced to depart were given sad presidential farewells and called "fine public servants."

This, to me, is the unexpectedly clear news in these transcripts— that, had he had the least civic, not to say moral, instinct, Richard Nixon could have been spared his agony. Had he known how to be forthright and, on discovering that the direction of the Watergate burglary came, in part, from his own official family, stood up and leveled with the public, he would have exalted his partisans and confounded his enemies, and, with a tremendous electoral victory in the offing, he would have held an undisputed national leadership. Nor is this as naïve as it appears; it seems believable that he need not have literally given the order to burgle Ellsberg's psychiatrist, was surprised by it, in fact. If, as also seems likely, he gave the nod to an intelligence operation against the Democrats at some previous meeting, it would not have been the first such strategy in political history, and he could have assumed the responsibility for that while disclaiming the illegal means for carrying it out. The nut of it all is that, even on the basis of self-survival, he marched instinctively down the crooked path.

So we are back with Plutarch, for whom character is fate, and in these transcripts Richard Nixon's character is our history. But to ask why he could not come forward and do his duty as the chief law-enforcement officer is to ask who and what Nixon is, and there is no one we can ask that question. All one can really affirm is that these transcripts show certain attributes which now are evidentiary. Like a good play these dialogues spring from conflict surrounding a paradox: his power as president depends on moral repute, at bottom; therefore, one would expect him to go after any of his associates who compromised him. Instead, something entirely different happens. He sits down with Haldeman and Ehrlichman and proceeds to concoct a double strategy: first, to convince the public that he was totally ignorant of the crimes, which is an intelligent decision; and, second, to make it appear that he is launching an outraged investigation of the facts in order to reveal them, when actually he is using his discoveries to keep his associates' infractions concealed. The latter objective is impossible and therefore stupid, and in short order he finds himself in possession of guilty knowledge, knowledge an honest man would have handed over to the requisite authorities. So the crux is always who and what he is. Another man need not have been swept away by events.

In the face of the sheer number of his appointees and their underlings who turn out to be unprincipled beyond the point of criminality, the issue is no longer whether he literally gave the orders for the burglary and the other crimes. The subordinates of another kind of man would have known that such despicable acts were intolerable to their patron and leader simply by their sense of his nature. That more than forty—thus far—are incriminated or in jail speaks of a consistency of their understanding of what this president was and what he stood for. Many of his staff members he barely knew personally, yet all of them obviously had caught the scent of that decay of standards emanating from the center, and they knew what was allowed and what was expected of them. The transcripts provide the evidence of the leader's nature, specifically his near delusionary notion that because he was "the president" he could not be doing what it was clear enough he was, in fact, doing.

At one point he and Haldeman and Ehrlichman are discussing the question of getting Mitchell to take the entire rap, thus drawing the lightning, but they suddenly remember John Dean's earlier warning that the two high assistants might well be indictable themselves.

NIXON: We did not cover up, though, that's what decides, that's what's [sic] decides . . . Dean's case is the question. And I do not consider him guilty . . . Because if he—if that's the case, then half the staff is guilty.
EHRLICHMAN: That's it. He's guilty of really no more except in degree.
NIXON: That's right. Then [sic] others.

EHRLICHMAN: Then [sic] a lot of . . .
NIXON: And frankly then [sic] I have been since a week ago, two weeks ago.

And a moment later, Ehrlichman returns to the bad smell:

EHRLICHMAN: But what's been bothering me is . . .
NIXON: That with knowledge, we're still not doing anything.

So he knew that he was, at a minimum, reaching for the forbidden fruit—obstruction of justice—since he was in possession of knowledge of a crime which he was not revealing to any authority. One has to ask why he did not stop right there. Is it possible that in the tapes he withheld (as of this writing) there was evidence that his surprise at the burglary was feigned? that, in short, he knew all along that he was protecting himself from prosecution? At this point there is no evidence of this, so we must wonder at other reasons for his so jeopardizing his very position, and we are back again with his character, his ideas and feelings.

There is a persistent note of plaintiveness when Nixon compares Watergate with the Democrats' crimes, attributing the press's outcry to liberal hypocrisy. The Democratic Party is primarily corrupt, a bunch of fakers spouting humane slogans while underneath the big city machines like Daley's steal elections, as Kennedy's victory was stolen from him in Chicago. Welfare, gimme-politics, perpetuate the Democratic constituency. The Kennedys especially are immoral, unfaithful to family, and ruthless in pursuit of power. Worse yet, they are the real professionals who *know* how to rule with every dirty trick in the book. A sort of embittered ideology helps lower Nixon into the pit.

For the Republicans, in contrast, are naïve and really amateurs at politics because they are basically decent, hardworking people. This conviction of living in the light is vital if one is to understand the monstrous distortions of ethical ideas in these transcripts. Nixon *is* decency. In fact, he is America; at one point after Dean has turned state's evidence against them, Haldeman even says, "He's not un-American and anti-Nixon." These men stand in a direct line from the Puritans of the first Plymouth Colony who could swindle and kill Indians secure in the knowledge that their cause was holy. Nixon seems to see himself as an outsider, even now, in politics. Underneath he is too good for it. When Dean, before his betrayal, tries to smuggle reality into the Oval Office—by warning that people are not going to believe that "Chapin acted on his own to put his old friend Segretti to be a Dick Tuck on somebody else's campaign. They would have to paint it into something more sinister . . . part of a general [White House] plan"—Nixon observes with a certain mixture of condemnation and plain envy, "Shows you what a master Dick Tuck is."

This ideology, like all ideologies, is a pearl formed around an irritating grain of sand, which, for Nixon, is something he calls the Establishment, meaning Eastern Old Money. "The basic thing," he says, "is the Establishment. The Establishment is dying and so they've got to show that . . . it is just wrong [the Watergate] just because of this." So there is a certain virtue in defending now what the mere duty he swore to uphold requires he root out. In a diabolical sense he seems to see himself clinging to a truth which, only for the moment, appears nearly criminal. But the *real* untruth, the real immorality shows up in his mind very quickly—it is Kennedy, and he is wondering if they can't put out some dirt on Chappaquiddick through an investigator they had working up there. But like every other such counterattack this one falls apart because it could lead back to Kalmbach's paying this investigator with campaign funds, an illegal usage. So the minuet starts up and stops time after time, a thrust blunted by the realization that it can only throw light upon what must be kept in the dark. Yet their conviction of innocent and righteous intentions stands undisturbed by their knowledge of their own vulnerability.

And it helps to explain, this innocence and righteousness, why they so failed to appraise reality, in particular that they were *continuing* to act in obstruction of justice by concealing what they knew and what they knew they knew and what they told one another they knew. It is not dissimilar to Johnson's persistence in Vietnam despite every evidence that the war was unjust and barbarous, for Good People do not commit crimes, and there is simply no way around that.

Yet from time to time Nixon senses that he is floating inside his own psyche. "If we could get a feel," he says, "I just have a horrible feeling that we may react . . . "

HALDEMAN: Yes. That we are way overdramatizing.

NIXON: That's my view. That's what I don't want to do either. [A moment later] Am I right that we have got to do something to restore the credibility of the Presidency?

And on the verge of reality the ideology looms, and they scuttle back into the hole—Haldeman saying, "Of course you know the credibility gap in the old [Democratic] days." So there they are, comfortably right again, the only problem being how to prove it to the simpletons outside.

Again, like any good play, the transcripts reflect a single situation or paradox appearing in a variety of disguises that gradually peel away the extraneous until the central issue is naked. In earlier pages they are merely worried about bad publicity, then it is the criminal indictment of one or another of the secondary cadres of the administration, until finally the heart of darkness is endangered, Haldeman and Ehrlichman and thus Nixon himself. In other words, the mistake called Watergate, an incident they originally view as uncharacteristic of them, a caper, a worm that fell on their shoulders, turns out to be one of the worms inside them that crawled out.

So the aspects of Nixon which success had once obscured now become painfully parodistic in his disaster. He almost becomes a pathetically moving figure as he lifts his old slogans out of his bag. He knows now that former loyalists are testifying secretly to the grand jury, so he erects the facade of his own "investigation," which is nothing but an attempt to find out what they are testifying to, the better to prepare himself for the next explosion; he reverts time and again to recalling his inquisitorial aptitude in the Hiss case, which made him a national figure. But now he is on the other end of the stick, and, after a string of calculations designed to cripple the Ervin committee, he declaims, "I mean, after all, it is my job and I don't want the Presidency tarnished, but also I am a law-enforcement man," even as he is trying to lay the whole thing off on Mitchell, the very symbol of hard-line law enforcement, the former attorney general himself.

Things degenerate into farce at times, as when he knows the Ervin committee and the grand jury are obviously out of his control and on the way to eating him up, and he speaks of making a "command decision." It is a sheer unconscious dullness of a magnitude worthy of Ring Lardner's baseball heroes. There are scenes, indeed, which no playwright would risk for fear of seeming too mawkishly partisan.

For example, the idea comes to Nixon repeatedly that he must act with candor, simply, persuasively. Now, since John Dean has been up to his neck in the details of the various attempts to first discover and then hide the truth, should Dean be permitted by the president to appear before a grand jury, eminently qualified as he is as the knower of facts? The president proceeds to spitball a public announcement before Ehrlichman's and Ziegler's sharp judgmental minds:

> NIXON: Mr. Dean certainly wants the opportunity to defend himself against these charges. He would welcome the opportunity and what we have to do is to work out a procedure which will allow him to do so consistent with his unique position of being a top member of the President's staff but also the Counsel. There is a lawyer, Counsel . . . [it starts breaking down] not lawyer, Counsel—but the responsibility of the Counsel for confidentiality.
> ZIEGLER: Could you apply that to the grand jury?
> EHRLICHMAN: Absolutely. The grand jury is one of those occasions where a man in his situation can defend himself.
> NIXON: Yes. The grand jury. Actually, if called, we are not going to refuse for anybody called before the grand jury to go, are we, John?
> EHRLICHMAN: I can't imagine (unintelligible).
> NIXON: Well, if called, he will be cooperative, consistent with his responsibilities as Counsel. How do we say that?
> EHRLICHMAN: He will cooperate.
> NIXON: He will fully cooperate.
> EHRLICHMAN: Better check that with Dean. I know he's got certain misgivings on this.
> ZIEGLER: He did this morning.
> NIXON: Yeah. Well, then, don't say that.

Refusing himself his tragedy, Nixon ends in farce. After another of many attempts at appearing "forthcoming" and being thwarted yet again by all the culpability in the house, he suddenly exclaims, "What the hell does one disclose that isn't going to blow something?" Thus speaketh the first law-enforcement officer of the United States. Excepting that this government is being morally gutted on every page, it is to laugh. And the humor of their own absurdity is not always lost on the crew, although it is understandably laced with pain. They debate whether John Mitchell might be sent into the Ervin committee but in an executive session barred to the public and TV and under ground rules soft enough to tie up the Old Constitutionalist in crippling legalisms.

NIXON: Do you think we want to go this route now? Let it hang out so to speak?
DEAN: Well, it isn't really that . . .
HALDEMAN: It's a limited hang-out.
DEAN: It is a limited hang-out. It's not an absolute hang-out.
NIXON: But some of the questions look big hanging out publicly or privately. [Still, he presses the possibility.] If it opens doors, it opens doors . . .

As usual it is Haldeman who is left to interpolate the consequences.

HALDEMAN: John says he is sorry he sent those burglars in there—and that helps a lot.
NIXON: That's right.
EHRLICHMAN: You are very welcome, sir.

(Laughter), the script reads then, and along with everything else it adds to the puzzle of why Nixon ordered his office bugged in the first place, and especially why he did not turn off the machine once the magnitude of Watergate was clear to him. After all, no one but he and the technicians in the secret service knew the spools were turning.

As a nonsubscriber to the school of psychohistory—having myself served as the screen upon which Norman Mailer, no less, projected the lesions of his own psyche, to which he gave my name—I would disclaim the slightest inside knowledge, if that be necessary, and rest simply on the public importance of this question itself. Watergate aside, it is a very odd thing for a man to bug himself. Perhaps the enormity of it is better felt if one realizes that in a preelectronic age a live stenographer would have had to sit concealed in Nixon's office as he exchanged affections with a Haldeman, whom he admired and whose fierce loyalty moved him deeply. At a minimum, does it not speak a certain contempt even for those he loved to have subjected his relationship with them to such recorded scrutiny? Can he ever have forgotten that the record was being made as count would show he has more broken speeches by far than anyone in those pages. He is almost never addressed as "Mr. President," or even as "sir," except by Henry Petersen, whose sense of protocol and respect, like—remarkably enough—John Mitchell's stands in glaring contrast to the locker-room familiarity of his two chief lieutenants. He can hardly ever assert a policy idea without ending with, "Am I right?" or, "You think so?" It is not accidental that both Ehrlichman and Haldeman, like Colson, were so emphatically rough and, in some reports, brutal characters. They were his devils and he their god, but a god because the Good inhabits him while they partake of it but are his mortal side and must sometimes reach into the unclean.

To turn off the tapes, then, when an elementary sense of survival would seem to dictate their interruption, would be to make an admission which, if it were made, would threaten his very psychic existence and bring on the great dread against which his character was formed—namely, that he is perhaps fraudulent, perhaps a fundamentally fearing man, perhaps not really enlisted in the cause of righteousness but merely in his own aggrandizement of power, and power for the purpose not of creativity and good but of filling the void where spontaneity and love should be. Nixon will not admit his share of evil in himself, and so the tapes must go on turning, for the moment he presses that STOP button he ends the godly illusion and must face his human self. He can record his own open awareness that he and his two bravos are quite possibly committing crime in the sun-filled, pristine White House itself, but as long as the tapes turn, a part of him is intrepidly recording the bald facts, as God does, and thereby bringing the day of judgment closer, the very judgment he has abhorred and dearly wants. For the hope of being justified at the very, very end is a fierce hope, as is the fear of being destroyed for the sins whose revelation and admission will alone crown an evaded, agonized life with meaning. The man aspires to the heroic. No one, not even his worst enemies, can deny his strength, his resiliency. But it is not the strength of the confronter, as is evidenced by his inability to level with John Mitchell, whom he privately wants to throw to the wolves but face to face cannot blame. It is rather the perverse strength of the private hero testing his presumptions about himself against God, storming an entrance into his wished-for nature which never seems to embrace him but is always an arm's length away. Were he alive to a real authority in him, a true weight of his own existing, such a testing would never occur to him. There are leaders who take power because they have found themselves, and there are leaders who take power in search of themselves. A score of times in those pages Nixon refers to "the President" as though he were the president's emissary, a doppelgänger. Excepting in official documents did Roosevelt, Eisenhower, Kennedy, even Truman, so refer to himself? Surely not in private conversation with their closest friends. But to stop those tapes would mean the end of innocence, and in a most cruelly ironic way, an act of true forthrightness.

If such was his drama, he forged the sword that cut him down. It was a heroic struggle except that it lacked the ultimate courage of self-judgment and the reward of insight. Bereft of the latter, he is unjust to himself and shows the world his worst while his best he buries under his pride and the losing hope that a resurrected public cynicism will rescue his repute. For it is not enough now, the old ideology that the Democrats are even more corrupt. The president is not a Democrat or Republican here, he is as close as we get to God.

And if his struggle was indeed to imprint his best presumptions upon history, and it betrayed him, it is a marvel that it took place now, when America has discovered the rocky terrain where her innocence is no more, where God is simply what happens and what has happened, and if you like being called good you have to do good, if only because other nations are no longer powerlessly inert but looking on with X-ray eyes, and you no longer prevail for the yellow in your silky hair. The most uptight leader we have had, adamantly resisting the age, has backhandedly announced the theme of its essential drama in his struggle—to achieve authenticity without paying authenticity's price—and in his fall. The hangout—it is a marvel, is unlimited; at long last, after much travail, Richard Nixon is one of us.

American Playhouse:
On Politics and the Art of Acting
2001

Here are some observations about politicians as actors. Since some of my best friends are actors, I don't dare say anything bad about the art itself. The fact is that acting is inevitable as soon as we walk out our front doors and into society. I am acting now; certainly I am not using the same tone as I would in my living room. It is not news that we are moved more by our glandular reactions to a leader's personality, his acting, than by his proposals or by his moral character. To their millions of followers, after all, many of them highly regarded university intellectuals, Hitler and Stalin were profoundly moral men, revealers of new truths. Aristotle thought man was by nature a social animal, and indeed we are ruled more by the social arts, the arts of performance—by acting, in other words—than anybody wants to think about for very long.

In our own time television has created a quantitative change in all this; one of the oddest things about millions of lives now is that ordinary individuals, as never before in human history, are so surrounded by acting. Twenty-four hours a day everything seen on the tube is either acted or conducted by actors in the shape of news anchormen and -women, including their hairdos. It may be that the most impressionable form of experience now for many if not most people consists in their emotional transactions with actors, which happen far more of the time than with real people. In the past, a person might have confronted the arts of performance once a year in a church ceremony or in a rare appearance by a costumed prince or king and his ritualistic gestures; it would have seemed a very strange idea that ordinary folk would be so subjected every day to the persuasions of professionals whose studied technique, after all, was to assume the character of someone else.

Is this persistent experience of any importance? I can't imagine how to prove this, but it seems to me that when one is surrounded by such a roiling mass of consciously contrived performances it gets harder and harder to locate reality anymore. Admittedly, we live in an age of entertainment, but is it a good thing that our political life, for one, be so profoundly governed by the modes of theater, from tragedy to vaudeville to farce? I find myself speculating whether the relentless daily diet of crafted, acted emotions and canned ideas is not subtly pressing our brains not only to mistake fantasy for what is real but to absorb this falseness into our personal sensory process. This last election is an example. Apparently we are now called upon to act as though nothing very unusual happened and as though nothing in our democratic process has deteriorated, including our claim to the right to instruct lesser countries on how to conduct fair elections. So, in a subtle way, we are induced to become actors, too. The show, after all, must go on, even if the audience is obligated to join in the acting.

Political leaders everywhere have come to understand that to govern they must learn how to act. No differently than any actor, Al Gore went through several changes of costume before finding the right mix to express the personality he wished to project. Up to the campaign he seemed an essentially serious type with no great claim to humor, but the presidential-type character he had chosen to play was apparently happy, upbeat, with a kind of Bing Crosby mellowness. I daresay that if he seemed so awkward it was partly because he had cast himself in a role that was wrong for him. As for George W. Bush, now that he is president he seems to have learned not to sneer quite so much, and to cease furtively glancing left and right when leading up to a punch line, followed by a sharp nod to flash that he has successfully delivered it. This is bad acting, because all the dire overemphasis casts doubt on the text. Obviously, as the sparkly magic veil of actual power has descended upon him, he has become more relaxed and confident, like an actor after he has had some hit reviews and knows the show is in for a run.

At this point I suppose I should add something about my own bias. I recall the day, back in the fifties, during Eisenhower's campaign against Adlai Stevenson, when I turned on my television and saw the general who had led the greatest invasion force in history lying back under the hands of a professional makeup woman preparing him for his TV appearance. I was far more naive then, and so I still found it hard to believe that henceforth we were to be wooed and won by rouge, lipstick, and powder rather than ideas and positions on public issues. It was almost as though he were getting ready to assume the role of General Eisenhower instead of simply *being* him. In politics, of course, what you see is rarely what you get, but Eisenhower was not actually a good actor, especially when he ad-libbed, disserving himself as a nearly comical bumbler with the English language when in fact he was a lot more literate and sophisticated than his public-speaking style suggested. As his biographer, a *Life* editor named Emmet John Hughes, once told me, Eisenhower, when he was still a junior officer, was the author of those smoothly liquid, rather Roman-style speeches that had made his boss, Douglas MacArthur, so famous. Then again, I wonder if Eisenhower's syntactical stumbling in public made him seem more convincingly sincere.

Watching some of our leaders on TV has made me wonder if we really have any idea what is involved in the actor's art, and I recall again a story once told me by my old friend the late Robert Lewis, director of a number of beautiful Broadway productions, including the original *Brigadoon*. Starting out as an actor in the late twenties, Bobby had been the assistant and dresser of Jacob Ben-Ami, a star in Europe and in New York as well. Ben-Ami, an extraordinary actor, was in a Yiddish play, but despite the language and the location of the theater far from Times Square, on the Lower East Side of Manhattan, one of its scenes had turned it into a substantial hit with English-speaking audiences. Experiencing that scene had become the in thing to do in New York. People who had never dreamed of seeing a Yiddish play traveled downtown to watch this one scene, and then left. In it Ben-Ami stood at the edge of the stage staring into space and, with tremendous tension, brought a revolver to his head. Seconds passed, whole minutes. Some in the audience shut their eyes or turned away, certain the shot was coming at any instant. Ben-Ami clenched his jaws. Sweat broke out on his face. His eyes seemed about to pop out of his head; his hands trembled as he strove to will himself to suicide. More moments passed. People in the audience were gasping for breath and making strange asphyxiated noises. Finally, standing on his toes now as though to leap into the unknown, Ben-Ami dropped the gun and cried out, "Ikh ken nit!" I can't do it! Night after night he brought the house down; Ben-Ami somehow compelled the audience to suspend its disbelief and to imagine his brains splattered all over the stage.

Lewis, aspiring young actor that he was, begged Ben-Ami to tell him the secret of how he created this emotional reality, but the actor kept putting him off, saying he would tell him only after the final performance. "It's better for people not to know," he said, "or it'll spoil the show."

Then at last the final performance came, and at its end Ben-Ami sat in his dressing room with the young Lewis.

"You promised to tell me," Lewis said.

"All right. I'll tell you. My problem with this scene," Ben-Ami explained, "was that I personally could never blow my brains out. I am just not suicidal, and I can't imagine ending my life. So I could never really know how that man was feeling, and I could never play such a person authentically. For weeks I went around trying to think of some parallel in my own life that I could draw on. What situation could I be in where, first of all, I am standing up, I am alone, I am looking straight ahead, and something I feel I must do is making me absolutely terrified, and finally that whatever it is I can't do it?"

"Yes," Lewis said, hungry for this great actor's key to greatness. "And what is that?"

"Well," Ben-Ami said, "I finally realized that the one thing I hate worse than anything is washing in cold water. So what I'm really doing with that gun to my head is, I'm trying to get myself to step into an ice-cold shower."

Now, if we translate this situation to political campaigns, who are we really voting for? The self-possessed character who projects dignity, exemplary morals, and enough forthright courage to lead us through war or depression, or the person who is simply good at creating a counterfeit with the help of professional coaching,

executive tailoring, and that whole armory of pretense that the
groomed president can now employ? Are we allowed anymore to
know what is going on not merely in the candidate's facial expression and his choice of suit but also in his head? Unfortunately, as
with Ben-Ami, this is something we are not told until the audition-
ing ends and he is securely in office. After spending tens of millions
of dollars, neither candidate—at least for me—ever managed to
create that unmistakable click of recognition as to who he really
was. But maybe this is asking too much. As with most actors, any
resemblance between the man and the role is purely accidental.

The Stanislavsky system came into vogue at the dawn of the twentieth century, when science was recognized as the dominating force
of the age. Objective scientific analysis promised to open everything to human control, and the Stanislavsky method was an
attempt to systematize the actor's vagrant search for authenticity as
he works to portray a character different from his own. Politicians
do something similar all the time; by assuming personalities not
genuinely theirs—let's say six-pack, lunchbox types—they hope to
connect with ordinary Americans. The difficulty for Bush and
Gore in their attempts to seem like regular fellas was that both
were scions of successful and powerful families. Worse yet for their
regular-fella personae, both were in effect created by the culture of
Washington, D.C., and you can't hope to be president without running against Washington. The problem for Gore was that Washington meant Clinton, whom he dared not acknowledge lest he be
challenged on moral grounds. As for Bush, he was forced to imper-
sonate an outsider pitching against dependency on the federal government, whose payroll, however, had helped feed two generations
of his family. There's a name for this sort of cannonading of Washington; it is called acting. To some important degree both gentlemen had to act themselves out of their real personae into freshly
begotten ones. The reality, of course, was that the closest thing on
the political stage to a man of the people was Clinton the Unclean,
the real goods with the six-pack background, whom it was both
dangerous and necessary to disown. This took a monstrous amount
of acting.

It was in the so-called debates that the sense of a contrived performance rather than a naked clash of personalities and ideas came to a sort of head. Here was acting, acting with a vengeance. But the consensus seems to have called the performances decidedly boring. And how could it be otherwise when both men seemed to be attempting to display the same genial temperament, a readiness to perform the same role and, in effect, to climb into the same warm suit? The role, of course, was that of the nice guy, Bing Crosby with a sprinkling of Bob Hope. Clearly they had both been coached not to threaten the audience with too much passion but rather to reassure that if elected they would not disturb any reasonable person's sleep. In acting terms there was no inner reality, no genuineness, no glimpse into their unruly souls. One remarkable thing did happen, though—a single, split-second shot that revealed Gore shaking his head in helpless disbelief at some inanity Bush had spoken. Significantly, this gesture earned him many bad reviews for what were called his superior airs, his sneering disrespect; in short, he had stepped out of costume and revealed his reality. This, in effect, was condemned as a failure of acting. In the American press, which is made up of disguised theater critics, substance counts for next to nothing compared with style and inventive characterization. For a millisecond Gore had been inept enough to have gotten real! And this clown wanted to be *president* yet! Not only is all the world a stage but we have all but obliterated the fine line between the feigned and the real.

Was there ever such a border? It is hard to know, but we might try to visualize the Lincoln-Douglas debates before the Civil War, when thousands would stand, spread out across some pasture, to listen to the two speakers, who were mounted on stumps so they could be seen from far off. There certainly was no makeup; neither man had a speechwriter but, incredibly enough, made it all up himself. Years later, Lincoln supposedly wrote the Gettysburg Address on scraps of paper while en route to a memorial ceremony. Is it imaginable that any of our candidates could have such conviction and, more importantly, such self-assured candor as to pour out his heart this way? To be sure, Lincoln and Douglas were civil, at least in the record of their remarks, but their attack on each other's ideas was sharp and thorough, revealing of their actual approaches to the nation's problems. As for their styles, they had to have been very different than the current laid-back cool before the lens. The lens magnifies everything: one slight lift of an eyelid and you look like you're glaring. If there is a single, basic requirement for success on television it is minimalization: whatever you are doing, do less of it and emit cool. In other words—act. In contrast, speakers facing hundreds of people without a microphone and in the open air must inevitably have been broader in gesture and even more emphatic in speech than in life. Likewise, their use of language had to be more pointed and precise in order to carry their points out to the edges of the crowd. And no makeup artist stood waiting to wipe up every bead of sweat on a speaker's lip; the candidates were stripped to their shirtsleeves in the summer heat, and people nearby could no doubt smell them. There may, in short, have been some aspect of human reality in such a debate.

Given the camera's tendency to exaggerate any movement, it may in itself have a dampening effect on spontaneity and conflict. There were times in this last campaign when one even wondered whether the candidates feared that to raise issues and engage in a genuine clash before the camera might set fire to some of the more flammable public. They chose instead to forgo the telling scowl or the passionate outburst in favor of that which ran less risk of a social conflagration: benign smiles on a glass screen.

No differently than with actors, the single most important characteristic a politician needs to display is relaxed sincerity. Ronald Reagan disarmed his opponents by never showing the slightest sign of inner conflict about the truth of what he was saying. Simpleminded as his critics found his ideas and remarks, cynical and manipulative as he may have been in actuality, he seemed to believe every word he said. He could tell you that atmospheric pollution came from trees, or that ketchup was a vegetable in school lunches, or leave the impression that he had seen action in World War II rather than in a movie he had made or perhaps only seen, and if you didn't believe these things you were still kind of amused by how sincerely he said them. Sincerity implies honesty, an absence of moral conflict in the mind of its possessor. Of course, this can also indicate insensitivity or even stupidity. It is hard, for example, to think of another American official whose reputation would not have been stained by saluting a cemetery of Nazi dead with heart-felt solemnity while barely mentioning the many millions, including Americans, who were victims of that vile regime. But Reagan was not only an actor; he loved acting, and it can be said that at least in public he not only acted all the time but did so sincerely. The second best actor is Clinton, who does occasionally seem to blush, but then again he was caught in an illicit sexual act, which is far more important than illegally shipping weapons to foreign countries. Reagan's tendency to confuse events in films with things that really happened is often seen as intellectual weakness, but in reality it was—unknowingly, of course—a Stanislavskian triumph, the very consummation of the actor's ability to incorporate reality into the fantasy of his role. In Reagan the dividing line between acting and actuality was simply melted, gone. Human beings, as the poet said, cannot bear very much reality, and the art of politics is our best proof. The trouble is that a leader comes to symbolize his country, and so the nagging question is whether, when real trouble comes, we can act ourselves out of it.

The first obligation of the actor, just as with the politician, is to get himself known. P. T. Barnum said it for all time when a reporter asked if he wasn't ashamed at having tricked the public. He had originated the freak show, which had drawn an immense audience to his Bridgeport, Connecticut, barn to see the bearded lady and the two-headed calf. But the show was such a great hit that his problem was how to get people to leave and make room for new customers. His solution was to put up a sign, with an arrow pointing to the door, that read, "This way to the Egress." Since nobody had ever seen an "egress" before, the place emptied satisfactorily, and the audience found itself in the street. The reporter asked if this ploy wouldn't anger people and ruin his reputation. Barnum gave his historic reply: "I don't care what they write about me as long as they spell my name right." If there is a single rubric to express the most basic requirement for political or theatrical success, this is it.

Whether he admits it or not, the actor wants not only to be believed and admired but to be loved, and what may help to account for the dullness of this last campaign was the absence of affection for either man, not to speak of love. By the end it seemed like an unpopularity contest, a competition for who was less disliked by more people than the other, a demonstration of negative consent. Put another way, in theatrical terms these were character actors but not fascinating stars. Ironically, the exception to all this lovelessness was Nader, whose people, at least on television, did seem to adore their leader, even after he had managed to help wreck Gore and elect Bush, whom they certainly despised far more than they did Gore. At this point I ought to confess that I have known only one president whom I feel confident about calling "the President of the United States," and that was Franklin Roosevelt. My impulse is to say that he alone was not an actor, but I probably think that because he was such a good one. He could not stand on his legs, after all, but he took care never to exhibit weakness by appearing in his wheelchair, or in any mood but that of upbeat, cheery optimism, which at times he certainly did not feel. Roosevelt was so genuine a star, his presence so overwhelming, that Republicans, consciously or not, have never stopped running against him for this whole half-century.

The mystery of the star performer can only leave the inquiring mind confused, resentful, or blank, something that, of course, has the greatest political importance. Many Republicans have blamed the press for the attention Bill Clinton continued to get even out of office. Again, what they don't understand is that what a star says, and even what he does, is incidental to people's interest in him. When the click of empathic association is made with a leader, logic has very little to do with it and virtue even less. Obviously, this is not very encouraging news for rational people who hope to uplift society by reasoned argument. But then, not many of us rational folk are immune to the star's ability to rule.

The presidency, in acting terms, is a heroic role. It is not one for comedians, sleek lover types, or second bananas. To be credible, the man who acts as president must hold in himself an element of potential danger. Something similar is required in a real star.

Like most people, I had never even heard of Marlon Brando the first time I saw him onstage not long after the end of World War II. The play was *Truckline Cafe*, a failed work by Maxwell Anderson that was soon to close, hardly a promising debut for an ambitious actor. The set is a shabby café on some country highway. It is after midnight, the place miserably lit and empty. There is a counter and a few booths with worn upholstery. A car is heard stopping outside. Presently, a young man wearing a worn-leather jacket and a cap strolls in, an exhausted-looking girl behind him. He saunters down to center stage, looking around for a sign of life. For a long time he says absolutely nothing, just stands there in the sort of slouch you fall into after driving for hours. The moment lengthens as he tries to figure out what to do, his patience clearly thinning. Nothing has happened, he has hardly even moved, but watching him, the audience, myself included, is already spellbound. Another actor would simply have aroused impatience, but we are in Brando's power; we read him; his being is speaking to us even if we can't make out precisely what it is saying. It is something like an animal that has slipped from its cage. Is he dangerous? Friendly? Stupid? Intelligent? Without a word spoken, this actor has opened up in the audience a whole range of emotional possibilities, including, oddly enough, a little fear. Finally he calls out, "Anybody here?!" What a relief! He has not shot up the place. He has not thrown chairs around. All he wanted, apparently, was a sandwich.

I can't explain how Brando, wordlessly, did what he did, but he had found a way, no doubt instinctively, to master a paradox—he had implicitly threatened us and then given us pardon. Here was Napoleon, here was Caesar, here was Roosevelt. Brando had not asked the members of the audience merely to love him; that is only charm. He had made them wish that he would deign to love *them*. That is a star. That is power, no different in its essence than the power that can lead nations.

Onstage or in the White House, power changes everything, even how the aspirant looks after he wins. I remember running into Dustin Hoffman on a rainy New York street some years ago; he had only a month earlier played the part of the Lomans' pale and nervous next-door neighbor, Bernard, in a recording session with Lee Cobb of *Death of a Salesman*. Now as he approached, counting the cracks in the sidewalk, hatless, his wet hair dripping, a worn coat collar turned up, I prepared to greet him, thinking that with his bad skin, hawkish nose, and adenoidal voice some brave friend really ought to tell him to go into another line of work. As compassionately as possible I asked what he was doing now, and with a rather apologetic sigh he said, after several sniffles, "Well, they want me for a movie." "Oh?" I felt relieved that he was not about to collapse in front of me in a fit of depression. "What's the movie?"

"It's called *The Graduate*," he said.

"Good part?"

"Well, yeah, I guess it's the lead."

In no time at all this half-drowned puppy would have millions of people at his feet all over the world. And once having ascended to power, so to speak, it became hard even for me to remember him when he was real. Not that he wasn't real, just that he was real plus. And the plus is the mystery of the patina, the glow that power paints on the elected human being.

The amount of acting required of both President Bush and the Democrats is awesome now, given the fractured election and donation by the Supreme Court. Practically no participant in the whole process can really say out loud what is in his heart. They are all facing an ice-cold shower with a gun to their head. Bush has to act as though he were elected, the Supreme Court has to act as though it were the Supreme Court, Gore has to act as though he is practically overjoyed at his own defeat, and so on. Unfortunately, such roles generally require hard work ahead of time, and the closest thing I've seen so far to deliberately rehearsed passion was the organized mob of Republicans banging threateningly on the door of a Florida vote-counting office and howling for the officials inside to stop counting. I must confess, though, that as a playwright I would be flummoxed as to how to make plausible on the stage an organized stampede of partisans yelling to stop the count and in the same breath accusing the other side of trying to steal the election. I can't imagine an audience taking this for anything but a satirical farce.

An election, not unlike a classic play, has a certain strict form that requires us to pass through certain ordained steps toward a logical conclusion. When, instead, the form dissolves and chaos reigns, the audience is left feeling cheated and even mocked. After this last, most hallucinatory of elections, it was said that in the end the system worked, when clearly it hadn't at all. And one of the signs that it had collapsed popped up even before the decision was finally made in Bush's favor; it was when Dick Armey, the Republican majority leader in the House of Representatives, declared that he would simply not attend the inauguration if Gore were elected, despite immemorial custom and his clear obligation to do so. In short, Armey had reached the limits of his actor's imagination and could only collapse into playing himself. You cannot have a major performer deciding, in the middle of a play, to leave the scene without utterly destroying the whole illusion. For the system to be said to have worked, no one is allowed to stop acting.

The play without a character we can really root for is in trouble. Shakespeare's *Coriolanus* is an example. It is not often produced, powerful though it is as playwriting and poetry, no doubt because, as a totally honest picture of ambition in a frightening human being, the closest the play ever gets to love is Coriolanus' subservience to his mother. In short, it is a truthful play without sentimentality, and truthfulness, I'm afraid, doesn't sell a whole lot of tickets or draw votes. Which inevitably brings me again to Clinton. Until the revulsion brought on by the pardon scandal, he was leaving office with the highest rating for performance and the lowest for personal character. People had prospered under his leadership, and, with whatever reluctance, they still connected with his humanity as they glimpsed it, ironically enough, through his sins. We are back, I think, to the mystery of the star. Clinton, except for those few minutes when lying about Monica Lewinsky, was relaxed on camera in a way any actor would envy. And relaxation is the soul of the art, because it arouses receptivity rather than defensiveness in an audience.

That receptivity brings to mind a friend of mine who, many years ago, won the prize for selling more Electrolux vacuum cleaners in the Bronx than any other door-to-door salesman. He once explained how he did it: "You want them to start saying yes. So you ask questions that they can't say no to. Is this 1350 Jerome Avenue? Yes. Is your name Smith? Yes. Do you have carpets? Yes. A vacuum cleaner? Yes. Once you've got them on a yes roll, a kind of psychological fusion takes place. You're both on the same side. It's almost like some kind of love, and they feel it's impolite for them to

say no, and in no time you're in the house unpacking the machine."
What Clinton projects is a personal interest in the customer that
comes across as a sort of love. There can be no doubt that, like all
great performers, he loves to act, he is most alive when he's on. His
love of acting may be his most authentic emotion, the realest thing
about him, and, as with Reagan, there is no dividing line between
his performance and himself—he is his performance. There is no
greater contrast than with Gore or Bush, both of whom projected a
kind of embarrassment at having to perform, an underlying tension
between themselves and the role, and tension, needless to say, shuts
down love on the platform no less than it does in bed.

On every side there is a certain amount of lamenting about the
reluctance of Americans to condemn Bill Clinton, but rather than
blaming our failed moral judgment I think we would do better to
examine his acting. Clinton is our Eulenspiegel, the mythical arch
prankster of fourteenth-century Germany who was a sort of mis-
chievous and lovable folk spirit, half child, half man. Eulenspiegel
challenged society with his enviable guile and a charm so irresist-
ible that he could blurt out embarrassing truths about the powerful
on behalf of the ordinary man. His closest American equivalent is
Brer Rabbit, who ravishes people's vegetable gardens and, just
when he seems to be cornered, charmingly distracts his pursuer
with some outrageously engaging story while edging closer and
closer to a hole down which he escapes. Appropriately enough, the
word "Eulenspiegel" is a sort of German joke: it means a mirror
put before an owl, and since an owl is blind in daylight it cannot
see its own reflection. As bright and happy and hilariously unpredictable as Eulenspiegel is, he cannot see himself, and so, among
other things, he is dangerous. In other words, a star. Indeed, the
perfect model of both star and political leader is that smiling and
implicitly dangerous man who likes you.

In part because Gore and Bush were not threatening, their offer of
protective affection was not considered important. Gore was so
busy trying to unbend that he forfeited whatever menace he may
have had. Bush did his best to pump up his chest and toughly turn
down the corners of his mouth, but it was all too obviously a performance, and for too long his opponents failed to take him as

anything more than the potential president of a fraternity. Risking immodesty, to say the least, he actually referred to himself as a "leader" and claimed that his forthcoming administration would fill the vacuum of "leadership." Caught time after time fouling up his syntax, thus shaking the image of manly command, he has improved since real power has descended upon him, and his sentences, saving on grammar, have gotten shorter and shorter—to the point where, at times, he comes close to sounding like a gunslinger in a Clint Eastwood film. He is, though, beginning to relax into his role and, like most presidents, may in the fullness of time come to seem inevitable.

The ultimate foundation of political power, of course, has never changed: it is the leader's willingness to resort to violence should the need arise. Adlai Stevenson may have seemed too civilized to resort to violence without a crippling hesitation, and Jimmy Carter was so clearly restrained by Christian scruple that a single military accident involving a handful of unfortunate soldiers destroyed all his credibility in one stroke. An American leader may deliver the Sunday lesson provided his sword is never out of reach, the two best examples being FDR and John Kennedy. But this type, which doesn't come along every day, is the aristocratic populist, and the aristocrat learns how to act at a very early age; it is part of his upbringing. A Nixon, on the contrary, has to learn as he goes along. Indeed, once he had ordered himself bugged, Nixon was acting during all his waking hours; his entire working life became a recorded performance.

The case of President Truman and the atom bomb is particularly rich in its references to acting and power. When several of the scientists who had built the first bomb petitioned Truman to stage a demonstration off the Japanese coast rather than dropping it on an inhabited city, he chose the latter course; the fear was that the first bomb might fail to work, encouraging the Japanese to refuse peace overtures even more resolutely. However frightful the consequences, it was better to bomb a city and in one flash bring the war to an end. The weakness in this reasoning is that if the bomb was so uncertain to explode, why drop it on a city, where Japanese scientists might examine and maybe even copy it? A more persuasive argument, I'm afraid, is that if the Japanese had been warned to expect a demonstration of a terrible new weapon, and it had been a dud, a dead iron ball splashing into the sea, Truman's unwillingness to kill would have threatened his leadership, and he, personally and symbolically, would have lost credibility. I'm not at all sure what I would have done in his position, confronted with the possibility of terrible American losses in a land invasion of Japan. But the issue is not Truman so much as the manifestations of power that people require their leaders to act out. Jesus Christ could not have beaten Hitler's Germany or Imperial Japan into surrender. And it is not impossible that our main reason for cloaking our leaders with a certain magical, extra-human, theatrical aura is to help disguise one of the basic conditions of their employment—namely, a readiness to kill for us.

Whether for good or for evil, it is sadly inevitable that all political leadership requires the artifices of theatrical illusion. In the politics of a democracy the shortest distance between two points is often a crooked line. While Roosevelt was stoutly repeating his determination to keep America out of any foreign war, he was taking steps toward belligerency in order to save England and prevent a Nazi victory. In effect, mankind is in debt to his lies. So from the tragic necessity of dissimulation there seems to be no escape. Except, of course, to tell people the truth, something that doesn't require acting but may damage one's own party and, in certain circumstances, the human enterprise itself. Then what?

Then, I'm afraid, we can only turn to the release of art, to the other theater, the theater-theater, where you can tell the truth without killing anybody and may even illuminate the awesomely durable dilemma of how to lead without lying too much. The release of art will not forge a cannon or pave a street, but it may remind us again and again of the corruptive essence of power, its tendency to enhance itself at the expense of humanity. The late director and critic Harold Clurman called theater "lies like truth." Theater does indeed lie, fabricating everything from the storm's roar to the lark's song, from the actor's laughter to his nightly flood of tears. And the actor lies; but with all the spontaneity that careful calculation can lend him, he may construct a vision of some important truth about the human condition that opens us to a new understanding of

ourselves. In the end, we call a work of art trivial when it illuminates little beyond its own devices, and the same goes for political
leaders who bespeak some narrow interest rather than those of the
national or universal good. The fault is not in the use of the theatri
cal arts but in their purpose.

Paradox is the name of the game where acting as an art is concerned. It is a rare, hardheaded politician who is at home with any
of the arts these days; most often the artist is considered suspect, a
nuisance, a threat to morality, or a fraud. At the same time, one of
the most lucrative American exports, after airplanes, is art—
namely, music and films. But art has always been the revenge of the
human spirit upon the shortsighted. Consider the sublime achieve-
ments of Greece, the necrophilic grandeur of the Egyptians, the
glory of the Romans, the awesome power of the Assyrians, the rise
and fall of the Jews and their incomprehensible survival, and what
are we left with but a handful of plays, essays, carved stones, and
some strokes of paint on paper or the rock cave wall—in a word,
art? The ironies abound. Artists are not particularly famous for
their steady habits, the acceptability of their opinions, or their conformity with societal mores, but whatever is not turned into art
disappears forever. It is very strange when you think about it,
except for one thing that is not strange but quite logical: however
dull or morally delinquent an artist may be, in his moment of creation, when his work pierces the truth, he cannot dissimulate, he
cannot fake it. Tolstoy once remarked that what we look for in a
work of art is the revelation of the artist's soul, a glimpse of God.
You can't act that.

Clinton in Salem
1998

A number of commentators have seen a resemblance between the extravaganza around President Clinton and the witchcraft hysteria in Salem three hundred years ago. There are some similarities and some important differences.

The tone of iron vituperation and the gut-shuddering hatred are reminiscent of the fury of the Salem ministers roaring down on the Devil as though they would grind their heels into his face. Though there were never any witches while there certainly is a Bill Clinton, the underlying emotions are not all that different—the evident wish is to end the Evil One's very existence.

In both cases there is a kind of sublime relief in the unearthing of the culprit's hidden crimes. The Salem church, which effectively controlled the village, had been so fractious that minister after minister had fled the pulpit or been dismissed. But with the discovery of Satan in town, the people understood in a flash what the source of their troubles had been, and a new era of social peace opened before them—provided they could root out the diabolically corrupt. Suddenly paranoia ruled and all were suspect and no one was safe.

What is very different now is the public reaction. Rarely does just about every newspaper and television commentator agree so thoroughly. Be it *The New York Times*, *The Washington Post*, or the television and print tabloids whose normal business is reporting news of the gutter, media outlets all became highly moral in a single stroke, as though an electric charge had passed through iron filings, instantly pointing them all in the same direction. Not often does one sinner raise so many so quickly out of their moral slumber.

But what is strange and interesting is how the public, that great stallion that is so often led to water, this time dipped its head but refused to drink, perhaps scenting the stale smell of political manipulation.

It may also be that with so many American marriages ending in divorce, and most of those surely involving a mate in the wrong bed, an unspoken self-identification with this kind of marital misery has restrained people from losing all sympathy for their leader, disappointed as they might be in his behavior.

Despite the lashings of almost all the press and the mullahs of the religious right, the people seem largely to have withheld their righteous anger. This did not happen in Salem, where the members of the clergy, who were also the leaders of the community, were strangers to mercy and indeed to common sense, and helped drive the public into a lethal panic.

There is, I think, a parallel in the sexual element underlying each phenomenon. Witch-hunts are always spooked by women's horrifying sexuality awakened by the superstud Devil. In Europe, where tens of thousands perished in the hunts, broadsides showed the Devil with two phalluses, one above the other. And of course mankind's original downfall came about when the Filthy One corrupted the mother of mankind.

In Salem, witch-hunting ministers had the solemn duty to examine women's bodies for signs of the "Devil's Marks"—a suggestion of webbing, perhaps, between the toes, a mole behind an ear or between the legs, or a bite mark somewhere. I thought of this wonderfully holy exercise when Congress went pawing through Kenneth Starr's fiercely exact report on the president's intimate meetings with Monica Lewinsky. I guess nothing changes all that much.

In any case, those who think it trivial that Mr. Clinton lied about a mere affair are missing the point: it is precisely his imperious need of the female that has unnerved a lot of men, the mullahs especially, just as it has through the ages. This may also help to account for the support he still gets from women. He may be a bit kinky, but at least he's not the usual suit for whom the woman is a vase, decorative and unused.

Then there is the color element. Mr. Clinton, according to Toni Morrison, the Nobel Prize–winning novelist, is our first black president, the first to come from the broken home, the alcoholic mother, the under-the-bridge shadows of our ranking systems. He is also the most relaxed and unaffected with black people, whose company and culture he clearly enjoys.

His closeness to blacks may, in fact, have contributed to the relative racial harmony we have been enjoying these past few years. But it may also be part of the reason for his estrangement from his peers, and it may have helped uncork the sewer of contempt upon his head, the Starr report.

The Devil in Salem was white, but two of the few black people in the village were his first suspected consorts, John Indian and Tituba. Both were slaves. Tituba was tortured into naming women she had seen with the Devil, thus starting the hunt on its way. The conflation of female sexuality and blackness in a white world is an old story, and here it had lethal results.

In Mr. Clinton's case, there comes an overflowing of rage reminiscent of that earlier explosion. If he lied under oath he of course broke the law, but it seems impossible that the Founding Fathers would have required Congress, as a part of his punishment, to study what parts of a woman's body the president had touched. Except for this hatred of Mr. Clinton, which sometimes seems to mount to a hellish fear of him as unclean, a supernatural contaminator, it would surely have sufficed for Mr. Starr to report that he had had an affair and falsely denied it under oath.

The Salem paroxysm left the town ravaged, accursed and almost deserted, a place where no one would buy land or farm or build for one hundred years. Salem's citizens had acted out the mythology of their dark subconscious and had eaten their own—all in the name of God and good morals. It was a volcanic explosion of repressed steam that gave people license to speak openly in court of what formerly would have been shamefully caged in their hearts—for example, the woman who testified that her neighbor flew in through her window one balmy night and lay upon her and had his way. Suddenly this was godly testimony, and the work of heaven was to kill the neighbor.

Salem purified itself nearly to death, but in the end some good may have come of it. I am not historian enough to assert this as fact, but I have often wondered if the witch-hunt may have helped spawn, one hundred years later, the Bill of Rights, particularly the Fifth Amendment, which prohibits forcing a person to testify against himself—something that would have stopped the witch-hunt in its tracks. It may also have contributed to the wall of separation between church and state in America, for in Salem theocratic government had its last hurrah. Or so one may hope.

The Nazi Trials and the German Heart
1964

There is an unanswerable question hovering over the courtroom at Frankfurt, where twenty-two Hitler SS men are on trial for murdering inmates in the Auschwitz concentration camp during World War II. Can the kind of movement which gave life-and-death power to such men ever again rise in Germany?

It seemed to me, sitting at one side of the courtroom one day last week, that as in all murder trials the accused here were becoming more and more abstract. Once the jackbooted masters of a barbed-wire world, they are now middle-aged Germans in business suits, nearsighted some of them, laboriously taking notes, facing the high tribunal with a blue-uniformed policeman at each one's elbow. The two exceptions are indeed extraordinary. One has an imbecile stupidity written on his face, the other shifts constantly in his chair, a free-floating violence so clear in his eyes that one would find him frightening if met on a train, let alone on trial for murder.

But the others could pass for anybody's German uncle. In fact, the lives most of them have lived since they scooted into oblivion before the allied advance show them entirely capable of staying out of trouble. Some have turned into successful business men, professionals and ordinary workers. They have reared families and even became civic leaders in their communities. When arrested they were not picked up drunk or disorderly, but at work or at rest in the bosom of their families.

For example, the one whose violence seemed to show in his quick roving eyes was, in fact, a real sadist. He was almost constantly drunk in the camp and liked to walk into a barracks and fire his pistol at random into the sleeping prisoners. If he didn't like the look of a passing inmate he would blow his head off.

But after the war this man got a job in a hospital as a nurse, and his patients have written to the court saying that he was an especially tender helper, an unusually warm person. "Papa Kaduk," they called him. No one knows anymore exactly how many defenseless people Papa Kaduk murdered in his four years at Auschwitz. A massive man, overweight now, his small eyes blaze with mocking victory whenever a witness sounds uncertain of a date or a fact, and he reaches over to nudge his black-robed lawyer who then rises to protest hearsay evidence. He seems, in short, to be quite convinced that he is indeed Papa Kaduk and not at all the monster being painfully described from the witness chair.

Another is a pharmacist who helped select prisoners for the gas chambers. He has become an important man in his town; the arresting officer had had to wait for him to return from a hunting expedition in Africa, and the local gentry showed real surprise on learning of the charges against him. Especially since it had been he who suggested that whenever the town leaders met to discuss civic affairs they wear tuxedos. How, it was actually asked, could a gentleman of such sensibility have done such awful things?

Yet, the doctor testifying hour after hour this day leaves no doubt about the facts. He was himself an inmate, but since he did get more food than the others he is here to tell the tale. And as he describes babies ripped from their mothers' arms, bed linen changed twice a year, the almost total absence of medicine, Red Cross trucks being used to transport prisoners to their deaths, tortures and beatings, and names one of the defendants after the other as the actual perpetrators, the German housewives who comprise most of the jury burst into tears or sit with open horror in their faces. And they are of an age which indicates they lived in Nazi Germany while this was happening: they were shopping, putting their children to bed, going on picnics on sunny days, worrying about a daughter's wedding dress or a son's well-being in the army while mothers like themselves and children no different from their own were forced to undress, to walk into a barren hall, and breathe the gas which some of the defendants now sitting here carefully administered.

Yet, lawyers on the tiny prosecution staff believe that ninety percent of the German people are opposed to this and other trials like it. They base their judgment on the mail they receive and on their own difficulties in getting local cooperation for some of the arrests they have made, and finally, on the absence of any clear voice or movement from among the Germans demanding that the country's honor be cleared by bringing such murderers to justice.

On the contrary, it is widely felt, according to these lawyers, that trials like this only give Germany a bad name; that it all happened so long ago why pluck men out of their lives at this late date, and so on. Time and again these lawyers have had to escort arrested men across Germany to the Frankfurt jail because they could not find a police officer to help. And the government has given them twenty-five marks a day for expenses on these trips; the most common lodging for a night costs eleven marks. This handful of Germans nevertheless intends to go on searching for every last man down to the truck drivers who drove prisoners to the gas chambers, until justice is done.

But is there really any long-range point in all this? They do not know. Some of them have been on these cases since 1959 when the first arrests were made in this particular group of cases. They have read through millions of words of testimony, stared at photographs of the camps taken by an SS man with a penchant for photography, showing the defendants actually at work separating the doomed from those temporarily spared for labor in the camp. By this they have lost any sensitivity about what others might think and are doggedly pursuing the goal.

And what is the goal? These lawyers are in their middle thirties, veterans of the Wehrmacht themselves, German through and through. They know their people and they know that even if every last SS man were convicted for his particular crime, it would not in itself prevent a new recrudescence of brutal nationalism which could once again confront the world with a German problem. It is something else they are after.

Imbedded in every word of testimony, and in the very existence of this trial, is a dilemma which is first of all a German dilemma, given the history of concentration camps, but is actually an unresolved

problem for all mankind. For the final defense of these accused is
that they acted under government orders.

When so many Germans oppose this trial, it is not simply an
insensitivity to suffering, or even an immunity to the question of
justice. Germans too weep for their dead and help the sick and care
very much about their children. As for a respect for law, they have
that even to an inordinate degree. What scares some Germans,
however, and makes the German to this day an enigma to many
foreigners, is his capacity for moral and psychological collapse in
the face of a higher command.

Several times during the course of this trial, newsmen covering it
were ordered to leave, for one reason or another, and the dozen or
so police who sit below the judges' tribunal are in charge of carrying out such orders. Not long ago three policemen were asked what
they would do if ordered to shoot a newsman who disobeyed the
court's command. One replied that he could not do that; the other
two said they would carry out orders.

The point which the prosecution is trying to open up first to Germany, and then to the world, is individual conscience and responsibility in the face of inhuman orders. A judge (who has no connection
with this trial) told me that his fears for Germany stemmed from
precisely this profound tendency to abjure freedom of choice, to fall
into line on orders from above. Another man of the law, a high official in this court, feels that the day is far off, but that his duty is to
work for its coming when the Germans would question authority.
He sees the root of the difficulty in the especially authoritarian role
of the father in the German family, which is the microcosm reflected
in the authoritarian state. The underlying point of these trials is
that there can be no mitigating excuse for the conscious and
planned murder of six million men, women and children, orders or
no orders. Some six thousand SS men did duty in Auschwitz during
its four years of operation, and not one is known to have refused to
do what he was told. And it is no mean irony that the Jew, whose
skepticism once leavened the authoritarian character of German
culture, is not around any more to help humanize the pompous
general with a little healthy doubt as to his real importance.

All of which sounds hopeless and dangerous, and perhaps that is
all that should be said. But there are a few unknowns which some

Germans would point to with some small and uncertain hopefulness. The young, they say, are less hermetically sealed in the old German ways than any younger generation of the past. Movies, television, books and plays from abroad flood Germany. Germans travel more than they used to, and tourists from abroad come in greater numbers than ever, and there are over one million foreign workers employed in the country now.

So that a German youth is perhaps more internationally minded than his parents and not as contemptuous of strangers and ways of life that are not German. Finally there is the more impressive fact that Germany for the first time in modern history is not flanked by a line of backward peasant countries whose defenselessness was all too tempting in the past. The equalization of industrial and hence military strength through the whole of Europe makes expansion by force a good deal less possible than before.

It is in this context, a context of much distrust and some hopefulness, that the prosecution presses for a German verdict of guilty upon members of the German armed forces. Thus far none of the accused has suggested he may have done something wrong; there is no sign of remorse, and they appear to maintain a certain unity among themselves even now. Some have been in jail two, three and four years awaiting trial and have undoubtedly read what the world press has had to say about their deeds, but no sign shows of any change of attitude toward the past.

In fact, one defendant carries out his familial duties from prison, and his authority and racial ideas are still so powerful (he dropped the gas cartridges into the gas chambers full of people) that his daughter broke off with her betrothed because he, the defendant, believes that no good German girl can possibly marry an Italian.

This trial will go on for about a year, during which time some three hundred psychologically and physically scarred survivors will face the high tribunal in Frankfurt, living evidence of how one of the most educated, technically developed, and artistic nations in the world gave itself over to the absolute will of beings it is difficult to call human. And while that testimony fills the silent courtroom, and the world press prints its highlights, German industry will pour out its excellent automobiles, machine tools, electronic equipment, German theaters will excellently produce operas and plays,

German publishers will put out beautifully designed books—all the visible signs and tokens of civilization will multiply and make even more abstract, more bewildering the answer to the riddle which the impassive faces of the accused must surely present to any one who looks at them. How was it possible in a civilized country?

It is the same question to which Cain gave his endlessly echoed answer, and I have often thought that this is why it is the first drama in the Bible, for it provides the threat, the energy for all that comes after. If man can murder his fellows, not in passion but calmly, even as an "honorable" duty leading to a "higher" end—can any civilization be called safe from the ravages of what lies waiting in the heart of man? The German government which Hitler destroyed had some of the most intelligent and advanced legislation in the world. The present republic also is buttressed by excellent laws.

What is in the German heart, though? Does the rule of law reach into that heart or the rule of conformity and absolute obedience? Surely, if the German police had picked up a twenty-two-man gang that had tortured and killed merely for money, or even for kicks, an outcry would go up from the Germans, a demand that justice be done. Why is there this uneasy silence at best, and this resentment at worst, excepting that in the Frankfurt cases these accused worked for a state under its orders? Perhaps the problem becomes clearer now, and not only for the Germans.

The disquieting, nagging truth which I think dilutes the otherwise clear line this trial is taking is that the human mind does in fact accept one kind of murder. It is the murder done under the guise of social necessity. War is one example of this, and all peoples reject the idea of calling soldiers murderers. In fact, the entire nation so deeply shares in this kind of killing that it must reject any condemnation of the individuals who actually do the killing, lest they have to condemn themselves.

The problem for the Germans is that they are being called upon to identify themselves with the victims when their every instinct would lead them to identify with the uniformed, disciplined, killers. In short, they are being called on to be free, to rebel in their spirit against the age-old respect for authority which has plagued their history.

This, I think, is why it is perfectly logical for the German house-wife on the jury to weep as any human being would at the horrors she hears, even as she and her millions of counterparts have, for at least a decade now, heard just such evidence a hundred times with no sign of public protest against Nazism. It is why the officers who tried to assassinate Hitler in 1944 have never been celebrated in Germany either: for they did the unthinkable, they took a moral decision against their obedience to authority.

So that the German looking at these twenty-two men may well be revolted by their crimes and yet feel paralyzed at the thought of truly taking sides against them. For part of his soul is caught in the same airtight room with theirs—the part that finds honor and goodness and decency in obedience.

But who, in what country, has not heard men say, "If I did not do this someone else would, so I might as well go along?"

So the question in the Frankfurt courtroom spreads out beyond the defendants and spirals around the world and into the heart of every man. It is his own complicity with murder, even the murders he did not perform himself with his own hands. The murders, however, from which he profited if only by having survived.

It is this profound complicity which the Frankfurt prosecution is trying to open up by sticking to its seemingly simple contention that all murder is murder. With the atomic bomb in so many different hands now it might be well to take a good look at the ordinariness of most of the defendants in Frankfurt. The thought is hateful, to be sure, and no one would willingly think it, but we do, after all, live in the century when more people have been killed by other people than at any other period. Perhaps the deepest respect we can pay the millions of innocent dead is to examine what we believe about murder, and our responsibility as survivors for the future.

Dinner with the Ambassador
1985

In March, Harold Pinter and I went to Turkey for a week on behalf of the International PEN Club. We made the visit not primarily to conduct an investigation of human rights—an impossibility in so short a stay—but to demonstrate to the country's writers and artists and to its political prisoners that the outside world cares about what is happening to them. It was to be an act of moral solidarity by the members of International PEN, and we hoped it might also have an effect on the country's military government.

We had wanted to talk to people of all political views, including Prime Minister Turgut Ozal and the martial law commander of Istanbul, Gen. Necit Torumtay. The prime minister was in Saudi Arabia, however, and the commander declined to see us, saying that the government is now controlled by Parliament—nonsense, since the military runs the country. We did meet with publishers and editors of conservative newspapers, who more or less support the regime. All of them, however, said that under censorship the truth about touchy issues could not be printed. We also attended the trial of a lawyer who had defended the Turkish Peace Association, a banned group which used to lobby for nuclear disarmament and détente, and we spoke with people who have been jailed and tortured without being accused of any act. We went to a dinner in my honor at the American ambassador's residence. Apart from the government-imposed news blackout on our press conference at the end of the trip, that dinner turned out to be the climax of the week.

It is important to understand that the 1980 military coup in Turkey was preceded by two years of terrorism, which had piled up some five thousand dead. At times, as many as twenty people a day were killed, and by all accounts the country appeared to be on the verge of civil war. Justification for the military takeover rests on this fact, which no one seems to deny. But some observers, including Suleyman Demirel, the prime minister at the time of the coup, find it suspicious that although seemingly helpless to curb the violence for two years, the military brought an amazing peace within a matter of weeks after taking power. In Demirel's view, the generals deliberately allowed the chaos to expand until their intervention would be gratefully accepted. Support for the military government is still based on fears that the violence will return.

A former high-level government official told us that there are currently about two thousand political prisoners in Turkey. In addition, seven thousand people are said to have been arrested as terrorists; most of them are under the age of twenty-four, and some are as young as sixteen. Many of these young people were picked up on the street for scrawling slogans on walls or arrested for harboring others in their homes. It is generally believed that about forty-eight "terrorists" have been hanged and that seventy more are awaiting execution.

The Turkish Constitution permits the police under martial law to detain a citizen for forty-five days without notifying his family or lawyers, and most instances of torture take place during that time. We met a respected Turkish publisher who had been arrested with his brother and had seen him beaten to death. In spite of his anguish as he related the details, he insisted on conveying the horror to us step by step. He told how he and his brother had been put in a van and, on their way to the prison, had been struck repeatedly by four guards. He believed he had survived because he had been handcuffed with his arms in front of him, allowing him to use them to protect his head. His brother's hands were cuffed behind his back, so he was helpless. When they arrived at the jail, the guards pulled them out and kicked his brother as he lay on the ground until he stopped moving.

Because of his prestige, the publisher was able to sue the police for assault. He won the case, but the four guards were sentenced to a few years in jail. Their superiors, who had ordered the arrests, were not mentioned in the proceedings.

We had looked forward to meeting U.S. ambassador Robert Strausz-Hupe, if only to hear the official U.S. view on the situation in Turkey. The dinner took place the day after we spent a deeply moving evening with the fiancée of Aly Taygun, a young director whose innovative work had created much excitement at Yale University's drama school a couple of years ago, and the young wife of a painter who, like Taygun, is serving an eight-year jail sentence for his membership in the Turkish Peace Association. The second woman's hope that we might help her husband in some way prompted her to show us several sepia drawings he had handed her during the five-minute visits she is permitted every two weeks. The drawings, mostly portraits of her, were packed with an almost palpable sensuous power.

When I found myself momentarily alone with the ambassador, I immediately began telling him about the imprisoned artist and his wife. To my surprise and pleasure, he was at once caught up in the story. He wanted to know their names, implying he would inquire about them. It seemed a good beginning. The ambassador, a spry, diminutive man in his eighties, is famous for his absolute deference to the Turkish military, with whom he has completely identified American interests. All I knew about him was that he had worked as a campaign adviser to Barry Goldwater. I learned later that he had been a professor at the University of Pennsylvania and has been considered a leading thinker of the far right.

That night he displayed a cultivated, literary air, not at all the image of a fiercely militant right-winger. He is an Austrian, naturalized in 1938; his rosy complexion and full head of silver hair, his blue baggy eyes with their soft drooping lids, his natty gray suit and sharp intelligence all suggested Vienna and civilized coffeehouse discussions. As we moved toward the dinner table, he confided to me that there might well be a declaration of amnesty in Turkey in the near future, giving the impression of cautious liberalism. "We can't push them too far," he said of the military. "We don't want to lose them."

Taking my seat across the table from the ambassador and to the right of his wife, I thought how functional the elegance of the table was, as though to protect power by enforcing good manners and empty conversations. The image of the imprisoned painter would not go away, but could such an unpleasant thought be introduced at a dinner given by my country's ambassador in my honor?

Harold Pinter was seated on the same side of the table as I was, half a dozen places down. The soup had hardly been served when I heard his strong baritone above the general babble and caught in it the flow of a quickened mind. On my left, Mayrose Strausz-Hupe, a beautiful woman who looks less than half her husband's age (the daughter, she volunteered, of a Ceylonese Ford dealer), was drawing a map of her country on the tablecloth with her fingernail, showing the demarcations between the religious factions that had been tearing the country apart in the years since the British left.

As the roast veal was served, Pinter's voice rose higher, his British diction sprouting angry ratchets. I could hear that he was engaged in a cross-table discussion with Nazli Ilicak, a widely read columnist whom we had met at the offices of her husband's newspaper, *Tercuman*, some days earlier, and Frank Trinka, the American deputy chief of mission, an unsmiling, tight-bodied man, with tinted glasses and a knife-like self-assurance. I could not make out what Pinter was saying, but I could hear Ilicak and the deputy chief replying, "That's your viewpoint. We have to see it in the round. You are only seeing part of it . . ." The ambassador, forking his veal, did not even glance in Pinter's direction as the playwright's voice reached the volume of an M.P. in the House of Commons. Madame Ambassador continued with her geographical drawing, maintaining an admirable aplomb. Her husband was trying to engage his neighbor in conversation, when Pinter, with open rage, shouted across the table at Ilicak, "That is an insult and was meant as an insult and I throw it back in your face!" As I learned later, she had told Pinter that although the Turks would have to remain and face the realities of their country, he could go home and put it all into a profitable play.

The ambassador quickly tapped his crystal water glass with a silver spoon and brought silence. "I wish to welcome Mr. Miller as our honored guest," he said, and went on to extol my work in the theater. He ended with a glance around the table which came to rest only for a moment on Pinter. "This demonstrates that all viewpoints are welcome here," he said. And then, pointing to the floor of his residence, his voice thick with emotion: "Here is democracy. Right here, and we are proud of it. Imagine this happening in a communist country!" Whercupon he thanked me for coming.

I understood that it was up to me to respond to the toast. Protocol must be observed, and the ambassador had been an engaging host. But as we sat there in the brightly lit room, an image popped into my mind: the painter's wife staring at an empty pillow; her husband lying on his mattress hardly a mile away, with six more years of prison ahead of him, all for an offense that, had I been a Turk, I surely would have committed myself.

I began by quietly thanking the ambassador for the dinner and the welcome, at which he looked relieved. "Whatever our political differences," I said, "we share the same faith in democracy." The ambassador nodded appreciatively. I went on:

As democracy enhances candor, my speech being without fear, it is impossible for us to ignore what we have witnessed in Turkey. We are playwrights, and playwrights are different from poets or novelists or perhaps any other kind of writer. We deal in the concrete. . . . An actor has to be moved from point A to point B, and so you cannot act in general, only in particular. We do not know what the situation in Turkey was last year, so perhaps it is better now, as is claimed. We don't know what it will be in the future. We do know concretely what we have seen, and what we have seen has no tangency with any democratic system in Western Europe or the United States. I wrote in *The Crucible* about people who were jailed and executed not for their actions but for what they were alleged to be thinking. So it is here; you have hundreds in jail for their alleged thoughts. We are told that Turkey is moving closer and closer to democracy, and that may turn out to be so, no one can say, but what it is now is a military dictatorship with certain merciless and brutal features. We are helping Turkey, and I am not saying we should not; but the real strength of a state in the last analysis is the support of her people, and the question is whether the United States is inadvertently helping to alienate the people by siding so completely with those who have deprived them of their elementary rights. Not a single action is alleged against the hundreds of Peace Association people in prison.

As I continued, I thought I saw the eyes of the ambassador glaze with astonishment or horror. But at the same time, he seemed to be listening to a kind of news: not political news, for he knew better than I did the state of affairs there, but news of an emotion, an outrage. After twenty minutes I ended my speech:

There isn't a Western lawyer who could come to this country and see what is happening in these military courts who would not groan with despair. The American part here ought to be the holding up of democratic norms, if only as a goal, instead of justifying their destruction as the only defense against chaos.

The ambassador turned, gazed at the faces around the silent table and asked Erdal Inonu, son of a former president and prime minister and head of a political party, if he would respond to my remarks. Inonu, sixty, balding and squinting, a man with a gentle face and long hands which he softly clasped above the table, said that in general he could not help agreeing with my views and wanted to add his welcome to that of the ambassador. I could hardly believe this apparent victory. The ambassador gestured toward Ilicak; she simply shook her head, her eyes rounded in shock. A bearded journalist was then invited to comment; he chose simply to rub his hands together, smile and welcome me to Turkey (though Pinter later revealed that this man had exchanged approving glances with him while I was speaking). And so, with no more takers, we all rose, as the ambassador said something to the effect that it had been a fascinating dinner. Before I could stop myself, I added, "This is one you won't forget soon," to which the ambassador responded with an uncertain smile.

The company adjourned to the sitting room for coffee, and I sought out the deputy chief, sensing that he occupied the center of power in the place. But I had hardly sat down when once again I heard the awesome baritone of Harold Pinter. Near the entry hall, Pinter was just turning away from the ambassador, who, half his size, was shouting something and walking abruptly toward an astonished guest. Pinter came directly to me and said proudly, "I have insulted your ambassador and have been asked to go."

Forced to be practical by Pinter's visible emotion, I wondered about transportation and found a guest whom we had met at a gathering of Peace Association supporters. He was happy to share his car, but the French ambassador intervened, at the risk of offending Strausz-Hupe, his colleague and friend, and offered to drive us to his residence. On the way out to the black Peugeot, Pinter explained that the ambassador had remarked that there can always be a lot of opinions about anything, and he had replied, "Not if you've got an electric wire hooked to your genitals." The ambassador had stiffened and snapped, "Sir, you are a guest in my house!" Whereupon Pinter had concluded he had been thrown out. Pinter was brimming with admiration for my peroration, as I was for his righteous indignation, without which I could not have launched my twenty-minute speech. We decided we ought to form a team that would visit American embassies around the world.

Throughout our stay we had declined interviews, promising instead to hold a press conference on our last day. It took place in the building of the Journalists' Association in Istanbul, and was attended by twenty-five or thirty men and women and a television crew from United Press International. What we said at the press conference was more or less what we had said at the ambassador's dinner. We understood that Turkish journalists would be forbidden to print more than scraps of such opinions, but we felt we had to speak candidly. The next day, in London, we learned that reporting about the press conference had been banned by the government and that an investigation was to be launched into the whole visit. But news of it has nevertheless penetrated the prisons, as we have indirectly learned, and has brought some hope that the world has not forgotten these people. Unhappily, Prime Minister Ozal could stand before the Washington Press Club a few weeks ago and declare there are no political prisoners in Turkey without causing a ripple in his audience. There is nothing farther away from Washington than the entire world.

What's Wrong with This Picture?
Speculations on a Homemade Greeting Card
1974

Here is a New Year's card I recently received many months late. Like couples everywhere, this one decided to celebrate the occasion with a humorous photograph. It could have been taken in any one of a number of countries. It happens to have been made in Czechoslovakia.

The wife is wearing just the right smile for a woman standing hip-deep in water with her clothes on. It is a warm and relaxed smile. The husband, likewise, expresses the occasion with his look of grave responsibility, his walking stick and dark suit, his reassuring hand on Eda, their beloved dog.

The wife's floppy hat and gaily printed dress and the husband's polka-dot tie and pocket handkerchief suggest that the couple might have started off for a stroll down a Prague boulevard when, for some reason unstated, they found themselves standing in the water. One sees, in any case, that they are fundamentally law-abiding people who do not make a fuss about temporary inconvenience. Instead, the couple displays almost exhilarating confidence in the way things are.

Actually—although of course it does not show in the picture—the man and woman are within a short drive from the encampments of the Red Army, which entered their country some six years ago to protect it from its enemies, and has never left. This contributes to the calm atmosphere of the photograph, for with the Red Army so close by there is no reason to fear anything beyond the Czech borders, or, for that matter, within them.

One can see, in short, that these people live in a country blessed by peace. True, a certain tension arises from one's not being certain whether the water they are standing in is rising or falling. But, either way, it seems certain these people will know how to behave. Should the water rise to their chins, the man and woman will swim away, without in the least altering the amused resignation that animates them now. They will be accompanied, of course, by their dog, whose life preserver they will continue to grasp.

So we may conclude that here is a couple that has learned how to live without illusions and thus without severe disappointment. He happens to be on a list of 152 Czech writers who are forbidden to publish anything within the borders of the Czechoslovak Socialist Republic or to have their plays produced on a Czech stage. But one does not see the man and his wife thrashing about angrily in the water, as might be expected.

Instead, they stand in the water for their New Year's photograph, not in the least resentful or angry but with the optimistic obedience the present leadership of Czechoslovakia expects of all its citizens. Since it has been decreed that the couple stand in the water, so to speak, then that is where they will stand, and nothing could be simpler. Their dog, of course, is not blacklisted, but she always follows them so closely that they allow her to share their fate.

Considering all this, one might conclude the husband and wife are expressing utter hopelessness, and there is indeed some truth in this interpretation. In its desire for peace, the United States, much as it might wish to, cannot officially raise the issue with the Soviet Union, and this leaves the writer and his wife standing in the water. On the other hand, the Soviet Union, much as it might wish to, cannot withdraw its military support of the regime it placed in power in 1968. At the same time, however, many Czechs believe the cultural cemetery their country has become is even too extreme for the Russian taste. The problem is that only mediocrities have been willing to take positions in the regime, and of course mediocrities lack the finesse to deal with the country's intellectuals, except to sentence them to an internal exile or force them to emigrate.

When some people, like the writer in this photograph, refuse to emigrate, they are nevertheless described in the controlled press as having left the country. A more bloodless and efficient solution is hard to imagine, but it is another reason why the writer is standing in the water fully dressed. When he and his wife are on dry land, walking down the streets of their neighborhood, they know that the official version is that they are living in another country; therefore, the couple's hold on reality—all that is really left for them—requires some expression, and so they occasionally stand hip deep in a lake or a river.

Yet another reason is that fellow intellectuals abroad, specifically those who espouse socialism or radical reforms in their own capitalist states, often march with placards denouncing tyranny in countries like Greece, Spain, Brazil or Chile, but none of these people seems to have noticed what is happening in Czechoslovakia. This is because Czechoslovakia is already a socialist country. And for this reason too the writer's wife smiles as cutely as she does and the writer himself shows no sign of surprise as the couple stands together in the water. Indeed, there is yet another reason for their expressions—namely, that the writer has for many years been advocating communism.

If the photograph could have been much wider, it would have revealed a veritable crowd of writers, professors, and intellectuals and their families, standing in the water. Not a few of these would be authors whose works come out in France, England, America—other places and other languages. For this these artists are not punished, although the government tries to discourage foreign publishers. Also, royalties are specially taxed so as to leave the artists with next to nothing. Thus they are quite successful in other countries but are forbidden to publish in their own language. And this also helps explain why the writer and his wife do not feel it so extraordinary to be standing hip-deep in water with their clothes on.

In Russia, quite otherwise, writers do not have themselves photographed in this curious way, because the Soviet government simply forbids their publishing abroad without official permission to do so. So Russian writers are photographed on perfectly dry land. The unique situation has therefore arisen whereby Czech writers would be delighted if foreign publishers or foundations would put out their work not only in foreign languages but in *Czech*. So persecuted a national pride is unequaled in any of the other socialist countries!

As matters stand, Czech writers can never read their work in other than strange languages, and this makes some of these writers feel they are instead the authors of translations. This is also why the couple is photographed standing hip-deep in water with their clothes on.

The man in the picture has had half a dozen plays produced abroad and receives press notices now and then from Paris, London, Frankfurt or New York, but he does not feel he has ever finished a play, since a play is usually finished inside a theater and he is not allowed inside a theater in Czechoslovakia to work with actors and a production. This is also why he is standing in the water with his clothes on.

At the risk of overelaborating on so simple a picture, it is nevertheless necessary to add that a path, so to speak, lies open before this couple, if they would only take it. It would be the work of half an hour for this playwright to secure for himself a place on dry land. He need only appear before the proper authorities and deliver a confession that he was wrong in 1968 to oppose the Russian invasion, the elimination of human rights, et cetera, ending with praise for the present regime and a confirmation of its correct and humane position. His confession would then be widely published—in Czech, of course—and with it his condemnation of friends who still insist on standing in water, calling upon them to come out against alien, imperialist ideas and to take up their part in the building of a new Czechoslovakia instead of pretending, as they do now, that their consciences are more valuable and right than the wisdom of the present rulers. With a few well-chosen words, the couple and the dog could dry off and become real Czechs.

That the playwright finds himself unable either to accommodate the government in this or to emigrate and write freely in a foreign country indicates a certain stubborn affection for his own land. This is also why his wife smiles as she does and why he seems on the verge of either laughing or crying, it is not clear which.

It is not to be assumed, however, that his seeming imperturbability extends into the depths of his heart, let alone that the scores of other writers who would be visible in a wider picture have left to them the humor which this playwright is still capable of showing. Some, for example, will say that they are writing more purely, more personally, now that they can only write for their circle of friends. But others feel reality is closing down around them, that in their enforced isolation they are losing their grasp on life itself. These last, if photographed, would be shown farther out, in deeper water, with only their noses visible.

If the whole crowd of intellectuals could be shown where they are—in the water, that is, and fully clothed—and if they could be heard announcing their preference as to what sort of system they would want for their country, hardly one would not declare for socialism. But a socialism that is not confused with absolutism. This leaves the government in the awkward position of having to forbid these people to publish in their own language. Awkward because it is doubtful that so total a silence was enforced even by the czars or Hitler himself. Yet the present regime is certainly anti-czarist and violently opposed to Hitlerism.

And so the writer and his wife and their dog wish us all a Happy New Year. Needless to say—but possibly advisable to say to the Czech police—all these interpretations are entirely my own and not those of the subjects in the photograph, who were doubtless moved by their very Czech sense of humor to send out such a New Year's card, whose symbolism, in all fairness, applies to many other countries, and not all of them Eastern or socialist. It's simply that in certain countries at certain times a rather universal condition is more palpable and clear. Where, after all, are the waters not rising? Who does not feel, as he positions himself to speak his mind in public, a certain dampness around his ankles? In the days of his glory, did not the United States president propose to dismantle the television news organizations in order to get himself a still more silent majority? Was he not setting in place a secret police force responsible only to himself?

All this photo does is rather wittily inform us of how infinitely adaptable man is to whatever climatic conditions, firstly; and secondly, that—as the numbers on the life preserver make so terribly clear—the year is 1974 rather than, let's say, 1836, 1709, 1617, or 1237 in, for example, Turkey.

The Measure of the Man
1991

What struck me strongly about Nelson Mandela in his American public appearances, as well as our Soweto interview for BBC TV, was the absence in him of any sign of bitterness. After twenty-seven and a half years with his nose against the bars he seemed uninterested in cursing out the whites who had put him there for the crime of demanding the vote in a country where his people outnumber their rulers by about six to one.

I suppose his rather majestic poise, unmarred by rancor, lowered white defensiveness to the point where reactionaries could join with liberals in applauding his speech to Congress. But such unanimous appreciation is bound to be suspect when an honest man can hardly please everyone with his views; after all, with all his charm and civility he was still the man who had organized the African National Congress's guerrilla force, for one thing.

Watching from a distance I had found him extraordinarily straightforward in his persistent refusal to pulverize his history to suit current American tastes, crediting communists for being the first whites to befriend his movement, sometimes at the risk of their lives. Likewise, he criticized Israel and in the same breath reminded us that the overwhelming majority of his earliest supporters had been Jews.

In short, he allows himself to remain complicated; with a grandson named Gadafi (which was not his idea, however), he has written that the highest expression of democracy is the British House of Commons and the best legal system the American, with its written Bill of Rights. To me in our interview he would say that he had never joined the Communist Party. He did not add that he had never been a Marxist, but whether or not he thought he had been,

I judge that he sees people in all their variety of character and deed in the foreground of events, rather than as shadowy creatures manipulated by forces, as a Marxist usually must.

I agreed to a conversation with Mandela after much hesitation, lasting a couple of weeks. The whole thing had begun with a London phone call from one Beverly Marcus, through whose South African English I discerned that she had proposed to the BBC that they film Mandela and me talking about life rather than politics, and that Mandela was receptive to the idea because he had called a halt to any more interviews in which the same simple-minded questions would inevitably be asked.

Lacking a reporter's killer instinct or investigative techniques I was simply very curious about the roots of this man's unusual character. How does one manage to emerge from nearly three decades in prison with such hopefulness, such inner calm?

But my main impulse came out of my background in New York, a racially splintered city with more than 2,000 people murdered last year. It has next to no inspiring black leadership, and so Mandela's success or failure seemed far from an academic question for me. If he can lead his riven country into a multiracial democracy the ripples could rock New York, Chicago, Detroit—and London and Europe and Israel, where the most explosive social problem is ethnicity and its unmet, often incoherent demands.

South Africa was full of surprises, the first being the fact that Beverly Marcus's younger sister, Gill, is Nelson Mandela's veritable right hand and a spokesperson for the ANC, and that their father was his accountant. I suppose I should have felt my integrity put at risk by this news, but I had never had any intention of drawing and quartering Mandela. I sought only a pathway into his nature and that of his movement. Gill, with her inside knowledge of the movement and unabashed admissions of its amateurish failings, as well as of the constantly shifting so-called tribal conflict, turned out, in fact, to be of great help in my grasping this situation.

Cape Town and the Cape area, which Beverly suggested my wife, Inge Morath, and I visit for a few days to unwind from the fourteen-hour plane trip, is an unlikely place to begin preparing for a talk with a revolutionary leader, since it is as close to Beverly Hills and the California littoral as you can get without tripping over a movie studio. Balmy air, a lazy Atlantic surf lapping white beaches, swimming pools and very good fish restaurants—I felt myself beginning to sink into its lovely lethargy.

But then one climbs a dune a hundred yards across a beach road in Hought Bay that fronts some extremely lavish homes and their tennis courts—and from the dune's ridge one looks down into a squatter town of hundreds of cardboard and tin shacks thrown one against the other right up to the edge of the sea. Don't the rich who live nearby object? Not all do—some happily sell drinking water to the blacks here who have no supply of their own. But of course this shantytown will have to go, for the view of the sea is superb here and the sand as white as sugar, a piece of prime real estate that will not be denied its promise forever.

One can drive around the Cape and Cape Town and indeed South Africa end to end without the slightest awareness that this sanitized prosperity involves only five million of its thirty million inhabitants. The famous South African schizophrenia is not hard to understand. To be sure, the back pages of the papers display ads for razor wire with which to surround one's home, and the walls surrounding most whites' homes show a metal sign reading "Instant Armed Response," and in many areas you are instructed not to stop at red lights at night lest your car be hijacked. But you quickly get used to this palpable fear, just as we have in New York, where as a child in Harlem I always carried my belongings with me to the blackboard or they'd be gone when I got back to my seat.

But South Africa is unique; it has state socialism for the whites—until very recent privatizations, sixty percent of all jobs were in state enterprises—and fascism for the blacks. Still, by the time we got back to Johannesburg after five days in the country I felt the place strange but comprehensible as merely one more kingdom of denial, unusual mainly for the immense proportion of its majority ghettoized and stripped of all civil rights.

Mandela's new house in the middle of Soweto has been criticized by some as one of Winnie Mandela's ostentations, standing as it does in the midst of the Soweto slum. Actually, donations built it. And there is a scattering of other quite good middle-class homes in the midst of the squalor, since the few successful middle-class blacks have been barred from white areas along with the poor. It is all part of a hopeless muddle of a modern technological state trying to sustain the most primitive, chest-pounding, Nazi master-race dogmas. So surrealism looms at every turn—a BMW dealership, black-owned, stands at the center of Soweto, a glass cube show-room exploding beams of white light toward houses yards away that have neither water nor sewers and whose occupants are no doubt unemployed and probably illiterate.

From the outside the Mandela house seems less elaborate than odd, a large chesty configuration of obliquely angular brick walls, an impromptu sort of construction until one is inside and realizes that it is a kind of fortress, its vulnerable dining and living rooms with their glass doors protected by a deep brick veranda extending outward some thirty feet. One drives into a receiving yard sur-rounded, as with so many other homes in this scared country, by a high wall with a steel, electronically controlled sliding door. And the doors of the main rooms are double-hinged to support a steel inner gate painted a discreet ivory to match the walls. Presumably these are barriers to an invading force.

Mandela's daughter, Zindzi, came into the living room pursuing her three-year-old son, both of them handsome, round-faced and no doubt accustomed to crowds of strangers in the place. Our crew was stringing its cables out; Gill Marcus was already on the phone; the floors and walls seemed covered with gifts, trophies and bric-a-brac; and now Winnie was here, explaining that she would not be eating with us because Nelson kept watching her calories and she liked to eat what she liked. Whereupon Mandela appeared, making a round gesture with both hands referring to her weight and saying "Africa!," both of them laughing while she bent to lift her rampaging grandson, whom she handed to a nurse. Even in his quick glances at her one saw his overwhelming love for his still-young wife, and she clearly basked in it. But her indictment in a murder case and impending trial seemed to hang in the air despite her tired jocularity.

Mandela was not wearing one of his formal London suits but a collarless short-sleeved African blouse with a gold-embroidered yoke—a chief's blouse, it looked to me. Gill hoped he would relax with me, and after a while he did come quite close. But he is by nature a formal, conservative man who in a peaceful country would have been chief justice of its Supreme Court or perhaps the head of a large law firm. My first question to him—after we had walked out on his veranda and looked down at Soweto, the dumping ground for human beings—was how he had been raised.

At first he sat pressed against the back of his couch, somewhat on guard, having been cornered by interviewers who find it impossible to believe that he simply means what he says. He was the son of a chief, and one could see how serious it was to be a chief's son; he had been taught early on that he would have the responsibilities of governing and judging. Even now he straightened a bit as he told with pride how, when he was ten and his father died, an uncle had taken over his education and his life. "My father occupied a position equivalent to that of prime minister in the tribe. . . . To me as a child the Transkei was the center of the entire world. . . . The missionaries tried to destroy the belief in custom and they created the perception that we have no history or culture." And with an amused grin: "When the 1939 war began we felt we were loyal subjects of the British monarch. That was the atmosphere in which we were brought up."

"And what went on inside you when the missionaries told you you had no history?"

"I'm not so sure I knew that I had a history." And later, "I must confess that Africa remained a dark continent in that I knew very little about it and I knew better about Europe, especially Britain."

This meticulous specificity, and his staid, almost Victorian structure of speech and demeanor suddenly had a root and expressed an innate authority which no doubt helped to keep him together through his prison decades. Mandela, to put it simply, *is* a chief.

And this may help explain why it has been so difficult for him to deign to confer with Mangosuthu Buthelezi of the Zulus, who have recently been on the attack against the ANC Xhosa people. Buthelezi, it is felt, helped to justify apartheid by accepting the headship of a concocted homeland where his people were dumped. It is the equivalent of a French maquisard guerrilla accepting political equality with a Vichy collaborator; there is not only a moral issue but his pride. Nevertheless, when Mandela did appear at a recent press conference with Buthelezi, the latter's people so threatened him that he was forced to leave the area.

The tribe, he insists, is basically an extended family. And in modern times there is no "natural" conflict between tribes, which are largely urbanized now, living side by side and intermarrying, joining the same unions and attending the same schools. It was the British and then the apartheid government that had always tried to tribalize Africa, pitting one against the other, setting up so-called homelands, newly founded territories that had never existed before. "There is one Africa and there will be one," Mandela said, creating a ball with his two hands.

The present conflict is "simply a conflict between two political organizations," a conflict that has failed to make headway in Soweto, as one example, because Soweto is more politically sophisticated rather than because the people are mainly Xhosa. "But when Zulus attack they never ask whether you are Zulu or something else, like the recent attack on people in the train, who do not sit according to tribes. They attack anyone."

And who would be interested in orchestrating these attacks? He pauses before his answer, which goes to the heart of his hopes. "My belief is that Mr. de Klerk wants South Africa to take a new direction, and it is therefore difficult . . . to say that the government itself is orchestrating this violence."

De Klerk still has Mandela's confidence, it seems, but the miasma remains dense and impenetrable where some of his government's lower officials are concerned. Last July Mandela's people had gotten information that an Inkatha (Buthelezi's political organization) attack on a township was being planned and had notified the police and higher officials. The attack came off, thirty were murdered, and the police did nothing to prevent it. "I immediately went to see de Klerk. . . . Why were they allowed to enter the township when we told you beforehand that this attack was coming? . . . Mr. de Klerk is a very smart man, a strong leader. He was unable to give me an answer." However, on the day of Mandela's visit to the scene of the slaughter de Klerk personally sent four helicopters and five hundred police to protect him. And besides, "When you discuss with Mr. de Klerk he seems to have a genuine sense of shock, unlike others."

And finally, "They have either lost control over certain elements of their security forces or those elements are doing precisely what the government wants. . . . They want to negotiate with a weakened ANC. . . . You are not dealing with tribal people from the countryside but people who are sophisticated in the use of weapons, who know how to move very swiftly with military precision. . . . There are efforts now to start the Renamo movement in South Africa." (Renamo was the Rhodesian-organized mercenary outfit that murdered thousands in Mozambique.)

I turned to a discussion of his prison time. He and his comrades had originally been assured by a prison officer that they'd be out in five years because the world was so outraged by their life sentences. But five years came and went. Winnie could visit only twice a year; his children were growing up with no father. Here his face showed pain at his inability to protect his family—the helplessness desecrated his chiefly role.

Government harassment of Winnie was driving her out of one job after another until "there were certain moments when I wondered whether I had taken the correct decision of getting committed to the struggle. But at the end of these hesitations with myself I would feel that I had taken the right decision. . . . The certainty of our final victory was always there. Of course I sometimes became very angry when I thought about the persecution of my wife and that I could not give her the support she needed. I felt powerless. And also my children were hounded out of one school after another."

His vulnerability was plain here, but over it his hardness flared. This was as close as he was able to come to acknowledging what must have been the loss of hope for release before he died; instead he preferred to find something positive to emphasize. When the world began to forget him and all black movements were suppressed, the government restated that a life sentence meant life, "but in the English universities they came all-out to oppose these harsh measures. . . . People tend to forget the contribution that was made by the National Union of South African Students, which was a white organization."

This was not an opportune, upbeat recollection but his ultimate vision of a nonracial South Africa. I am convinced it is more than a tactic to recognize the absolute future need for whites who have advanced education and business prowess. It was striking how he never seemed to categorize people by race or even class, and that he spontaneously tended to cite good men even among the enemy.

"That came from my prison experience. It gets very cold on

Robben Island and we had no underwear. Some warders went strictly by regulations—you were allowed two blankets. But another warder would slip you an extra one. I made some good friends among the warders; some of them visit me now."

In fact, toward the end of his imprisonment he ran "Mandela University" on Robben Island, and white warders were among his pupils. But there wasn't time to talk about this. We'd scheduled two sessions and at the last minute had to settle for one because he had to rush off to deal with the murders going on all over the place and the government's inability—or unwillingness—to keep order.

On the way back to Johannesburg that night, Gill Marcus pressed the driver on no account to stop at red lights and to drive as fast as possible through the darkness.

The Parable of the Stripper
1994

The Yugoslav catastrophe raises, for me, an especially terrible and comical memory. In the 1960s I presided over the congress of International PEN that was held in Bled, a beautiful resort town built around a crystal-clear lake high in the lovely mountains of Slovenia. Bled had been the watering hole for generations of Europeans, a fairy-tale place. And it was already more than a decade since Tito had broken with Moscow.

Marxist intellectuals in Yugoslavia were remarkably open in their criticisms of the economy and politics of the country. That the system needed deep changes was taken for granted, and new concepts were being floated that would free individual initiative while retaining the social gains of the communist system. Worker ownership of factories was being tried, and identical consumer products, such as radios, were given different names in order to spur competition between factories, in the hope of raising quality and lowering prices. Yugoslavia was prodding the limits of socialism; and to come there from the dictatorships of Hungary, Czechoslovakia, East Germany, not to mention Russia, was to experience the shock of fresh air. In the Sixties Yugoslavia the place seemed filled with enormous energy. These were the proudest, friendliest people I had met in Europe, and the most frank and open.

There was one taboo, unmentioned but obvious: the ethnic nationalism that Tito had ruthlessly suppressed. I knew, of course, that Slovenians, Bosnians, Serbs, Croatians, Montenegrins and other nationalities made up the Yugoslav delegation to the PEN congress, but to me they all looked alike and conversed in a mutually understood language, so their differences might be no more flammable than those separating the Welsh and the English, or maybe even

Texans and Minnesotans. And when I asked an individual, out of curiosity, if he was Croatian or Slovenian or whatever, and the question caused a slight uneasiness, it seemed minimal enough to be dismissed as more or less irrelevant in this rapidly modernizing country.

Then one evening a group of four writers, one of them a Serb journalist friend called Bogdan, invited me out for a drink after dinner. Two of my companions were poets, a Croatian and a Montenegrin, and one a Slovenian professor. We walked down the road to the local nightclub that usually catered to tourists. The room was very large, like a ballroom. There were maybe fifty bare, plastic-covered tables, only a few of them occupied by stolid, square-headed Alpine types. The cold night air was not noticeably heated. The place had the feeling of a big Pittsburgh cafeteria between meals.

Then a three-piece band took places on a platform up front and began tootling American jazz standards, and a woman materialized and stood unsmilingly facing the audience. Small and compact, she wore a matching brown skirt and jacket and a shiny white rayon blouse. In a businesslike way, she began undressing, in what I was informed was to be a delightful striptease. The scattered audience of men and their chunky women silently gulped beer and sipped slivovitz as the dancer removed her suit jacket, her shoes, her blouse and her skirt, until she stood looking out upon us in her pink rayon slip and bra. It was all done rather antiseptically, as if preparing for a medical examination. Each garment was tidily laid out and patted down on the piano bench, there being no pianist.

Then she stepped out of her slip, and in her panties did a few routine steps in approximate time to the music. She had very good legs. Things were heating up. From somewhere she picked up a heavy blue terry cloth robe and, wrapped in it, she slipped off her bra and flashed one breast. My fellow writers broke off their dying conversation. I don't know what got into me, but I asked a fatal question: "Can you tell from looking at her what her nationality is?"

My Serb friend Bogdan, depressed by his wife's absence in Belgrade, since it had left him for an entire week to the mercies of his melancholy mistress, glanced across the room at the stripper, and gave his morose opinion: "I would say she could be Croatian."

"Impossible!" the Croatian poet laughed. And with a sharpened eye and a surprising undertone of moral indignation, he added,

"She could never be Croatian. Maybe Russian, or Slovenian, but not Croatian."

"Slovenian!" The mocking shout came from the Slovenian literature professor, a tall, thin fellow with shoulder-length hair. "Never! She has absolutely nothing Slovenian about her. Look how dark she is! I would say from the South, maybe Montenegrin."

The dark-skinned Montenegrin poet sitting beside me simply exploded in a challenging "Ha!" Just a few minutes earlier, he had been ethnically relaxed enough to tell a joke on his own people. Montenegrins are apparently famous for their admirably lethargic natures. One of them, said the poet, was walking down a street when he suddenly whipped out his revolver and, swiveling about, shot a snail on the sidewalk behind him. His energetic Serbian friend asked what the hell he had done that for. The Montenegrin explained, "He's been following me all day!"

When it came to the stripper, however, humor had noticeably evaporated, as each of the men kept handing her over to somebody else. And in the middle of this warming discussion of ethnic types, I noticed that the dancer had left the platform in her thick terry cloth robe, with her clothes cradled neatly in her arms. She was just about to pass us when I stuck out my arm and stopped her. "May I ask where you come from?" With a wan, polite smile, she replied "Düsseldorf," and continued on her way.

None of the writers allowed himself to laugh, though I thought one or two blushed at the irony of the situation. A bit tense, struggling awkwardly to reconstruct the earlier atmosphere of comradely warmth, we strolled through the dark Balkan night, the president and four distinguished delegates of the writers' organization established after World War I by H. G. Wells, George Bernard Shaw, Henri Barbusse and other war-weary writers as an attempt to apply the universalist tradition of literature to the melting down of those geographical and psychological barriers of nationalism for whose perpetuation humanity has always spent its noblest courage, and its most ferocious savagery.

Uneasy About the Germans:
After the Wall
1990

Do Germans accept responsibility for the crimes of the Nazi era? Is their repentance such that they can be trusted never to repeat the past? When people worry about the unification of Germany, these are the usual questions. But for me there is a deeper mystery, and it concerns the idea of nationhood itself in the German mind.

Three attempts to create a successful state have been smashed to bits in the mere seventy-two years since Germany's defeat in 1918. And although we are now in the presence of a great victory of a democratic system over a one-party dictatorship, it is not a democratic system of German invention. The nation about to be born is one that never before existed. And in apprehension over what this may mean, the Jews are by no means alone. The British are concerned and so are the French, not to speak of the Russians and numerous others whose lives were ruined by German aggression.

I have more than the usual contact with Germans and German-speaking people. My wife, Austrian by birth, spent the war years in Germany, and her family is involved in German industry; I have German journalist friends, as well as colleagues in the German theater and the film and publishing industries. If I were to announce that I am not too worried about unification and have confidence in the democratic commitments of the younger generation, my friends would doubtless be happy to hear it—and proceed to worry privately on their own.

No one can hope to predict what course any country will take. I believe that for Germans, including those who are eager for unification, the future of German democracy is as much of an enigma as it is for the rest of us. They simply don't know. More precisely, they are almost sure it will turn out all right. But that's a big almost.

Several weeks ago in West Berlin, one of my wife's high school friends, a woman in her late sixties who never left Germany through the rise of Nazism, the war and reconstruction, had some conflicted, if not dark, things to say about the question. "In Germany it will always be the same," she said. "We go up very high, but in the end we come down. We are winning and winning and winning, and then we lose. And when we are in trouble we turn to authority; orders and work make us happiest."

She is using a cane these days, after a fall on the ice. She has a broad-beamed peasant air, thinning hennaed hair, ruddy cheeks. A survivor of a battered generation, she seems to refer to her own observations rather than to things she has read. "We must go slowly with unification," she said. "It is all darkness in front of us." And if the future is murky to West Germans, she wondered: "What is in the minds of the East Germans? We don't know. For us it was bad enough. We had twelve years of dictatorship, but after that we have had nearly fifty years of democracy. They have had nothing but dictatorship since 1933. To become democratic, is it enough to want a good job and a car and to hate the left?"

She has come to visit, despite her injury, because in her circle it is hard to find an open-minded conversation. "I fear it is all very artificial," she said. "It is the same old story, in one sense. We are not like the French, the British, the Americans. We never created our own democracy, or even our own regime, like the Russians; ours was handed to us by the Allies, and we are handing it to the DDR people. But we had a memory of democracy before Hitler. Even their fathers have no such memory now. Who will influence whom— we over them or they over us?"

She talks about the Republicans, a far-right extremist party that won ninety thousand votes in the last West Berlin election after only a few months of existence. "People say they are nonsensical, a tiny minority," she said. "I remember the other tiny nonsensical minority and how fast it took over. And mind you, we are prosperous now. What happens if we run into hard times and unemployment?"

That conversation could be repeated as many times as you like in

Germany. But it is entirely possible that two-thirds of the Germans—those under 50, who can barely recollect Nazism—have only the remotest connection with the woman's sentiments and underlying worry. So hostile are they to any government intrusion in their lives that some of them made it nearly impossible to conduct a national census a few years ago because the questions being asked seemed to threaten them with regimentation from on high. Questions had to be altered, and some census takers were even accompanied by inspectors to make sure more personal questions than those prescribed were not asked.

Nevertheless, the Berlin woman's apprehensions do leave a nagging suspicion. Does the Federal Republic of Germany arouse lofty democratic feelings in its citizens' minds, or is it a system that is simply a matter of historical convenience invented by foreigners? To be sure, this system has helped the nation to prosper as never before, but the issue is how deep the commitment is to its democratic precepts, how sacred they are, and if they will hold in hard times.

I have often sensed something factitious about German society in the minds of Germans, regardless of viewpoint. Discounting the zephyrs—or clouds—of guilt and resentment that obscure conversations with foreigners, especially Jewish liberals like me, it seems that the very reality of the German state is still not quite settled in their minds. I have never, for example, felt that Germans have very transcendent feelings toward the Federal Republic; it does not seem to have imbued them with sublime sensations, even among those who regard it as a triumph of German civic consciousness risen from the ruins of war.

Nothing, at least in my experience, approaches the French emotions toward their republic, the British toward their confusing monarchy, the Swiss toward their multilingual democracy, or Americans' feelings toward their country (which at least once every quarter century is pronounced imminently dead from depression, war, racial conflict or corruption, and therefore requires the loudest avowals of patriotic fervor on the face of the earth).

In a word, the German ship, in the German mind, increasingly powerful and promising though it may be, seems to float slightly above the surface without displacing water. Again, I may get this impression because of the tendency of Germans to apologize for themselves implicitly, which in some is a form of secret boasting, given the incredible success of the German economy.

The Berlin woman's sense of the system as having been conferred on Germans rather than created by them—a routine enough idea in Germany—nevertheless expresses the insubstantiality or, as she put it, the artificiality of the society that is now being merely multiplied by unification. It has sometimes seemed to me in Germany that there is a feeling of walking on Astroturf rather than natural sod. Or maybe it is simply a feeling that the other shoe has not yet dropped.

But when one recalls the polities they did unquestionably create on their own—Frederick the Great's Prussia, Bismarck's state and Hitler's—they were all dictatorial or at least heavily authoritarian and in their time remarkably successful. This is also what my wife's Berlin friend was trying to say to me, namely that as a German she does not quite trust her compatriots' civic instinct when it comes to constructing a free society. And I wonder whether, unspoken, this is the source of the distrust a great many people feel in and out of West Germany, especially now that its territory is to be reunited with the East.

Of course, for the foreigner, Germany's civic failure is most perfectly expressed by the Holocaust and military aggressions of Hitler. But I have wondered whether, foreigners and their accusing attitudes on these counts apart, a different and less obvious historical experience is not more active in creating an uneasiness in them, an experience uniquely German.

It has often been said that Germans alone among the major peoples have never won a revolution. Instead, Germany's intense inner integration of social services, economy and culture was conceived and handed down by kings, princes and great chancellors like Count Bismarck (who though elected was kingly and sternly paternalistic), then a ferocious dictator and, since 1945, by her wartime victors. It is as though George Washington had accepted the widespread demand that he be crowned king, and proceeded to carve out a new society with little or no contribution or interference by elected legislatures. America might well have emerged with a fine well-ordered society in which the rules were very clear and life deeply organized from cradle to grave.

Instead, the state's decisions became the American citizen's rightful business, a conception that destroyed the time-honored relationship in which he was merely the subject of the state's attentions and efforts. The image of himself as citizen was thus vastly different from that in other post-feudal societies of the time—and from that of most people of our time.

Besides a lack of revolutionary past, the Federal Republic is unique among the great powers in another way: it came to life without a drop of blood being shed in its birth. No German soldier can say, "I fought for democracy." It was not given him by history to do so. West Germany is the creation not of arms, but work. The Japanese system, also practically America's creation, is a quite different case, in that the monarchy and government were never destroyed as such; indeed, MacArthur took great pains to make its continuity with the past obvious to all.

The German break with Hitlerism, the last German-made system, had to be total and condign. And German society had to be started almost literally from a pile of bricks under which the shameful past was to be buried, put out of mind, deeply discredited.

If these observations are in fact operative, and I cannot imagine how they can be proved or disproved as such, then what Germans lack now is the consecration by blood of their democratic state. The torrent of German blood that has flowed in this era in the Hitler-launched wars was, in fact, to prevent any such state from coming into existence.

For me, this is what keeps sucking the life out of German protestations of a democratic faith and casts suspicion on the country's reassurances that its economic power is no menace to the world. The fact is, West German civic practice has been as democratic as any other society's for more than forty years and is less repressive and all-controlling than, for example, that of France, whose bureaucracy is positively strangulating by comparison.

I know Germans who are as certain as it is possible to be that democracy will hold; I know other Germans who do not believe that at all. The world, it seems to me, has no choice but to support the positive side of the split and to extend its hand to a democratic Germany. By giving it the recognition it deserves, German democracy can only be strengthened, but meeting it with endless suspicion may finally wither its hopes. A recent *New York Times*/CBS News poll shows a large majority of Americans in favor of reunification, a vote of confidence with which I agree. At the same time, no German should take umbrage at the reminder that his nation in a previous incarnation showed that it had aggressive impulses that brought death to forty million people. This memory should not vanish: it is part of democratic Germany's defense against the temptation to gather around some new extreme nationalism in the future.

It does not really do any good to remind Germans of those horrendous statistics if the purpose is simply to gratify an impulse to punish. But it is necessary never to forget what nationalistic blood lust can come to, so that it will never happen again.

Likewise, German resentment at such reminders has to be understood. No one can live in a perpetual state of repentance without resentment. In the scale and profundity of its degradation Nazism has no equal in modern time, but each country has had some level of experience with contrition, some taste of it, as a repayment for oppression of other people. What if every nation guilty of persecution were to own up? Are we really prepared to believe in their remorse? And while penitence in the persecutors may be a moral necessity for those who survived victimization, it will not bring back the dead. So is it not infinitely more important that the descendants of persecutors demonstrate something more than contrition, namely political responsibility?

What do I care if a Nazi says he's sorry? I want to know what the constitution and educational system of Germany are doing to defend democracy under possibly difficult future circumstances. That is important to me and to my children. It is equally important that democracy live not only in institutions but in the German heart. But in all candor how are we ever to know that it does, except as crises are faced in a democratic spirit?

The world has a right—its World War II dead have earned it the right—to reproach and criticize and make demands of Germans if and when they seem to revert to bad habits. For a long time to come, the Germans are going to have to face the legacy of their last attempt to dominate other nations.

But there is another Germany—the Germany of high aspirations. It does truly exist, and it must be welcomed wholeheartedly in the hope that one day its permanent dominion over the country will be unquestioned by any fair-minded person. In short, the time has come to look the worst in the eye but to hope for the best.

A German journalist in her mid-forties, typical of many of her generation despite an upper-class Black Forest origin, has struggled with her country's past all her life and by turns is in despair and hopeful. "The problem," she says, "or part of it, is that the world is still thinking of Germany as it was in the Nazi time or shortly after. But a lot has happened in Germany in the last forty years!" As her voice rises, I am struck by an odd resemblance to the attitude of the Berlin woman. They both seem to doubt that they are *registering*; it is as if events were wild horses flying past with no one really pondering how to tame them. "For example," she goes on, "the impact of the 1968 French students' rebellion. It overturned Germany's educational system and for the first time made it possible for German workers to go to universities, the way it happens in America. Until then, we had a very narrow elite system. In fact, ours is now far more democratic than the French or the English, and we are now paying people to go to university, eight hundred marks a month if their parents together earn less than fifteen hundred a month. University education is free. This has had good and bad results—a lowering of standards, actually—but socially it has broken the class system."

Slim, elegantly dressed and a stubbornly heavy smoker, she is unable to come psychologically to rest. "This generation cannot be confused with the stupid, lumpen people who flocked to Hitler," she said. "Moreover, there is an immense amount of travel by this generation. They are not the parochial, isolated mass that Hitler poisoned so easily with antiforeign propaganda. This is not in any sense the pre-Hitler German people."

Then, hardly a moment later: "The problem with the German, the one great weakness of his character, is his worship of loyalty. Loyality! Loyality! It's the supreme virtue, the chain around his heart. . . ." And she is quite suddenly angry, and, for a few minutes, blue and uncertain and perhaps fearful.

In short, the uneasiness about national character is subjective, difficult to catch in the nets of rationality, but it may turn out to be more decisive than any other.

The anxiety shown by the journalist and my wife's Berlin friend transcends political viewpoints, I believe. Nor is it purely a product of the catastrophic last war and the Holocaust. I know some liberal Germans, a couple of radicals and some very conservative business types, and from all of them I have felt a similar emanation of uncertainty as to what, in effect, the German is—and consequently what kind of society fits him, expresses his so contradictory nature. And this is what I think the perplexity comes down to.

The Federal Republic is not a nation like others, born of self-determining revolution. Paradoxically, perhaps, West Germany is the first great society born of peace; if it is to achieve a deep sense of identity it will have to be real, not slyly apologetic, an identity reflecting the evil past and the present resurrection together.

If Germany remains implicitly on trial for a long time to come, release must come through good works and a demonstrated devotion to democratic ideals and practice. The past cannot be changed, but the future of democracy is in the nation's hands. Perhaps Germany can one day even stand as an example to other new societies of how to win a place in the world by work and the intelligent use of science rather than arms.

There is now a generation that cannot remember the war or Nazism, and in fact finds it difficult to understand them, especially what to it is the incredible degree of Nazi regimentation to which Germans submitted. Maybe it is time for Germans to take a look at how and why their society began, not for the sake of cosmetizing an image, but to make themselves more real in their own eyes. If I may quote *Incident at Vichy*, when the Jewish psychoanalyst confronts the self-blaming Austrian prince, "It's not your guilt I want, it's your responsibility." That is to say, to relinquish denial and take to heart the donations of history to one's character and the character of one's people, the most painful but rewarding job a people can undertake.

The Sin of Power
1978

It is always necessary to ask how old a writer is who is reporting his impressions of a social phenomenon. Like the varying depth of a lens, the mind bends the light passing through it quite differently according to its age. When I first experienced Prague in the late Sixties, the Russians had only just entered with their armies; writers (almost all of them self-proclaimed Marxists if not Party members) were still unsure of their fate under the new occupation, and when some thirty or forty of them gathered in the office of *Listy* to "interview" me, I could smell the apprehension among them. And indeed, many would soon be fleeing abroad, some would be jailed, and others would never again be permitted to publish in their native language. Incredibly, that was almost a decade ago.

But since the first major blow to the equanimity of my mind was the victory of Nazism, first in Germany and later in the rest of Europe, the images I have of repression are inevitably cast in fascist forms. In those times the communist was always the tortured victim, and the Red Army stood as the hope of man, the deliverer. So to put it quite simply, although correctly, I think, the occupation of Czechoslovakia was the physical proof that Marxism was but one more self-delusionary attempt to avoid facing the real nature of power, the primitive corruption by power of those who possess it. In a word, Marxism has turned out to be a form of sentimentalism toward human nature, and this has its funny side. After all, it was initially a probe into the most painful wounds of the capitalist presumptions, it was scientific and analytical. What the Russians have done in Czechoslovakia is, in effect, to prove in a Western cultural environment that what they have called socialism simply cannot tolerate even the most nominal independent scrutiny, let alone an opposition. The critical intelligence itself is not to be borne and in the birthplace of Kafka and of the absurd in its subtlest expression absurdity emanates from the Russian occupation like some sort of gas which makes one both laugh and cry. Shortly after returning home from my first visit to Prague mentioned above, I happened to meet a Soviet political scientist at a high-level conference where he was a participant representing his country and I was invited to speak at one session to present my views of the impediments to better cultural relations between the two nations. Still depressed by my Czech experience, I naturally brought up the invasion of the country as a likely cause for American distrust of the Soviets, as well as the United States aggression in Vietnam from the same détente viewpoint.

That had been in the morning; in the evening at a party for all the conference participants, half of them Americans, I found myself facing this above-mentioned Soviet whose anger was unconcealed. "It is amazing," he said, "that you—especially you as a Jew, should attack our action in Czechoslovakia."

Normally quite alert to almost any reverberations of the Jewish presence in the political life of our time, I found myself in a state of unaccustomed and total confusion at this remark, and I asked the man to explain the connection. "But obviously," he said (and his face had gone quite red and he was quite furious now), "we have gone in there to protect them from the West German fascists."

I admit that I was struck dumb. Imagine!—The marching of all the Warsaw Pact armies in order to protect the few Jews left in Czechoslovakia! It is rare that one really comes face to face with such fantasy so profoundly believed by a person of intelligence. In the face of this kind of expression all culture seems to crack and collapse; there is no longer a frame of reference.

In fact, the closest thing to it that I could recall were my not infrequent arguments with intelligent supporters or apologists for our Vietnamese invasion. But at this point the analogy ends, for it was always possible during the Vietnam war for Americans opposed to it to make their views heard, and, indeed, it was the widespread opposition to the war which finally made it impossible for President Johnson to continue in office. It certainly was not a simple matter to oppose the war in any significant way, and the civilian casualties of protest were by no means few, and some—like the students at the Kent State University protest—paid with their lives. But what one might call the unofficial underground reality, the version of morals and national interest held by those not in power, was ultimately expressed and able to prevail sufficiently to alter high policy. Even so it was the longest war ever fought by Americans.

Any discussion of the American rationales regarding Vietnam must finally confront something which is uncongenial to both Marxist and anti-Marxist viewpoints, and it is the inevitable pressure, by those holding political power, to distort and falsify the structures of reality. The Marxist, by philosophical conviction, and the bourgeois American politician, by practical witness, both believe at bottom that reality is quite simply the arena into which determined men can enter and reshape just about every kind of relationship in it. The conception of an objective reality which is the summing up of all historical circumstances, as well as the idea of human beings as containers or vessels by which that historical experience defends itself and expresses itself through common sense and unconscious drives, are notions which at best are merely temporary nuisances, incidental obstructions to the wished-for remodeling of human nature and the improvements of society which power exists in order to set in place.

The sin of power is to not only distort reality but to convince people that the false is true, and that what is happening is only an invention of enemies. Obviously, the Soviets and their friends in Czechoslovakia are by no means the only ones guilty of this sin, but in other places, especially in the West, it is possible yet for witnesses to reality to come forth and testify to the truth. In Czechoslovakia the whole field is preempted by the power itself.

Thus a great many people outside, and among them a great many artists, have felt a deep connection with Czechoslovakia—but precisely because there has been a fear in the West over many generations that the simple right to reply to power is a tenuous thing and is always on the verge of being snipped like a nerve. I have, myself, sat at dinner with a Czech writer and his family in his own home and looked out and seen police sitting in their cars down below, in effect warning my friend that our "meeting" was being observed. I have seen reports in Czech newspapers that a certain writer had emigrated to the West and was no longer willing to live in his own country, when the very same man was sitting across a living room coffee table from me. And I have also been lied about in America by both private and public liars, by the press and the government, but a road—sometimes merely a narrow path—always remained open before my mind, the belief that I might sensibly attempt to influence people to see what was real and so at least to resist the victory of untruth.

I know what it is to be denied the right to travel outside my country, having been denied my passport for some five years by our Department of State. And I know a little about the inviting temptation to simply get out at any cost, to quit my country in disgust and disillusion, as no small number of people did in the McCarthy Fifties and as a long line of Czechs and Slovaks have in these recent years. I also know the empty feeling in the belly at the prospect of trying to learn another nation's secret language, its gestures and body communications without which a writer is only half-seeing and half-hearing. More important, I know the conflict between recognizing the indifference of the people and finally conceding that the salt has indeed lost its savor and that the only sensible attitude toward any people is cynicism.

So that those who have chosen to remain as writers on their native soil despite remorseless pressure to emigrate are, perhaps no less than their oppressors, rather strange and anachronistic figures in this time. After all, it is by no means a heroic epoch now; we in the West as well as in the East understand perfectly well that the political and military spheres—where "heroics" were called for in the past, are now merely expressions of the unmerciful industrial-technological base. As for the very notion of patriotism, it falters before the perfectly obvious interdependence of the nations, as well as the universal prospect of mass obliteration by the atom bomb, the instrument which has doomed us, so to speak, to this lengthy peace between the great powers. That a group of intellectuals should persist in creating a national literature on their own ground is out of tune with our adaptational proficiency which has flowed from these developments. It is hard anymore to remember whether one is living in Rome or New York, London or Strasbourg, so homogenized has Western life become. The persistence of these people may be an inspiration to some but a nuisance to others, and not only inside the oppressing apparatus but in the West as well. For these so-called dissidents are apparently upholding values at a time when the first order of business would seem to be the accretion of capital for technological investment.

It need hardly be said that by no means everybody in the West is in favor of human rights, and Western support for Eastern dissidents has more hypocritical self-satisfaction in it than one wants to think too much about. Nevertheless, if one has learned anything at all in the past forty or so years, it is that to struggle for these rights (and without them the accretion of capital is simply the construction of a more modern prison) one has to struggle for them wherever the need arises.

That this struggle *also* has to take place in socialist systems suggests to me that the fundamental procedure which is creating violations of these rights transcends social systems—a thought anathematic to Marxists but possibly true nevertheless. What may be in place now is precisely a need to erect a new capital structure, be it in Latin America or the Far East or underdeveloped parts of Europe, and just as in the nineteenth century in America and England it is a process which always breeds injustice and the flouting of human spiritual demands because it essentially is the sweating of increasing amounts of production and wealth from a labor force surrounded, in effect, by police.

The complaining or reforming voice in that era was not exactly encouraged in the United States or England; by corrupting the press and buying whole legislatures, capitalists effectively controlled their opposition, and the struggle of the trade union movement was often waged against firing rifles.

There is of course a difference now, many differences. At least they are supposed to be differences, particularly, that the armed force is in the hands of a state calling itself socialist and progressive and scientific, no less pridefully than the nineteenth-century capitalisms boasted by their Christian ideology and their devotion to the human dimension of political life as announced by the American Bill of Rights and the French Revolution. But the real difference now is the incomparably deeper and more widespread conviction that man's fate is *not* "realistically" that of the regimented slave. It may be that despite everything, and totally unannounced and unheralded, a healthy skepticism toward the powerful has at last become second nature to the great mass of people almost everywhere. It may be that history, now, is on the side of those who hopelessly hope and cling to their native ground to claim it for their language and ideals.

The oddest request I ever heard in Czechoslovakia—or anywhere else—was to do what I could to help writers publish their works—but not in French, German or English, the normal desire of sequestered writers cut off from the outside. No, these Czech writers were desperate to see their works—in Czech! Somehow this speaks of something far more profound than "dissidence" or any political quantification. There is something like love in it, and in this sense it is a prophetic yearning and demand.

A Visit with Castro
2004

Like a lot of other people's feelings toward Cuba, mine have been mixed in the past decades. A part from press reports, I had learned from film people who had worked there that the Batista society was hopelessly corrupt, a Mafia playground, a bordello for Americans and other foreigners. So Castro storming his way to power seemed like a clean wind blowing away the degradation and subservience to the Yankee dollar. What emerged once the smoke had cleared finally turned into something different, of course, and if I chose not to forget the background causes of the Castro revolution, the repressiveness of his one-man government was still grinding away at my sympathy. At the same time, the relentless US blockade at the behest, so it appeared, of a defeated class of exploiters who had never had a problem with the previous dictatorship seemed to be something other than a principled democratic resistance.

The focus of all these contradictions was Castro himself; this man, in effect, was Cuba, but when my wife, the photographer Inge Morath, and I were invited in March 2000 to join a small group of "cultural visitors" for a short visit, we went along with no thought of actually meeting the Leader but merely to see a bit of the country. As it turned out, soon after our arrival he would invite our small group of nine to dinner and the following day, unannounced, suddenly showed up out in the country where we were having lunch in order to continue the conversation.

By March 2000, the time of our meeting, the future of Cuba was the big question for anyone thinking about the country. Our group was no exception. We were, apart from my wife and myself, William Luers, former head of New York's Metropolitan Museum of Art and ambassador first to Venezuela and later to Czechoslovakia, and his wife, Wendy, a committed human rights activist; novelist William Styron and his wife, Rose; book agent Morton Janklow and his wife, Linda; and Patty Cisneros, philanthropist organizer of a foundation to save Amazon culture. The only nonspeakers of Spanish were the Styrons, Janklows and I.

Expecting to simply wander in the city and perhaps meet a few writers, we were surprised our second day by the invitation from Castro to join him for dinner. Later, it would come clear that "Gabo" (Gabriel Garcia Márquez), Castro's friend and supporter as well as a friend of Bill Styron, had most probably been the author of this hospitality. I was greatly curious, as were the others, about Castro and at the same time slightly guarded in my expectations.

Having had a certain amount of experience with Soviet and Eastern European officialdom in the arts, particularly as head of International PEN for four years, I expected to have to do a lot of agreeable nodding in silence to statements manifestly silly if not at times idiotic. Unelected leaders and their outriders are unusually sensitive to contradiction, and the experience of their company can be miserably boring. However, Castro was mythic by this time, and the prospect of an hour or two with him was something to look forward to.

I'll mention only two or three observations I had made in Havana before our dinner. The city itself has the beauty of a ruin returning to the sand, the mica, the gravel and trees from which it originated. The poverty of the people is obvious, but at the same time a certain spiritedness seems to survive. Poor as they are there is little sense of the dead despair one finds in cities where poverty and glamorous wealth live side by side. But this is all appearances, which do count for something but not everything. A guide I happened upon with whom I had a private chat—answering my questions, I should add, and not volunteering—said that it was simply not possible for anyone to live in Cuba on a single job. Educated, clearly disciplined, he could not keep his deep frustration from boiling over as he explained that he worked for a government tourist agency that charged large fees to foreign clients for his services while he received a pittance. If this was not exploitation he did not know the meaning of the word.

But there may be another dimension to unhappiness like his. I walked around near the lovely old Hotel Santa Isabel, where we were staying, and a few blocks away sat down on a park bench facing the pleasantly meager traffic on the Malecón, the broad road around the harbor. Presently, two guys showed up and sat beside me, deep in discussion. They were exceedingly thin, neither had socks, one wore cracked shoes and the other disintegrating sandals, their shirts were washed and unironed with shredded collars, they were both in need of a shave. They had a way of sitting crouched over crossed knees while sucking on cigarettes and staring at the flowing away of time as they talked, reminding me of street people in New York, Paris, London. A taxi pulled up to the curb in front of us and a lovely young woman stepped out.

She was carrying two brown paper bags full of groceries. Both men stopped talking to gape at her. I saw now that she was beautiful and tastefully dressed and, more noticeable in this proletarian place, was wearing high heels. One white tulip arched up from one of the bags and drooped down from its long slender stem. The woman was juggling the bags to get her money purse open, and the tulip was waving dangerously close to snapping its stem. One of the men got up and took hold of one of the bags to steady it, while the other joined him to steady the other bag, and I wondered if they were about to grab the bags and run.

Instead, as the woman paid the driver, one of them gently, with the most tender care, held the tulip stem between forefinger and thumb until she could get the bags secured in her arms. She thanked them—not effusively but with a certain formal dignity, and walked off. Both men returned to the bench and their avid discussion. I'm not quite sure why, but I thought this transaction remarkable. It was not only the gallantry of these impoverished men that was impressive, but that the woman seemed to regard it as her due and not at all extraordinary. Needless to say, she offered no tip, nor did they seem to expect any, her comparative wealth notwithstanding.

Having protested for years the government's jailing and silencing of writers and dissidents, I wondered whether despite everything, including the system's economic failure, a heartening species of human solidarity had been created, possibly out of the relative symmetry of poverty and the uniform futility inherent in the system from which few could raise their heads short of sailing away.

A VISIT WITH CASTRO

The poverty is apparently close to catastrophic. On this same lively harbor road are stoplights that, when they turn red, are a signal for a dozen or so young women and girls to approach the halted cars as though out of nowhere. They are not garishly dressed and their makeup is subdued. I asked our driver what they were doing, and he said they were "hitching rides." He did not turn to meet my gaze but kept his eyes straight ahead, obviously unwilling to pursue the subject. This kind of display was forbidden during the Soviet-dominated years, probably because the economy was not quite so desperately bad and perhaps as well out of deference to Soviet puritanism. Now the pressure of outright hunger was too great to hold back.

I met with an acting class in the theater school after they had shown me a beautifully modulated performance of a surreal student play in which a crucifixion suggests a symbolization of the HIV/AIDS anguish. On the lawn outside, I faced about a hundred of them, young and avid and bursting with hope and energy, wanting to know all about "Broadway." When I told them that "Broadway" had been captured almost exclusively by musicals and pure entertainment and that the few straight plays were limited runs for stars, they looked unhappy and really didn't want to hear the bad news. Nothing, it seems, can tarnish the success and hopefulness that most things American convey. One thing is sure, given the chance they'd have rushed in a body to Times Square.

On arriving in the Palace of the Revolution for our dinner, my wife was immediately required to give up her Leica before meeting Castro. The man taking the camera promptly dropped it from a high bin to the stone floor. The palace is pre-Castro, very modern and aggressively opulent, with gleaming black stone walls and checkered floors, all of it immaculately kept. We entered an anteroom leading into the dining room and suddenly there was Castro, not in uniform as one always sees him in photographs but in a blue pencil-striped suit that, unpressed as it was, must not have been worn very often. Despite the suit, my quick impression was that had he not been a revolutionary politician he might well have been a movie star. He had that utterly total self-involvement, that need for love and agreement and the overwhelming thirst for the power that comes with total approval. In this crowded antechamber his retinue, as with most leaders everywhere, were supremely agreeable and one sensed immediately their absolute submission to the Leader. Whatever else he is, Castro is an exciting person and could probably have had a career on the screen.

Luers, in effect our senior shepherd, introduced our members in Spanish, and Gabo added a few words of explanation to identify us for Castro. Garcia Márquez is quite short and the rest of us men are six feet or over, so that he stood looking up at Castro and the rest of us like a new younger boy in school. His friendship with Styron and his English started things off fluently, so that between them and Castro's conversations with Luers and Wendy, his wife, and Patty Cisneros and Inge, a loud hubbub banged against the walls. Suddenly Castro looked at me over the heads of the others and nearly shouted, "What is your birthday!"

"October 17, 1915," I replied, pretending I was not astonished at the question.

He now pointed his long index finger at his right temple. All went silent. An expression of deep-delving sagacity settled over his face as he kept the finger pressed against his head. I sensed hambone overacting, but then recalled paintings of Cervantes's Knight of the Sad Countenance, the heaven-directed gaze, the scraggly beard, the slanty eyebrows, the immemorial dark Spanish mournfulness, and Castro began to look normal. Now he raised the finger to point upward like a censorious teacher. "You are eleven years, five months and fourteen days older than I." (I can't recall the exact figures, but this will do.) Congratulatory laughter burst out and brightened the air. There was something almost touching in this childish demonstration of his calculating ability, and one recognized again his boyish hungering for the central distinction in a group. I thought of his idolization of Hemingway, another star who I am sure had felt the same driving need in himself. It was easy to imagine how they must have appreciated each other.

Now, with a wicked look in his eye, he turned to Wendy Luers. In midafternoon she had gotten us all out of the minibus the government had provided and into taxis that had taken us to the home of a dissident, Elizardo Sanchez. There we learned what was rather obvious—that despite the man's having been jailed a number of

times for writing and distributing antigovernment publications, he
was presently free but without any detectable influence. Knowing
that his house was bugged he felt free to say whatever he liked,
since his positions were already well-known. And if any of us had
imagined that the visit was secret, we were disabused by the friendly
TV cameraman who photographed us out in the street as we left.
So much for our taking taxis instead of the government bus.

Now, addressing Wendy Luers primarily, Castro leaned forward
and said, "We hear you were all missing for a couple of hours this
afternoon! Were you shopping?" A flash of fierce irony crossed his
face before he joined in our laughter. And so to dinner.

A meeting had been arranged the previous afternoon, no doubt
through the writers union, with some fifty or so Cuban writers. Initially the organizers had expected only a few dozen on such short
notice, but they had had to find a larger space when this crowd
showed up. We encountered a rather barren auditorium, a speaker's
platform and an odd quietness for so large a crowd. What to make
of their silence? I couldn't help being reminded of the fifties, when
the question hanging over any such gathering was whether it was
being observed and recorded by the FBI.

It was hard to tell whether Styron's or my work was known to
this audience, almost all of them men. In any case, with the intro-
ductions finished, Styron briefly described his novels as I did my
plays, and questions were invited. One man stood and asked, "Why
have you come here?"

Put so candidly, the question threw my mind back to Eastern
Europe decades ago; there too it was inconceivable that such a meeting could have no political purpose. Styron and I were both rather
stumped. I finally said that we were simply curious about Cuba and
were opposed to her isolation and thought a short visit might teach
us something. "But what is your message?" the man persisted. We
had none, we were now embarrassed to admit. Still, as we broke up
a number of them came up to shake hands and wordlessly express a
sort of solidarity with us, or so I supposed. But in some of them
there was also suspicion, I thought, if not outright, if suppressed,
hostility to us for failing to bring a message that would offer some
hope against their isolation. But back to the dinner with Fidel . . .

There were fantastic shrimp and spectacular pork, dream pork,

Cubans being famous for their pork. (Castro, however, ate greens, intending to live forever.) Our group sat intermixed with Cubans, government ministers and associates, several of them women. Styron sat alongside Castro and his fabulous instantaneous interpreter, a woman who had been in this work the past quarter-century. Surrounding the table was a plastic tropical garden beautifully lit, possibly to suggest the sort of jungle from which the Revolution had sprung.

It quickly became clear that instead of a conversation, we were to have what seemed a rather formalized set of approaches to various ideas springing from the Leader's mind. Most of these have left my memory (after seven or eight months), but I can recall Castro suddenly looking severe as he spoke of the Russians' dumb stubbornness in all things, and his imitating their basso voices as they stuck to some absurd proposition despite all contrary evidence. What he seemed to hold against them primarily was their disloyalty amounting to perfidy—they had not stuck it out as real revolutionaries had to. But Luers, who next day would have a private conversation with him lasting hours, learned that his principal beef was the Soviets' refusal to back his attempts at starting revolutions in various Latin American and other countries. They wanted no confrontation with the United States and in his view were contemptibly unrevolutionary.

At the dinner he also took a few stabs at the CIA and its numerous assassination attempts against him, but here he affected to be more amused than angry, if only because they had blown back in American faces. And one couldn't miss a certain air of settled or even haughty confidence vis-à-vis America; it was almost as though Cuba were the great power and America some sort of unpredictable adolescent who periodically threw stones and broke his windows. However, he is said never to sleep twice in the same house, and his private movements are known to very few. What I do clearly recall is his leafing through a book of Inge's photographs, given to him that evening, and on seeing them promptly ordering an underling to return her her camera. And he had no objection to her photographing him the rest of the evening.

We had sat down at about 9:30. At 11:30 I began to wilt, and I recalled that Castro, who was clearly gaining strength with every passing moment, enjoyed staying up all night because he slept during most of the day. I was hardly alone in my deepening exhaustion; clearly his retinue, having no doubt heard his stories and remarks numerous times before, were cranking up their eyelids. Now it was 12:30, and then inevitably it got to be 1:30, and Castro was filling with the energy of his special vitamin pills, perhaps (a bag of which he later gave to each of us). I saw that García Márquez was, as far as one could tell, in a deep doze sitting upright in his chair. Castro was now in full flight, borne aloft by a kind of manic enthusiasm for sheer performance itself. Be it some perfectly well-known scientific discovery or somebody's intelligent perception of whatever sort, he spoke of it as though personally exposing it for the first time. But charmingly, not without ironical self-deprecation and some wit. He was remorselessly on, obviously anxious to occupy as vast a space around him as he possibly could. And how, I realized, could it be any different, when he had been the chief of state for close to half a century, longer by far than any king or president in modern times, except perhaps Emperor Francis Joseph of Austria. And what effect had his endless rule had on Cubans, most of whom had not even been born when he came to power? Indeed, I had asked at our meeting with the writers how the country was going to move from Castro to whoever or whatever was to follow him, and the uneasiness in the audience was palpable and no one would venture a reply. As we were leaving that meeting one man came up to me and said, "The only solution is biological."

At around 2 in the morning I realized that this veritable human engine of sheer joy might well expect us to stay until dawn. Desperate for sleep, before I could really think it through, I raised my hand and said, "Please, Mr. President, forgive me, but when we arrived you will recall that you said I was eleven years, five months and fourteen days older than you." I paused, struck by his sudden brow-lifted look of surprise or even some small apprehension at the interruption. "It is now fifteen days."

He threw up his hands. "I have transgressed!" He laughed and stood up, ending the dinner. When our group departed we were applauded in the street by the grateful retinue.

Next day we were lunching far out in the country, on the porch of a reforestation institute that over the years had planted hundreds of acres of various species of trees on the rolling hills that surround the rustic headquarters building. The air was pure and the silence refreshing. Suddenly, the roar of engines, and in a cloud of dust three large, recent-model Mercedes raced to a halt and the door of the middle one swung open and there was Castro, this time in his green uniform. He mounted the porch to our general greetings and took a chair and settled in.

Styron seemed to be the center of his interest today, and Castro asked him for the names of the best American authors, but of the nineteenth century, explaining with a grin that he wanted to avoid arousing our competitive instinct.

He had never really studied American literature, he said, and knew very little about it. This admission seemed strange, given Hemingway's iconic position in Cuba, with his home a veritable holy site. In fact, it made one wonder whether for Castro there was something almost forbidden in the idea of the enemy's even having a literature, or for that matter a spiritual life, at all. As Styron, unprepared for this display of Castro's remoteness from the culture he was unceasingly castigating, tried to improvise a brief lecture on American literature's high points, I wondered whether Castro might have been as remote from his own country as from ours. One is forever attributing informed wisdom to power, but in the face of the privation around him, should not a wise ruler who even in a free election would doubtless be reelected, nevertheless recognize that after almost fifty years in supreme control the time had come to make way for a regime with new people and possibly more effective ideas?

Watching him at lunch—he ate two leaves of lettuce—one saw a lonely old man hungry for some fresh human contact, which could only get more and more rare as he ages. He might very well live actively for ten years, perhaps even longer as his parents reportedly had done, and I found myself wondering what could possibly be keeping him from a graceful exit that might even earn him his countrymen's gratitude?

The quasi-sexual enchantment of power? Perhaps. More likely, given his history, was his commitment to the poetic image of world revolution, the uprising of the wretched of the earth with himself at its head. And in plain fact, as the chief of a mere island, he had managed to elevate himself to that transcendent state in millions of minds. The more so now, after all other contestants had fallen away and conditions in Latin America and Africa gone from bad to worse, the possibility needed only its right time to erupt again. After all, he had thrown Cuban forces into action in many countries around the world despite his country's poverty and the obstinate resistance of his main sponsor, the now-abominated Soviet leadership.

It would have been too much to expect that after half a century in power he would not become to some important degree an anachronism, a handsome old clock that no longer tells the time correctly and bongs haphazardly in the middle of the night, disturbing the house. Notwithstanding all his efforts, the only semblance of a revolt of the poor is the antimodern Islamic tide, which from the Marxist point of view floats in a medieval dream. With us he seemed pathetically hungry for some kind of human contact. Brilliant as he is, spirited and resourceful as his people are, his endless rule seemed like some powerful vine wrapping its roots around the country and while defending it from the elements choking its natural growth. And his own as well. Ideology aside, he apparently maintains the illusions that structured his political successes even if they never had very much truth in them; to this day, as one example, he speaks of Gorbachev's dissolution of the Soviet Union as unnecessary, "a mistake."

In short, there was no fatal contradiction inherent in the Soviet system that brought it down, and so there is nothing in the Castro system or in his take on reality that is creating the painful poverty of the island. The US embargo created this island's poverty out of hand, along with the Russians by their deserting him. It is Don Quixote tilting at windmills which, worse yet, have collapsed into dust.

The plaza before the Hotel Santa Isabel is lined with some fifteen or twenty bookstalls displaying for sale battered old Marxist-Leninist tracts, which two caretakers stock each morning and empty each evening, their positions on the shelves undisturbed during the days. Is it possible that someone in the government—Castro, perhaps—imagines that sane persons will be tempted to buy, let alone read, these artifacts of another age? What, one wonders, is keeping it all alive? Is it the patriotic love of Cubans, conformist or dissident, for their country, or is it the stuck-in-cement manic hatred of US politicians, whose embargo quite simply gives Castro an insurance policy against needed change, injecting the energy of rightful defiance into the people? For it is the embargo that automatically explains each and every failure of the regime to provide for the Cuban people. It will need the pathos of a new Cervantes to measure up to this profoundly sad tale of needless suffering.

Why Israel Must Choose Justice
2003

I wish to thank you for this honor and for allowing me to join the distinguished list of authors who were past recipients of the Jerusalem Prize. The awarding of this prize in recognition of my work as a writer also cites my activities in defense of civil rights. As a past president of International P.E.N., the association of writers from around the world committed to the defense of the freedom to write, I have visited many countries with various political systems, at times to try to get writers out of jail, at other times simply to reinforce local P.E.N. centers in their struggle, quite often, to continue to exist. To tell the truth, I never wanted to spend time away from my desk, but it may be that as a Jew of a certain generation I was unable to forget the silence of the 1930s and '40s, when Fascism began its destruction of our people, which for so long met with the indifference of the world. Perhaps it is because I have tried to do something useful to protect human rights that I know how hard it is to make good things happen. At the same time, my experience tells me that most people by far continue to believe in justice and wish it to prevail.

Because I have at least a sense of the many terrible contradictions in Israel's situation vis-à-vis the Palestinians. I am also conscious of my distance from the day-to-day realities. So I am not going to lecture or try to persuade. The fundamentals of my views are simply that Israel has the right to exist, and the Palestinians likewise, in a state of their own. With the expansion of settlements I have witnessed, initially with surprise and then with incredulity, what seemed a self-defeating policy. I am not going to pursue conflicting arguments with secondhand knowledge, but merely to say the obvious—that the settlement policy appears to have changed the very nature of the Israeli state and that a new birth of a humanistic vision is necessary if the Jewish presence is to be seen as worth preserving. To put it perhaps too succinctly—without justice at its center, no state can endure as a representation of the Jewish nature.

I might fill in some of the background of these views, because this background is what provides the stark contrast for me with the present tragic situation. I have not been without some small experience with political Israel. I was invited to attend the Waldorf dinner in 1948 to celebrate the Soviet Union's recognition of the State of Israel, which was the first and for a time her only international acknowledgment. The very idea of a nation of Jews existing in modern times was hard to imagine then. It was almost as though a scene out of the Bible were being re-enacted, but this time with real people smoking cigarettes. Imagine! Jewish bus drivers, Jewish cops, Jewish street sweepers, Jewish judges and the criminals they judged, Jewish prostitutes and movie stars, Jewish plumbers and carpenters and bankers, a Jewish president and parliament and a Jewish secretary of state. All this was something so new on the earth that it never dawned on me or, I think, on most people, that the new Israel, as a state governed by human beings, would behave more or less the same as any state had acted down through history—defending its existence by all means thought necessary and even expanding its borders when possible. In 1948, from the prospect of New York at any rate, the very idea of a Jewish state was defensive, since it was under almost perpetual attack. It existed at all as a refuge for a people that had barely escaped a total genocidal wipeout in Europe only a few years earlier. And so it was, I think, that the predominant sense of things at that Waldorf celebration was that, having passed out of the control and domination of others, the time had come for Jews to act normal.

Naturally, it never occurred to most people, certainly not to me, what normal really meant. In that ebullient Waldorf moment and afterward one heard little or nothing of the dark side of the history of new states, especially their sharp collisions with other peoples in the same or contiguous areas. For some years, especially in the United States, a certain idyllic Israel existed in the public imagination, and for some it probably still does. The Israel of the kibbutz,

of the rescued land, of the pioneers and the pioneering cooperative
spirit reminiscent of summer camp. There was inevitably a lot of
psychological denial in this picture, just as there always is in the
nationalist picture of any nation. I was not a Zionist, but I certainly
participated, however unwittingly, in this kind of denial—although
it did seem rather odd to hear Golda Meir responding to a question
about the Palestinians by saying, "*We* are the Palestinians." But
this seemed about as harmless as the American President's habit of
resolving the harsh inequalities in American society by pridefully
declaring, "We are all Americans."

The Jewish obsession with justice goes back to the beginnings, of
course. Job, after all, is not complaining merely that he has lost
everything; he is not some bourgeois caught in an economic depression. His bewilderment derives from a horrendous vision of a world
without justice, which means a world collapsed into chaos and
brute force. And if he is called upon to have faith in god anyway, it
is a god who in some mysterious manner does indeed still stand for
justice, however inscrutable his design may be.

Israel in that Waldorf moment meant the triumph of sheer survival, the determination to live a dignified life. Israel also signaled
the survival of a temperament, the continuing Jewish entanglement
in the mesh of life, and somehow the Jewish engagement with eternal things. In short, Israel was far more than a political entity, let
alone a geographic place, probably at least in part because it was so
far away and the distance turned it into something approaching an
artistic expression, a sort of bright vision of productive peace.

However it may have evolved, it appears at this distance that
from the assassination of Rabin onward the settlement policy and
the present leadership's apparent abandonment of Enlightenment
values before the relentless suicide bombings and the inevitable fear
they have engendered have backed the country away from its visionary character and with it the Waldorf prospect of a peaceful, progressive, normal society like any other. What is left, so it appears,
is its very opposite—an armed and rather desperate society at odds
with its neighbors but also the world. That it remains the only
democracy in the area is easily glossed over as though this were not

of great consequence, such is the hostility surrounding the country in many minds. Maybe the hypocrisy in this conflict is no greater than usual, but it is certainly no less.

Is it because the country is the country of the Jews that this hostility has found so little resistance? I think so, but not for the obvious reason of congenital anti-Semitism, at least not entirely. It is also because the Jews have from their beginnings declared that god above all means justice before any other value. We are the people of the book and the book, after all, is the Bible, and the Bible means justice or it means nothing, at least nothing that matters. The shield of Israel, it seems to me, was that here in this place a kind of righting of the scales of justice had at last taken place, this people had in fact survived the mechanized genocide and had come back to once again work the land and raise up new cities. This Israel, in my experience, soon earned the admiration and respect of people, many of whom, to my knowledge, had had no special regard for Jews or were even hostile to them. This refusal of death and embrace of life resonated out into the world, and it seems to me now as it did half a century ago, this was Israel's shield, quite as much as her valor in arms.

It may be futile to argue with a repeated story that every modern nation has gone through in its development—a democratic system for its own citizens, and something quite different for others outside its physical and psychological boundaries. Israel's misfortune, as the current leadership and its partisans no doubt see matters, is the lateness of its arrival on the scene, long after a colonial mentality was thought not only normal but praiseworthy. Whole long blocks of very solid buildings still stand in London, Vienna, Paris, which were once filled with offices whose function was the administering of the lives and fates of peoples thousands of miles away in climates that no European would ever see. Post-Rabin Israel, no doubt as an act of defense, is nevertheless asking not only that the clock stop but that it turn backward to allow Israel's expansion into lands beyond its borders.

Finally, I believe it would be a mistake to attribute so much of the world's resentment of this policy to anti-Semitism. The United States, incredibly to most Americans, is experiencing a very similar aversion in the world, and very possibly for similar reasons. The American Administration has turned an extraordinarily hard and uncompromising face to the world, and along with a certain arrogant self-righteousness in its tone has alienated a lot of people who only a short while back were genuinely commiserating with us over the bloody attacks of 9/11. It was not long ago, after all, that the French—yes, the French—were declaring in some banner headlines, "We Are All Americans Now."

It may have struck some of you that what I have been talking about is basically public relations—the impact of Israel as an image before the world—rather than the hard questions of security and new arrangements with the Palestinians. But my inspiration in this goes a long way further back into history than the public relations industry. Thomas Jefferson, writing the American Declaration of Independence, inserted into it a phrase no doubt to help justify the new democracy's decision to break away from the British Empire. Thus he hoped to appeal to the forbearance of a hostile world of monarchy and imperialism. The Declaration, he said, was written "In decent respect for the opinions of mankind. . . ." In short, the weak, newly born society needed the world's friendship or at least its toleration even as it was prepared to go to war for its independence.

There too something unique was being ushered into a largely hostile world; the British were the enemy and French support was purely strategic, the monarchy having no use for this new democracy whose influence it suspected might endanger the regime. But Jefferson and his friends understood and accepted that no nation can for long endure, whatever the urgency of its defenses, with less than respect, let alone contempt, for the rest of mankind in its longings for justice and equity for all. But my own belief is somewhat less than pessimistic. A nation's history does count a great deal in determining its future. Jewish history is extremely long and is filled, as I have said, with an obsession with justice. It is a terrible irony that, in a sense, the State of Israel today is being attacked by those wielding visionary ideals that were born in the Jewish heart. It is time for Jewish leadership to reclaim its own history and to restore its immortal light to the world.

SATIRE

A Modest Proposal for the Pacification of the Public Temper
1954

There being in existence at the present time a universally held belief in the probability of treasonous actions;

And at the same time no certain method of obtaining final assurance in the faithfulness of any citizen toward his country, now that outright Treason, dallying with the Enemy, and other forms of public and private perfidy have been abundantly demonstrated in and among persons even of the highest office;

I herewith submit a Proposal for the Pacification of the Public Temper, and the Institution among the People of Mutual Faith and Confidence;

Having clearly in mind the Damages, both financial and Spiritual, which have already accrued due to the spread of Suspicion among Citizens, the said Proposal follows, namely:

THE PROPOSAL

1. That upon arriving at his eighteenth (18th) birthday, and every second year thereafter so long as he lives, providing said day does not fall upon a Sunday or nationally proclaimed Legal Holiday; in which case performance shall take place on the first regular day of business following, every Citizen of the United States of America shall present himself at the office of the United States Marshall nearest his place of residence;

Duties of Marshal

1. That said Marshal shall immediately place the Citizen under what is hereby officially described and determined as Patriotic Arrest or National Detention, which shall in every way conform to regular and ordinary incarceration in the prison, jail, or other Federal Detention Facility normally used in that locality;

Duties of Incarcerated Citizen

1. That without undue delay the citizen shall be informed that he may avail himself of all subpoena powers of the Government in order to secure for himself all documents, papers, manifolds, records, recorded tapes or discs, witnesses and/or other paraphernalia which he requires to prove his Absolute and steady Allegiance to this Country, its Government, Army and Navy, Congress, and the Structure, Aims, and History of its Institutions;
2. That upon assembling such documents and/or witnesses in support, he shall be brought before a Judge of the United States Court of Clearance, which Court to be established herewith;

Duties of Judge in Court of Clearance

1. That said Judge shall hear all of the defendant's witnesses and examine faithfully all evidence submitted;
2. That said Judge shall, if he deems it necessary, call upon the Federal Bureau of Investigation to refute or corroborate any or all claims submitted by the Citizen in defense of his Loyalty;
3. That if said proofs then be found invalid, untruthful, immaterial, irrelevant, or inconclusive, the Citizen shall be so notified and may thereupon at his option demand a Second Hearing meanwhile being consigned by Warrant and Seal of said Judge within one of the three Classifications hereunder described as Class CT, Class AT, or Class U.

CLASSIFICATIONS

Classification CT (Class CT)

1. Classification or Class CT shall be deemed to signify Conceptual Traitor;

Classification CT (Class CT) Defined

1. Class CT signifying Conceptual Traitor is herewith defined as including, but not exclusively,

   a. Any person otherwise of good character, without police record of felony, who has been adjudged at his or her Clearance Trial and/or Second Hearing as having engaged in Conversations, talks, public or private meetings, lectures, visits, or communications the nature of which is not illegal but on the other hand not Positively Conducive to the Defense of the Nation against the Enemy;

   b. Any person who, on evidence submitted by the FBI, or in the Absence of Evidence to the Contrary, has shown himself to have actually expressed concepts, parts of concepts, or complete ideas or sentiments Inimical to the Defense of the Nation against the Enemy;

   c. Persons who have not actually expressed such concepts in whole or part, but have demonstrated a receptivity to such concepts as expressed by others;

   d. Persons who have neither expressed themselves, nor shown a receptivity to expressions by others of concepts or sentiments Inimical to the Defense of the Nation against the Enemy, but on the other hand have failed to demonstrate a lively, visible, or audible resentment against such concepts or sentiments as orally expressed or written by others;

All the above described, but not exclusively, shall be classified Conceptual Traitors by the duly constituted Court of Clearance.

Classification AT (Class AT)

1. Classification or Class AT shall be deemed to signify Action Traitor;

Classification AT (Class AT) Defined

1. Class AT signifying Action Traitor is herewith defined as including, but not exclusively,

    a. Any person who has been proved to have actually attended meetings of any group, organization, incorporated or unincorporated body, secretly or publicly, whose title is to be found upon the Attorney General's list of proscribed organizations;

    b. Any person who has committed any of the acts attributable to Conceptual Traitor as above defined, but in addition, and within hearing of at least one witness, has spoken in praise of such groups or affiliates or members thereof, or of non-members who have themselves spoken in praise of said groups or organizations so listed;

    c. Any and all persons not falling under the categories above described who nevertheless have been summoned to testify before any Committee of Congress and have failed to testify to the Expressed Satisfaction of said Committee or any two members thereof in quorum constituted;

Penalties

1. Penalties shall be laid upon those classified as Conceptual Traitors, as follows, namely:

    a. The Judge of the Court of Clearance shall cause to be issued Identity Card CT. Upon all correspondence written by said Class CT Citizen the words Conceptual Traitor or the letters CT shall be prominently displayed in print or in ink; as well upon any and all books, articles, pamphlets or announcements whatsoever written by said Citizen; as well any appearance on radio, television, theatrical or other public medium by said Citizen shall be preceded by the clearly spoken announcement of his Classification; and in addition his calling or business cards shall be so marked as well as any other cards, (Christmas, birthday, New Year's, etc., but not exclusively), which he may mail to anyone beyond his own family so connected by blood;

    b. Any organization or person employing said citizen with or without remuneration in money or kind, shall, upon agreeing to such employment, apply to the Federal Bureau of Clearance, to be established herewith, for a Conceptual Traitor Employment Permit;

c. It shall be an infraction of this Act to refuse employment to a citizen Classified as Conceptual Traitor, or to discriminate against said Citizen for having been so Classified, and the employer, upon receiving his Conceptual Traitor's Employment Permit, shall cause to be imprinted upon all his stationery, vouchers, public circulars, and advertisements, the following words or legend—"We Employ A Conceptual Traitor"— or the initials, "WECT."

Release of Incarcerated CT's

1. Conceptual Traitors, upon being duly classified by the Court of Clearance, shall be instantly released and guaranteed all the rights and privileges of American Citizenship as defined in the Constitution of the United States.
   a. No Conceptual Traitor duly classified shall be detained in jail or prison more than forty-eight hours (48) beyond the time of his Classification;
   b. No person awaiting Classification shall be detained more than one year (1 year).

Penalties for Action Traitors

1. Persons classified Action Traitors shall be fined two thousand dollars and sentenced to serve not more than eight (8) years in a Federal House of Detention, nor less than five years (5 years).

UNCLASSIFIED PERSONS

1. Persons who are neither Classified as Action Traitor nor Conceptual Traitor shall be classified as Unclassified, or "U."

Unclassified Persons Defined

1. Unclassified persons, (U), shall be defined, although not exclusively, as those persons who are:
   a. Unable to speak or understand the English language or any language for which an accredited Interpreter can be found, or can be reasonably thought to exist within the Continental United States or its Territories, Possessions, or Territories held in Trust;

b. Able to speak the English language or any of the languages for which an Interpreter may be found, but unable to understand the English language or any of the languages for which an Interpreter may be found;

c. Committed to institutions for the Insane or Homes for the Aged and Infirm;

d. Accredited members of the Federal Bureau of Investigation;

e. Accredited members of any Investigating Committee of the Congress of the United States;

f. Officers of the United States Chamber of Commerce;

g. Persons who are able to read, write, and understand the English language but have not registered their names in any Public Library as Lenders or Borrowers; and persons who have been registered as Borrowers in Public Libraries, but whose cards have never been stamped;

h. Listless persons, or persons who cannot keep their minds attentive to the questions asked by the Judge of the Court of Clearance;

i. All Veterans of the War Between the States;

j. All citizens who have Contributed to the Walter Winchell Damon Runyon Cancer Fund or who have been favorably mentioned in the newspaper column written by Ed Sullivan;

k. Most children, providing;

That none of the entities above mentioned be constituted as exclusive; and that no abridgment is made of the right of Congress to lengthen or shorten any of the defining qualifications of any of the above categories.

Release of Unclassified Persons (Class U)

1. All Unclassified Persons shall be instantly released, but with the proviso that any and all Unclassified Persons may be recalled for Classification.

POSSIBLE OBJECTIONS TO THIS PROPOSAL

The author of the above proposal, or Act, is well aware of certain objections which are bound to be made. All argument will inevitably reduce itself to the question of Civil Liberties.

The author wishes to state that, as will soon become apparent, it is only his devotion to Civil Liberties which has prompted creation of this Proposal, and in order to Enlighten those who on these grounds feel a reservation about this Proposal, he states quite simply the most vital argument against it which is that it sends absolutely everybody to jail.

This, unfortunately, is true. However, the corollary to this objection, namely, that this is exactly what the Russians do, is emphatically not true. I insist that no Russian goes to jail excepting under duress, force, and unwillingly; hence, he loses his liberty. But under this Act the American Presents himself to the prison officials, which is a different thing entirely. Moreover, he Presents himself without loss of liberty, his most precious possession, because he Presents himself with Love in his Heart, with the burning desire to Prove to all his fellow-citizens that he Is an American and is eager to let everybody know every action of his Life and its Patriotic Significance. It may as well be said that if an American boy is good enough to fight he is good enough to go to jail for the peace of mind of his Country.

The author can easily Visualize that going to the local Marshal for his Patriotic Arrest will soon become a kind of Proud Initiation for the Young American. He can Visualize the growth among the Citizens of Coming Out Parties when the young member of the family is released, and there is no doubt that the national Radio and Television Networks will do their best to popularize this form of Patriotic Thanksgiving, and the entire process of Waiting, Classification, and ultimate Deliverance will eventually become a hallowed Ritual without which no young man or woman would feel Complete and At Ease. It is, after all, nothing more than the Winning of Citizenship, something we who were given the blessing of American Birth have come to take for granted.

I would go even farther and say that the psychological significance of Arrest is beneficial. At the age of eighteen, or thereabouts, a person is just getting out of his adolescence, a period marked by strong feelings of guilt due to Pimples and so forth. This guilt, or Pimples, leads many an individual of that age to feelings of high idealism at which point he is amazed to discover the presence of Evil in the world. In turn, the recognition of Evil is likely to cause him to scoff at the Pretensions of the Older Generation, his parents and teachers, who in his new and emotional opinion have Failed to make a decent world for him. He is then wide open to the Propaganda of the Enemy.

It is at this very moment, when his spiritual pores, so to speak, are open, that under this Act he is sent immediately to Jail, and then through a Court of Clearance, to which institution he may Open his Heart. Under this Act, in short, every American over the age of eighteen (18) is automatically regarded as technically and momentarily Guilty. This, of course, represents no profound novelty, but instead of making it possible for only Traitors to Be Discovered, as at present, under this Act everyone will have the opportunity of being, so to speak, Discovered, but as a Patriot, which after all is what most Americans are.

The simple and pervasive Logic of this proposal will be completely evident if one reflects on the fact that in almost every other sphere of human activity the Society does in fact "clear" and give its stamp of Approval beforehand rather than afterwards; in most states we have to renew our dog licenses every year, and no dog with, for instance, rabies, is entitled to a license; we inspect cattle, motorists, buildings, railroads, elevators, sprinkler systems, teachers, and fish markets, for instance; nor do we wait until any of these have caused damage to the community. On the contrary, you have no need of suspecting an elevator, for instance, upon entering it because you know that it has been cleared, in effect, Before you arrived and you may therefore repose in it your utmost Confidence, nor do you take a Driver's Test after you have killed a pedestrian, you take it Before.

It is necessary to imagine, or Project, as the psychologists say, the National Situation as it will be after this Act is operative.

When walking down the street, buying in a store, waiting for a street car or bus, getting gas, buying stocks, Meeting Someone hitherto unknown, answering the doorbell, listening to a lecture, seeing a movie or Television Show, the Citizen will automatically know where everybody around him Stands. A sense of Confidence and Mutual Trust will once more flow into the Land. The Citizen will need have no fear of reading anything, attending any meeting, or being introduced to anyone; instead of an atmosphere of innuendo, suspicion, aborted conversations and low vocal tones, we shall have a situation in which you know and I know that you were in jail and I was in jail and that we are therefore good Americans, and if there was anything Wrong one of us, or both of us, would not be out here talking like this. That is, by and large.

Aside from avowed enemies there are, unfortunately, Patriotic people who will unquestionably be found in opposition to this Act. Mothers, for instance, may shudder at the idea of sending their boys to Jail. But they will quickly see that a short stay in Jail will be the Hallmark of every Good American.

To sum up, then, it can be said that the current sensations of Confusion, Ferment, Distrust, and Suspicion are obviously not being dissolved by any present methods of Investigation and Exposure. A Permanent, Regular, and Uniform Clearance Procedure is vitally necessary, therefore. Everyone knows that a Man is Innocent until proved Guilty. All this Act is meant to provide is a means for securing that proof. God Forbid the day when in America a man is guilty without Proof. Once it was a Land that millions of Americans were trekking thousands of miles to find; later it was Gold; recently Uranium has been sought for at great effort and expense. But it is fair to say that with our characteristic energy we are devoting more time, more concentrated effort, and more Patriotic Concern with discovering Proof than any other material in our Nation's History. Now, in a dignified manner, in a Regularized and profoundly American manner, we shall all have it.

Get It Right: Privatize Executions
1992

The time has come to consider the privatization of executions.

There can no longer be any doubt that government—society itself—is incapable of doing anything right, and this certainly applies to the executions of convicted criminals.

At present, the thing is a total loss, to the convicted person, to his family and to society. It need not be so.

People can be executed in places like Shea Stadium before immense paying audiences. The income from the spectacle could be distributed to the prison that fed and housed him or to a trust fund for prisoner rehabilitation and his own family and/or girlfriend, as he himself chose.

The condemned would of course get a percentage of the gate, to be negotiated by his agent or a promoter, if he so desired.

The take would, without question, be sizable, considering the immense number of Americans in favor of capital punishment. A $200 to $300 ringside seat would not be excessive, with bleachers going for, say, $25.

As with all sports events, a certain ritual would seem inevitable and would quickly become an expected part of the occasion. The electric chair would be set on a platform, like a boxing ring without the rope, around second base.

Once the audience was seated, a soprano would come forward and sing "The Star-Spangled Banner." When she stepped down, the governor, holding a microphone, would appear and describe the condemned man's crimes in detail, plus his many failed appeals.

Then the governor would step aside and a phalanx of police officers or possibly National Guard or Army troops would mount the platform and surround the condemned. This climactic entrance might be accompanied by a trumpet fanfare or other musical number by the police or Army band, unless it was thought to offend good taste.

Next, a minister or priest would appear and offer a benediction, asking God's blessing on the execution.

The condemned, should he desire, could make a short statement and even a plea of innocence. This would only add to the pathos of the occasion and would of course not be legally binding. He would then be strapped into the chair.

Finally, the executioner, hooded to protect himself from retaliation, would proceed to the platform. He would walk to a console where, on a solemn signal from the governor, he would pull the switch.

The condemned man would instantly surge upward against his bindings, with smoke emitting from his flesh. This by itself would provide a most powerful lesson for anyone contemplating murder. For those not contemplating murder, it would be a reminder of how lucky they are to have been straight and honest in America.

For the state, this would mean additional income; for the audience, an intense and educational experience—people might, for example, wish to bring their children.

And for the condemned, it would have its achievement aspect, because he would know that he had not lived his life for nothing.

Some might object that such proceedings are so fundamentally attractive that it is not too much to imagine certain individuals contemplating murder in order to star in the program. But no solution to any profound social problem is perfect.

Finally, and perhaps most important, it is entirely possible that after witnessing a few dozen privatized executions, the public might grow tired of the spectacle—just as it seizes on all kinds of entertainment only to lose interest once their repetitiousness becomes too tiresomely apparent.

Then perhaps we might be willing to consider the fact that in executing prisoners we merely add to the number of untimely dead without diminishing the number of murders committed.

At that point, the point of boredom, we might begin asking why it is that Americans commit murder more often than any other people. At the moment, we are not bored enough with executions to ask this question; instead, we are apparently going to demand more and more of them, most probably because we never get to witness any in person.

My proposal would lead us more quickly to boredom and away from our current gratifying excitement—and ultimately perhaps to a wiser use of alternating current.

Let's Privatize Congress
1995

It is great news, this idea of selling a House office building now that the Republicans are dissolving so many committees and firing their staffs. But I wouldn't be surprised if this is only the opening wedge for a campaign to privatize Congress. Yes, let the free market openly raise its magnificent head in the most sacred precincts of the Welfare State.

The compelling reasons for privatizing Congress are perfectly evident. Everybody hates it, only slightly less than they hate the president. Everybody, that is, who talks on the radio, plus millions of the silent who only listen and hate in private.

Congress has brought on this hatred, mainly by hypocrisy. For example, members are covered by complete government-run health insurance—while the same kind of coverage for the voters was defeated, with the voters' consent and support, no less.

The voters, relieved that they are no longer menaced by inexpensive health insurance administered by the hated government, must nevertheless be confused about not getting what polls show they wanted.

The important point is that even though they are happy at being denied what they say they want, they also know that the campaign to defeat health insurance was financed by the big private health insurance companies to the tune of millions of dollars paid to congressional campaigns. The net result is that with all their happiness, the voters are also aware of a lingering sense of congressional hypocrisy.

Health care is only one of many similar issues—auto safety, the environment, education, the use of public lands, etc. The way each issue is decided affects the finances of one or another business, industry or profession, and these groups naturally tend to butter the bread of members of Congress.

We can do away with this hypocrisy by making Congress a private enterprise. Let each representative and senator openly represent, and have his salary paid by, whatever business group wishes to buy his vote. Then, with no excuses, we will really have the best representative system money can buy. No longer will absurdly expensive election campaigns be necessary. Anyone wanting the job of congressional representative of, say, the drug industry could make an appointment with the council of that industry and make his pitch.

The question arises whether we would need bother to go through the whole election procedure. But I think we must continue to ask the public to participate lest people become even more alienated than they are now, with only thirty-nine percent of the eligible voters going to the polls in November.

A privatized Congress might well attract a much higher percentage of voters than the present outmoded one does because the pall of hypocrisy would have been stripped away and a novel bracing honesty would attract voters to choose whichever representative of the auto or real estate industries or the date growers they feel most sympathy for.

Once Congress is privatized, the time would have come to do the same to the Supreme Court and the Justice Department. If each justice were openly hired by a sector of the economy to protect its interests, a simple bargaining process could settle everything. The Auto Industry justice, wishing to throw out a suit against General Motors or Ford, could agree to vote his support for the Agribusiness justice, who wanted to quash a suit by workers claiming to have been poisoned while picking cabbages.

Some will object that such a system of what might be called legalized corruption would leave out the public and its interests. But this is no longer a problem when you realize that there is no public and therefore no public interest in the old sense. As Margaret Thatcher once said, "There is no society," meaning that the public consists of individuals, all of whom have private interests that to some degree are hostile to the interests of other individuals.

Possible objections: the abstract idea of justice would disappear under a system that takes only private economic interests into account. Secondly, the corporate state, which this resembles, was Mussolini's concept and resulted in the looting of the public by private interests empowered by the state.

Objections to the objections: we already have a corporate state. All privatization would do would be to recognize it as a fact.

Conclusion: we are in bad trouble.

Index